WINNING AT LEADERSHIP

HOW TO BECOME AN EFFECTIVE LEADER

SAL MONASTERO

iUNIVERSE, INC.
BLOOMINGTON

Winning at Leadership
How to Become an Effective Leader

iUniverse books may be ordered through booksellers or by contacting:

iUniverse
1663 Liberty Drive
Bloomington, IN 47403
www.iuniverse.com
1-800-Authors (1-800-288-4677)

ISBN: 978-1-4502-7834-8 (sc)
ISBN: 978-1-4502-7835-5 (dj)
ISBN: 978-1-4502-7836-2 (ebk)

Library of Congress Control Number: 2010918461

Printed in the United States of America

iUniverse rev. date: 1/20/2011

To Kathie, with your love and support you made my career possible. And to Kimberly, Todd, Craig, and Courtney, who made it worthwhile.

CONTENTS

Acknowledgments

I would like to thank my leadership team: Verene Torres, Dana Valius, and Jack Mitchell.

PREFACE

This book is written with the belief that most of us are not born natural leaders. My goal is to give you practical, realistic information on the winning leadership traits I learned over the thirty-seven years I was a leader. More importantly, I want to save you from making the frustrating mistakes that most new leaders make early in their careers. This book will give you the knowledge to make decisions like a veteran leader. If you are already a veteran leader, use this book as a refresher course in leadership. I know there were many times I needed refreshing and am thankful to those who provided it for me.

INTRODUCTION

Learning to become an effective leader begins with developing harmony between your head and your heart. My concentration is on the leadership traits that you must possess to successfully handle the issues all leaders are faced with day after day. You can approach the issues either with your intellect alone or with your heart and intellect working in unison. Most new leaders are very good at using their intellects to make decisions but learn only after many years to allow their hearts to show to those they lead.

I use the terms *manager* and *leader* interchangeably. Strictly speaking, the definitions of the words are not interchangeable. A leader is defined as someone "who can enlist the aid and support of others in the accomplishment of a common task."[1] A manager is defined as someone who can *organize* and *coordinate* the *activities* of an enterprise in accordance with certain *policies* in order to achieve clearly defined *objectives.*[2] Leaders influence and enlist the support of followers. Managers tend to act based on defined policies and objectives under the direction of a leader.

However, my belief is that managers who do not see themselves as leaders are only administrators. In the marketplace of business, education, sports, or even the military, a leader is worth more than an administrator, who fulfills only the technical aspects of a position. A leader-manager possesses the ability to inspire others to follow but also has the organizational skills needed to be successful in the chosen business. If you choose to be a leader-manager, you are guaranteed to be successful.

This book is divided into three sections. Section one, "Learning to Be a Leader," covers some of the most important personal skills that effective leaders must possess. In this section, you will learn the importance of constantly being open to learning from any situation in which you find yourself. In addition, motives, listening, communication, and empathy skills are covered. Finally, I end section one with the secret key to success that all winning leaders eventually learn—everyone is a volunteer.

Section two, "The Value Skills," addresses the need for leaders to be consistent, decisive, positive, inspiring, honest, and confident. These are the make-it-or-break-it personal values that will either assist you in earning volunteers or cause you be an ineffective leader. Each chapter will give you practical suggestions on how to be effective as a leader.

Section three, "The Action Skills," will help you with the most frequent issues that you face as a leader. I start this section with learning to think like an owner. There is no lesson more important to leadership and no skill that helped me more over a thirty-seven-year career than this. In the following chapters, you will see the importance of setting and monitoring priorities, managing conflicts, and being a coach.

No book can cover every skill, value, and function of leadership. Every leadership book will address these and other aspects of leadership. My goal is to give you a practical book with ideas that can be put into action immediately.

Finally, I should address an obvious question that may be on your mind right now: "What can I learn about leadership from someone who was not a famous CEO, politician, or sports figure?" The simplest answer is that you can learn a lot. Day after day for thirty-seven years, I handled the same issues that you will handle. The leaders who are at the highest levels in an organization don't deal with the same situations as us. Frankly, they have people just like you and me who handle the issues for them.

I hope you find this book helpful.

SECTION ONE

LEARN TO BE A LEADER

Chapter One

Learning to Be a Leader

In his book *Coaching*,[3] Ferdinand F. Fournies described what I was like when I was promoted into my first management position. I think he was describing almost everyone who receives a promotion into a first leadership position. He probably was describing you too. He said that when someone is promoted, the person who does the promoting thinks this: "You are a manager because I just made you one; therefore, you must know how to do the job." In other words, the person making the promotion is thinking, "I promoted him to his position; therefore, he must be qualified. If he wasn't qualified, I wouldn't have promoted him." Fournies goes on to say that "when the new manager fails, the primary reason for failure is assumed to be unchangeable, inherent limitation in the individual, rather than an inability to do something because he or she does not know how to do it."

Most superiors in an organization will not admit that they picked the right person but just did not put enough time into coaching the new leader properly. So when the newly promoted person fails, they think it has to be because he or she failed to do something. In truth, the superior made a mistake by not realizing that technical qualifications are not the same as leadership qualifications. Technical qualifications involve proficiency in a particular function of the business, such as sales ability or accounting or financial skill. A person who is technically proficient is not necessarily ready for leadership.

The second mistake is more unfortunate, because the newly promoted people think that because their superiors promoted them, they must be qualified. In reality, the only people who know that the newly promoted leader lacks leadership training are the ones who work with and for that leader. They not only see it but often are called upon to become the coaches and trainers of their new leader. This kind of coaching can sometimes be harsh, particularly when the new leader is not prepared. In these situations, the employees often will provide negative coaching and either be critical or show their frustration in other ways.

Employees may ask for transfers. They may complain to coworkers. They may leave the company. My goal is to give you the tools to be a successful leader so that you avoid some of the mistakes many of us made and still make. The solution is to learn to be a leader.

LEADERSHIP CAN BE LEARNED

Learning to be a leader does not have to be difficult, but it does require learning. The reason is that people follow a person, not methods, and most new leaders start out with methods. They emphasize job-specific methods or rules rather than seeing that the leadership function is people oriented.

It was perhaps a little easier for me because I was a leader in a sales organization. When you lead a sales organization, it quickly becomes obvious that there is no way you can be successful unless your salespeople and their support staff are both personally successful and supportive of your leadership. If you don't figure that out on your own, they will be sure to tell you. Every dime of my revenues came from the people I managed. I did not personally produce anything of value. They did! More importantly, I learned that my success or failure was not going to be dictated by the corporate leaders in New York. It depended on my success or failure in gaining the support of the people who worked with me locally. I needed them!

It is possible that it is more difficult to understand how important your employees are in a non-sales leadership management position, because the fruits of their efforts are not as immediately measured as in a sales management position. However, it is important to remember that whether you are in a sales organization or perform an administrative function—in any leadership position—you will fail if those you lead are failing. It is interesting to me that there are so many leaders who have the ability to divorce themselves from the failures of their employees yet are willing to own the successes they achieve. I have known people who believed they were good leaders even though their business units were failing. For example, one of my former employees was responsible for the development of new salespeople. He was not good at it and had a dismal track record. When I would press him on the trainees' poor performances, he would terminate them rather than improve them and then come back and say, "I showed them the door." I would then press him on the poor performance and his response was never to take any personal responsibility. It was always the trainee's fault, not his.

These leaders believe that circumstances cause their lack of performance and that they earned a promotion based on effort not results. It's similar to playing a sporting event where the score doesn't matter.

WE START LEADING IN MIDDLE MANAGEMENT

For most of us, our first meaningful leadership position will be in what is often described as middle management. Middle management, though, can mean a lot of things. For our purpose, I will use middle management to mean any position, in any endeavor, where you lead people directly and not through intermediaries. You could be leading a platoon, a basketball team, a department, a school, or a charity, and by my definition, you would be in middle management. I think the textbook definitions of middle management miss the point of leadership and management in real life. Most definitions describe a middle manager as someone who heads a specific department or business unit. One definition states that a middle manager is responsible for implementing the top management's policies and plans.[4] I believe that in real life, in real businesses, most of us are in middle management according to my working definition. All of us—even the CEO of a corporation or the coach of the finest team in sports history—have people to whom we report and people we lead. The CEO reports to the board of directors who report to the shareholders. Everyone reports to someone. We are

5

all in the middle. We all receive leadership and policy from those above us in the organization, and we all take what we receive and provide leadership and policy for those we lead.

In the book *Competitive Strategy*, authors Pearce and Robinson talk about "stakeholders." Every one of us in business has stakeholders. The board has shareholders. The CEO has the board. We also have stakeholders "below" us, for want of a better term. The CEO is also responsible for the employees, who are stakeholders as well. There are stakeholders above and below us on the organizational chart. We are all in middle management in some way.

The decisions made by the CEO of a corporation or the owner of a team may be critically important to their organizations and affect many people. But the decisions made locally to bring about the CEO's decisions are of greater importance to local people, because their careers are more affected by the local leader than by the CEO. If the local leader is ineffective, it doesn't matter how dynamic the CEO is—you will have an unrewarding career in the environment he creates. On the other hand, a gifted local leader can create an environment that provides a career experience that is truly rewarding even if the CEO is ineffective.

Corporations are often global, but corporate success is achieved locally in remote locations or in small departments. Local leaders, unknown to shareholders or owners or CEOs, are called upon to implement the corporate strategy. They are the ones who either make or break the organization. Local leaders generally manage a small, local part of the business and are therefore commonly in middle management. Many times they are new to their leadership positions, because they are managing a smaller type of endeavor than the corporation itself. Middle-management leadership is the area, however, where we find the new leaders who have not been trained properly for their roles. They typically have recently been promoted because they possessed the technical knowledge or sales ability to do the jobs of the people they are leading, but they have not received training on how to lead others. For example, take a person who is a successful accountant and is promoted to run the finance department but may not be prepared to organize, motivate, and inspire others. Middle management is also the place where we find veteran leaders who have not progressed to more senior positions. For them, keeping vital and personally motivated is as important a leadership task as motivating the people they lead.

LEADERSHIP TAKES HEART, NOT METHODS

I was a local leader in a major corporation. I was a middle leader-manager by my definition. I reported to a regional director and had salespeople who reported to me. I had to grow a business, lead others to do business and grow, and manage the profit and loss of the business as well as performing all the administrative functions that go along with those responsibilities.

When I started in management, I made the most common rookie mistake of a new leader—I was too dogmatic. I knew all the policies and procedures and expected that everyone else knew them too. Because I had been successful as a salesman, I knew what it took to build a successful client base. I knew how hard someone had to work to be successful. My problem was that I expected everyone else to do it just like me, and it turned out that everyone was different. They weren't bad different—just different. Some, in fact, were differently better, but all I saw was the different.

> **I relied too much on the methods and not enough on the passion.**

I relied too much on the procedures and methods of management and not enough on putting heart into management. I knew what those above me wanted, and I knew that my career depended on their approval. I didn't know yet that it was the approval of those on my local team that mattered more. I didn't know yet that the secret to success for all of us in middle management is to show respect to the people above us but show heart to the people we lead. I had to learn that there was no such thing in management as being the boss. In fact, leaders quickly learn that as soon as we think we are the bosses, we're on our way to failure. It is very difficult for a boss-type person to be a leader, because the boss person thinks people must follow, and the truth is that people have to want to follow.

> The secret to success is to show respect to the people above us and show heart to the people we lead.

YOU CAN'T BE A LEADER WITHOUT FOLLOWERS!

All of us in leadership roles need people to lead, and we have to earn each person we want to lead one by one. We can't tell them to follow us because we are appointed—we have to earn them. Leaders need consenting followers. Surprisingly, this is one of the least-discussed concepts in leadership training. Most leadership training programs focus on the methods of leadership. They focus on the technical aspects of leadership, not the winning over of followers. All successful leaders eventually understand that their success is the result of earning followers who consent to their leadership.

One of my first leaders did this very service for me.

After a number of people resigned from my sales office, my regional director asked me to join him for lunch. He told me that I was all about the methods and was not getting to know my people; I was not showing that I cared about them as individuals. All I cared about was the business as a whole, and I had not recognized yet that the business was nothing more than the sum of the people. I was about efficiency, not people. He told me that leadership required a heart. He was saying nicely that it was obvious that I did not care enough about the people on my team. I was cold and distant, and I was on my way to failing. People were not consenting to follow me. I was the appointed leader but not the accepted leader. He was right, and I worked at changing. The fact that I survived thirty-seven years in management hopefully shows that I changed for the better. You can too.

The job of being a middle manager—or really a leader in the middle—is the most difficult one in a company, because the middle managers are the ones called upon to be the implementers of policy. On the other hand, the job of being a local leader within a national company can be one of the most rewarding from a career standpoint. It is the daily equivalent of living Basic Leadership 101, not in college but in real life. It is the best position, because it gives you the opportunity to manage face-to-face and one-on-one. You learn almost immediately if your leadership is effective or not. You see the results of your leadership in person, not through sales reports or cost-reduction studies. Frankly, you also learn whether or not you have the ability to earn followers almost immediately.

A veteran of my industry summed up the benefits of local leadership away from the home office in very graphic terms for me years ago. I was the manager of a local sales office, and I asked him for his advice when I was asked to take a position in our home office. He said, "You have the best job in the company. It's like being the governor of one of the original thirteen colonies. As long as you keep sending taxes back to the mother country, you'll be well favored. And as long as you send more taxes back than the other colonies, you will be very well compensated." I took his advice, and he was correct. People came and went in the home office, but I managed to survive in the colony.

The most important lesson of this chapter is that while people earn their first promotion because they possess the technical knowledge to do a particular function (e.g., sales ability or knowledge of any specific job or task), they will succeed or fail based on different skills—leadership skills. And, most times, no one spends the time to train new leaders in the value and action skills addressed in this book.. These are the people skills that no one spends time talking about but that become most important in a middle-management leadership position. They are skills apart from technical know-how. For some of us, they are skills we learned early in our lives at home, on sports teams, playing music, or on our first jobs. My goal in this book is to give you the heart skills to be successful in management so that whatever your career goals are, you will be in a position to achieve them.

Below, I've recounted some experiences that affected my future and helped prepare me for leadership. We are preparing for future leadership every day of our lives. Every experience we have will influence the kind of leader we later become. Unfortunately, for most of us, we don't realize until later that a particular person or event was instrumental in our future success. I don't want to get caught up in my career when we should be talking about yours. However, in order to speak about leadership, I have to draw on my experiences. I want to share just a few of the very important experiences that helped form my future leadership style. Perhaps giving you these examples will allow you to keep your eyes and ears open and seek out experiences and people who are part of your leadership development. If you are a veteran leader, perhaps reading this will encourage you to be a better leader to someone on your team.

Take the Initiative to Ask Why

When I graduated from college, I decided I would take a job that would allow me the time to go to law school at night. It did not matter what the job was, because it was not going to be my career—it was just a job to get me through law school. Being a lawyer was my goal. The job I took was as a management analyst (GS-5) in the Navy Department. In two words, the job was *very boring*. All I did all day long was prepare staff reports for the people I reported to. I wrote papers on boring topics. It was like being back in college. I would prepare a report, and then someone would correct it for content, grammar, and spelling. Here I was, a college graduate, and someone was correcting everything I did every day. I can remember walking the circular halls of the Pentagon with my papers, wishing I had a real job. Well, in retrospect, it was a real job. Our country was entering the Vietnam War in earnest, and the work I was doing was part of the planning process. The problem was that I could not see how my specific function fit into the big picture. There was a general lack of inspiration among the long-term civil servants, so they could not inspire new people like me.

Here is a word of advice. If you are already a leader or supervisor of even the lowest, entry-level person in your company (like I was), take the time to tell that person not only what to do but also *why* it is important to you and the organization. If you're the one who doesn't know, then you should ask why you are doing what you are doing. I had no idea why I was writing those reports, and I didn't know enough to ask. The work might not have been boring if I had known the importance or relevance it had to current events in the country.

Do you have people who you supervise? How many people report to you? Do you take the time to tell them why their efforts are important? When they do their assigned tasks under your direction, do you give them both positive and critical feedback? Do you give the feedback in person, or do you send it via e-mail with a curt note? Remember this when it comes to e-mail. You may not be a gifted writer, and what you say in an e-mail may be received in a different manner than you intended.

If the person you report to is not giving you the guidance you need, be bold and go ask for it. I can tell you that the men and women I have respected most over the years—and the ones who eventually became the most successful—were the ones who weren't afraid to wear a path to my door. I learned early in my management career that the people who came into my office to ask "How would you do this?" or "Can you help me understand this?" or "What did you mean at the meeting when you said …?" or "This is what I am working on; what do you think?" are the ones who went on to be successful. The people who never came in to see me or to ask questions had several things working against them:

1. I never really **got to know them**.
2. I never knew **what they were working on**.
3. They never **got the help** that might have made the difference in their chances for success.

They wanted to be successful on their own, so they didn't seek guidance and eventually failed on their own. In person is always better, both for the person guiding and for the person being guided. However, even with direct, person-to-person interaction, you must be careful to ensure that interactions are meaningful and that important questions are resolved. In my case, in my first position, I did receive hands-on guidance on my writing of reports, but I received no guidance on why my work was important. Therefore, to me, it was boring. My leader could have made it different. I could have made it different if I had known to ask. But it was "just a job," so what did I care? Whenever an employee views his or her work as just a job and lacks any further understanding, the result is a far less rewarding experience.

LEARN SOMETHING FROM EVERYTHING YOU DO

Everything was going according to plan until six months later, when I got my draft notice. I was faced with two years of service as an enlisted person or three years of service as an officer in the Medical Service Corps. Easy choice! I chose the three-year option, and I was sent to Letterman General Hospital in San Francisco. Once again I found myself writing staff reports. This time I was writing them for two colonels who reported to the hospital commander. I led a team of four other officers who served as management analysts for the hospital.

I was concerned that the boredom of writing reports was about to start again. It didn't! The reason is that one of the colonels cared about the work I was doing, and it showed. Each time I took a report in to him, he made me sit down in front of his desk, and he corrected the content, grammar, and spelling *with* me. He explained to me why he was making the changes, and he told me what he was looking for in my reports. He corrected me on the spot. Immediately, I received both positive and negative feedback for my efforts. If he gave a report back to me to redo it, I would rewrite it and go back in again. Once again, I would sit while he read and corrected it. I went back and redid it. Finally, he had it the way he wanted it, and he complimented me on the job I did. This is an important point! He expected that I would not be able to produce the quality of work he desired, but he was willing to personally take time to show me what he wanted. He was willing to develop me, and he was patient with his coaching.

> **[My boss] expected that I would not be able to produce the quality of work he desired.**

Later, he asked me to present the report to him as he would report it to the general. This time, I stood as if I was presenting, and I had a slide presentation. I made presentation after presentation for him as he *privately* corrected my delivery and content. Then, he asked me to attend the general's briefings while he delivered the report. Finally, when he knew I was ready, he allowed me to deliver presentations to the general and his staff.

Here is what I learned from my three years working for this very demanding, meticulous colonel.

- He taught me to be thorough and to check my work carefully.

- He taught me the value of leadership—his leadership and what would become mine some day.
- He taught me how to be a coach.
- He taught me to be patient.
- He taught me the value of immediate, constructive feedback.
- He taught me to give people more and more responsibility.
- He taught me that the way we, as leaders, show people we care is to give of ourselves to them.
- He taught me that by giving our team members our time and knowledge, we gain their trust and loyalty.
- He taught me how leaders earn consenting followers.

EVERY EXPERIENCE HAS FUTURE VALUE FOR YOUR CAREER IF PROPERLY APPLIED

My first position after the army was as an account executive for a stock brokerage firm. In those days, we were *salesmen*, not *financial advisors* like today. I was fortunate and was able to grow my client list and earn a good living. I was a salesman for three years and decided I might enjoy a career in management. My wife said she would be willing to move to the South, and we decided Atlanta would be a good place to go. My company did not have an office in Atlanta, and I was familiar with the area because several of my clients were there. Remember my colonel? I did what came naturally! I wrote a staff report on why my firm should have an office in Atlanta. My experience from working for the demanding colonel was now going to be a benefit to me. His coaching and leadership guaranteed that I was going to prepare the best staff study my sales organization had ever seen. I gathered the data on the market for a financial services office in Atlanta and wrote the report. Naturally, I checked it many times before sending it to the leaders in New York. Eventually, I was invited to New York to meet with the eastern region director. He said that he had read my report and was appreciative. I assumed he was going to ask me to go to Atlanta to open a new office. Instead, to my surprise, he asked me to take over management of the office in my own city.

Every experience has future value to your career. In my case, my experiences at the Pentagon and in the army provided the knowledge to write the report that got me noticed and promoted to a management position in my own location. If you are a new leader, try to see the value in each position and in each experience you have. Apply each experience to improving your skills. If you are a veteran leader, try to remember circumstances or people who were instrumental in your success. Perhaps think also about leaders who failed to influence your future and why they failed you. Take a moment to be sure you are not that kind of leader today. Ask yourself if there are people you need to serve better and people who need more of your time. We all learn from our bad and good experiences!

PREPARATION FOR LEADERSHIP TAKES MANY FORMS

You are prepared for leadership from birth. First, you are influenced by your parents. Either you are taught to take responsibility or not. You are encouraged and motivated by them or criticized and defeated by them. You are taught dependence or independence. You are taught to work hard or not to work at all. From what I have seen in my career, our basic natures are set very early in our lives under the tutelage of our parents. By the time we go to school, our personalities and view of how things work are well formed.

Then our teachers influence us. Are they patient and encouraging, or are they critical of us? Are they just doing their jobs, or do they really care about their students? Then there is the influence of our coaches, our music directors, our peers, and really almost everyone who walks through our lives. Everything goes into the kind of leader we will be to others. Notice I said "to others." We provide leadership to people. It is an outward exercise. They don't have to follow us. When my children became teenagers, I realized that it was ultimately up to them to choose whether to obey or to rebel. At a certain age, our children become volunteers in following our parental leadership. We all have seen rebellious children and realize that sometimes parents are unable to stop those children from walking into terrible life mistakes. It is the same with the people we lead. They either choose to follow us or not. Our job as leaders is to be the kind of leader who others will voluntary agree to follow.

The fact that our leadership traits are formed early in life does not mean that what we are is what we always will be. While we can't change our natures or our basic personality traits, we can change the methods and procedures we follow. For example, we can change how we speak to people. We can change how we see people. Fortunately, we can change enough so that even those of us who are not natural leaders can be successful.

CHAPTER ONE SUMMARY:

1. We become leaders because we are appointed.
2. Most new managers are promoted based on technical knowledge.
3. Most new managers have not received enough leadership training.
4. You are "qualified" to lead because your boss said you were qualified.
5. If you fail, it's your fault and not because of the level of training provided by your boss.
6. Leadership can be learned.
7. You will fail if those you lead fail.
8. Everyone is really a middle manager.
9. Leadership requires heart. If no one takes the time to tell you, ask.
10. Learn something for your future from everything you do. Every experience has value.
11. Preparation for leadership can take many forms.

CHAPTER TWO

LEADERS MUST POSSESS THE RIGHT MOTIVES TO EARN FOLLOWERS

LOOK AT YOUR CONGRESSPERSON

For most new leaders, the most difficult task is to turn the people you are leading into consenting followers of your leadership. In this vein, if you want to be a leader people will follow, look at your local congressperson. Look first at the method he or she uses to run for office. The congressional election is a local election. The person running knows he or she needs to have the support of the constituents. To get their support, the congressional candidate has to make sure the voters *know* him or her better than the opponent. He or she will hold meetings in local sites like union halls, libraries, train stations, or churches. He or she may go door to door to meet business owners and home owners. You will often find him or her shaking hands outside of groceries or train stations. In short, the congressional candidate knows that the only way to win votes is one by one. It's a person-to-person election. The candidate's goal is to personally meet as many people as possible and certainly more than his or her opponent. The middle-management leader should be no different. We win followers or lose followers one by one. Because we typically start out leadership careers in small units,

17

we are, from our first leadership day, in immediate, direct contact with employees. Very often the home office senior leaders are in contact with far fewer people than the local leaders. The home office senior leaders have layers of managers in between them and the majority of employees. They manage with internal television broadcasts designed to keep people up-to-date. They send out policy updates. Periodically, they take brief field trips. But for the most part, they rely on the middle managers to funnel issues up and down the line. Middle managers are different. We can't hide behind memos. We would look foolish sending out taped versions of our updates. We have to be just like the congressional candidates, but instead of being outside a grocery or train station shaking hands, we have to be out with our teams in the local offices or factories or stores we work in. We have to have daily contact with our teams. In fact, I personally would start having withdrawal fear if I missed a day walking around my office speaking to people. Local leaders cannot hide; we have to be visible. We have to think like that congressperson every day!

> **We have to have daily contact with our teams.**

You Earn the Right to Lead by Having the Right Motives

Congresspeople know they will get reelected if they get things done for their constituents. They get bridges, jobs, aid, hospitals—anything that will show the voters that they are on the job and care about them. Politicians know that people vote for them based less on credentials and more on their view of the politician's value to the district. By the same token, as a leader you must show that you have value to your constituents—your employees. You will earn the right to lead if you have the right motives. Every successful leader says that he or she wants to lead (to be elected or to keep your job) in order to *serve his or her constituents.* You will never see anyone win an election or keep a leadership role if he or she claims to be in it for him or herself. Leaders always point to what they can do for others as their motive for seeking a leadership position. Politicians don't always mean it, but leaders must always mean it.

The problem for many middle managers is that sometimes they really are in it for themselves. Remember that I said this is a practical book based on what is realistic? The obvious reason a middle manager could be in it for him or herself is that most middle managers want to become higher management. Usually, they are in a particular position to show that they can do a good job and excel in order to be promoted out of that position. In a home office environment, everyone understands the notion that many people are there to do a good job and get promoted. It is accepted by the employees in the various departments. It's not a negative, because that's the way it's always been done in a headquarters environment. In the field, though, it's different. In the field, the local employees are typically local lifers, and if the new leader (manager) is an outsider, there is immediate suspicion as to his or her intentions. The new leader sometimes says to him or herself, "I can stand this town for now, but I really want to be in XYZ." Everyone who arrives in a new position like this will normally tell everyone how excited and happy they are to be there. They talk long-term because that is the appropriate way to talk and it is accepted business practice. The real test comes a few months later. That's when the long-term local employees start making an opinion on whether the leader is in the job for the right reasons (in their minds) or is there just for a promotion. There has been no shortage of Hollywood movies about the small-town plant getting a new big-city manager. The manager comes to the town to save the plant or shut it down. He or she starts out badly, but after various conflicts comes to love the factory, the town, and sometimes even a person in it. It's great for movies, but it seldom turns out that way in real life. When a new manager starts out badly, the story generally has an unhappy ending.

One way employees can see the leader's commitment is in his or her personal life. Does he or she buy or rent a home? Does his or her family move to the town in a timely manner? Does he or she get involved in the community? With the local school? In business life, the right motives can be seen in the kind of relationships the leader makes. Does he or she take the time to really get to know the people on his or her team or manage from a distance? Does he or she take the time to develop talent for the future, or is he or she interested just in what someone can do today? Does he or she promote people who are doing a good job to positions outside of the department or location or hold on to good people just to help him or herself? The most obvious way that the leader's intentions can be seen is in the decisions he or she makes.

> **All leaders can manage in one of two ways. The first way is to do the things that make the business unit look good for a short time but steal from future performance.**

For example, research and development can be cut to reduce expenses today. However, the future may not be as bright if the introduction of new products is hurt. Another example is that training of new and existing employees can be eliminated or reduced today at the expense of future growth. The better way is to build the business unit as if you are going to be there forever. If you act as though your department, team, or really anything you lead is a place you are going to build forever and then turn over to your child, you will always make the right decisions.

Then you know that no matter what the outcome is, you had the right intentions.

THERE CAN'T BE TWO YOUS

The following statement was attributed to Warren Buffet: "When you get out of bed in the morning and think about what you want to do that day, ask yourself whether you'd like others to read about it on the front page of tomorrow's newspaper. You'll probably do things a little differently if you keep that in mind."[5] What did he mean? Well, to me, it relates to everything you do in leadership. There are many ways to describe it. We could say you can't fake it. You can't be two-faced. You must have your own style. You can't say one thing and do another. You have to be the same yesterday, today, and tomorrow. You have to be the same in and out of the office. I put it this way—personal traits matter in leadership. In the final analysis, your possibility for success is this—it's all about you, you, and you again. Let's talk about the you that your team members might see.

I mentioned this earlier. Leadership is not about policy, procedure, goals, and mission statements alone. It starts with having a heart for managing other people. Yes, I was too dogmatic when I began my management career. Most new middle managers start out trying to prove to everyone that they are the boss. Ego often gets in the way of the reality of the situation. We managers need our teams. Maturity is in knowing that the organization got along fine before it came under our leadership and it will get along fine after we are gone. I did not have the leader's heart, and fortunately one of my early leaders took an interest and told me I needed to improve. Do you have the heart for leadership, or is it more important for you to go by the book and follow procedures?

> **Leadership is about having a heart for managing other people.**

I had a sales manager many years ago who was promoted into his first management position. My advice when I sent him off to his first location was to take a month or so to get to know everyone, learn what everyone did, take a look at the business being done, see what needed to be changed, and then go slowly with any changes needed. I don't know where the confusion came from, but he started changing virtually everything in the new location during the first week. The reception area was rearranged. The conference room was rearranged. He started reassigning office space without regard to how a person would feel about moving and without regard for tenure. He started reassigning administrative staff. In short, he tried to change everything. You can imagine what happened! Revolt! His career was over before it started, and he was replaced. You are only the leader as long as you have followers. Followers are consenting volunteers. Never forget it! But if you do, don't worry, because your team will remind you immediately.

THEIR EYES ARE ALWAYS ON YOU

The next time you go to your place of business, take a moment and think about this. Their eyes are always on you! I mean your employees' eyes. Do you realize that they have an opinion about you? Do you realize that some of them are envious of you? Some of them think that they should have your position, and they are jealous.

Some think that your job is easy. This is particularly common in a sales organization where the producing salespeople think their job is harder than their sales manager's. As far as they are concerned, they work harder and you get the benefits of their hard work. The salespeople have a term for your role—they call it "management net living." So they watch you and come to know you better than you know yourself. Their eyes are always on you! They notice everything that you do. If you are on the phone too much or too little, they notice. If you close your door or don't close it, they notice. If you wear the same tie twice in a row, some will notice. They notice when you come in and when you go out. They notice how many vacations you take, and they somehow know where you went and for how long. Some will count the days you are out of the office and will assume that whenever you are gone, it's for fun and not for a business meeting. They know who you take to lunch and how many times you take each person. If you have an office cafeteria, they know who you sit with and how often. Take a moment and reflect on what you are like in your office, store, factory, etc. What do people see? Is it a video you are proud to watch? Would people say you have the right motives?

You Are the Leader Now

Do you remember your first leader? Did you idolize him or her? Did you have some amount of awe for something he did or how she handled herself? When he or she came into the area where you were, did you try to get his or her attention? Did you hope he or she would acknowledge the work you did? Did he or she offer a word of encouragement? I am asking you these questions because, if you are a manager-leader, you are that person to someone today. You are the person who people are looking up to. You are the person who someone holds in awe and talks about when he or she goes home at night. For example, what's the first thing your spouse says when you arrive home from work at night? "How was your day?" Leaders are the table talk in each employee's home. Everything you say and do is highlighted each night of the week.

You are the one who needs to offer words of encouragement. You are the one who needs to acknowledge someone in a room.

On the other hand, did you have a leader who faded in your esteem? Did you have a leader for whom you lost respect? Was there something he or she did that caused you to go home and tell your spouse or a friend that you no longer respected your leader? He or she could have been a parent, teacher, coach, colonel, boss, or captain of a team. But something happened, and the luster faded, and you lost respect for your leader. It might have been something as simple as failing to remember your name. My first manager called everyone buddy. We figured out that he called everyone buddy because he didn't know our names. Maybe he or she passed you by and did not say hello. Maybe he or she criticized you within hearing of someone else. Maybe he or she used foul language in speaking to you. Whatever happened, you changed your opinion. You could become that person! You could become that person because it's all about you. Just as Warren Buffet implied, there can't be two yous.[6] The good and the bad in you will eventually come out. Your motives will eventually show through.

THEY NOTICE EVERYTHING YOU DO

In middle management, we work in such close proximity to our employees that anything can happen at a moment's notice that can change someone's opinion of our leadership. That's why middle management can be so demanding and why it is a perfect proving ground for higher management responsibility. In middle management, more people notice your mistakes because they are right there with you. I could give you good examples and bad examples. For personal ego reasons, I'll give you a good example first. At a recent dinner, one of my managers was describing my leadership, and he brought up an occasion I had forgotten. He spoke about a visit I made to his location. He said that when I went into the office, I stopped at the receptionist's desk and introduced myself. He went on to say that I asked the receptionist about herself and how long she had been with the company. I also asked her what functions, other than receptionist, she had in the office. This little gesture, a perfectly normal conversation, was apparently discussed in the office after I left that day. My conversation probably lasted one minute, but the aftereffect was very positive. That minute of time showed that one person that I cared about her.

> **In middle management, more people notice your mistakes.**

23

Have you ever lost your temper? Of course you have! So have I. So here's a negative example. Something happened in our office that caused me to become agitated with a particular employee. What I said to the individual was not in poor taste in any way, but my mistake was in reprimanding the employee in front of his coworkers. The issue wasn't that big a deal either, but my actions made it a big deal. You see, we in leadership roles need to handle problems discerningly. In this case, I reacted too quickly. When we react too quickly, without reflection, we will almost always say the wrong thing. I said the wrong thing, and I said it harshly. The biggest problem was that I said it in earshot of other people in the office. You see, for those of us in middle management, everyone we manage is typically within earshot. That's what makes reflection so important. What happened? First, everyone who heard my reprimand of this employee felt sorry for him. They were right to feel sorry for him. Second, the individual receiving the criticism looked at me differently after that, and regardless of what I said, our relationship was never the same. Third, I felt terrible and immediately realized how badly I had handled the situation. Fourth, the incident that caused the blow up didn't even matter that much. Of course the way I should have handled it was to reflect first. Then I should have asked the individual to come into my office. The door should have been closed. And I should have used the occasion as a teaching opportunity. I could have been firm, but I could have put my coach's hat on and not only corrected the individual but gained a supporter. Instead, I temporarily lost the respect of the employee I reprimanded, and it took some time for tension in the office to dissolve. That's how fast you can lose the luster.

THEY HAVE AN OPINION ON YOUR VALUES

You're not off the hook yet. Their eyes are still on you. Do you realize that they have an opinion on your values? You might think that it's debatable whether or not they should have an opinion on such a personal thing as your values. After all, as an employer, you shouldn't pay, promote, or demote someone based on his or her values away from business. That may be so, but your employees are not doing any of those things to you either. They are just deciding if they respect you enough to follow your leadership. They are listening to what you say to them and then reflecting on whether they respect you enough to trust your leadership.

Is that big enough for you? They can't fire you, but they can decide if you're worth following.

> **[Employees] are just deciding if they respect you enough to follow your leadership.**

Here's an example. Have you ever tried to use humor in a meeting? Do you think you're funny? The truth is you probably are not as funny as you think, and you will most likely end up offending someone. In a sales meeting, I once used a story to describe a particular scenario. It was humorous, I thought. In the story I inserted the name of one of our salespeople as an example. It wasn't even a bad story—just an example. Later, the employee came in and was angry with me. He said, "You're no Johnny Carson. Don't ever use me as an example again." Fortunately, he became a friend and supporter. I never tried to use humor again. I heard a more damaging example of a business leader trying to be funny. In this situation, the individual told a group of people about a recent trip he had made to a small Southern town. He spoke about the people in the town and how they acted toward him. He described how they spoke in what he thought was his finest Southern accent. He described how the hot, humid weather caused everyone, including him, to perspire profusely. Unfortunately, he offended the Southerners in his audience, who did not find the description of the people he encountered humorous. He later gave the same impersonation in an even larger venue—on closed circuit television. From the reaction his comments received, he too learned that he was no Johnny Carson.

You have no idea who you may offend with your language.

Do you use bad language? Some words that were universally considered improper in my early years are now common terms to a younger generation. The words may be common now, but many people still find them offensive in conversation. The most common example is that young leaders will think nothing of saying in a meeting that something pissed them off. They use the term as a regular vocabulary word. Yet many people cringe whenever they hear the term. You have no idea who you may offend with your language. If you were brought up on a steady diet of casually vulgar language and use it in your business life, you may offend others and lose the ability to lead. The point is this. Bad language can never be good for your career, but it can be bad for it. If the only outcome can be bad, or at best neutral, why use it?

Are you sports crazy? Too much sports talk from the leader can be offensive to someone. Do you think your employees really care that you *love* the Yankees? A story was related to me about a home-office leader who loved his New York Yankees so much that no matter what the occasion was, he managed to fit them into his talks. It became almost a game at meetings to bet on how long into his speech it would be before the beloved Yankees were mentioned. If it was football season, it would be the Giants. He missed the point that people in Alabama or California didn't care that his beloved teams were winning or losing. Is it important that you love golf? Maybe your employees can't afford to play golf, and to them the fact that you play every Wednesday afternoon is another sign that you have it easier than them and get paid more than them. Values matter, and being relevant to those you are leading matters as well. Your employees see your motives in everything about you.

They Even Keep Notes on You

Do you realize that there are some people in your organization who keep notes on you? I was in a business with relatively high turnover. One day I was talking to one of the salesmen about our business. He brought up the turnover as an issue. I said that I didn't think it was unusually high. He said it was and immediately pulled out of his drawer the various phone lists we had put out for the business over the last ten years. His point was that every time someone left or joined, we put out a new phone list. If there were so many lists, we must have had high turnover. In his mind, there was a problem with my leadership because of all the phone lists. I saw that we were achieving growing revenues and profits greater than our peers. He saw high turnover, and I saw that the sales force was increasing in total size.

In summary, their eyes are always on you, and there can't be two yous. Your employees will have an opinion on your values, your character, and your family and will make decisions about your leadership based on what they see, hear, and think. So what do people see when they look at you? Are you proud of how you act? Are there some things you want to work at changing? If people are going to agree to follow your leadership, they will first determine whether or not they respect you. They will look at everything about you, including your work effort, knowledge, values, social skills, and methods. Think carefully every day you go to work! Who are your employees seeing when they look at you? Are they seeing a leader who, in their view, possesses the right motives?

CHAPTER TWO SUMMARY:

1. Leaders need consenting followers.
2. Look at your congressperson. Every successful leader is a successful servant.
3. You can't be in it for yourself.
4. There can't be two yous.
5. You're not the boss.
6. We need our teams more than they need us.
7. Their eyes are always on you.
8. Everything matters to someone.
9. Never correct people in public.
10. Never show personal anger.
11. They see your values.
12. You're no Johnny Carson.
13. No one cares if you love the Yankees.
14. They keep notes on you.

CHAPTER THREE

SUCCESSFUL LEADERS ARE GOOD LISTENERS

If you want to be a leader who people look up to and want to follow, here's the easiest place to start. Be a good listener! I don't think there is a single trait more important than being a good listener. Your employees—and everyone else—will love you if you listen to them. They will tell you everything you need to know to be a good leader to them. I'm sure you were promoted into a leadership position because you were technically proficient in your field. The problem, though, is that very often new leaders feel that they have to prove to everyone they manage that they are smart. The issue in management isn't that you are smarter or know more than everyone else. Maybe you do and maybe you don't. Certainly if you feel compelled to let everyone know how much you know, you're not very smart. I'll bet that there is always someone on your team who knows more than you do about the functions of your endeavor. In fact, I wanted people on my team who knew more than me about their functions and mine too. I sought them out and hired them. I knew that if I had the best people, my job would be easier. You should be suspicious of the manager who is always trying to prove he's got the answer. I worried about that kind of manager, because I knew he or she was not a listener. He or she was most likely insecure in his or her role. If you are always talking about yourself, you're taking the focus off of the employees, which is where it belongs. If you have to prove your quality of leadership by talking about it all the time, you probably are not leading very well.

THEY WILL TELL YOU EVERYTHING

You need to listen to the people who work for you. They will tell you everything you need to know about them and the business. You will hear amazing things if you listen. You will hear ways to get a job done better. You may hear an innovative way to manufacture a product better. You may hear what is bothering your employees before there is a blowup. They may tell you how you can save money and deliver stronger profits. You will hear everything, including some criticism directed at you. Everything you hear should be taken constructively. If one person criticizes you, never be offended, because there may be a dozen other people thinking the same thing. The person telling you to your face is actually helping you. Listening, however, can be difficult. It takes time and patience to be a good listener. You probably have an agenda for the day. You probably have your next team meeting all planned. You may be pressed to get a report done. You may have fifty e-mails to read. The problem is that there is always something that can keep you from listening. Forget those things and listen.

CONTROL THE LISTENING ENVIRONMENT

The hard thing, once you decide to be a listener, is to be a good listener. If you want to be a good listener, take control of the listening environment. In other words, you should carefully pick the listening location. In fact, you should control the listening environment as much as possible. Here are some suggestions. Carefully pick *where* you want to do the listening. If someone stops you in a hallway or in the front of your building and they want to tell you something, invite them into your office. Try never to listen in an environment where there are distractions. If you are listening in a hallway or outside, there will most likely be too much going on around you. You will not be able to take notes. Always take notes so that you never forget to follow up. By inviting the employee into your office, you are confirming that you take his or her issue seriously and that you respect him or her enough to spend some personal time together.

ALLOW ENOUGH TIME

Allow enough *time* to be a good listener. The worst thing is to appear rushed. You need to be relaxed so that your employee is relaxed. I remember one very senior leader who asked me to join him in his office many years ago when I was visiting our home office. He started out by saying that he wanted to get my thoughts on some of the changes the company was making in the new fiscal year. He first told me about the changes he was thinking of making. Then he asked my opinion. Within one minute of speaking, I realized he had no interest in my opinion and that our conversation was over. Here's how I realized it. Body language! First, he started rocking back and forth in his chair. Not a little rocking motion—a big one. Then he started running his index finger around the inside of his shirt collar. He was getting itchy, and it was noticeable. I quickly thanked him for his time and excused myself. Later, I was telling the story to one of my associates, and he said that the same thing had happened to him. Apparently, it was well known in the home office that when this person started pulling at his collar, the conversation was over. It was time to get up and leave. Staying beyond the collar action could be perilous to your career. Allowing enough time to listen is critical. You want to get the most out of the listening meeting in two ways:

1. You should want to hear what is on your employee's mind.
2. You want to get the right PR out of the meeting. You want the employee telling everyone that you really cared about what he or she had to say.

SET THE LISTENING STAGE

When an employee came in to speak with me, I asked my assistant to hold my calls. This was a way to set the listening stage. I wanted the employee to hear me ask that my calls be held. I could have done it before the employee came in, but I wanted him or her to hear me say, in effect, that his or her thoughts were important to me and I did not want to be interrupted while hearing them. It let the employee know that I was not rushed and had time to listen. Staging is very important to being a good listener. I found that I could not be a good listener if my computer was turned on and if it was in front of me. Even if my guest was a little to the right of the computer, I would find my eyes going to the screen if something popped up on it. I realized that the computer was becoming my collar when someone remarked that I wasn't interested in what he had to say because I kept looking at the computer during our conversation. Unfortunately, he did not say that to me but to other people in the office. I tried after that to move away from my desk and sit at a couch whenever I was in listening mode. If you don't have a location in your office to get away from the computer, then turn off the monitor. Let your guest see that you are turning it off.

> **Staging is very important to being a good listener.**

So now you have held your calls and turned off the computer. What's next? Of course you should turn off your cell phone or Blackberry. To me there is nothing more ridiculous than being in a meeting when everyone has their Blackberrys on the conference table right in front of them. Sometimes they vibrate on the table. These people seem to be required to look at every e-mail that comes their way. Put your Blackberry away and turn it off. I have had people ask me a question and then look at their Blackberry while I answered. I know they are not listening to me. Then they start typing with their thumbs and listening too. It can't be done.

CHOOSE AN ENVIRONMENT WITHOUT DISTRACTIONS

Everything is now turned off. Let's talk about eye contact and distractions. This can be a big problem. It was for me. I found that I was easily distracted by movement. I had glass walls in my office, and sometimes people would see me speaking to someone in my office with the door closed. They would stand outside looking through the glass, using hand signals to get my attention. Move away from a spot where you can see movement behind your guest. For sure, something will catch your eye, and you will be distracted. If even for a second, your guest will notice. If you are in a restaurant, try to get a table with the least distraction and train yourself to look only at your guest. For example, at one restaurant

I often visited, I used a particular table that was behind a post and next to a fireplace. It provided privacy both visually and verbally.

Good eye contact is critical. Just as important is to choose a quiet location free of distractions. The point is to take the time to think about it before you start listening. You'll be glad you did.

DON'T JUST LISTEN TO THEM, HEAR THEM

How you listen is important. Be an engaged listener and listen for what your guest is really saying. In particular, your employees may feel that they cannot tell you what they really feel. You have to listen for what is not said. Someone may want to speak to you because he or she are having difficulty at home and he knows it is hurting their job performance. He doesn't know how to say it, so they tell you about the symptoms, not the reason behind the symptoms. Years ago, when our children were in elementary school, my wife and I took a parenting class from a local psychologist. This psychologist told us that there would be times when our children would come home very agitated from school or act out in what appeared to be an irrational way over something very small. She told us to say, "Kimberly, it sounds like you had a difficult day—are you okay?" or, "Todd, it sounds like there is something on your mind—do you want to talk about it?" I found that when I used the "sounds like" idea in business, it worked on adults successfully. I would say, "It sounds like you're frustrated over XYZ." Sometimes, while listening, I would realize that my employee was not happy and wanted to leave the firm but didn't know how to admit failure. I would say that it sounded like they were not *enjoying* their work rather than that they were not achieving the desired progress. Then they would agree that they would rather do something else. Sometimes, they weren't happy with something I did, and I would invite them to tell me by saying "It sounds like you're not happy with the way I handled such and such." It gave them the opening to tell me what they didn't like about what I did. More often than not, they were not the only one thinking what they thought, and I was able to correct my actions. The point is not just to listen but to hear what your employee is saying. Good listening requires you to be engaged and to ask leading questions. If someone wants to speak to you, it is always for a reason. Find out the reason before she leaves you.

ENCOURAGE OPEN COMMUNICATION

Part of being a good listener is to create an environment of open communication among the people on your team. Some leaders, particularly those in senior-management positions, do everything but create open communication. Unfortunately, those of us in middle-management positions sometimes do the same thing. As a leader, you need to hear everything. You need to hear the good, the bad, and the ugly. If all you ever hear is the good and you are sheltered from the bad, you will never improve yourself, those around you, or the organization you lead. I know that I not only survived but excelled at times because people who were on my team told me the straight scoop, not just what I wanted to hear. There are leaders who don't want strong-willed, bold, independent people working on their immediate staffs. They are wrong! My immediate staff could tell me anything. We were a team—the same team. I wanted to hear what they had to say even though it was not what I thought at first. More often than not, their collective thinking was correct, and I had to change.

Open communication, though, needs to go beyond your immediate staff. It should extend to everyone who works with and for you. Anyone should be able to say anything that is on their mind to you as long as it is done with respect and in the right venue. You should be able to listen with an open mind to what they say. Respect and venue are important, though. I told the people who worked for me that they could tell me anything that they didn't like about what I was doing as long as it was privately delivered. Sometimes, it wasn't privately delivered, and it was said in a group meeting. I found the best thing was to listen and move on to the next topic. Later, I would remind the individual that they should come in to see me when they were frustrated and not save it for a meeting. They got the message without me reprimanding them. I used the word *frustration* because I think it is one of the biggest issues we deal with as leaders. People need a release for their frustrations, and as leaders, we have to be sensitive to that need. Open communication got me through my career, because the people who reported directly to me were empowered to make decisions and to act. Because they were dealing with all the issues of management, they saw the results of my decisions firsthand. They gave me quick feedback on the effectiveness of what I was doing so I could quickly correct course before I crashed.

YOU NEED A THICK SKIN

A thick skin, or not taking things personally, is important to being a good listener. If you are going to listen and have open communication, you have to be ready for some hurtful things to be said. Sometimes it's not pretty. We don't always say things just right, and the people who work for us don't either. If we ask someone what they think about something and get an outburst of frustrated anger, we need to try not to get upset. Over thirty-five years ago, I heard a management speaker say that we should think of every employee as carrying around a bucket every day. Into that bucket, each day, dripped various issues, frustrations, angers, and hurts.

> **He said that eventually the bucket was going to be full and the employee would have to dump the bucket.**

I remembered that phrase my entire career, because it helped me stay on course and not take the buckets that got dumped on me periodically personally. When someone was really angry with me and just let me have it, I would remember the picture of the bucket getting filled up to the point of overflow. In many management positions, we work in such close proximity to our employees that we have to have thick skin and not take things personally. The bucket could have been filled to overflow because an employee has a bad marriage or because he or she has too much debt and finally can't take it anymore. It may be events outside of work that filled the bucket almost to the top. However, if the final drip in the bucket comes at work, it will be dumped at work. When the bucket is dumped, you have to take a step back, not take it personally, and you have to find out what the cause really is. We are back to "sounds like." You can't get angry when the bucket is dumped on you, because if you do, that is what the employee will remember later. He or she may forget the original issue later, but your anger and how you handled the situation will be remembered for much longer.

YOU NEED EMPATHY TO LISTEN

Good listeners have empathy for their employees. There is no point in listening to people if you don't really care what they think or why they think it. I think the most important thing to remember about empathy is this. If you take a moment prior to making a decision to realize that every decision you make affects someone in your department, office, plant, or firm, you will dramatically improve your management performance. It took me time to realize this, but it's true. Every decision you make affects some person in your business. Not only the people under your supervision but sometimes, if you make a terrible decision, the people above you also. Many times the decisions you make not only affect the employees but also their families. Every decision you make affects someone. Even very small things affect people.

I realized this when I decided to stop ordering pens for our employees. We always had boxes of the cheap, plastic ballpoint pens in the supply room. We would go through them by the hundreds, because when someone went home from work, they took the pens home and then forgot them when they came back to work. I decided we were ordering too many pens and stopped ordering more. Everything was fine until we used up our supply of pens. People started asking the supply person where the pens were, and he quickly put the blame on me and said that I had stopped ordering them. Then the word got around that I had stopped the pens. Soon, what I call "the management oversight committee" came in to see me. We were not unionized, but if we had been, the committee would probably have shut the business down over the pen fiasco. Needless to say, more pens were ordered, and I never stopped or cared to stop ordering pens again.

What does this have to do with empathy? I was at an office party after the pen incident, and an employee's spouse asked me why I had stopped providing pens for my workers. "Didn't I want them to be able to work?" she asked. Obviously, the pen decision was big enough to this employee that it was mentioned at home. You can imagine what was said about "that cheap manager"—me! Now, think about all the other decisions, policies, changes, and reorganizations that we in middle management are expected to manage through. If a pen is a big issue, how big is a compensation change? How big is a work-hour or dresscode change? How big is a reorganization of your office or division? How big is a layoff?

You see, when you are in early leadership management roles, you work closely with your employees, but most often the big policy changes are coming from people who don't live with the employees. A new policy is decided from afar, and it comes down to you to enforce. Or a layoff is determined to be necessary, and you must carry it out. You have to take the decisions of senior management and enforce them locally. Every decision will affect someone, and you must have *empathy* for them. If you are putting through a reduction in health benefits or an increase in co-pay, your employees will have less to spend on something else at home. If you announce a change in the work-hour policy, someone may have difficulty in finding proper child care. You have to put the heart to these decisions. You can't pass the buck and say it wasn't your decision. You have to support the firm. But you have to be sensitive to the fact that there are concerns in the minds of all your employees. When you speak to them, particularly when you announce a change, you have to be honest, direct, and compassionate at the same time. You have to listen to their feelings.

If you are reducing some benefit or compensation, say so directly but compassionately. I can remember a time when we were making a compensation change. It was supposed to be revenue neutral, meaning we were going to pay out the same amount of money to the sales force but it was going to be allocated differently. The firm sent out elaborate meeting materials to show that the changes would be good for most people. Unfortunately, there were a lot of people in my location who saw right away that the changes were not good for them. In fact, it seemed like everyone at the meeting who looked at the changes was negatively impacted. The meeting became a disaster. It taught me a lesson. Less is less, and no matter how you package it, less is less. That was the last time I used the prepared materials to deliver the message of change to my employees in a meeting. After that, I delivered my own message so that there was no spin to it.

Having empathy means putting ourselves into the seat of the person we are speaking to and trying to see the topic from her point of view. Doing that puts a different light on every decision. If you are in middle management, it is critical that you empathize, because you will quickly learn that your support and success comes from your own people. If you understand that, you will want to deal with what they are dealing with and what they are concerned about. That's how empathy works.

How to Show You Listened and Care

The final point of listening is this. You not only have to be a good listener but you also have to show that you care about what you have heard. The way you show that you care is to respond immediately to the person. You can do it in various ways, but the one I found best is to try to handle the person's issue while you are still together. Many times, the issues I encountered had to do with an operational or administrative process that did not appear to be handled in a prompt or effective manner. Sometimes the problem was local, and sometimes it was in the home office. While the person was still with me, I called the department handling the matter and attempted to solve the problem over the phone. Sometimes it required that I ask one of our local administrative people to join me in the meeting to assist us. In any event, my goal was to show the person with the problem, while we were together, that I took the problem seriously and that I would do everything possible to handle it promptly. If the issue we were discussing was something that I personally needed to decide, I did my best to give a decision at the meeting. Many times these discussions may take place while you are away from your office, perhaps in the office of the person you are listening to. In that case, I used my cell phone to try to immediately reach the person needed to fix the issue in question. Finally, as I was walking through a branch office, I found that I was often stopped by one of the administrative assistants who had an issue. We often had no place to speak except at the person's workstation. In that case, I took careful notes. If I could not handle the issue in question immediately myself, I got one of my staff people in my main office to deal with it immediately. The next day, I followed up personally with an answer. The point is that you must do something immediately to validate the importance of the discussion you just participated in. The person you listened to will know then that you care.

You Are Always in the Right Seat

The best conclusion I can give to this chapter is something that was said by my friend Dean Curry, senior pastor at the Life Center in Tacoma, Washington. He said that "you are always in the right seat" when you are with another person. In other words, as a pastor, Dean sees his seat as one in which he can help others who may need him. This is something that leaders should take and own. If we approached every conversation with every person with the belief that we were in that particular chair with that particular person for a reason, we would all be the most successful and most loved leaders anyone could have. I admit that I did not approach every conversation with that level of conviction. Just think how carefully you would listen if you believed that you were always in the right seat.

Chapter Three Summary:

1. Be a good listener. If you listen, people will tell you everything you need to hear.
2. It's not about being smarter than everyone else. You want the people on your team to know more and be smarter than you.
3. Never be personally offended.
4. Control the listening environment.
5. Allow enough time to listen.
6. Don't be an impatient listener.
7. Set the listening stage.
8. Keep good eye contact.
9. Limit the possibility for distractions.
10. Be an engaged listener.
11. Remember "sounds like."
12. Have a thick skin.
13. Have empathy.
14. Everything matters to someone.
15. Handle the issues immediately.

CHAPTER FOUR

SUCCESSFUL LEADERS COMMUNICATE PERSONALLY

Are you a leader who leads from behind the computer? The computer is one of the greatest inventions for improving productivity but also one of the greatest ones for destroying productivity. It can become your personal leadership destroyer, because it has the potential to hinder person-to-person dialogue. I would also add your hand-held device to the list of dialogue killers. Anyone in any capacity in business knows the problem with the computer. Though e-mail cannot be overlooked as an integral part of the modern business world, it causes its share of problems. The mail starts coming to us overnight or in the wee hours of the morning. When we get to work, we are already behind for the day. Before the invention of e-mail, we could do some thinking, relationship building, or coaching before the mail arrived. Now we arrive at the office only to find ourselves behind on our work. The e-mails come from every department in your company. If you work for a big company, you get more e-mail than in a little company, because there are more departments and people who are personally trying to torment you. At least that's the way it seems some times. The e-mails also come from the people who report to you.

I'm on the Computer

I can remember mornings when there were so many e-mails on my computer that it would have taken all morning to get through them. It's the same with you probably. The problem, though, is that this can put you in danger of becoming the kind of leader who is on the computer all day. Think about the phrase "I'm on the computer" and how often you use it at home and at the office. It's part of our common language. Even my wife, who didn't have a computer until last year and now gets volumes of e-mails from her friends, will say she's on the computer. She will tell me that she has a hundred and fifty e-mails to get through. She thinks that it's rude to delete them without a thorough review and at least a return thank-you. It goes on that way in business too. I tried to stop sending thank-you e-mails, because I didn't want people sending them to me or sending me e-mails that said only "you're welcome."

E-mail Is Too Easy to Send

The reason we are all inundated with e-mails is that it's too easy to send. A single person can send e-mails to dozens or even hundreds of managers like us all over the country with one easy key stroke. Imagine what it would be like if the sender had to first dictate the memorandum. Then it would have to be typed. Then the person would have to proofread it, send it back for one more round of typing, proofread it again, initial it, and send it to corporate communications for review. Once approved, it would have to be sent to legal for final review, then sent to the duplication department, then come back and be placed in an envelope (by hand), stamped (by machine), and mailed out. Guess how many memos you would get? I can tell you not many, because I've experienced it both ways—before and after e-mail. It's far worse now.

We have come a long way in business. We are now at the point where e-mail is preferred over person-to-person or telephone conversations. It wasn't that way just one generation ago. I can remember an incident in the first few months of my management career. It was 1972, and I had just been appointed to manage a branch sales office. I had a great idea about something that I noticed needed to be fixed in the way the home office did something. So I did what came naturally after three years in an army administrative position. I wrote a memo to my supervisor in

New York. It was a good memo. About a week later (it took that long for mail to get from Philly to New York), he called me. The conversation went something like this: "Do you know my phone number?" (I wasn't given a chance to say yes or anything else!) "Don't you ever send me a memo again! If you have something to say to me, pick up your phone and call me. I don't ever want to receive anything in writing from you." Needless to say, after he was through, I felt the political thing was not to ask him what he thought of my very fine memo.

He reacted so harshly about the memo because it was an unwritten rule on Wall Street to speak directly to people and to have as little in print as possible. Though this is an outdated concept these days, the point is that leaders back then knew that they were not great writers and that whatever they put in memo form could eventually be misconstrued. I am writing this on April 26, 2010, and the scrolling news headline on CNBC this morning was about the release of various Goldman Sachs e-mails regarding Goldman's participation in the mortgage bond market collapse. The e-mails are between employees who could have spoken on the phone or in person.

SAY IT, DON'T WRITE IT

The point is that in business years ago people spoke in person or on the phone. There weren't any of the lost-in-translation problems of knowing what you wanted to say and something different coming across in your e-mail. Most of us should just assume we are not good writers. Pick up the phone and say it, don't write it! It reminds me of the commercial on TV years ago in which the salesman kept saying, "Set it and forget it!" Now people put their thoughts quickly into an e-mail and then send it and forget it. That's really the biggest problem—it is too easy and too fast. In the old memo days, there were many, many times when I wrote a memo and then, after seeing the rough draft, decided not to send it. I would think it was too harsh or too petty. Sometimes my assistant, who typed the rough draft, would be the one to tell me diplomatically that it was a terrible memo. I hate to think what I would have sent out in my early leadership years if all I had had to do was type my thoughts and hit send. I most likely would have been terminated many years ago for stupidity—or at least poor grammar.

I recently Googled my name to see what was on the internet about me. Unfortunately, one of the items was a reprint of a memo I sent to my managers in 2002. It brought back bad memories of a day a year or so later when I was riding the train to work and was reading the *Wall Street Journal*. As I turned the page to section C, I was confronted by a memo regarding a sales contest at Morgan Stanley. It took only a few seconds to recognize it as my memo. At the time the memo was written, sales contests were standard industry practice. However, in the brief period between when it was written and when it was made public, sales contests had become ancient history. In the new environment, it became news. It was personally embarrassing and certainly violated the old Wall Street adage. So say it. Don't write it. Assume that whatever you send by e-mail will eventually be on the front page of a newspaper.

MANAGEMENT COMFORT FOOD

Another problem with the computer for managers is that it's the equivalent of management comfort food. We figure that if we are on the computer, we must be working. If something comes to us, it must be important, so we must have to deal with it right now. Here is an example of what I mean by management comfort food. I retired one month ago. I noticed that in the mornings, the first thing I did was to check my computer for e-mails. I was shocked to find that there weren't any. Then I checked various publications relating to investing. I spent a fair amount of time on the computer. It became my retirement comfort food, because it reminded me of how I started my day when I worked. It made me feel as if I was still employed. The moral of this story is that you should not assume you are working just because you are on the computer. The computer might be one of the least productive things you do. It creates the feeling that you are being productive because you are doing something. It's usually only a feeling. Often, what we do on the computer is nothing more than busywork that takes us away from leading people.

One of the best people leaders I knew did not read his own e-mail. He had his assistant read it and determine what was important. Many of the e-mails his assistant could handle directly. The ones he couldn't handle were given to the leader for review. The leader wrote his comments on the e-mail copy and the assistant responded. This leader freed himself from the computer by reverting to the days when he had an in-box on his desk. You might try it!

WHY DIDN'T YOU ANSWER ME?

Have you ever gotten this call? It goes something like this: "You didn't answer my e-mail!"

"What e-mail?"

"The one about—"

"Well, no; I'm not in my office."

"Don't you have your Blackberry?"

"Yes, but I'm driving on the turnpike."

"So?"

"I'm going seventy-five miles an hour."

"Okay, well get back to me as soon as you see it." This person didn't have the time to tell me what the e-mail was about, but he had the time to ask a dozen questions about why I didn't read it. It doesn't make sense. People assume that we will instantly see and respond to any e-mail they send. Here is a simple rule to follow. We should use the phone if something requires an instant answer. We should start thinking of e-mail as if it's a letter going into a mailbox. When all we had were letters, we used the phone to get answers. We knew it was far easier to talk to someone than to sit down to write a letter. Make this your new policy. If the person you are thinking of e-mailing is in the same office as you, go to see them. If they are in a different location, call them on the phone. My experience was that over the years I created a personal bond with many home office people just from speaking with them on the phone. You can tell so much about people from the sound of their voices. They get to know you as well. We became phone friends who would do things for each other. These home office administrative associates become invaluable to you when you need to get things done quickly. Guess how many friendly associates I would have earned by using e-mail instead of the phone? How about none! If the person you need to contact is your supervisor, make an appointment to see or call him or her. If you are thinking of career advancement, speaking directly to your supervisor is always more impressive and safer than an e-mail that you may not write well. It will also give your supervisor the chance to see how you present yourself. Those kinds of meetings are invaluable for your career. Make this your new motto—"Say it, don't write it."

ARE YOU A POLICY LEADER?

One example of a person who is not a people manager is the policy manager. Many new leaders start out making policies for everything. They think that if they have clearly defined policies, everyone in their responsibility area will know exactly what to do, and therefore things will run smoothly. New leaders think that the only reason people don't do what they are supposed to do is that they weren't told what to do. They assume that if they put it in writing, people will certainly know exactly what to do and therefore do it. Once again, by putting it in policy form, the new leader doesn't have to discuss the issue in person with people. His policy will do the talking for him. Plus, there is less stress on him because a policy memorandum doesn't argue with him.

These policy managers will many times find themselves faced with a small, individual matter caused by a particular person in the group. They *should* handle the matter directly and privately with the individual. But then the policy manager thinks, "If Craig has this problem, maybe there are others just like him. If I make a new policy, I don't have to confront Craig directly, and I can cover everyone else too." This is the great wimp out. Here is what happens as a result of this style of management. The entire group receives a copy of the new policy. They read it and immediately know that Craig was the one who caused the new policy. They then resent Craig and lose respect for the manager, because they know he didn't handle it directly with Craig. Any time you do not handle issues immediately and directly, you are wimping out. I have seen managers who would rather stand up in front of their entire teams and admonish everyone not to do something that was done by only one person than talk with that person directly. How is that easier? Now you have the entire group wondering why you didn't handle Craig directly.

ARE YOU A MEMO LEADER?

The next example of the person who is not a people-to-people manager is the one who leads through memorandums. I'm not talking just about negative memos. I'm talking about the uplifting, motivating, informative, heartwarming documents meant to stir everyone to new career heights. Often, these are the daily informational memos that many of us send out. Many of these memos serve a very useful purpose. They are useful because it becomes impractical to have a meeting or conference call every single morning. They provide an efficient way to keep people informed. They become a problem, though, when they become the sole source of contact between the leader and the employees. There is a species of manager called a *memo leader*. They pour themselves into their memos instead of their people. Here is what I mean. We went through a particularly difficult business environment in the 1970s. At one point, just to keep all of us in my business on some kind of positive track, I started holding a meeting every day at 4:00 p.m. with any of the salespeople who could attend. I am certain that those daily meetings, where we talked about how our day went and what we accomplished, got us through each day. It gave us the chance to dump our buckets before we went home to our families. Daily meetings are helpful during high-stress periods when morale is at its worst.

No motivational memo could have taken the place of those meetings. Think of this. Did you ever hear of a football coach sending out a great halftime memo? Don't try to motivate through memos!

If you have difficulty confronting individual actions or speaking directly to people about their actions, get assistance early in your career. You owe it to your staff to be able to correct the things they are doing wrong.

THE BIGGEST PROBLEM

The biggest problem faced by executives in business today is that they are in danger of becoming high-priced administrative assistants and not efficient executives. The computer causes them to:
- open and sort their mail,
- type and edit their responses,
- determine responsibility and assign tasks, and
- handle items others would have automatically handled if they had come in via mail.

If you want to be an effective leader, you have to concern yourself with highly effective and productive functions, and everyday administrative functions are not ones most of us would put on that list.

Chapter Four Summary:

1. You can't lead from behind a computer in your office. Saying "I'm on the computer" is a leadership nightmare.
2. Though e-mail is necessary, it also can become overly intrusive.
3. Be rude! Don't send back thank-yous.
4. Use the telephone; it's a wonderful instrument.
5. Say it, don't write it.
6. The computer is high-calorie management comfort food, and it clogs arteries.
7. Don't be a policy manager.
8. Don't be a memo leader.

Chapter Five

Successful Leaders Know the Needs of Their Teams

Everyone Has a Different Commitment

One of the most important points that leaders should learn is that the people they lead may have different commitments and interests than they have. And if the leader attempts to manage as if the group he or she is leading has the same interests, the result can be bad in many ways. The most common way is that the leader will be seen as being out of touch with the needs and desires of his employees. First, though, we should look at why the commitments and interests are different. The most common reason is that the leader normally has a stronger bond with the corporation or organization. The leader is looking to move up in the organization and therefore knows that she has to cooperate with and achieve the organization's goals. Very often, the leader's annual compensation is directly tied to the achievement of the organization's goals.

The salaried employee's compensation, though, is not tied directly to the organization's goals, and it may be the product of circumstances not tied to corporate success at all. The salaried employee, in fact, may not personally produce a level of work effort that warrants a salary increase even though the department or corporation achieves its goals. Conversely, the salaried employee may get a pay increase based on superb individual achievement even though the department or corporation does not achieve its goals. So how does this affect the leader? It can have this effect: If the leader focuses too much talk on the corporate goals he or she has been given rather than the local needs of the group, he or she will not be an effective leader.

In the beginning of my management career, I did not realize that every single employee was not as interested in the goals I had been given as I was. I thought that if they knew each one of the annual critical objectives assigned to me, they would become supporters in the achievement of the goals. So I spent too much time holding meetings with anyone who would listen to me about my goals rather than holding meetings on the subject of what was important to them.

What do you think the people you are leading are thinking about your goals? They are thinking, "Okay, you have these goals, but what's in it for me if you achieve them?" They may know from past experience that you get a bigger bonus or a faster promotion if they achieve your goals. But what do they get? Doesn't everyone in business want to know what's in it for them? Many people go to work every day, work hard, go home, spend time with their families, and have only one objective for their work effort—to support themselves and their families. I know it's hard for some leaders to realize this, but there will be times when your employees have no interest in your critical objective goals.

The task for you, then, is to take the goals you have been given and tailor them to fit the group you lead. Some goals may directly benefit them, and they will want to hear about those. Those are the goals you should emphasize. You need to take the "What's in it for me?" question and turn it into a workable local goal. Here's what your employees will be thinking—"Okay, you're the leader, but what does it mean to me if we get to where you are leading me?" You have to fine-tune the local delivery of the corporate goals. You have to communicate those goals so that the people you are leading understand what the achievement of them means to them and why they are good for them. Then they will buy into your goals.

> **You need to take the "What's in it for me?" question and turn it into a workable local goal.**

Every one of your corporate goals can generally be communicated in a manner that is beneficial to the local organization. Once I learned that the local employees saw my goals differently than I did, I started taking the time to look at each one to determine what it meant locally before sharing it with the team. Then, once I had what I thought was the right plan, I began communicating it at every opportunity. Let me emphasize that I said "at every opportunity." Even if the goals are presented in a positive, workable, local plan, you have to communicate that plan over and over again to keep it as a focal point. They will forget your goals as soon as they get back to doing their jobs. The reason is that they know that the quality of the job that they personally do will benefit them directly. What you do may or may not benefit them.

The last thing to remember regarding local communication of the corporate goals is that even the most senior leaders sometimes don't understand how local employees think. I have memories of senior leaders coming to my location and, in the depth of the most horrible, terrible business climate, tell everyone how wonderful things were going in the home office. They would tell them how we were doing terrific (relative to everyone else in the industry). The only problem was that my employees could not see relative performance in their paychecks or eat it. The most senior leaders can sometimes be the biggest offenders when it comes to not keeping the message relevant to the audience. If your audience is in Philadelphia, for example, don't spend ten minutes telling them how great morale is in Atlanta, Houston, and Dallas—the last three cities you visited. Be relevant to your current audience. Sometimes senior leaders are so accustomed to dealing with the big picture that they forget the little pictures that make up the big picture. If you have the opportunity, take the time to brief any visiting leader who comes to your location—whether you are in the home office or the field. Brief any visitor on the issues of concern to your staff and then ask him or her to address them directly. If you don't brief and direct, you may be disappointed in the outcome of the meeting.

EACH PERSON'S VIEW OF LOYALTY IS DIFFERENT

Currently the average worker stays in a job for about four years. The short job-duration rate sheds light on the amount of effort that people are willing to put into working through difficulties.

It is no wonder, then, that people are constantly looking for greener career pastures and do not possess the company loyalty that their parents or grandparents had. It is also the reason that when there is difficulty in your department, you will find very few people willing to work through it with you. Or if you have a personal conflict with a particular person, how many times does the person leave rather than stay and work through the problem? I don't want it to seem that I am saying that employees have become disloyal, because we could also show how corporations have become disloyal. When there is a reduction in force, past loyalty to the company is not one of the items taken into consideration by most companies. The human resources people and the attorneys who advise them have their own set of parameters that don't always have anything to do with past loyalty to the company. In fact, past loyalty is not one of the parameters used, and most employees know it.

So what do we do? Should we take a fatalist view and just assume that the people we lead and the companies we work for are both disloyal and we are the only pure ones? That's not the answer. It is this: Understand what we all learned in college economics, and then take a look at real life. A company is not a person. A company is not your family. A company does not have a heart. You will work for the company for as long as it suits the company's purpose and you have value for it. You will work for the company for as long as it has value for you. You know it works that way. So if you know it, don't be surprised that your employees may leave you, and don't be surprised that you may leave the company or the company may ask you to leave. You can be laid off too!

> **Understand what we all learned in college economics, and then take a look at real life. A company is not a person.**

Here is an example. Many years ago, I was in our home office at the World Trade Center. I was there for a meeting with several of our leaders. One, in particular, was fond of telling the people in the home office that they were his wing men. Everyone was his wing man and he was their wing man too. It was a very clubby, warm, friendly meeting. Everything was going great until about a month later, when there was a corporate realignment. Well, you guessed it; the wing men all suddenly needed to fly solo and take care of themselves. First, the person who was most fond of using the wing man term was no longer with us, and then some of the people he used it with were no longer with us. Ironically, one of his wing men was the person who decided what to cut and who to cut. Later, he was cut too. Again, it's not bad that these reorganizations take place. They happen all the time. It has nothing to do with competence. Anyone in any position of leadership should know that corporations work that way. In one of the talks I give, I tell new leaders that they are only great in the eyes of their mothers! No one loves them like their families love them. Don't ever confuse corporate love with family love. It's not the same!

LEADING SALESPEOPLE IS UNIQUE

Being a sales leader (sales manager) can be one of the most rewarding forms of leadership. It can also be one of the most frustrating! It is rewarding because it is the closest we business leaders can come to being the coach of a great sports team. Sales leaders have the benefit of seeing immediate results. They see their wins and losses almost every day. There is no career in the business world where you can see results faster. It is frustrating, however, because typically the sales managers and the salespeople have very different interests and are very different personality types. The best salespeople I have known are individualists and are extremely high on the ego scale. In general, they would do very poorly in a structured, corporate type position. In particular, they do not see conformity, teamwork, policy, or administrative manuals as helpful to their sales efforts. The top salespeople are individualists, have total self confidence, have their own goals, and believe they are solely responsible for their success. Maybe I am overstating the top salesperson's uniqueness, but if I am, it's not by much. Finally, one last very big thing to remember—salespeople are the least loyal employees to a corporation. The reason is simple and also makes total sense from the salesperson's point of view. If you were the salesperson, you would be exactly the same.

> **The reason the salesperson is the least loyal is because he or she sees immediately if there is anything wrong in the organization.**

He or she is the first to see poor quality control, because he or she hears about it immediately from his or her clients. Salespeople are also the first to realize that product innovation has slipped. They are the first to realize that certain products or services are not what the marketplace is looking for. In short, if there is anything wrong, the salesperson feels and sees it immediately. His or her lack of loyalty is a proper business outcome and is the truest form of capitalism at work in corporate life. The salesperson is properly loyal to his or her clients first and the corporation second. If you want an honest assessment of how your organization is doing, always ask the salespeople.

Now let's think about the kinds of personality traits that most management leaders need to possess in order to climb the corporate ladder. First, you won't see too many true individualists in the higher ranks of management. Certainly self-motivation and self-confidence are traits of top managers. But the ingredients that often get them to the top are these:
- They do well in a structured environment.
- They know how to conform.
- They are team players.
- They understand policy and, more importantly, follow it.

Manager-leaders are also different because many of them would rather not confront corporate decisions or oversights directly. Unlike the salesperson, who will leave the company to go to another company with a more competitive product, the leader will try to manage through it. Unfortunately, and this is the biggest problem, managers are often the last people in an organization to know that the company has the wrong products, that the quality of the products is poor, and that the end user has checked out. The salesperson knows it before anyone else.

So how should you lead the salesperson? Listen to your salespeople! It's the easiest way to learn about your products and services. I have spoken to many automobile salespeople who say that they realized that the American-made autos they were trying to sell were out of step with what the customers wanted. The salespeople who saw it most vividly were the ones who sold both domestic and foreign products. The owners of dealerships I spoke with consistently would say, "My foreign car store is doing well, but my domestic store is doing terribly." Senior leaders need to listen to the people closest to the customer, and no one is closer than the salesperson. Lead them by listening to them.

BE RELEVANT TO THE PEOPLE YOU LEAD

Why does being relevant relate to knowing who you are leading? You can't be relevant if you don't know them. It goes back to something I discussed earlier regarding how leaders communicate with their followers. I mentioned the big-picture leaders who frequently visited my business unit and spoke to our local employees about issues they had no knowledge of or interest in. There was an occasion several years ago when one of our salespeople had earned a particularly large amount of money in one month. Obviously, a substantial amount of income tax was withheld from his pay check. When he got his check, he proceeded to walk through the office complaining to anyone who would listen about the amount of tax he had to pay. To the average salaried worker and to the average salesperson, the amount of just the tax would have been enough to live on for many months. Naturally, instead of feeling sorry for him, they looked at him as a bragger who was out of touch with the reality of their lives. The salesperson wasn't consciously trying to brag. He wanted sympathy from the people around him. The problem was that all he thought about was himself. He didn't stop to think that his personal problem of having paid a five-figure tax bill for one month had no relevance to anyone else.

Now this is a very vivid example of being out of touch, but leaders do the same thing in a more subtle manner. Maybe it's just my industry, but it's very common for higher income leaders to talk about their fine wine collection and their cellars. For most of us, the cellar is a storage location for junk, but to others it's a location for wine. The average employee wants to say, "Who cares about how many bottles of wine you have?" but they can't say it to the leader. I can give you many more examples of out-of-touch leaders. The point for you is not to become one yourself. Know at all times who you are speaking to and who you are leading. Speak about what is important and relevant to the person or people you are addressing. As the leader, you are never off duty to your employees. They have the right to expect that you are relevant to their needs. Be a relevant leader!

CHAPTER FIVE SUMMARY:

1. Everyone has a different commitment.
2. Each person's view of loyalty is different.
3. Leading salespeople is unique.
4. Be relevant to the people you lead.

CHAPTER SIX

SUCCESSFUL LEADERS
KNOW EVERYONE ON THEIR
TEAM IS A VOLUNTEER

"I'M IN CONTROL HERE," OR, WHY SHOULD PEOPLE FOLLOW YOU?

On March 30, 1981, following the attempted assassination of President Ronald Reagan, Secretary of State Alexander Haig uttered the famous words, "I'm in control here." In the confusion of everything going on, his well-intentioned attempt to reassure the country resulted in the end of his political career. Rather than being reassured, everyone wondered why he as the secretary of state didn't realize that there was a constitutional line of succession that controlled the situation. As it turned out, he knew what he meant to say—it just didn't come out right. I wonder if leaders are ever like General Haig. You may not say, "I'm in control here," but you might think it. The controlling leader has always caused me the greatest concern for the health of local business. I had offices reporting to me in three states, and each one had a branch manager. The most common issue of local concern from the staff in those offices was an overbearing, controlling manager. The controlling manager seems to think that his position automatically gives him the authority to lead, and as we learned earlier, that's not the case. Leading is not about control of anyone; it's about earning consenting followers.

I Win or You Win

The controlling manager views every decision as a situation in which he or she personally wins or loses. He or she sees rules, changes in personnel assignments, changes in office environment, and changes in procedures as signs that he or she is the leader. The controlling manager does not look at these things from the perspective of whether they improve the environment, improve productivity, or improve his or her people. The controlling manager makes changes because he or she wants it his or her way and not the way it was when he or she took over. This is something you have to be particularly careful about as a manager in a new position. Too often, new managers think that the way they show their staff and their bosses that they are leading is to make changes. They think that if they reorganize the business, everyone will see that they know what they are doing. I have seen managers who get locked into the I-win-or-you-win mentality with their staffs. They don't see people as partners in accomplishing a goal. They see them as employees on duty to do their assigned tasks under the rules and policies the managers have set up.

Controlling Leaders Fail

The controlling leader typically will be ineffective and distant. This kind of leader never connects with his or her employees. There is never a true bond with anyone, because everything the leader does is designed to show authority. The controlling leader never sees the purpose of forging a bond with people, because the people are not as important as the job he or she has to accomplish. The controlling leader is focused on the goal, but nobody else is or cares, because he or she does not take the time to create a team atmosphere. To create that atmosphere requires getting deep with people, treating them as partners, and giving them the authority to act as leaders themselves through delegation. That never happens in a controlling environment, because to the controlling leader, there can't be more than one leader.

EVERYONE'S A VOLUNTEER

In this chapter, I want to expand on chapter two and discuss further what it takes to earn followers. In particular, it is my belief that it is through earning the consent of those we lead that we become leaders. If you accept this as a reasonable premise, then it is reasonable to ask why anyone should consent to follow you. It's a big question, because it gets to the heart of what you offer as a leader. One of my salespeople, many years ago, said that as soon as I figured out that everyone was a volunteer, I started improving as a manager. In a sales management position, it is very clear that we deal with volunteers. In other organizations, it's less clear but still true. In the administrative world, people can come into their places of work, do their jobs, and go home without accepting your leadership. How can that be? It's very simple. It happens every day, because there are many quiet people who do their jobs, don't ask questions, are not inspired to excel; work the required hours, have long careers, and never feel a particular attachment to you as a leader. I think this is particularly true in the case of the passing-through middle manager who the employees feel only needs to be tolerated for a little while.

WHERE ARE YOU LEADING TO?

Let's dissect leadership. The definition of leadership is the ability to lead, guide, direct, or influence people. By definition, then, you are leading people to some location or result. Your leadership is not an empty exercise of exerting control over people. That's the attitude of the control leader we discussed above who only cares about proving he or she is a leader. There are people who take positions of leadership just to prove that they can be the leader, and they have no clue as to what they want to accomplish as the leader. Or they hold on to leadership for their own gain and not because they are interested in helping others to succeed.

Sports coaches are the best example of leaders who understand why they are leading and what the purpose of their leadership is. They understand that a large part of coaching (leading) is teaching. They get to know their players and understand how each one's talents fit the team's goal of winning games. The coach doesn't have to spend time telling anyone that he or she is the leader, because all of his or her actions are seen by the team as steps toward winning more games through the development of each player individually and the group collectively. The coach wants to win but knows that winning comes from the development of the team.

WHAT CAN WE LEARN IN THE BUSINESS WORLD FROM SPORTS COACHES?

- **To ask ourselves if we have communicated the goal for the team we lead**. In order to communicate the goal, we have to know and believe in the result we want to achieve. Most companies will set annual critical objectives for each level of the organization. The objectives will be disseminated at the beginning of the year, typically from the top down. One objective might be better quality control. Another person may be required to increase sales in general or sales of a particular product line. Another might be to improve diversity in the organization. Companies put out many objectives to their leaders, which then get passed down the chain of command. When you get your objectives, you can do several things with them. One thing for sure is that you can't ignore them. I'm not being facetious! I have known managers who decided that they really didn't need to participate in all of the objectives. They thought that if they really did well in a few of them, no one would care about the ones they ignored. That worked in the old days when companies accepted quirky managers who were individualists. Today, with the level of competitiveness in most companies, there is no room for the renegade manager who does it his or her way.
- **It doesn't matter what the goal for the year is if the people on your team don't trust your motives**. If you are going to get your team (your employees) to follow your leadership to achieve the critical objectives set for your department (winning the game), you need to follow the proven principles that all coaches utilize. You have to possess personal values that the people on your team respect. Or put a different way, they need to see a level of personal integrity

on your part that gives them the confidence to follow your leadership. That gets back to the kind of person you are. It has to do with your character, your integrity, your honesty, and how you act in and out of the office. It's the two-yous issue we discussed earlier.

- **You have to know it to lead it**. Next, you have to know your business (know the sport) and be dedicated to constantly improving your knowledge of it. The coach may not have played the sport, and even if he or she did, may not have been a star. But the coach most likely has prepared him or herself meticulously for the role. He or she generally knows the fundamentals of the sport better than any of the players. He or she continually works on personal development by attending conferences, watching game tapes, reading journals, and improving communication skills. The coach knows it is necessary to stay current on the changes taking place in his or her sport. He or she is committed to his or her own education and to the education of the players. You probably have not done the job of every person you are leading, but you will have direct reports who know the jobs of the people under them. Your direct reports have to become your specialty coaches. They will educate you on their areas, and you will work through them. Just like the sports coach who didn't play the sport, you will read, watch, go to seminars, and learn so that you can improve your knowledge of your business and put yourself in a position to be a good teacher.

- **You have to lead each individual.** The coach knows that his or her efforts can't be directed at the group exclusively. He or she will have to teach the fundamentals individually to each player. To do that, he or she has to take the time to observe each player and determine what skill the player needs to improve. The coach is, in effect, forming a personal relationship with the player and forming a bond that creates the trust that is necessary to earn consenting followers. I loved training new salespeople and did it for my entire career. The joy that came from seeing a new trainee join our firm, go through our training program, start as a rookie salesperson, build a clientele, and grow into a successful advisor to his or her clients was the single most rewarding part of my management career. After I retired, someone said, "Have you ever thought about all the people you trained, about how many are now successful and the wealth that they have created based on you giving them an opportunity and the skills to succeed?" For those of us in the business world, that statement should feel like a game-winning touchdown. In order for you to achieve your goals, you must get down to the level of the individual person just like the coach does. You will form bonds within your team that will be strong enough to get you through good and bad times. You will earn the loyalty of the people you lead if they see that you are instrumental to their success. Talent development of others should always be your primary measure of success.

- **Create a team to be a leader.** The coach also knows that after the individuals know their fundamentals, it's up to him or her to create a winning team. The coach knows that she has to take the individuals and determine how to put them together for the maximum benefit. We business leaders have to do the same thing. We have to be able to look at the talent on our teams (our departments, divisions, or factories) and determine the most effective way to achieve our goals. We have to take individuals who are interested in their personal success and show them the value of the group achieving its goals. I have to say that this became easier to do as I moved up the corporate ladder. The reason is that in my last position, I had ten people who reported directly to me, all of whom were in a bonus pool that was based on the overall success of the team. It's easy to get individuals to pull together when the achievement of the goal benefits each person individually as well as collectively. It's like when the team wins the game. There may be a most valuable player, but everyone shares the glow of the victory equally.

Getting the same teamwork is more difficult when the employees on your team do not benefit directly from the achievement of your critical objectives. I have found, however, that it is still possible to create a team in that environment. The key is to find people who love what they do. Their work effort is not commensurate with their pay or titles. These people, frankly, are the people who keep every company going. They are the lifers I spoke about earlier or the people who possess a technical skill in a very narrow area.

You will be successful in building a team in this environment if you get to know these people just like you get to know your star performers. It will be difficult to spend as much time individually with them, so you have to use your time wisely. It was easy when everyone who worked in my department was in one building. I could speak to them as I walked around, or I could have a quick meeting. The critical thing was informing them what the goals were (the critical objectives). They worked hard, and they deserved to know what the end result was. I found that I got to know them very well, because they tended to stay with us for many years. We asked for their input at the meetings to learn how we could do our jobs better to achieve corporate goals. We were willing to experiment with their ideas and use them if they worked in our business. We had a continual education program in place so that every person knew they could improve themselves in both position and pay. All of us on my management team had an open-door policy. Anyone and everyone was welcome and listened to.

It was more difficult when my business unit was spread out over twenty locations. But the same method worked. Whenever I visited a location, I made sure I visited with as many people as possible. Generally, there would be a meeting with the sales staff scheduled either early in the morning or at lunch time. In many of our locations, both the sales staff and the administrative staff attended these meetings. In some locations, we held separate meetings. Our goal was to communicate to everyone that we cared about them and wanted them to know what was going on in the firm. Everyone knew that we had an open-door and open-communication policy, and they were encouraged to ask questions. Many times, after visiting a location, I would get e-mails from the people I visited giving me suggestions or ideas for the business. You can form a successful team from any group of people if you treat them with the professional respect they deserve.

I started this chapter speaking about the controlling, authoritative manager who never can grow into a leader of others. We can sum it up this way:

- You will seldom succeed as a leader if you emphasize your authority instead of your commitment.
- You will seldom succeed if you emphasize who you are rather than who the others are.
- You will seldom succeed if you don't lead by example.
- You will seldom succeed if you don't realize that you need consenting followers who are volunteers on your team.

CHAPTER SIX SUMMARY:

1. Are you an I'm-in-control-here leader?
2. New managers are very often controlling managers.
3. "I win, you lose" is a bad leadership philosophy.
4. Every employee is a volunteer.
5. Leaders guide, direct, and influence—they don't control.
6. The best leaders learn to be teachers.
7. To accept your leadership, people have to accept your values.
8. Love your work.
9. Know your business.
10. Keep improving yourself.
11. Get around and speak to people so you get input.
12. Communicate that you care about people.

SECTION TWO

LEADERSHIP VALUES AND SKILLS

CHAPTER SEVEN

SUCCESSFUL LEADERS
ARE CONSISTENT

Consistent! The various synonyms for *consistent* describe the qualities that are necessary to be a good leader. One is *coherent*—to be reasonably or logically harmonious. Another is *reliable*—to be able to maintain a particular standard or repeat a particular task with minimal variation. Finally, it is said that a consistent person is free of contradictions. I think we can all agree that a leader-manager should be coherent, reliable, and free of contradictions. The reason is simple. If you, as the leader, are inconsistent, your employees will never know which you they are hearing from and relating to on any given day. We are back to the idea that there can't be two yous. Yet so many new and experienced leaders fail because they are inconsistent and have too many contradictions. How you lead today or tomorrow or next week can't depend on what side of the bed you woke up on. Your leadership style can't be based on the size of your raise or bonus. It has to be the same every day so that your employees are comfortable and can do their jobs. I found that if I could keep my managers focused on the goal at hand and be a consistent influence on them, they in turn would be more consistent in their dealings with their employees. If they felt supported and comfortable in their roles, they would comfort others. If I managed from a negative or punitive stance, they would pass that style on to others.

> **If you, as the leader, are inconsistent, your employees will never know which you they are hearing from on any given day.**

CONSISTENCY BREEDS CONSISTENCY

As I said earlier, I was a leader in one market for my entire career. I had to be consistent! I had no choice! If I was not, my reputation would have been so poor after just a few years that no one in their right mind would have wanted to work for me. Consistency was not hard for me, because I have a consistent personality. I have plenty of bad traits, but fortunately one is not inconsistency. I can do the same things in life and business every day and not get bored. I know people who need to do something different every day or do the same thing in a different manner every day. They are always looking for a new way to do the same thing. Innovation is certainly not bad, but it can be confusing if you are practicing it on real people every day.

ACT IN THE SAME WAYS EVERY DAY

For better or worse, you have to be the same person every day. People appreciated my better and forgave me for my worse, because eventually they knew what my worse was and they were comfortable with it. We become comfortable even with bad traits if they are always the same and we know there is some good to compensate for them. Most people have a good nature and will look for the positive in us. I have never had a perfect leader but have learned something from every one of them. Showing that you are the same person every day is one of the most important tasks you have as a leader. You have to start with knowing who you are and accepting your own strengths and weaknesses. I know that I am a serious type of person. I am analytical. I am able to take the long-term view of things. I like to develop talent. I am not frivolous or gregarious. If I tried to be frivolous and gregarious and therefore be something I'm not, I couldn't keep it up long.

Could this be you? One of the managers in my region was in my estimation one of the best we had. I thought he had tremendous qualities that were improving every year. As good as I thought he was, he had one problem. It certain situations, he became a different person than the one I knew. It was as if he was acting the part of the person he thought he should be. When he did that, he came across to people as insecure and not genuine. By trying to be too confident, he appeared not to be confident at all. Sometimes he tried to be overly friendly with people. He assumed a level of intimacy that did not yet exist. He was trying to be the person he thought he should be rather than being the person he was. The real him was a much better leader than the person he thought he should be. So the first part of being a consistent leader is to know your good points and bad points and to use both to your advantage by emphasizing the good and working on improving the bad. Never try to make believe the bad ones don't exist. And never try to be someone you're not.

HANDLE SIMILAR ISSUES THE SAME WAY

Next, your *actions* have to be consistent. In particular, you have to handle similar issues in a similar manner from day to day. Imagine the chaos in your business if you handled similar issues differently on different days. Yet, without realizing it, many leaders do just that. Everyone knows how you previously handled a particular issue, so they have the right to expect it to always be handled the same. If a particular infraction of policy resulted in a verbal reprimand, the same thing shouldn't be a termination a month later. That's an easy one for most managers to understand, but there are many subtle decisions made about small issues that managers tend to change depending on circumstances. One of those circumstances is often whether the manager likes one employee more than another. Don't think this doesn't happen to you in real leadership situations. No leader wants to admit it, but it's perfectly normal to like one person more than another. The problem occurs when the decisions you make are influenced by your feelings. First, to do so is wrong, and second, without you realizing it, everyone on your team already knows who you like and don't like. They will be looking for any opportunity to say you play favorites. If you do play favorites, people will say, "See? You can't get a fair chance unless he likes you."

Handle Different People the Same Way

For that reason, you have to handle similar issues with different people in the same manner from day to day. Every one of your employees already knows how you handled Courtney yesterday or last week when she failed to get a payroll report done on time. So if you handle Jane in a different way when she fails to have it ready, everyone will say you are playing favorites or that you just don't know how to handle circumstances that come up. You will find that your employees are looking for opportunities to think that you have your favorites so they can't get a fair break. If you are inconsistent, you will feed that thought process. Today, the people issues are far more complicated, because most big issues will fall under some kind of labor law or internal policy. Most organizations will have specialists who are well trained in human resources' issues to handle these situations. The kinds of decisions that you have to be consistent about are the ones that are part of the daily effort of getting the work done. Any one decision is not critical, but as a group, the many daily decisions you make become the legacy your team judges you by.

Manage with an Open Book, Because the Book Is Already Open

You have to be consistent in your words. You can't say one thing today and another two days or two weeks from now. In other words, always tell the truth. Your exaggerations—or worse, lies—will always catch you. Assume that whatever you say to one person is known by everyone in your business. I tell every leader that there are no secrets within a team. Everyone knows everything! You might as well manage with an open book, because the book is already open. I missed this point when I started my leadership career. If you do something for one person, you better be prepared to do it for everyone else. Their eyes are always on you, your actions, and your words. Remember that you are the leader, and just like you look up to your leader for direction, your employees are looking to you.

There is something else that new leaders don't realize. Every one of your words has meaning to your employees. They are listening to you carefully to see what you think of them and the job they are doing. They are listening carefully to hear what you really mean. Your words should never be frivolous or casually said. Remember, you are the leader! You are never not the leader. Finally, never tell someone about something that is confidential. It won't be confidential for long. If something is confidential and future implementation requires planning by your immediate management team, still understand that there will probably be a leak. The White House can't contain leaks, so don't think you're any better.

MAKE A CONSISTENT EFFORT

You have to be consistent in your effort. Level, consistent work effort will pay off in the long run. I am a morning person, so I always got to the office early. The people who worked in my business knew that they could get me either by phone or in person any time after 7:00 a.m. If I wasn't there by then, they knew that I was probably visiting one of our business locations. Then they knew they could get me on my cell phone up to 8:30 p.m. My schedule was always the same. There was comfort for the people who reported to me because they could count on that schedule.

You also have to be consistent in your long-term effort. This is the part of being a consistent manager that tends to trip up many managers. I spent thirty-seven years building one market. It took long-term thinking and a steadfast vision of what I wanted to achieve. I did not have the luxury of sprinting to the finish line, because I was in a marathon race. Many middle managers want to quickly achieve just enough to get promoted to the next higher position, and they really don't care about the long-term consequences of their decisions. Early leader-managers tend to be sprinters—always seeking immediate gratification—but the people who work for them tend to be marathon runners—long-term thinkers. Conflict will often arise when managers with short-term priorities fail to listen to the long-term concerns of employees.

Consistent effort means that you don't have up-and-down days. One day you are leading the charge to get a particular thing done, and the next day you have no interest in what you did yesterday. Is that ever you? Do you jump from one thing to the next, giving conflicting signals as to what's important? I spent a great deal of time continually telling my management team first what the mission was and second what we had to do to accomplish it. A common statement I heard from my former managers after I retired was that they always knew what I expected of them. They always knew what the mission was. The mission lasted continually. It was to provide a growing, nurturing environment for our employees; grow market share; be the best-known firm in our market; recruit more salespeople; provide a high-quality, compliant service to our clients; and increase profits for the corporation. I spoke about the mission every time I spoke to the managers. It gave them comfort to know what was expected. Do you have a clear sense of your mission, and do you clearly and consistently keep it in front of your team?

HAVE A CONSISTENT PHILOSOPHY

> **No matter what business you are in, you have to determine your philosophy.**

Your philosophy can't change to suit the occasion. You have to have a consistent philosophy. Obviously every reader is in a different circumstance and in a different business. My philosophy was both unique to the business I was in and general enough to fit any business. It was general because I had a long-term philosophy. My philosophy was that I had value as long as I supported the efforts of my sales and administrative staff. I had a philosophy of delegating authority to others to assist in our growth. I had a philosophy of doing a high-quality business that would be beneficial to our clients, employees, and shareholders. I wanted to build our market for our firm on a long-term basis. I wanted to treat all our staff in a professional, respectful manner. My philosophy was with me for my entire career. The people who worked with me knew what I represented, and they had the comfort of knowing it was not constantly changing. No matter what business you are in, you have to determine your philosophy. If you don't have one, you should sit down and work on one. Here are three simple things to think about to form your philosophy.

1. Determine what your philosophy of life is. You can't have a philosophy about business issues if you don't have a life

philosophy. Know what you stand for and have a value-based view of your life.

2. Determine your career philosophy. Determine what you want out of your career. Be realistic about how you want to balance your career and your personal life.

3. Determine your professional philosophy. Have a vision of not only what the current environment is but also what the environment will be in the future. If you don't have an opinion about the future, why should anyone follow you? If you don't have an opinion about the future, get out of leadership as soon as possible for everyone's benefit.

Next, you have to be able to communicate your philosophy to those on your team. Then you have to be consistent in your philosophy. If you follow those steps, you will be a successful, consistent leader.

CHAPTER SEVEN SUMMARY:

1. Be free of contradictions.
2. There can't be two yous. You have to be the same person every day.
3. Handle similar issues in a similar manner from day to day.
4. Handle similar issues with different people in the same manner.
5. You can't say one thing today and another tomorrow. You need to be personally consistent with a consistent philosophy.

Chapter Eight

Successful Leaders Are Decisive

Don't Be a Definite Maybe

To be a successful leader-manager, you have to be decisive. Probably the most frustrating thing to employees is working for a leader who can't make a decision. The phrase "don't be a definite maybe" is well known. The problem is that no one believes *he or she* are a definite maybe. The term itself is demeaning by what it implies. We all think we make decisions in a prompt or decisive manner, but I wonder if that is true and if that is what our employees think. I found that most leaders could make decisions about *things* quite easily. It's making decisions about *people* that is difficult. In many cases, middle managers can't make people decisions, or they vacillate over them. When it becomes apparent to people in the organization that they are working for a definite maybe, they begin to lose confidence in that person's leadership completely. Before getting into how to correct the definite-maybe factor, we need to look at its potential causes.

The first cause goes back to my earlier description of the newly promoted manager who the boss assumes is qualified for leadership just because the new manager is in the seat. We are back to Fournies's description: "I promoted you, so you must be qualified, because I would not have promoted an unqualified person."[7] Then you think, "Well, I was promoted to this position, so I must be qualified." And then, once you are in your position and you are in the middle of your first high-tension day, with a constant line of employees at your door looking for decisions on various issues, the panic sets in. It is then—if you are smart and hopefully a little self-analytical—that you realize you need help. When I went into management, I had no idea how difficult the people decisions were. I truly was not professionally prepared to handle the issues that came up. I could handle the technical issues, but not the people who had them. The interesting thought is that I don't know how much training it would have taken to properly prepare me. On-the-job training was the only training I had for decision-making skills—perhaps it was also yours.

Here are some definite-maybe warning signs:

1. You can't make a decision.
2. Any decision you do make can be changed from day to day.
3. Any decision made can be changed under pressure.
4. You typically find yourself taking the path of least resistance.
5. No one gets a direct answer.
6. There is never a prompt conclusion to matters.
7. You say "Let me get back to you" frequently.
8. You don't say it out loud, but you mean "Maybe yes, maybe no."
9. When people ask, you find yourself saying, "I haven't decided yet." When the pressure grows, you ask the person to give you a few more days. If it's a Friday, you put off the decision until Monday. Then you worry and lose sleep all weekend because you know a decision is due Monday morning.
10. When you make an unpopular decision, you pass the responsibility for it to someone else.

Do any of these ever describe you? Maybe not every item describes you, but do some of them describe you some of the time? Of course some do, because not all decisions are easy, and the ones that involve people are hardest. Let's discuss some things you can do to assist you in being a decisive decision maker.

QUALIFIED PEOPLE MAKE BETTER DECISIONS

The easiest issue to tackle is your qualifications for the position you are in. Simply put, if you are qualified, it's easier to make decisions. Do you know what it is that the people who work for you do? You see, there are times when managers are promoted to run something that they never actually did themselves. In my industry, in the early years, every branch manager had been a financial advisor to clients prior to becoming a manager. Then, after we were appointed to be branch managers, we continued to service our former clients as well as managing the local branch office. So we not only knew the functions taking place in our office but were actively living in the same environment as those we managed. We were player coaches! If there was an administrative problem in the business, we sensed it immediately, because it affected us as well as our employees. We really were qualified in the skills that our employees possessed. If something was broken in the business, we caught it immediately.

Later, we started requiring that branch managers cease handling their own client accounts and devote their time exclusively to management. The various investment firms wanted to be sure there were no conflicts of interest between the manager, the employees, and the clients. They also wanted to be sure that the employees were getting the right amount of management support and that industry regulations were being followed. In theory it made sense, but here is what happened. As soon as managers did not have their own clients, they lost that immediate knowledge of what was working well and what was working poorly in the business. Now they had to hear it from someone else, and they might not hear it promptly. The fact is that most times we don't hear about problems until it's time for someone to dump his or her issue bucket.

> **The fact is that most times we don't hear about problems until it's time for someone to dump his or her issue bucket.**

We progressed from managers handling clients to not handling clients and finally, in some cases, to never having had clients at all. Now there are managers in our industry who never were financial advisors themselves but manage a business made up of financial advisors. They never handled the needs of clients, but they are expected to make decisions based on what's right for the client. They do not think like the people they manage and have little ability to empathize with them. To that kind of manager, everything is theory. Everything is easy because it's theory, and everything this manager knows is from what he or she hears. That's when it gets hard to make decisions. When you haven't done it and you only know what you hear, it's tough to make decisions. The good news is there are ways to overcome this handicap and improve your chances for success.

But You Won't Always Know Enough

There may be a time when you are assigned to lead something that you would not have chosen to lead but could not turn down diplomatically. So you may not have the knowledge of the intricacies of the business you are leading. If that is the case, be honest with the people on your team and tell them the truth. There is no upside to faking it. Be honest and ask for help. Tell your staff you want to learn what they do. Let them know that you have broad knowledge of what the function is and where it fits and benefits the company but you want to know more. You can lead them by letting them see how what they are doing benefits the organization. Let them see that you are their advocate and can help them get the resources they need to be successful. You are comparable to a congressperson. Congresspeople may not be versed in the problem itself, but they know who to go to when they want to get something done. You have to build your go-to resources within your own organization to get things done for your constituents.

There is a lot you can offer. Let them see that you have qualifications that can help them to do better but you also need their help. Qualifications, if not learned from doing, can be learned from asking. Not all sports coaches were the best athletes, yet they can lead because they have learned the fundamentals of their sports; they can teach, can analyze their players' abilities, and can enhance those abilities. Business leaders can do the same thing.

Some Leaders Wilt in the Heat

Sometimes, even if they possess the proper qualifications, people are definite maybes because they can't make decisions. No one likes to admit that they can't make decisions, but there are people who are so concerned that their decision might be incorrect that they think and think of every possibility and still can't decide what to do. This happens frequently with analytical, scientific people. They assume that proper research and analysis will clearly define the perfect decision and then are surprised when it doesn't. So then they analyze again but still can't reach the perfect decision. Or they are so concerned that someone might be offended by their decision that no decision is made.

There are managers who are very effective as long as everything is going well. Then as soon as there is a difficult message to deliver, they tell everyone that it (the tough message) was from above them. If you are going to have a career in leadership, you might as well decide now that you can trust your knowledge and instinct and make your decisions promptly. Then move on to the next decision! We all make some good and some bad decisions—no one is perfect.

A person is an ineffective leader when he or she changes his or her decisions from day to day under pressure. You might think you never do this, but have you ever given a budget to one part of your business and then reduced it because another department heard you gave the first department money and wanted it too? Or maybe you set up a work schedule and then someone complained so you changed the schedule. Then someone who was affected by the change you just made complained, and you changed it again. Well, maybe it's not so clear, but there are times when you change, and when you do, it's disconcerting to your employees.

THE PATH OF LEAST RESISTANCE

Some managers find the easiest decision is the one that follows the path of least resistance. In other words, they make the decision that has the fewest negative consequences or effects the fewest people. That decision might not be best for the organization, but it provides the most peaceful environment. It might mean that they don't challenge their employees to reach for the next level and everyone under them becomes mediocre. The result is that they don't succeed because their business is less productive than it could be. Everyone was calm, including those managers, but they didn't succeed because they couldn't decide that excellence was worth making people a little uncomfortable. Those under them were not motivated to excel. The easy path was to ignore poor performance and not make a decision for excellence.

DON'T PASS THE BUCK

Some of the most disconcerting phone calls I have received are the ones that go something like this: "I asked my manager three times now if I could have additional administrative assistance, and he keeps saying he's waiting for a decision." It really could be any topic, but it's always the same type of conversation. "My manager says that he made the request and hasn't heard back yet." The implication is that this manager was waiting for a decision from me. Then I would call the manager to find out what was going on, and the manager would say that his budget did not allow for more administrative support. When I asked why he had not given his decision, he would say that he was trying to find the right time. The right time was as soon as the manager knew the answer, not a week or two later. Here is a fact that every veteran leader knows: When people don't get a prompt, direct answer to a request that they see as reasonable, they lose confidence in their leaders. A prompt no is acceptable if it's backed up with a prompt, logical reason. The lack of an answer is what frustrates people and sometimes causes a level of anger beyond what would have arisen from a simple no delivered immediately.

> **The right time was as soon as the manager knew the answer, not a week or two later.**

HANDLE EACH ITEM ONCE

To be a successful manager, you have to be able to handle many tasks and decisions and you can't let old ones sit on your shoulders for too long. Early on, when I was still a salesman, the president of a major corporation taught me to only handle each item (either paper or verbal) once. I had gone to his office to try to get him to do business with me. Instead, as I sat in front of his desk, he gave me a valuable lesson. I asked him how he rose to become president of his company. He said, "I will tell you exactly how I got to where I am today. If you pick it up, deal with it, finish it, and don't handle it twice. If you're asked—decide and move on. But don't keep dealing with the same things, because tomorrow there will be more things to deal with, and that's when they start piling up." If you find yourself saying, "Let me get back to you," or, "I haven't decided yet," you're on the wrong track. If you find you are losing sleep over your decisions, it means you didn't make them promptly enough. Otherwise, you wouldn't be in a position to lose sleep. If the to-do folder on your desk has items left over from yesterday or the day before, you are not leading efficiently or decisively.

> **If you pick it up, deal with it, finish it, and don't handle it twice.**

How to Be a Decisive Leader

I can't include a chapter on being a decisive leader without telling you the only tried and true way to be one. This is what worked for me, and it will work for you too. It starts with having the self-confidence to be sure that you are making the right decision. But you can't have confidence about a decision if you are not sure in your own mind that your decision is the right one. I always found that determining the right thing to do was the proper starting place. By the right thing, I mean that there is a moral compass that leaders must have in order to be successful. There is a heavy responsibility that leaders must carry, and no decision can ever be divorced from doing what is morally right. We have all seen leaders get caught doing what is wrong, and I don't need to list the examples. Just know this: you will never make a bad decision because you did what was morally right.

Next, never forget that you have a responsibility to the people you lead, the people you report to, and the people who use whatever good or service you provide. We already established that you are not in leadership just for your own gain. I found that remembering all three constituencies was important. I had a strong loyalty to Morgan Stanley and to the employees and believed that we were truly the best place for our clients to invest. I could be decisive about our firm and its people because I believed in our value to our clients. Just as importantly, I had a strong loyalty to our clients and found that decisions were easy to make if they were always based on doing what was right for them. Your leadership must be based on doing what is right for the customer at all times. It takes a generation to build brand loyalty, but it can be ruined overnight. The right decisions will be easy to make if they are always based on doing what is right for all three constituencies.

Remember that being decisive does not mean that you have to make quick, on-the-spot decisions all the time. There will be situations and decisions that, with experience, will be easy, because you will have seen them many times before. Those are the repetitive issues that come up over and over in all businesses. Most of the time, it's just a different person asking for a decision on an issue you have seen many times before. If you remember to be consistent with these decisions, you will be able to be decisive. It's different in the case of unusual and difficult issues. In these cases, be sure you get all the facts from all interested parties before deciding. The worst thing you can do is get partial input from a single source that will most likely be biased and use that to formulate your decision. I can remember numerous situations where I was asked for an immediate decision. These situations were usually the product of a long-festering issue or disagreement between two parties. Or they were the result of inactivity by a support department in accomplishing something for one of my star financial advisors. Suddenly, the situation was on my doorstep, and the interested parties always wanted an immediate answer and vow of support. My experience was that there was always more to the story I was being presented and there was always bias in what I was hearing. You must get all the facts to make a decisive decision. The person standing in front of you will be irate that you won't give that initial vote of unequivocal support, but there is a nice way of saying that you have to get all the facts. Wanting the facts doesn't make you a definite maybe, and it may take time to get them.

> **There was always more to the story I was being presented, and there was always bias in what I was hearing.**

Lastly, but importantly, get input from your immediate staff. They probably have already heard about the issue in question and will have the most unbiased input. Trust them! Then, once you have consulted your moral compass, remembered all your constituencies, gathered all the facts, and received input from your staff, it will be time for your decisive decision. Now it really is on your shoulders, and this is when you risk being a definite maybe if you can't make a decision.

A definite-maybe manager is harmful to the organization for all the reasons I have given. The biggest one, though, is that the employees see that they have a leader who can be maneuvered or intimidated into making only popular decisions. When this happens, the function that the manager was assigned to perform, that of leadership, is eliminated. Then there is no leadership at all, because the manager-leader becomes another employee in his or her own organization who sees not rocking the boat as the ticket to success. He or she becomes an administrator instead of a leader. In senior management, we know this has happened when a manager's employees call us with questions that could have easily been handled locally. For this reason, I purposefully gave everyone in my business my cell phone number—it was on everything I sent out—just to be sure I would hear directly if something was boiling up to the frustration level.

Learn to make decisions promptly. Finish what you start. You and your employees will be happier. If you have a family, they will be happier too, because you'll be more relaxed at home.

CHAPTER EIGHT SUMMARY:

1. Don't be a definite maybe. No one thinks he or she is a definite maybe, so it could be you.
2. Thing decisions are easier than people decisions.
3. It's easier to make decisions if you are qualified.
4. People need to dump their buckets.
5. Be decisive even when delivering a difficult message.
6. No one is decisively perfect, so make the decision and stop worrying about it.
7. Don't take the path of least resistance all the time.
8. Don't pass the buck on difficult decisions.
9. Handle each item once.

Chapter Nine

Successful Leaders Are Positive

I never would have guessed that some leaders find it so difficult to be positive—or put another way, that so many leaders start out with a negative personality. We all have met people in our lives who we instantly think of as being positive or negative. There is something about them that brings us to that instant judgment. The most obvious kind of negative person is the one who always sees things as insurmountable. "The deadline is too short to get a report done." "The annual goals are so high that I'll never attain them." "I'll never get promoted." These are the easy and obvious kinds of negativity. But there are more subtle kinds. For example, there is the manager who motivates with negatives. He says, "If you don't do this, I won't do that." "If you don't hit this goal, you'll lose $25,000 of your bonus." "If you're not in the top 50 percent of your peer group, you'll be replaced." "I don't see how your department can ever catch up." I knew a manager who used these kinds of incentives to motivate people. Everything was about what his managers would not get if they didn't do what he expected. Life in his region became intolerable. There was so much intimidation, so many threats of terminations and actual terminations, that even excellent managers left the organization rather than work for him.

TAKE-AWAY LEADERS

Many times, leaders like this don't realize how negative they are. They may have been brought up in a negative home where every motivation was through taking something away. "If you don't get an A, you can't have the car." Everything was an "if you don't" proposition. That's how the manager sees his or her leadership—"if you don't." These leaders probably don't realize how they come across to the people they are leading, because negativity is all they have ever known. I can remember a very stark example of a manager telling his staff that if they didn't achieve a particular goal then he would know they didn't care about him. He said, "If you don't care about me, I won't care about you." Actually, he used much more colorful language to get his point across. That's what I mean by a person who manages with take aways. He made two errors. One was that he made performance or lack of performance all about what it meant to his career, and the second was that he was too confrontational with the people whose support he needed to be successful.

THERE'S NO SUCH THING AS NEUTRAL

You can be a negative leader without realizing it, because you are automatically a negative leader if you are not a positive leader. The lack of being positive makes you negative. There are no neutral leaders. Thinking you are in the middle does not exempt you from being considered negative. When I have questioned managers about why they appear negative, they often say they don't want their staff to think they are a cheerleader for the company. They want to be neutral so that their staff will see them as intellectually honest, I suppose. Their teams know that the leader represents the organization. Why else is he or she there? Leaders do nobody any good by being neutral. They don't see themselves as others see them. If you are not positive, you are already negative.

Here's an example. I sat in on a sales meeting in one of my locations where the manager was describing a new initiative to his staff. He seemed depressed in the presentation. He had no voice inflection. He was monotone. He was clearly unexcited, and the people in the meeting could tell. I asked him later why he sounded the way he did. I asked if he had a problem with what the company was trying to accomplish. He said that he thought the initiative was excellent. "So," I said, "what happened?" His answer was simple and very honest. He didn't want his people to think that he was trying to impress me by being too enthusiastic. He thought he was playing to his audience. I was happy he told me the truth, because it gave us the opportunity to discuss his need to be accepted by his staff as one of them rather than being their leader. Leaders who want acceptance above all else are essentially ineffective, because they're not leading. My experience with this ineffective leadership became a coaching opportunity with positive results.

Another time, I sat in on a meeting where a manager was again so unenthusiastic that he appeared to be trying not to get people interested in a particular new service. I got up to speak after the manager, and I felt it was important to review the new service that he had just spoken about. I asked the manager later what had happened. He normally was a good public speaker. Again, he was honest and said he had not had the time to prepare his presentation. That explained his fumbling delivery—he wasn't prepared. Lack of preparation will always come across as you being negative. If you are not positive, you are negative.

LOVE WHAT YOU DO

The most successful leaders are people who are passionate about their sports, businesses, family lives, or whatever it is that they are doing. Try to imagine an unenthusiastic sports coach. Try to imagine a non-passionate politician. Try to picture how boring an opera singer without passion would be. Many leaders want to appear neutral to their employees so that they are seen as unbiased and not company parrots, so to speak. These leaders think that by being neutral. they will be seen as unbiased and out for the interest of the employees. Rather, they are seen as people who don't care enough about what they do to be enthusiastic. You have to start first with loving what you do. If you love what you do and believe you are good at it, you won't have a problem in communicating positively to those you lead. How many times has someone told you to pick a career that you love? In college, we all were probably instructed to pick a major we loved or to play a sport we loved. That's the advice many of us have received from the first time our parents coached us about life. It's still the same today, only it's not your parents or teachers coaching you—it's you who needs to coach yourself.

> **My worst days were better than everyone else's best days.**

I interviewed, recruited, and trained many new salespeople. In their first interviews, most candidates would ask me what I liked about my business. I said the following to every person who asked: "This is the greatest business in the world. I have been doing this for years, and I can honestly say that my worst days are better than everyone else's best days." I truly felt that way about the business I was in, the company I worked for, and the people with whom I worked. I loved to go to my office because I loved what I did. My worst days were better than everyone else's best days. How would it have made the candidate feel if I had said, "Well, I have enjoyed the business, but you have to decide for yourself if it is something you would enjoy." How would that make you feel coming from the person who ran the business? Would you go home thinking, "He was so honest with me"? Or would you think, "Why does this man represent his company?" I think it would be the latter.

MOTIVATION IS NOT OPTIONAL

As a leader, it is expected that you will be a motivator. Motivating others is not an optional part of leadership in management. Neutral or negative people cannot motivate. Just like you can't motivate through intimidation, you can't motivate through neutrality and passive acceptance of whatever comes your way. You either have something to offer people, or you don't. You've heard the phrase "an empty shirt." That's you if you don't have something in you worth following. If you love what you do, it will be easy for you to have something to follow.

DON'T HAVE NEGATIVE MEETINGS

> **A simple rule is to handle uplifting issues in a group meeting and handle negative issues door to door.**

I had a few simple rules to keep myself positive. One was that I tried never to have a negative meeting. You know before you start how a negative meeting will end up. You know before you start who the people are who will break up the meeting and turn it into a disaster. Finally, you know how you are going to feel after the meeting. So why have it? A simple rule is to handle uplifting issues in a group meeting and handle negative issues door to door. Does that sound like a cowardly way to handle negatives? A rookie leader would say, "Stand tall and handle negatives up front and in a meeting. Take it like a man." It sounds cool! But with the maturity that comes from many leadership years, I have found that going door to door with the delivery of a negative issue is more effective, because it makes it possible to handle the personal questions everyone will have on the spot. In a group meeting, one person tends to ask all the questions, and he or she ends up monopolizing the meeting. He or she determines the meeting's outcome. His or her agenda is not your agenda! Going door to door allows everyone to vent immediately rather than leaving the meeting, going home, venting to a spouse or friend, and then coming into the office the next day ready to pounce. Everyone is more positive if you handle as many issues as possible personally with your staff. And, as an added benefit, people are more courteous in a private meeting than in a group meeting. Every good coach knows the value of having a good relationship with his or her players. Every coach knows to treat everyone as an individual. Dealing with issues face to face lets people know you care about how they are going to react to the message you are delivering.

THERE'S ALWAYS SOMETHING POSITIVE

You can always find something positive to highlight. Maybe it's just one product line or one person. Maybe it's something that was good yesterday or today. Leaders can always find something good to highlight.

> **You should be as visible as possible to everyone who reports to you.**

But let's assume that you really are in a difficult environment and business is terrible. You look around, and there is nothing to get positive about. You are concerned that you will appear to be a Pollyanna, an eternal optimist, if you are too positive. You fear that those who report to you will think you are unrealistic and out of touch with what's really going on. What do you do in that case? You should be as visible as possible to everyone who reports to you.

- The worse things get, the more visible you should be. The worse things are, the more your leadership is needed.
- Remember that their eyes are always on you. When things are unusually difficult, the people who you lead will be watching your face, your posture, and particularly your eyes to see how bad it really is. Your employees will be listening to every word you say, and they will analyze everything you say.

How you behave in a crisis situation will often define how others view your leadership. There are leaders who miss the greatest opportunity of their careers to be relevant to the people on their teams by abdicating leadership in a crisis.

So what can you do when *you think* there is nothing positive to talk to your team about?

- First, notice the emphasis on *you think*. Maybe you see things more pessimistically than everyone else. I have known times when managers were far more negative than was warranted by general business circumstances. Don't confuse your personal circumstances with all business in your company. Your department might be closing because another department is responsible for a technology that your firm finds can replace what your department does. Productivity might have risen so dramatically because of innovation that your firm can reduce your staff level. What is bad for you and the people on your team might be very good for the corporation as a whole.
- Second, there are leaders who allow personal circumstances to dictate how they view the general environment. In particular, when a leader is passed over for a promotion, there is the greatest opportunity for a general letdown. The loss of a promotion can cloud the thinking of some of the most positive people.

IF THINGS ARE REALLY BAD, THEN ENCOURAGE

If things are genuinely bad, you need to *encourage* the people who work for you. We leaders earn our worth in the bad times more than in the good times. In the boom times, you can sometimes put your business on autopilot and everything will be great. It's not so in difficult times. Encouraging the people you lead and giving them confidence that someone is in control of the business is your most important task in difficult times. As a veteran manager, I saw that the times senior management was most relevant to the firm came during the worst crises. Our firm was a major tenant in the World Trade Center on September 11, 2001. Of course, at first we were most concerned for the people who were directly involved in the tragedy at all levels. Then the press and public wondered how badly the attack had damaged our firm. There was a question as to whether we would be ready to operate on the day the New York Stock Exchange opened for business. What happened was a lesson in corporate communications. Starting the day after the attack, a new command center was set up across the river from Manhattan in New Jersey. Our senior leaders were on the internal speaker system speaking to the entire company on September 12. Our president had his entire operating committee with him. He encouraged us, because he was visible and was obviously dealing with the crisis. Every day, sometimes twice a day, he told us how the firm was progressing in order to be ready to open again for business. It was an example of leadership in a difficult situation. On the day the NYSE opened, we opened, our leaders were successful. They knew that everyone in the company was looking to them for encouragement that everything would be okay.

> **Encouraging the people you lead and giving them confidence that someone is in control of the business is your most important task in difficult times.**

In October 2008, the financial system of our nation was reeling, and our firm was under siege like many others. Once again, the thing that stands out in my mind are the daily in-house television briefings from our leaders. Everyone knew things were bad, but our leaders encouraged us by letting us know that the firm was doing the right things for the employees, investors, and shareholders. We were told exactly what was going on each day. We found that we could trust what we were told because it was true. Leadership pulled us through. Our leaders were able to pull us through because they encouraged us and we had confidence in them.

That's the kind of leader you have to be. The worse things become, the more visible you have to be and the more you have to encourage people. You encourage your team by letting them know what you are doing to get them back on track. When times are bad, you need to communicate more than you ever did before. You are being a positive leader when you communicate with people. You are a positive leader when you take a difficult situation and turn it into a learning experience for your team. If your department failed to attain the goals set by the firm, communicate that fact to your team. You can deliver the message in a coaching manner rather than a punitive manner. After the fiscal year is over, it's pointless to beat everyone up over their poor performance over and over again. Once you deliver the bad news, get on with deciding what has to be done to improve in the new year. You encourage people by showing them you have a plan that will allow them to do better.

KEEP SCORE OF THE POSITIVES

One way to gauge whether or not you are a positive and encouraging leader is to keep score on yourself. We teach athletes and sales professionals to keep score. We have always measured anything important by keeping score. You should have your own daily positive-encouragement score card. You don't need to show it to anyone else. It's for you to see. Write down the actions that you would categorize as positive and encouraging. Log in the time of day, who it was you encouraged, and what the end result or action step was. This exercise will tell you several important things about yourself:

1. You will see how many times each day you engage in dialogue with the people you lead. We all know that there are many distractions in management that can fill your day. Logging

in the time will start to give you a picture of whether there is a time of day you are more or less productive.

2. With this exercise, you also have the opportunity to grade yourself on the amount of time you spend in the task of leading and encouraging. **For most managers, the time put into actual leadership tasks is less than the time put into administrative tasks**.

3. Next, because you have written the name of the person you encouraged, you will have a record of how many positive influences (opportunities to provide leadership) you have had with each person.

4. You will also have a record of what you discussed for future follow-up.

5. You will know if you are spending too much time with some people and too little time with others. I found that if I didn't keep track there would be people I missed. Keeping track kept me from spending too much time with the people who were already positive and growing and too little time with the more difficult personalities.

Here is the simple truth of leadership. There are people who are easy to lead. They are the people who are a leader's dream. You already know who they are in your organization. We leaders don't speak openly about it, but there are people we like to be around because they make us feel good when we speak to them. They confirm our vision of the model employee. They do everything we ask and do it well. It's only natural to want to spend more time with these people than with some of the other employees, but that's a mistake. Logging your interactions can help you to avoid this problem. Writing down the action steps you've agreed upon with an employee also gives you what you need for a follow-up meeting.

Finally, judge your conversation with each individual by asking yourself these questions:

*   Would the person who you spoke with say that you encouraged him or her in some manner?
*   Would you say he or she felt good after speaking to you?
*   Third, did the person feel better when leaving your office than when he or she came in?

Keep a scorecard on yourself.

SAY POSITIVE THINGS

Encourage people by taking the time to say something positive to them. I was responsible for twenty locations in three states, so I couldn't be every place every day. But I could work the phones on a daily basis and speak to people almost instantly. The phone made my geography small. No matter where someone was, I could speak to them within seconds. Some people were early people, so I called them first. Others, I knew, arrived at the office later, so I called them in the afternoon. Here's what I found by calling people on the phone: They would tell me more on the phone than in person. They would tell me everything that was on their minds. I assume it was because on the phone we were just voices—no presence—and they were comfortable speaking that way. I think we are all so accustomed to communicating by phone, computer, or Blackberry that person-to-person dialogue is more difficult. Leaders encourage by communicating. Encouraging others is a positive act of leadership.

> **My employees would tell me more on the phone than in person.**

We are positive leaders when we have a vision to share with our teams that is more enduring than the immediate circumstance. In a later chapter, we will talk about vision, but here it is important to say that vision should trump the current environment if you communicate properly.

CHAPTER NINE SUMMARY:

1. Don't be a negative or a take-away manager.
2. You are automatically negative when you're not positive.
3. Being positive requires preparation.
4. Love your work.
5. Remember my motto: "My worst days are better than everyone else's best days."
6. Motivating is not an optional leadership function.
7. Don't be an empty shirt.
8. Handle negatives one-on-one.

9. There is always something positive to highlight.
10. If things are really bad, encourage people more.
11. Keep your positive activity score.
12. Say positive things to people.

CHAPTER TEN

SUCCESSFUL LEADERS ARE INSPIRING

Did you inspire someone today? Does that sound like a strange question? With all you have going on in your personal and professional life, how would you have time to inspire someone? I'm talking about the kind of inspiration where you allow somebody to achieve a level of performance beyond what they thought was possible. *Inspire* is a remarkable word. We don't use it much in business. It should be what we leaders are about. If you are like me, there are probably times when you do inspire people, times when you fail someone miserably, and times when you are merely average.

DO YOU ENCOURAGE OR INSPIRE?

> **Being an inspirational factor in someone's career should be a part of your leadership responsibility every day.**

In looking back over my leadership career, I have to admit that most of the times that I thought I was inspiring, I was really only *encouraging* people who were already self-inspired. I encouraged people who were not self-inspired but were average and needed a lift to do a little better. But there were too few cases when I took an average person and made that person far better than he or she would have been without me. However, if we are going to be leader-managers, I submit that inspiration is something we should think about every day. My only regret after thirty-seven years in sales leadership is that I did not do more inspiring work with the people I managed. I did do it—sometimes! I just should have done more of it. That's the point of this chapter. I want to give you a heads-up that being an inspirational factor in someone's career should be a part of your leadership responsibility every day.

To be an inspiration to someone, you first have to realize that people need and want your leadership—*if* you are worthy to lead them. For now, we will assume that your employees accept you as a worthy leader. In those situations where the leadership was accepted, the biggest problem I encountered as a supervisor of managers was that most managers are too timid to perform the inspirational aspect of their jobs. In fact, most managers abdicate the inspirational part of leadership because they do not believe that they can do it successfully or that their employees need it. Being inspirational requires that you have a vision. It starts with you, not the employee! I can think of plenty of examples where highly motivated people came to me with a vision and a plan to attain greater success and I supported their activities. Most of us confuse being inspirational with being encouraging or supportive. I did! There were fewer cases when I saw that someone could achieve more and inspired them to do so.

Learn How to Inspire

The reason that business leaders don't inspire is that they lack a vision, don't know how to inspire, or are timid. Great political leaders know how to inspire and are not bashful about doing it. Their egos drive them to believe that they have the answers we need. Think about the creators of our Declaration of Independence. They not only had a vision but could inspire our country to go to war for their vision. Can you imagine how powerful the British Army must have seemed to the general public at that time? Yet the leaders and the public risked their lives and fortunes because they were inspired. President Ronald Reagan had a vision of a world without the Soviet Union and knew how to inspire us to greater heights than we thought possible. We could go on and name many more political and religious leaders who possessed the skill to take their vision from thought to words to action. We business leaders rarely possess that same talent or the belief that we can and should inspire people.

Sports coaches inspire routinely, perhaps because it's expected of them, but also because they know that they can win more games with an inspired team. They probably know that they don't have to inspire every single person on the team to win on any given day, but by trying to inspire everyone, they know they will inspire someone. If they get just a few players to deliver far beyond the norm, they will win. The coach's preparation starts well before the game and then builds into the great locker-room pre-game pep rally. If that's not enough, there is still the halftime locker-room oration to inspire every player to give his or her all in the second half.

INSPIRATION REQUIRES TIME AND KNOWLEDGE

What can you do to be an inspirational leader to the people who report to you? You have to realize it is easier to come up with a grand vision for your business than to come up with a vision for an individual. It is a unique challenge to inspire an individual. The reason for this is that the individual vision takes a one-on-one knowledge of the person and the levels of achievement that person can attain. It requires you to go deep and really know your people and their talents. It also requires you to accept that people want your leadership, because in most cases they can do better than they are doing but need help to achieve more. It means that you have to stretch your thinking about what is possible for each particular person to achieve. Finally, it requires that you be willing to devote time to each person you want to inspire. In fact, the task of inspiring will require a lot of time from you if you choose to do it.

> **It is easier to come up with a grand vision for your business than to come up with a vision for an individual.**

Perhaps you are a leader who was an average employee who did not personally excel before your promotion. Yet you are called upon to inspire those who work for you to attain great heights. Do you think you can call on others to achieve something that might be beyond your personal reach? As you will see in a later chapter, sports coaches do it all the time. It's really just a matter of knowing your business and the individual you want to inspire. If you have confidence that your vision of what the individual can achieve is the correct one, then you should be able to communicate it properly. To do this, you have to have knowledge of the business, the function, and the individual.

If you get to know the individual, you will see what is possible. It's important to realize that there are people on your business team who are far more accomplished than you are or were. They want to grow but need someone to inspire and coach them. Even people who want and have the ability to be great in their careers need leaders. Your role as an inspiring leader is to motivate people to grow today when they would rather grow tomorrow. Then, once they start growing, it's your job to motivate them to grow beyond their comfort level when they would rather stay comfortable.

EVERYONE HAS A COMFORT ZONE

Most people settle into a comfort zone and will not grow their careers beyond their self-imposed limitations without an interested leader. The problem is that most people will not admit that they are in a comfort zone. They will look for any excuse not to grow. If they are in sales, they will say they are too busy with their existing clients to add additional clients. They will say that they don't have enough administrative support to grow. They will say that they need more advertising money. Believe it or not, the comment I heard most was, "I am growing—why don't you see it?" I wanted to bluntly say, "I do see it, and you're not growing." Fortunately, I found a more diplomatic way to get my point across. I would ask them to help me understand why my conclusion was wrong, to show me how they saw their business growing. If they were in administration, they would often say that they needed more staff to do better. Most underachievers will not, on their own, take themselves into an uncomfortable zone from a comfortable zone. It's not a reasonable expectation. I have seen people get angry at any mention that they are in a comfort zone. Because of that, we leaders have to find ways to get people out of something (a comfort zone) that they don't know they're in and into something (an uncomfortable zone) that they won't admit they're not in. It's almost like we have to be stealth inspirational leaders to achieve our goals.

Early in my career, I thought all I had to do was show someone objective data that proved that he or she was not growing and that then that person would immediately agree to participate in a growth program. So I tried the objective approach and found that people would get very defensive. The direct, fact-based approach was most likely a result of all the industrial management courses I took in college. We were taught things like motion and time study, workflow analysis, and ways to improve productivity. Too bad that I forgot the Hawthorne effect, the idea that productivity improves because of attention and interest shown in people. The greatest leaders instinctively know that it's the attention and interest they show in people that gain them willing, consenting followers, not the objective, cold facts of performance. Fortunately, I learned sooner rather than later that to be an inspirational leader requires that same ingredient I mentioned in an earlier chapter—caring about each individual. Caring takes time and requires that you see people as your greatest asset.

RECOGNIZE TALENT

To be inspiring leaders, we also need to possess the ability to recognize talent in people and then develop that talent. When I look back at my career, I can say with complete conviction that the decisions I made to select certain people for advancement in *their* careers were the decisions that advanced *my* career. Let me repeat that! The success you have in your career will be determined by the success you foster in the careers of the people on your team. Looking back today, I can go through my career and list almost every person I promoted or inspired to do better and show how their successes created my success. If you can't do that yourself, you can use this book as a refresher course in leadership. As you learn to become an inspiring leader, you will eventually come to the same conclusion that every successful leader comes to—it's about them, not you! You will also realize that there is some risk to you that is acceptable risk. That's because you won't always be right when choosing which people to inspire or promote.

> **The success you have in your career will be determined by the success you foster in the careers of the people on your team.**

Now let's look at a very common example of the kind of person you may be called upon to inspire. For this purpose, I am going to assume that you have a vision that a certain person has the ability to double her sales volume in five years. That's about a 15 percent growth rate, but more importantly, it is far beyond the 5 percent this particular person has historically grown. The person is very satisfied with the 5 percent growth rate, because it provides her and her family with the standard of living she desires. She often says that she has everything she wants and considers herself very successful. She is not unhappy; to the contrary, she is very satisfied. However, you know that this person has the ability to accomplish far more than what she is currently accomplishing. If you are a new leader, believe me when I tell you that this example of the relatively successful, comfortable, happy, and somewhat complacent employee is the type you will meet more often than not. You will find that the bell curve is alive and well in business.

This is important! Your team will also include a few of the highly motivated, success-oriented people all managers dream about who only need our encouragement and support to excel. These people are your bread-and-butter, so treat them like gold. Give them whatever they need to grow further. I looked at these high achievers as hungry tigers pacing back and forth, impatient for the achievement of greater success. All I had to do was throw raw meat into their cages. I knew they would always take the raw meat and turn it into valuable new revenues. Everyone knows the eighty-twenty rule, which states that 80 percent of your revenues will come from 20 percent of your people. Stop and think every day about those in the top 20 percent. Be sure you have done everything possible to further their efforts through your inspiration.

There will be a few who are completely unmotivated, and any effort you put into them will be nothing more than career life support and a waste of your time. Many leaders, however, think that they are just the people to turn their underachievers around. At the beginning of their careers, many leaders put more time into the unmotivated than the highly motivated. It's a poor use of your time and will not bear fruit.

> **At the beginning of their careers, many leaders put more time into the unmotivated than the highly motivated. It's a poor use of your time and will not bear fruit.**

The vast majority of the people you lead will be average individuals who do an average job and are very content doing it. The good news for you and me is that this type of person is the exact reason companies need leaders, and these people can be very enjoyable to inspire! In the long run, we will define our success by how we inspire and motivate average people to excel.

BREAK THINGS DOWN INTO MANAGEABLE TASKS

The key to inspiring people is to start with setting a goal and then to break it down into manageable parts. This is the aspect of inspiring that most leaders fail to grasp. Professional athletes and coaches understand the concept very well. Baseball spring training is a great example. Professional major league baseball players represent a small percentage of the thousands of excellent baseball players who play in the minor leagues or on college teams. They are the best there is. Yet, every spring they show up for spring training to prepare for the coming season. They know that to be the best, they have to work on all the fundamentals that make a great professional. They first work on conditioning so that their bodies are ready. They work on reviewing fundamentals. The batting coaches work with the players. The fielding coaches work with their players. The pitching coach works his players. Everything is broken down into a series of small, manageable goals. Then, as each skill is remastered, the team starts practice games. Eventually, when the season starts and the players take the field for the opening game, the team is at its peak of performance.

As an example, the immediate concern of the salesperson you want to see double sales in five years is what she does today! If you can't get that salesperson to accept the fact that she can do more today than yesterday, you will never accomplish the five-year goal. You have to create the vision of doubling sales for her, but then you have to be able to define the actions that she has to execute today. So you really have two jobs—one is to get this average, happy person to agree to grow at the rate you want, and the other is to get that person to buy into the daily actions required. Inspiring leaders are not only great at defining a vision; they also define the actions required to achieve the goal. They have the ability to get people to perform beyond their comfort levels.

> **Inspiring leaders are not only great at defining a vision; they also define the actions required to achieve the goal.**

The Successful Achievement of Small Tasks Will Define You

The truth in all this is that if you want to be an inspiring leader, you have to start with you. You really are the one who has to have a vision for your people. Next, you have to inspire yourself to want to act on the vision. Then, you have to be willing to do the small tasks today and tomorrow that are necessary to make even the average person feel inspired. So for you, just like for your employees, it's the small tasks that will define you. If you don't take the time today to do the people-to-people coaching necessary, you will never be inspirational. Do you want to know what to do? Pick one person right now who works for you and decide today that you are going to inspire that person. If you start with one person today, then you can pick another tomorrow. There is no sense worrying about tomorrow if you don't start today. In fact, try to do it in the next hour!

Chapter Ten Summary:

1. Most of us encourage rather than inspire.
2. People want and need leadership.
3. We need a vision ourselves in order to be inspirational.
4. Don't confuse support with inspiration.
5. You need knowledge, and you can't be timid.
6. We don't have to inspire every person, but we need to inspire some.

7. We can't inspire without a deep knowledge of our people.
8. An average person can become an inspirational leader.
9. Everyone has a comfort zone, but many people won't admit it.
10. Our people are our greatest asset.
11. Objective data doesn't motivate anyone.
12. We need to recognize talent to be inspirational.
13. Their success creates our success.
14. There is some risk involved.
15. People tend to fit the bell curve.
16. Go for the lowest common denominator.
17. Inspiring leadership starts with your activities today.
18. Pick one person today and another tomorrow. There's no sense worrying about tomorrow if you don't act today.

Chapter Eleven

Successful Leaders Are Honest

I mentioned this chapter topic to a friend, and his first reaction was, "Of course a leader should be honest!" He was correct, because he was thinking about the traditional honesty all leaders should possess. We certainly should be honest whether we are at the office or at home. It is too simple, though, to look at leadership honesty in the traditional manner. We need to expand on what it means to be honest specifically in a leadership context. In this chapter, I want to discuss some of the more subtle issues of honesty that will arise in your leadership career.

Being Honest with Yourself

You have to start with being honest with yourself. There is no point worrying about anything else if you are not honest with you. It comes down to knowing yourself and what you want from your career. The place to start is to ask yourself how hard you are willing to work to be a successful leader. If you love what you are doing, you will love the hard work it takes to be a success. I know in my heart that I was not more talented than the many leaders I outlasted in my organization. You don't have to be the most talented person to rise to the top, but you do have to be the hardest worker. Here is an example: I went through training with two very talented salespeople. They had all the right credentials, including a long history of sales success. I came to my company directly

107

from the army, and I had minimal sales experience. They had sales experience, and all I knew how to do was follow orders. We all received the exact same technical training and heard the same lectures regarding the level of difficulty involved in building a successful business. We all heard how to build a business from successful salespeople. Naturally, the two people with sales experience were far more successful than me—in the beginning! By the second year of our careers, two of us were still working fourteen-hour days, and the third had left the business. The one who left finally had to be honest with himself and admit that he wasn't willing to continue to sacrifice his time with his family. I can remember him telling me that his spouse was tired of putting the children to bed alone every night. If success requires fourteen-hour days and you don't want to give that much time, then you have to be honest with yourself and not make-believe you want something you have no interest in pursuing.

Honesty with yourself also means knowing what you are willing to give up for your career. An example would be relocation. If the top jobs in your company are in Houston and you have no interest in moving there, then we can agree that you either have to limit your ambitions by staying away from the home office or find another company whose home office is in an acceptable location. I have known many people, including me, who would not relocate under any circumstance. Relocation is a qualitative decision that everyone will be faced with at some point. I decided that the fourteen-hour days were worthwhile if my family was in a stable, consistent, and familiar location. With the support of family and extended family, I was free to pursue success in our home town. In my company, relocation was not forced on people. In other companies, employees have to choose between relocating and leaving. In any event, honesty requires that if you are not willing to relocate and promotions require relocation, you shouldn't complain when others get the positions you think you deserve.

I can't possibly list all the areas in which you should be honest with yourself. Perhaps in later editions I'll complete the list, but for now—be honest with you so that you can be honest with others!

BE HONEST WITH YOUR EMPLOYER

I suppose that I have an old-fashioned view of what it means to be honest with my employer. As a pre–baby boomer, I was brought up in the era of strong loyalty to country (World War II had just ended), family, friends, community, church, and employer. In the decade following World War II, patriotism was at a fever pitch. I can remember the Memorial Day parades in our town of Valley Stream, NY. It seemed as though the parade went on for hours. Every organization in town marched. People cheered the veterans, who came out to march in their old uniforms. Even as late as 1961, the level of patriotism and belief in the system was incredibly strong. I was at the Devon Horse Show in Devon, PA, when President Dwight Eisenhower visited the showgrounds. He had just left office. He came into the grounds in an open Jeep. I can still picture the cheering crowd, many of whom had tears streaming down their faces as he passed them. People stretched their arms just to touch the jeep he rode in.

It was easy to be loyal and honest with an employer with that kind of background. Our elders, perhaps because of the Depression, taught my generation to cherish our jobs and our employers. We were taught the value of an honest day's work. Now, let's fast forward to 2010! We are far from the era of the Depression and World War II. Our children have been brought up in a much more cynical environment. Patriotism, except for the period following 9/11, has been relatively low. Employees' confidence in their employers is low. It seems almost impossible to have a life-long career with one organization. And here is the biggest change that I have seen over my career: many employees, even within leadership teams, view their employment as just a job and not a career to be cherished. They are willing to give just enough to their jobs to earn a reasonable living and not so much that it detracts from their other interests.

> **Many employees, even within leadership teams, view their employment as just a job and not a career to be cherished.**

Honesty with our employers means that we should examine our personal goals for our lives and then determine what level of leadership position is appropriate. We all make decisions between our careers and personal lives every day, and we should be honest about those decisions. As a leader, my most difficult task was finding truly committed individuals to join our firm and lead in my area of responsibility.

BE HONEST ABOUT WHAT'S REALISTIC

Have you ever worked for an unrealistic person? Or have you ever been with someone who had no sense of reality and was always striving for the pot of gold? It's sad when someone you lead is always dreaming about great success but never puts out the effort required to achieve it. The individual is dishonest, because while he or she has dreams, he or she has no intention of performing the many small tasks required for success. It is equally dishonest when you, as the leader, set lofty goals but then fail to provide the leadership required to achieve them. Rookie leaders almost always overreach when setting the goals for their teams. Wise leaders know that the goals they set should be realistically achievable by the organization. There is no point in setting people up to fail. Yet leaders often do just that. I remember being at one of those annual meetings that all companies have when the goals for the new year—and more importantly, the bonus program—were announced. An elaborate stage was set in the front of this large auditorium. Uplifting music played as we entered the room. Then it came time for the official presentation of goals and compensation. All of us in the audience knew that the goals had been set too high, and to make matters worse, the compensation formula almost took achievement for granted. And without the achievement of the unrealistic goals, we were all going to make much less money. We had just finished one of the most incredible years of increased revenues, profits, and margins. It seemed the new compensation formula took profits for granted, and my experience suggested that as soon as you take any part of business for granted, you are guaranteeing failure. So, naturally, we went from one of the best years ever to one of our weaker years. In short, leaders should be honest in setting goals for people so that those striving to achieve them believe that they are getting a fair deal.

BE HONEST ABOUT HOW PEOPLE ARE DOING

I mentioned earlier that one of the hardest things for new leaders to learn is one-on-one interaction with employees. This is particularly difficult when it falls upon the new leader to give an employee an honest assessment of his or her quality of performance. Our company, like most companies, had an annual performance assessment of all employees. Everyone received a formal performance evaluation in writing and in person. If you haven't done it already, it is something you will certainly be called on to do. For these performance evaluations to be effective, the leaders are required to be completely honest in their assessments. On one occasion, a manager told me that one of his management people was not doing a good job. At the end of the year, though, the performance evaluation was quite the opposite, and the employee was ranked relatively highly. It turned out that the leader-manager was reluctant to confront the employee with his shortcomings, because he would have had to do it in person, and he was not prepared for that kind of conversation. It turned out that he had not properly coached the individual during the year and felt it was unfair to rate poor performance that had not been addressed before.

This may be an extreme example, but how often do you fail to give the constructive criticism necessary for the improvement in someone's performance? Everyone knows they are not perfect in everything they do. Why do leaders pretend people are perfect? I had the finest assistant any leader could possibly have, but even then, proper coaching mixed with constructive criticism was sometimes necessary. I would have been dishonest to my assistant if I had not provided proper coaching. That person is far better today than twenty or ten or five years ago because I was honest with her over the years. And by the way, she was honest in her assessments of me too. She became my local eyes, ears, and conscience. Because my leader was a hundred miles away, no one really viewed my daily actions and decisions except the people who worked for me. Frankly, it is hard to get direct, constructive criticism from people who work for you. They are uncomfortable providing it. Now here is the very positive outcome of me providing coaching to my assistant over a period of thirty years: She became my unofficial coach. She coached me when I needed it and there was no one else around to do it. That's how being an honest leader who gives honest assessments benefits both you and the organization.

> **Because I was honest and offered coaching, she was honest and offered coaching in return.**

Remember this: Early coaching benefits an employee the most. Great leaders see everything that goes on around them. The great ones that I have known don't miss much. We will discuss the failure of micro leaders later. They fail because they spend their time *doing micro functions*, not because they *see micro needs*. The great leaders see micro and then they lead macro. So if you see someone performing in a less than excellent manner, it is your responsibility to address it immediately. By addressing it immediately and not waiting for a formal quarterly review, you are doing the employee a great favor. He or she has the opportunity to improve immediately and therefore get a far better review.

Here is an example. As I previously mentioned, I had sales offices spread around three states. Because of this, I used the phone to touch base with different salespeople every day. My calls served two purposes. First, they gave me valuable ear time with my top producers. Second, the calls gave me the opportunity to assess the client service model in the various offices. I always called on the office's main phone number as if I did not know the direct dial number. I wasn't a big policy maker, but because our livelihood was based on high-net-worth investors, I had set in place a certain service model. One part of the model was that everyone who answered the phone would give a name as part of the standard greeting. Very often, when I called our offices, the people who answered the phones omitted their names. I had two choices! One was to ignore the oversight and assume that the person usually provided a name. The other was to use the occasion as a coaching opportunity and remind the person that our policy was to offer our names when we answered the phone. Leaders are honest when they provide immediate, honest coaching.

Sometimes honest leadership means that we have to tell people that they are not performing at a high enough level to keep their positions. When that happens, don't wimp out and tell the person that he or she does a great job but you are just cutting back staff numbers. If you are properly leading, the person in this situation should have had several conversations with you regarding the poor performance, and the termination should be no surprise. My rule of thumb regarding how effective coaching conversations have been is this: If I felt any insecurity or had any question in my mind that the termination was coming as a surprise to a person, I re-reviewed the circumstances leading up to the termination to be sure that there had not been a breakdown in our leadership procedures. The termination session should not be the coaching session. It's too late at that point.

BE HONEST WITH YOUR CLIENTS

For our discussion, we will assume that any end user of your product or service is a client. If you are leading a sports team, your clients are the spectators. If you are leading an orchestra, your clients are the audience. If you are leading a factory, your clients are the people who eventually buy your products. In my case, our clients were the thousands of people, companies, trusts, and institutions who entrusted us with billions of investment dollars. These clients were the ultimate beneficiaries of our honesty with ourselves, our employers, and our employees. Because we were honest inside the business, we had the opportunity to be honest with our clients. For our industry, the primary opportunity to be honest was providing proper investment guidance given the unique circumstances surrounding each person's economic and life situation. Defining *honest* was pretty easy for us. As a managing director of Morgan Stanley, I believed that we could provide a level of honest service to our clients that could not be matched anywhere else. Our worldwide research analysts provided our financial advisors with the finest information possible. That's what I believed about what I did. I gave you that commercial on Morgan Stanley for a reason. Do you believe that the end user of your service or factory or team is receiving the finest that your organization has to offer? Do you feel that the quality of what you are providing is worthy to be called honest service? If you don't feel it's the best service in your particular industry and you are clearly second or third, then you are not providing honest service. Rather, you are being dishonest to your clients, because you really should be telling them to do business with the top provider instead. If you're not leading your team to be the best, then you are dishonest to your team and your clients.

> **Do you feel that the quality of what you are providing is worthy to be called honest service?**

Finally, see honest leadership as your calling. Seek to provide nothing less than the best you have. Your career will fly by, and you will go from being the new leader to the retired leader almost overnight. If you retire knowing that you gave your best every day to your employer, employees, and clients, you will be truly satisfied with your career.

CHAPTER ELEVEN SUMMARY:

1. Be honest with yourself.
2. Be honest about what can be achieved.
3. Be honest with your employer.
4. Be honest about how people are performing.
5. Be honest with your clients.

CHAPTER TWELVE

SUCCESSFUL LEADERS INSTILL CONFIDENCE AND GAIN LOYALTY

This chapter will explore what it takes to instill confidence in those we are leading. Then, I will discuss the result of the confidence we have earned. I have already touched on many of the ways leaders can build confidence:

- have the right motives,
- always be the same person (there can't be two yous),
- have the right values,
- be a good listener,
- be consistent,
- be decisive,
- be positive,
- be inspirational,
- communicate directly and openly,
- lead—don't push—and have knowledge of the people you are leading.

There are a few other traits that are extremely important, and if any of them are missing in us, everything else we want to accomplish will be impossible. Each one, joined with the others mentioned above, forms the basis for instilling confidence.

CONFIDENCE BUILDERS
COURAGE

The first confidence builder is *leadership courage*! You can be certain that there will be times in your leadership career when you are called upon to be a courageous leader. The problem is that these courageous moments will sneak up on you. Because they are unannounced, you will not have time to prepare ahead, and you may miss the opportunity to be courageous and show true leadership. Also, because they take you by surprise, you may make a wrong or indecisive decision. This is the most common area where many leaders become definite maybes. Obviously some decisions you make will require more courage than others. The most common ones that I was involved in were related to some type of human resources' infraction. The easiest example is that of the sales or sports leader who is faced with a top producer or star player who has done something egregious enough to warrant dismissal. It could be the case, though, that the leader may find that there is some gray area involved in the infraction that makes the decision to terminate the employee a qualitative judgment. The gray is often directly proportionate to the amount of business the star brings in. In this case, you could be faced with either terminating your star and standing up for your standards or keeping the star employee and allowing your other employees to see that you will stretch your standards under the right (for you) circumstances. Clearly, the second choice is unacceptable. The consequences of lowering your standards are as follows:

- Little by little, your standards will drop lower and lower.
- You will not have any definitive standards.
- When you subsequently speak about standards, the people on your team will know that there is always a possibility that under the right circumstances the standards will be changed.

A business, team, or office is no different than a family with young children. All parents know you can't say one thing and do another. The children will do as they see you do. It's the same in business, only it's the adults who will do as you, the leader, do.

Here is another example of a situation where courage is needed. Sometimes you, as the local leader, have to choose between supporting your people and supporting a decision made at your home office. Sometimes, as in the case of a general reduction in force (RIF), you may be called upon to terminate a person or persons who you believe are superior to others being retained. Here is what I have seen! The RIF decisions are generally made on a nationwide basis by HR specialists and attorneys. They are looking broadly at a cross-section of the company. My experience is that you will not be successful in overturning those kinds of decisions. The real courage you will need is the kind that allows you to sit and tell excellent employees that their employment is terminated. You will learn that a RIF requires all the courage and empathy you possess.

The real courage we leaders need is subtle. We need to have the courage to lead our teams into the future when the future is not clear. I have been a leader in one industry spanning five different decades, and there always were a few clouds on the horizon that caused leaders and team members alike to wonder if the future might not be as bright as the past. Let me review a few of the changes we faced. Forty years ago, there was no such thing as a workstation or desktop computer in our business. The commission rates that we charged our clients were set by the New York Stock Exchange and could not be independently negotiated. There was no such thing as no-load mutual funds. There was no such thing as a money market fund. There were no discount brokerage firms. Now, as each of these items came into being, some people thought that the ability of financial advisors to earn a living would be severely hampered. If that happened, the earnings ability of the corporation would be greatly reduced. Quickly, not one but all of the future negatives arrived, and we were required to lead our teams through them. It was assumed that the full-service investment firm model would become a corporate dinosaur. It took courage to lead into the future when the future looked bleak, but we overcame the obstacles.

JUDGMENT

The second confidence builder is good judgment. Leaders prove their value to their companies and to their followers by how they show judgment. You will be faced with a few major judgment decisions and many, many little judgment decisions. While the leader will remember the major ones for his or her entire career, the team members will remember the many little ones, particularly the ones that involved them. Making the right judgments requires a moral compass that provides the basis for knowing right and wrong. You can't make a good judgment if there is no sense of right and wrong in you. The *Encarta Dictionary* gives the following as one of the definitions of judgment: "discernment or good sense—the ability to form sound opinions and make sensible decisions or reliable guesses." It should be noted that the first two definitions provided in the dictionary are religious in nature and have to do with God's judgment. It is God who provides the moral compass that gives us the ability to make sound judgments. I think most people would be insecure in accepting the judgment of an immoral person.

> **Making the right judgments requires a moral compass that provides the basis for knowing right and wrong**

Next, to make good judgments, you must be knowledgeable about the subject matter. I would love to coach a college basketball team in the NCAA championship game! Come to think of it, I would really enjoy being on the US Supreme Court! That's the job for me. I would put on the robe of a justice, go out on the bench, and set the judicial system straight. The only problem is, except for being a season ticket holder, I know nothing about coaching basketball. As for the Supreme Court— well, you can guess! Most of us think we are knowledgeable about our careers. I know that there was a point when I would have said I was very knowledgeable. As time progressed, though, I know I became less knowledgeable. What happened? Well, it happens to everyone. Times change, new products come out, procedures are updated, programs change, regulations change, and suddenly we are outdated. It happens very slowly, and no matter how young you may be as a new leader, it has already started happening to you. Unless, of course, you realize that it is happening and make a conscious effort to stay knowledgeable. You know what you have to do to stay knowledgeable in your profession and how much effort it will require. My recommendation is that at the beginning of each year, you set a training schedule for yourself. Don't expect your company to do it for you, because a home-office staff educator's idea of what training you need will be totally different from what you know you need. It takes self-confidence to make sound judgments, and self-confidence comes from knowing that you possess the knowledge necessary to make sound decisions.

SELF-CONFIDENCE

The third confidence builder we need to possess is self-confidence. When I took my first leadership position, I had too much self-confidence. I was the youngest branch manager in the firm (at that time), and I was typical of a brand new leader. I was the perfect example of the person who got promoted and assumed that because I had been promoted, I was suddenly a qualified leader. Unfortunately, Fournies's book in which he describes the promotion process had not come out yet, and I truly needed the education that comes from being on the job to know that I had a lot to learn and really wasn't qualified. In fact, I came to realize that I knew very little. I started out as a policy leader and made every possible mistake in the early months of my career. I probably invented a few new leadership mistakes along the way. Well, you can guess what happened. I went from being a cocky, dogmatic, over-confident leader to the most humble, timid, and unconfident leader in a few short months. I was totally unprepared for leadership in a non-military environment where people failed to salute their leaders.

Don't all new leaders have similar stories? Almost every person I promoted over thirty-seven years went through some leadership growing pains. I mentioned earlier the leader who changed everything about the business he took over in the first week. Obviously, he failed. Another person took over a very successful business that had been run by a very popular leader and was so dogmatic that within thirty days morale was in total chaos. I could give many examples of new leaders doing dumb things early in their careers. The end result, if we survive the dumb things, is that our self-confidence plummets. Then we need to make the decision that all leaders must make at some point in their careers, which is to stay, fight, and learn or else to leave and give up leadership.

Leaders need to be like the watch in the old Timex commercial that kept on ticking and ticking after taking a beating. If you are going to be a successful leader, you have to be able to take a beating, get up, and start leading again. You will be tested in every new leadership position you assume. It is automatic! You will be tested! Sometimes the person who tests you will be someone you know well who is jealous of your promotion. Who tests you becomes irrelevant, because it is part of your initiation to the new position. It's like fraternity hazing. As you are going through it, remember that the testing is part of your leadership growth. Accept it as a help for your future.

> **Leaders need to be like the watch in the old Timex commercial that kept on ticking and ticking after taking a beating.**

You will gain confidence with each successful thing you do. I gained it day by day as I got feedback from my associates. Success breeds success.

As you handle more and more situations, you will become more self-confident, because you will realize that you have seen almost everything before. Eventually, there are fewer and fewer curve balls that come your way. Your self-confidence rises as time passes.

RIGHT MOTIVES

Lastly, the people you lead will have confidence in you if they believe that you have the *right motives*. We spoke earlier about the fact that leaders always claim that their goal in leading is to serve others. Think about this! In Congress, there are two years between each election. In the senate, there are six years between elections. Even the resident of the United States gets four years before learning whether the electorate still trusts his motives. As a business leader, you don't have the luxury of years to prove your motives. You prove your motives every day in every decision you make. The people you are leading assess your motives minute by minute. At first, I didn't realize I was being assessed by the people I led. Early on, all I cared about was what my superiors thought of me. In time, though, it became painfully obvious to me that what really mattered was what my team thought of my motives. As for you, it's exactly the same.

> **You prove your motives every day in every decision you make.**

The easiest way for you to judge whether your motives are being perceived well is this: If the people you lead can't determine your motives by your actions, you are doing something wrong. If you have to tell people what your motives are, you're not leading properly. For example, if one of my functions as a sales leader is to assist my salespeople to grow, then my actions should appear to lead to that purpose. If I say I want to assist people to grow sales but never actually do it, then whatever I say to people has little impact. If I want to have a reputation as an ethical business leader but everyone knows that I lead an immoral life style, it doesn't matter what I say about my reputation. If the leader cheats on his or her spouse, the followers have the right to believe that he or she could cheat on them. The point is that we wear our motives on our sleeves. There might as well be a two-sided poster over our shoulders—one in the front and one on our backs. On the front would be what we say, and on the back would be what we do. I said this earlier, and it is valuable to say it again: There are absolutely no secrets about you, your lifestyle, your purpose, or anything you do. Just assume that everyone on your team knows everything about you, and then be certain that your actions match your publicly stated motives.

> **If the people you lead can't determine your motives by your actions, you are doing something wrong.**

Let's talk a little about what your leadership motives should be. Your primary motive should be to improve, in all ways, the entity you are leading. You should not take any position, whether in business or not, unless you have a vision of how you can make it better. If you don't believe you can make it better, it will be difficult to be an effective leader. Of course, there are times when you don't get to pick the entity you will be leading. If you work for a large corporation, you don't always get to pick your next assignment. In cases like that, you have to be able to quickly assess the landscape and determine what can be improved. The person promoting you may tell you when the position is offered what he thinks needs to be improved. I mentioned earlier that rookie leaders sometimes try to do too much too soon when going into a new position. You should look for the areas that will make the greatest initial impact if you can improve them.

There was one merger where the business I took over had a very poor profit margin. There was plenty of revenue but no profit. In studying the income statement, I learned that the percentage paid out in compensation was unusually high. Frankly, the number jumped off of the page it was so high. It took some digging to find out why, and it soon was fixed. In another situation, the first improvement needed was housekeeping. The sales office had been permitted to fall into disrepair, and it was filthy. Every employee brought up appearance as a top concern. The point is that to have the right motives, you have to believe you can make the business better.

ASK QUESTIONS—BE CURIOUS GEORGE

I found that asking people what needed to be improved always served me well. In one of our firm's realignments, I took over a significant number of additional sales offices. On my first tour through the offices, I spent a full day in each one asking questions about the local business and what needed to be done to make things better than they were. There is no substitute in business for a simple, open-ended question like "What would you like to see me get done?" Recently, a leader took over a new territory, and all I heard about him was that in every office he visited he spent the entire time speaking about his accomplishments and his style of management. He ruined his opportunity to be seen as a leader who wanted to make improvements for the good of his followers. He telegraphed that the employees should care about him—not that he cared about them.

> **Having the right motives also means that you have the servant mentality.**

Having the right motives also means that you have the servant mentality. By making myself vulnerable and becoming the employees' servant, I was able to hear what my early goals should be. I used the term *vulnerable* in an earlier chapter. I cannot emphasize it enough! You need to make yourself vulnerable by putting yourself at the service of those you lead. I tried never to forget that I worked for the company, the local team members, and the clients. Because I managed a sales organization, it was easy to stay responsive to the sales staff. They paid the rent! It was even easier to be responsive to our clients, because they paid the salesmen who paid the rent. And since nothing would function without the hard work of the administrative support staff, it was easy to remember that I worked for them. I was telling a business leader recently that I was writing this book and mentioned the servant mentality to him. His quick response, without prompting, was, "Yeah! As soon as you think you're the boss, you're finished." It's okay for others to call you the boss. Sometimes it can be an endearing expression. But don't you ever be the one to say or think you are the boss. Having the servant mentality means that you are willing to do whatever needs to be done to further your team's success.

LOYALTY

You earn loyalty from leading with the right motives, showing proper judgment, being consistent, and, frankly, being everything that we have discussed so far in this book. Loyalty is the measurement of our leadership success. You will never succeed as a leader without loyal supporters. I have touched on loyalty in almost every chapter. The loyalty equation is simple: The servant leader who possesses and then leads with proper motives and judgment will always be successful and earn the loyalty of those he or she leads.

> **Loyalty is the measurement of our leadership success.**

CHAPTER TWELVE SUMMARY:

1. Leaders have courage.
2. Leaders use good judgment.
3. Leaders have self confidence.
4. Leaders have the right motives.
5. The leader's reward is loyalty.

SECTION THREE

ACTIONS OF SUCCESSFUL LEADERS

Chapter Thirteen

Successful Leaders
Think Like Owners

They See Micro But Lead Macro

The easiest way to relate the micro-macro leadership concept is to tell you a story about two leaders— me and a colleague. We were both considered good leaders and had similar experience. We worked for the same company but in different cities. Actually, we originally worked for two different companies, but our firms merged and now we were in the same one. That's where the story begins—at the merger of the firms. Both firms were in the investment business and therefore were very dependent on the ability to report key data to their clients and other investment firms. The two companies knew that an undertaking as large as their merger would be difficult, so they naturally planned ahead. They were very thorough and held many joint meetings prior to the merger. At one meeting, representatives of our computer company (we both dealt with the same service provider) told us that on the Monday morning of the merger, the magical merger switch would be turned on and the two operating systems would become one. So on that Monday morning, the merger switch was turned on, and by Wednesday morning everyone knew that the two companies' systems were not talking to each other and that disaster was at hand.

Within two weeks, the administrative processes had broken down to such a great extent that it was almost impossible to provide accurate purchase and sales data to clients. In fact, every area of accounting became problematic. The two investment firms had branch sales offices throughout the country that dealt with the public, and that's where the brunt of the administrative chaos was felt. It was in the branch offices that the public would come in or call to inquire about their accounts. Each branch office had its own administrative department devoted to customer service, and because the home office administration had deteriorated, service locally was also in disarray. The situation was this: The clients were irate because they could not get an accurate picture of their accounts and therefore their money. The investment representatives who managed the client relationships were irate because they could not maintain good relationships with their clients or handle their financial affairs accurately. The people in the administration area of the branch offices were frustrated because everyone locally blamed them but in reality it was the home office administration that was to blame. The local branch administration people were working almost around the clock to keep up with the workload, and no one appreciated their efforts. That brings us to our two leaders and the micro-macro leadership concept.

Both of us accurately and equally recognized the issues—poor client service and inaccurate accounting would eventually lead to the loss of clients, particularly because other similar firms that were not involved in a merger were not experiencing the same difficulties. We both understood that a loss of clients would lead to a loss of the investment representatives responsible for the clients. If we lost the clients and the representatives, we knew that we would eventually be out of business. So each of us independently developed a plan to deal with the issues and save our respective local businesses.

THE MICRO LEADER

My associate was a micro leader. He decided that the way to show leadership was to personally and physically throw himself into the administrative department of his branch. It was his assessment that he and his staff could overcome the home office administrative difficulties and somehow provide accurate reporting where none existed. He literally worked around the clock to clean up the mess. He was always in the back office administrative area behind the cashiering window working hard. His leadership style was to be a team player by being the utility outfielder and playing any position to win the day. He became one of the accounting staff and worked alongside them. It was an admirable leadership decision made with the highest standard of unselfishness. Unfortunately, the real problem was not a local one, and no matter how hard he worked, he couldn't fix administration. He soon became personally negative, because he blamed the home office for failing to deliver accurate data. He became emotionally involved in the failure of the merger, and his feelings were evident to anyone who spoke to him. He blamed the problems on the firm's leaders rather than taking responsibility for what he could do realistically.

THE MACRO LEADER

> **I saw the micro issues but realized that the solution was a macro one!**

I took the macro approach. I saw the same issues but viewed them differently. I felt that the real problem was the inability of the firm's home office accounting department to deliver accurate client reporting. I understood that no matter what I did locally, the reporting would still be inaccurate to the clients and my staff, because it was the home office and not the branch office that provided the accounting. I decided that the main objective was to provide out-front leadership to our clients and employees and to be the person who would provide confidence to them during the crisis. I knew that I had a very competent administrative manager, and I worked closely with him. I saw the micro issues but realized that the solution was a macro one!

- I met with the investment representatives and told them that they were the ones who were closest to the clients and that **they knew better than anyone what should or should not be in the accounts**. Therefore, it was the representatives' responsibility to personally keep accurate posting records so that at any point there would be a local record of the account. I took a risk, because the representatives could have resisted and said that accounting was not their function. Fortunately, the representatives understood their responsibility and acted professionally.

- Next, whenever clients visited the office to request information, I tried to meet with them. I attempted **to be the face the clients needed to be comfortable with the company**. Along with the client's representative, I showed the client the process we were following to ensure that their accounts were eventually going to be accurately reported.

- Finally, **I became a frequent phone and in-person communicator** with the accounting department in the home office and utilized these relationships to correct the most difficult and long-standing administrative issues little by little. The end result was a bond of teamwork between the investment representatives and administrative staff that had not existed before. A bond was also created between the clients and their representatives. And I was able to develop a lasting relationship with many clients. In short, it was macro leadership activities that solved micro issues.

Think Like an Owner

I found that by leading and managing as if I were the owner of my business unit, I naturally led in a micro-macro manner. In my opinion, thinking like an owner is the only way to be an effective leader. An owner sees everything, because the business is her business! Let's face it—when everything and every penny belongs to you, you have a much greater interest in the business. This strategy carried me successfully through my career. Unfortunately, it is not the philosophy of most leaders today. My philosophy was formed in the first few years of my career. It was born from necessity. When I first took over my sales office, my compensation was based on a draw (no salary) and a 25 percent share of the profits. I was smart enough to understand that I could not live on the draw for long and that it was the share of profits that would allow me to earn a reasonable sum of money. The only problem with the formula was that the business I inherited had no profit. Some of you will also find that your first leadership position will be in a location or business that is not doing well. That is probably why you are receiving the position. It is exactly the reason I was promoted. In any event, the combination of a low draw, a percentage of profits that did not exist, and a strong desire to eat daily drove me to watch every penny. I was driven to look at every expense item in a micro manner to determine if the expense was a contributor to increasing revenues. I did that successfully. I noticed everything about the expense side of the business, but I also noticed everything about the revenue side of the business. I reduced expenses but could see that we would not be profitable without a major increase in revenues. In fact, it was obvious that no level of expense control would in any way bring the business back to profitability! My problem was similar to one that many businesses face. I had a revenue deficiency, not an expense issue. I also learned to notice everything else about our business. A business is not just about revenues and expenses. It's about everything that goes into the business.

> Let's face it—when everything and every penny belongs to you, you have a much greater interest in the business.

It is important to realize that there will be times when those who lead you will have a different view of the business you manage, and there may be conflict as a result of it. You may someday be in the position of being told to do something that you know is not the correct course of action for your business. I do not mean that you will be asked to do something unethical. On the contrary, that may never happen. Here is an example! I ran a very profitable profit center for my company, and as a result, I had the reputation of being very tight on expense control. The truth was that I focused very little on expense control, because I didn't have to. I happened to have a region consisting of many rural locations that had highly productive, conservative, revenue-producing salespeople who did not require huge capital outlays to be effective. The region also had low overhead because our occupancy cost was low in comparison to major metropolitan areas.

That is the background to a day in the winter of 2007 at the height of the bull market when I went to our home office. After spending time reviewing the year's performance, I was told that I probably wasn't spending enough money growing the business because my region was too profitable. It was assumed that I must not have been reinvesting in the business if I was so profitable in comparison to the other regions.

In fact, the high level of profitability came from operating in a low-cost region of the country. It was an example of leaders not understanding the local nature of a business profit center. I returned to my location and continued to manage as I had before. In the spring of 2008 and continuing into the winter, the business turned precipitously weak, and revenues decreased dramatically. My region remained profitable throughout the downturn. Had I spent the additional money as my leaders suggested, it would not have been as profitable. Think like an owner!

Thinking about it from an owner's perspective, I realized that the job I had was too big and too encompassing to do it alone. I saw so many areas of micro need that it was obvious that only through macro solutions would I succeed. Once I understood the macro need, the logical solution was to develop a management team to work through. Still today, I can remember making it my goal to organize my business so that it could run itself. I was fortunate in realizing two principles early in my career. Both of them I learned from calling on successful leaders and business owners as a salesman. The first I mentioned earlier! Handle each item or decision only once. The second is to delegate to competent associates. That is, to touch an issue, make a decision about it, and then hand it off to someone else for action. Delegating allows you the luxury of being a macro leader. It has been said that President Jimmy Carter was a micro leader who had difficulty delegating responsibility. The media reported that he would take the time to review the allocation of tennis court time at the White House. Not the best use of time for the president of the United States!

SEE EVERYTHING—TAKE PRIDE

There is something else I learned from my many sales visits to successful entrepreneurs. The business owner was interested in everything about his or her business, and he or she had pride in every aspect of the business. I think I earned an account relationship from every business owner I visited in person *if* I could get the owner to give me a tour of his company. I found that the owners were so proud of what they had accomplished that the tour was almost automatic if I asked for it. The tours were always the same! We would go into the factory to see the production of the products. The newest equipment would always be highlighted. Very often, I would be shown the very first piece of equipment from the beginning of the business, which had been lovingly preserved. The owner would introduce me to the people in the factory, and *he or she knew every person by name.* The owner knew the entire workflow process and could describe it to me. I noticed that if something was out of place or if there was a piece of trash on the floor, the owner dealt with it immediately and picked it up. I noticed that owners never told someone else to do what they could do on the spot. If an owner noticed something that needed fixing, he or she called someone over to deal with it right away. If there was a finished product that had an imperfection, he or she showed it to a foreman. The owner did all this while talking to me. I noticed that the owner noticed everything. He or she saw micro but acted macro.

We then would go back into the office, the owner would close the door, and I would ask how he or she started the business. That's when the pride came through. If you want to get an entrepreneur talking, ask how the business was started. Entrepreneurs will tell you every step they went through to build and grow. They will show you pictures of the first building. You will see pride like you never saw it before. These many visits, which were intended to earn business, became my on-the-job training in leadership. Do you remember the concept discussed earlier—learn something from everything that you do? I put everything I learned about these entrepreneurs into my memory bank. I loved my visits with my entrepreneurial clients and went back frequently to learn more. I did learn from them, and until the day I retired, I would walk around my offices looking at everything. I would remove clutter from the shelves. If something was out of place, I would put it where it belonged. If someone was not dressed properly, we would discuss it immediately. If someone appeared distressed, I would ask if he needed to talk. Pride in what we do in life is a prerequisite for success in life. Success in business comes from pride in what we do in business. The entrepreneur sees micro and leads macro. He or she has tremendous pride in what he or she has done, is doing, and will do in the future.

> **Pride in what we do in life is a prerequisite for success in life. Success in business comes from pride in what we do in business.**

MACRO LEADERSHIP REQUIRES A SUPERB SUPPORT TEAM!

You need to find, employ, train, and then develop the finest direct support team possible. It is impossible to be a successful macro leader without an able, effective, and loyal team behind you—and even more importantly, in front of you. In addition, a loyal, effective team allows you to see micro, because you have more eyes seeing. Anyone who knows me or has heard me speak has heard me say that I didn't run the business. My team did! I wanted an autopilot, business, and my team was my autopilot equipment. We worked together for over thirty years, and each one of us could do the others' jobs and we could think alike. There were three key people, and I trusted them with the business and my career completely. I gave them the authority and the support to manage the business, thereby giving me the freedom to grow the business. Whether you are new in a leadership role or experienced, you need to do a team assessment to be sure you have the best team possible on your field.

The great leaders whom I have met all had one thing in common. They were excellent judges of character, and all of them surrounded themselves with talented people who were the best they could find. The leaders were fiercely loyal to their teams, and the teams were loyal to their leaders. I wanted strong people on my team. Some leaders are afraid of bringing strong people onto their teams for fear they may offend others or take their jobs. My view is that as leaders, it is our function to provide the proper coaching to our strong team members so that their strengths are properly channeled. There will certainly be occasions when you need to take one of your support staff aside and tell her them that she did not handle a given situation properly. If you do it in a coaching session that is positive in nature, your team member will grow stronger. Of course you will do it privately.

Part of your leadership is to set the parameters of acceptable actions and outcomes for your support team. Here is how I described my team to our employees: I told them that my support team was given the authority to manage the business as long as they did not make exceptions to industry or corporate regulations. Frequently, they would be asked to make an exception to policy, and it was comforting for my team to be able to say that they were not permitted to do so. In my meetings with our employees, I periodically reminded them that my staff could not make exceptions so that the staff would be off the hook in trying to explain it themselves. The reason I gave was that I did not want other people risking my money and career by making the wrong exception. If there was going to be an exception, I wanted to make it based on all of the facts. Then, if I made a wrong decision, I would have no one to blame but myself. You will recall that I spoke about open communication earlier. No place is open communication more important than with your own staff. You have to keep them informed regarding the critical elements of the business and what you expect from them. They have to be taught which issues you want to hear about.

CHAPTER THIRTEEN SUMMARY:

1. Remember the micro leader and the macro leader.
2. Think like an owner.
3. See everything and take pride.
4. Macro leadership requires a superb team.

CHAPTER FOURTEEN

SUCCESSFUL LEADERS SET
AND MONITOR PRIORITIES

I have a gate at our shore home. Actually, there are four gates at the house, and every one of them was in desperate need of repair when I got down to the shore in June 2009. I should tell you that the "shore" or "down the shore" is Philadelphia slang for going to the Southern New Jersey beaches. In any event, when I first arrived in Ocean City in June and saw that the gates were broken, I decided my first task would be to at least fix the back gates, because they had the highest traffic. The problem was, though, that I don't like to fix things. Fortunately for me, the gates were not quite ready to fall off, so in the absence of anyone prodding me to finish my job, I was able to put the task off. I figured I had just got there and I might as well enjoy the first week before starting on maintenance. The second week came and went, and so did many other weeks. There seemed always to be something that was more pressing to spend time on. The more pressing things just happened to be both the things I was good at doing and the things that were more enjoyable to do.

WE NEVER NOTICE OUR OWN WEAKNESSES!

Now here is the important point for leaders! I went through the broken gate from June to late August and didn't feel bad about myself. I didn't look at myself as a failure. I knew I had to fix it, but I kept telling myself that I was busy doing other things. Periodically, my wife would ask me how the gate was coming. I made excuses! One was that I didn't have the new hardware I needed for the repair. Another was that I had to get cedar pickets from a lumber yard in Pennsylvania. The gate finally got so bad that the only thing I could do was to remove it and lean it against the fence. It remained against the fence for several weeks. Finally, knowing that we would be leaving the shore on the day after Labor Day, I fixed the gate in early September. I felt pressured to fix it too! Have you ever noticed that your most unproductive employees are always the ones who feel the most pressured? The productive people never complain about pressure, because they never feel that they are under pressure. They are never under pressure because they are always one step ahead of both what you want them to do and what they already know they want to do themselves. Unproductive employees are like me with the gate. First, they don't see what you think should be obvious to them. In my case, the gate was broken and I planned to fix it. In my mind, as long as I had an active plan to fix it, I was doing my job. Thinking I was going to fix it was good enough. Is there something in your business life that is similar to the gate? Is there a particularly poorly run sales office that you have been planning to reorganize? Is there a factory that has slipped in the quality of its output that you have been planning to improve? Is there a manager in one of your departments who has not been performing to the level you expect and who you have put off replacing? You may have a gate right now that needs fixing.

> **In my mind, as long as I had an active plan to fix it, I was doing my job.**

Once you realize that even we leaders don't see our own weaknesses, your effectiveness will improve. Leaders are no different than anyone else when it comes to critically analyzing our own actions. The question, then, is how to overcome the fact that you can't be objective with yourself. The answer is that you need a plan, and you need to set milestones for yourself just as you would for anyone else. Also, you need associates you trust who will give you objective feedback on your own performance. One of the senior leaders in our company would periodically call me and say, "How am I doing?" Sometimes, immediately after a conference call, he would call to see if he got the proper message across. One leader would call me to see what issues I was facing and then he would ask how I handled them. He figured if he wasn't facing the issues currently, he would be sooner or later. In my case, I used my own team to keep me on track. I would ask both my immediate staff and my most productive salespeople how I was doing. Frankly, even if I didn't ask, the salespeople, who were never shy, would tell me how I was doing. But your own staff may be reticent about critiquing your performance, so it is up to you to develop the open communication that I spoke about earlier. There are leaders who know what they want to hear, and, not surprisingly, they always hear it. If you ask those who report to you for advice but never act on the advice, it won't take long before you don't get the kind of advice you need. It doesn't take long for even the best intentioned leaders to become isolated and begin making decisions based only on what they think and what they want to hear. We never notice our own weaknesses. Open communication is the only way leaders improve themselves.

> **There are leaders who know what they want to hear, and, not surprisingly, they always hear it.**

SOME EMPLOYEES DON'T CARRY THEIR WEIGHT

The gate was so bad that I leaned it against the fence. In a way, the fence was being asked to hold up that poorly performing gate. The fence couldn't complain about holding up the gate, and the opening in the fence became the gate. Are there departments or employees who report to you who are not carrying their weight? Does one employee constantly have to make up for another who is ineffective? Do you recognize when that happens, and do you do anything about it? I know there were times when I overlooked the fact that one person was constantly doing the work of another. The fence couldn't speak, so it held up the gate in silence. Are there employees who feel they can't speak and hold up someone else in silence? Be perceptive and notice what is going on around you. For some unexplainable reason, we can always see when some other leader misses something that we think is completely noticeable, but when it happens to us, it's a total surprise. I mentioned that I used the telephone constantly to stay in touch with people in the various locations that reported to me. The calls were not random. I was looking for information. Every parent knows that the times when we are driving a car and are seemingly intent on the road are the times when our children will give us the most information. It is the same with employees, only the road is the phone. Finding out who is a fence and who is a gate is as simple as calling people to wish them happy birthday. I tried to call as many people as possible to wish them happy birthday or happy anniversary. I learned more in those conversations than almost any other way.

WITHOUT LEADERSHIP PEOPLE SET THEIR OWN PRIORITIES!

Why didn't I feel bad about not fixing the gate? Why wasn't my self-esteem damaged by my obvious procrastination? One reason was that the gate was very low on my list of priorities. The house was fine—the gate was broken, and it didn't affect the operation of the house. I wonder how many businesses have failed because people did not see their roles or functions as important to the business as a whole. The house was fine—just the gate was broken. Is there a business analogy? Are there companies where employees do not see their roles as important so they slack off? How many people slacking off does it take to bring a company down? As a leader, you have to deal with those who are successful and those who are unsuccessful. There are people, like me with the gate, who are not doing a good job and who don't feel even the slightest amount of remorse. In fact, they feel good about themselves and think they are doing fine. Their departments are still doing well even though they are not doing their part. They go unnoticed. The fence is holding up the gate.

It is the absence of leadership that causes businesses to fail. If the quality of a factory's output drops, it is because a leader permitted the quality to drop. The leader's priority was not excellent quality. Therefore, the leader's immediate management team did not stress quality as a priority to their teams, and so on down the ladder. Should it have taken as long as it did for the American automobile industry to recognize that the quality of its output was poor and that buyers were buying output from another country? The leaders had to recognize it and had to have made a conscious decision to ignore quality as a priority. Can there be any other explanation? Finally, our auto industry is stressing the quality of its output again, and that is because it is now a priority for the leaders. Is it possible that the drop in quality started with one broken gate in one part of the manufacturing process? Maybe then a fence saw that the gate was not doing its part and got tired of holding up the gate. Then the fence said to itself, "Well, management doesn't care, so why should I always have to make up for the gate?" That's how poor performance spreads.

You, as the leader, set the priorities for your own team, and you set them every day. You set the expectation for performance and quality in whatever you are leading.

LEADERSHIP LESSONS FROM THE GATE

The first lesson is that very few of us can be our own leaders. Certainly we all want to believe that we are self-motivated, but the truth is *we all need leaders*. In fact, we all need hands-on leaders, because most of us have a very difficult time being our own boss. It's not that we don't know what we should do. It's that we do the things first that come easiest and put off the difficult things. For the salesperson, it's easier to service an existing account than to find a new account. It's more pleasant to speak with an existing client than to be rejected by a prospect. In my industry, for years the financial advisors have said that their ideal manager was someone who left them alone. Perhaps it is the same in all industries. "I love my manager because he leaves me alone." Is that what most of us want in a leader? That was the best that could be said about the advisor's leader—he leaves me alone. Isn't that a sad indictment of a leader? The person might as well have said that he didn't have a leader. The next lesson of the gate is that when people are left to their own schedules, nothing will get done in a timely manner. If I had had a leader who had set a completion date for the gate repair, it could have been finished in the first week.

PROCRASTINATION IS THE DEVIL THAT GETS IN THE WAY OF PRODUCTIVITY

Another lesson of the gate, then, is that with infinite time, tomorrow is better than today—particularly if I don't like whatever I'm supposed to be doing. It doesn't matter what it is. It goes like this: with infinite time and no accountability, if I feel busy, I must be busy. Tomorrow is better than today! Leaders must set goals for their followers, but even more importantly, they must monitor and hold people accountable for their performance. Goals without monitoring and accountability are completely useless. I performed a monthly review with all of my salespeople who had less than three years of experience. Periodically, though, I would assign a weekly task to someone if I felt that person was not doing well. I would give them an assignment to accomplish and then say something like, "Come in to see me next Friday with the results." Virtually every time I did it, Friday would come and go without the person coming in to voluntarily report on his or her progress. If I didn't call to tell him or her to come to see me, there would have been no report. The person was hoping that because of all the other things I had on my plate, I would forget about the task I had assigned. Further, if I had not called that person in, the next time I gave him or her a time-sensitive assignment, he or she would have ignored that too. Plus the local office gossip would have been that the boss doesn't follow up so there's no reason to worry about getting back to him or her. I had a leader who was just that way. He would bark out over conference calls all of the reports he expected to receive on any number of topics. I knew he rarely followed up, so I rarely sent the reports to him. I never heard that he missed them, and he never brought it up to me. Leaders must hold people accountable for their performance. And people crave accountability!

> **Goals without monitoring and accountability are completely useless.**

KNOW WHEN TO USE AVAILABLE RESOURCES

The next lesson from the gate is that because I didn't like to fix things, especially that gate, I really should have gotten someone else to fix it. Had

I done that, there is a good chance it would have been done promptly and correctly. Even though I finally fixed it, it still is not operating properly and is in need of a true carpenter. One of the functions of leadership is to properly assess the talent within your team and assign the right person to any given task. In the basketball world, it's obvious that a coach shouldn't make a point guard play as a center. It takes a great deal of time to assess talent and put the right people in the right places. In addition, we leaders need to be honest with ourselves and properly assess our own talents. This is possibly the most important lesson. In the example above with the gate, I had good intentions, but I lacked the talent required. Deep down, I knew I shouldn't try to fix it. At the beginning of our leadership careers, we think we can do everything and do it well. We also try to do everything, because we want to show everyone else that we are the leaders and therefore competent.

> **One of the functions of leadership is to properly assess the talent within your team and assign the right person to any given task.**

DON'T LEAVE THEM ALONE!

I think the most important lesson of the gate is that all good leaders know that being a good leader is not about leaving people alone. Yes, people need to have the feeling that they can fly free and excel, but their flight pattern must always be under the guidance of the leader. The guidance can be looser sometimes and tighter other times, but there has to be guidance. I remember an occasion when one of the sales offices in my region was transferred to another region. One of the top salespeople in my region was in the office that was transferred. The region he transferred to was more administratively liberal and tended to have less management oversight than mine had. Because of the liberal policies, the salesman eventually got sloppy and failed to adhere to the firm's procedures. He eventually had to leave our firm. Now here is the point of this story. After he left, I called him to wish him well, and here is what he said. He said, "If I had stayed in your region, this would never have happened. You would have stopped me from doing …!" His point was that with proper controls, he would have been constrained in his activities early on and would not have run afoul of the firm's policies later on. The most productive salespeople are very often so focused on their goals that they lose sight of the administrative requirements that every business has. They don't mean to circumvent policies. It's just that they are focused on something other than administration.

The person we are speaking about, the top salesperson, can also be the top research scientist in a pharmaceutical company who is so focused on the research that he or she loses sight of the administrative requirements of the position. My experience is that the more focused the individual is on his or her endeavor, the more leadership is needed. The most highly motivated people need management to maintain the infrastructure supporting their efforts and to provide the boundaries for them to operate within. Just as a leader can't be successful without highly motivated team members, the highly motivated team members will not be successful without excellent leadership behind them. I know I said "behind them," but make no mistake: for even the most highly motivated worker, salesman, or teammate, leadership also has to be out front. As a leader, I sometimes performed a support function, handling whatever issue my highly motivated people required. But there were just as many times when I needed to show that I was as highly motivated as they were and could be instrumental in helping them to be even more successful. Think about this! Why would a highly motivated, successful person want to work for someone who had nothing to offer in the way of career advancement? If you are leading in a sales organization, it's easy to understand, because the salesperson wants to make more money, and our job as leaders is to increase sales volume. In that case, it's a win-win, and everyone is successful together. However, it's just as important in any other endeavor for a leader to have both a vision for the future and the technical knowledge to implement it for every person on the team.

We can sum up this section by saying that leadership is not about leaving anyone alone. Here is what people really meant when they said, "My manager is great—he leaves me alone." The leader had the common sense to give just as much leadership as was needed in any given circumstance. Not too much and not too little! The experienced leader knows when to let them play the game and when to get back to teaching and leading. That's the kind of leader you want to be. Good leadership means that you recognize gates and fences and that you are proactive in weeding out the gates.

PROACTIVE LEADERSHIP

Proactive leadership is a ridiculous term. There is no other kind of leadership. I really dislike the word proactive, so I want to add a little section about why I feel that way. It was just a few years ago—maybe ten years—that I started hearing leaders say that you have to show proactive leadership. Or they would say, "Be proactive—get out and lead this sales effort!" It seemed that the more I heard it, the more it kept being used. Over and over, we were being encouraged to be proactive leaders. Okay! The term was cute at first. Proactive sounds good to me. I would hate to be a reactive leader. But words get started in business, and then they get repeated over and over again. A few years ago, the president of our company used the word *robust* to describe something about the firm's accomplishments. All of a sudden everything was robust. Our earnings were robust. Our training facility was robust. Every leader in the organization found ways to insert the word *robust* into their vocabularies. Then I heard the term used on CNBC by another business leader. Some words just get overused, and *proactive* is one of them! The opposite of proactive leadership would be passive leadership, which isn't leadership at all.

So in conclusion, watch out for your gates and fences, recognize when someone is becoming a gate, don't be a passive leader, and go out and be a positive, hands-on leader.

CHAPTER FOURTEEN SUMMARY:

1. We never notice our own weaknesses.
2. Some employees don't carry their weight.
3. Without leadership, people set their own priorities.
4. Remember the leadership lessons from the gate.
    a. We can't be our own leaders.
    b. Tomorrow is better than today.
    c. Know when to use resources.
    d. Don't leave them alone.
5. Proactive leadership is assumed.

CHAPTER FIFTEEN

SUCCESSFUL LEADERS MANAGE CONFLICTS

Conflict resolution is one aspect of leadership that most of us would rather not be involved in. It is one of the most stressful things about a leadership career. I always found that growing a business was far easier than dealing with all the conflicts that came at me. I touched on the issue earlier when I discussed how and where to correct someone. Now I want to go deeper into the kinds of conflicts that typically arise and then discuss ways to deal with them. Conflicts fall into five main categories:

1. Conflicts between employees of equal status.
2. Conflicts between employees of different status.
3. Conflicts between you and employees.
4. Conflicts between you and other leaders.
5. Conflicts between employees and customers.

There are more conflicts that leaders deal with, but these are the ones that I came upon most frequently, and they are varied enough for our purposes. These conflicts have subtle differences but more fundamental similarities. The similarities are very important, and by knowing what they are and by being prepared in advance, you will be successful in handling the conflicts that come your way. Here are some general rules that pertain to almost all conflicts:

EVERY CONFLICT WILL APPEAR TO BE A MAJOR CRISIS AT THE TIME IT FIRST OCCURS

Whenever there is any conflict (personal or business), it always seems to be at its worst as it is happening. As time passes, the severity becomes more muted. This is particularly true in the case of conflicts between individuals. People are always at the angriest point with each other as the conflict is taking place. Then as time passes, even an hour or two, the people involved in the conflict move on to their next thing and leave you scratching your head wondering what just happened. There are times when I involved myself in these conflicts unnecessarily; the right thing to do was to let those involved in the conflict work the issues out themselves. When conflict arises because a client feels that he or she has not received proper service or because he or she feels a product has not lived up to expectations, a leader will often be called upon to resolve the issue—whatever it is. Sometimes the client is in what can only be described as a furious state when you receive the call, and you have to do everything you can to refrain from becoming emotionally involved in an argument with the client. It was always my habit to try to answer my own phone calls, and over the years, I received my fair share of irate ones. Most of the calls I handled in a calm, dignified, and professional manner just as I am recommending for you to do. But every once in a while, there would be that totally rude, crude, profane barbarian of a person who was not calling to resolve an issue but rather to release all of the stuff he had been carrying around in his or bucket of life's ills. This was the kind of person with whom there was no reasoning at all. I am sure you have met this person! Here is my confession—and please try to refrain from this kind of behavior, because it's not professional. There were a few times over the years (and it felt so good for just a few minutes) when I found myself pulled into an incredibly bad argument either on the phone or in person. I can still remember some of the worst blowups I had in these situations, and here is the point—the reason I remember them is that they only felt good for a few minutes and did not do any good for either our business or my emotions in the long term. It's hard to remember at times, but it is true that the customer is always right. I was inspired recently when I had dinner with a friend and fellow board member. He owns multiple automobile stores, as he calls them. He built his business on customer service. He gave me his business card, which still has his direct phone number on it. He gave his card to everyone who bought a car from him over the years. He took all the calls. When someone called to complain, he said, "What would you like to see me do?" Often, the person would be reasonable and not ask for more than what was fair. He would take care of it. Sometimes, the requests were unreasonable, and he would still take care of the request. He knew the customer was always right, and he is one of the most successful businessmen I know.

The same can be said about blowups with employees. Most leaders have an open-door policy. Mine was always open, and people were not shy about coming through it. There were occasions when the only thing missing in the demeanor of an employee was foam at the mouth. I can remember occasions when, after listening to a major tirade, the only thing I could say was, "Wow! What happened to you?" There are times when the employee is so distraught with what has just happened that there is almost nothing you can say or do that will be beneficial in any way. There are times when the only thing you should do is be a good listener and remember that it's not personal. I had occasions when employees were in tears, and there was truly nothing to do except listen. Listening is a wonderful leadership secret! This brings me to the next point.

DEALING IMMEDIATELY WITH THE CONFLICT IS NOT THE BEST COURSE OF ACTION EVEN WHEN YOUR INSTINCT TELLS YOU IT IS!

Most conflicts will not be as serious on conflict-day-plus-one as they appear on the day of the conflict. Time out works in business as well as it works at home. Of course, if the conflict is causing disruption to the work environment, you need to diffuse it as soon as possible by separating the people involved. Never allow a conflict between individuals to affect other people. However, a cooling-off period is beneficial to all parties in a conflict, and many times the individuals solve their problems without your intervention. Resolutions that the parties arrive at on their own are always better than forced arbitrations. There are also times when reacting too quickly can make a conflict worse than it is. You have the least information when a conflict first arises or comes to your attention, and if you are too hasty in reacting, you will invariably make the wrong decision. Make sure you get all the facts before acting, and remember that most of us do not possess the wisdom of Solomon. You will never make the perfect decision in haste. In fact, you may never make any perfect decision. Personally, I always saw issues more clearly after I had some reflection time. I can tell you that in any conflict, the most important thing for you to do is to remain objective and keep an open mind.

> **You have the least information when a conflict first arises or comes to your attention, and if you are too hasty in reacting, you will invariably make the wrong decision.**

The important thing to remember is that you are the leader and the conflict is being brought to your attention for a resolution. You must remain objective, or you will not be successful in resolving the conflict. Once I realized that everyone makes mistakes, I became more successful in dealing with conflict. It's true! We all make mistakes, so why should we hold someone to a standard of performance or behavior that does not allow for mistakes?

> **Why should we hold someone to a standard of performance or behavior that does not allow for mistakes?**

There are also occasions when a department or a sales office is in conflict with a leader who you have appointed. I was involved in one situation where an entire sales office was irate with the manager I had appointed to run the office. I received phone calls from employees in that office telling me that either the manager had to go or they would ask for a transfer. Others asked me to meet with them to tell me how bad the work environment was in the office. After meeting with the employees, I met with the manager to tell him about the issues. He was shocked and thought that he had an excellent relationship with the people who were complaining about him the most. I could tell that he cared about the people in his office and truly wanted to do a good job for them. The things that he was doing that upset his employees were ones that could easily be corrected and did not warrant the level of anger that existed. In speaking to the employees, it was clear that they felt strongly that he did not care about them. The issue was how to bridge the gap.

I did something that I had never done before. I decided that the only way I was going to bring the issue to any reasonable conclusion was to get everyone—manager and employees—into the same room at the same time. I felt it was the best way, because both the group and the leader seemed to have good intentions, but they did not know how to tell each other what was bothering them. What I did was simple. We all met in a conference room and placed our chairs in a circle. I explained as best I could what the issues were and then threw the meeting open for discussion. I asked everyone to be respectful of each other, and we began. Each person had an opportunity to speak and say what was on his or her mind. The session became very emotional with the manager virtually heartbroken over the level of distrust and lack of confidence in him. It turned out that he also felt hurt that he had not been accepted by the group. After everyone spoke, we discussed how to proceed. The manager apologized to the group, and one by one, the members of the group also apologized. Everyone agreed to try harder to understand each other and to be more open.

The session was successful because we all spoke together in the same room; there was no opportunity any longer to complain just to me, and the employees were able to see firsthand how upset the manager was when he realized that the group thought he was not doing a good job and did not have their interests at heart. As soon as we were seated in that circle, even the harshest critics became more civil. We never would have solved the conflict successfully separate from each other. The branch went on to be very successful, and the manager, who learned well from this experience, was promoted several times. The role of the leader is to bring about group reconciliation, foster a spirit of cooperation within the participants, achieve a result that brings about progress toward the team's goal, and refrain from getting personally involved in the disagreement that brought the meeting about in the first place. The last thing you want to see happen is for no resolution to be achieved and the various factions to leave thinking that you were really supportive of the other person or persons. This can happen more easily than you think, and it will happen if you have not prepared properly for the meeting. By preparing, I mean that *prior to the meeting* you have spoken to the various participants and know that you can make progress toward reconciliation and cooperation.

In many cases, including some of the worst conflicts imaginable, I found that the conflicting person (the antagonist) really just needed a venue to back down or calm down with dignity. Most of us regret our own blowups and arguments, and our employees are just like us. Perhaps that is something for new leaders to remember when they are involved in a conflict—the other person is most likely just like the leader. You will find that the more you err on the side of compassion, the better you will be at resolving conflicts. You will find that the more you listen, the more you say "sounds like," and the more you refrain from quickly giving advice, the better you will be at resolving conflicts. Leaders need to allow the employee as much time as needed to vent, release emotions, and then come to their own conclusions about how to resolve the conflict. Remember that what everyone will remember about a conflict-resolution meeting is who talked the most. You don't want your employee remembering that you monopolized the conversation. In those cases, you will be remembered as being too opinionated.

There is another kind of conflict, and that is the quiet conflict that occurs in all businesses and is a normal part of business life. Some of these conflicts are healthy, because they can create orderly change in processes or functions. Without conflict, there would be no improvement. You should allow this kind of conflict to take place. An example would be when two of your managers have differing views on how to achieve a goal and each feels strongly that his or her plan is the best one.

THERE WILL BE CONFLICTS BETWEEN EMPLOYEES

Virtually all business conflicts are caused by people who are unwilling to see one another's points of view. In the case of conflicts between equally ranked employees, the cause can also often be jealousy. In fact, let me say this—most often, the conflict *is* caused by jealousy. Typically, the jealousy will be a result of compensation levels or workload. As far as compensation is concerned, jealousy will be caused by one person not getting as substantial a raise in pay as another person or by a new employee being hired to do a similar job as an existing person at a higher pay level. The first situation (that of one person getting a better raise in pay than another) is relatively easy to handle. It is easy to handle if each raise was based on merit. The problem, however, is that even if the raises or promotions were based on merit, the conflict will still exist between the two people if it is not handled properly. In virtually all companies, employees are told that compensation matters are strictly confidential. Yet compensation never seems to be as confidential as we think it should be. How the conflict affects the relationship between the jealous employee and the other employee can sometimes get ugly, particularly if it spreads to other employees. Our first step in this situation should be to sit down with the wounded employee and show that we take the person's concern seriously. We have to do that within the context of not getting into a discussion about why the other person received a larger pay increase. I have been in many of these discussions, and invariably the wounded person will try to make the discussion about why he or she should have received a bigger increase and why he or she does a better job than the other employee. He or she will try to tell you everything the other person does wrong. You have to control the parameters of the meeting and ignore these attempts to discuss the other person's performance. You may have to be forceful in keeping the discussion away from a performance evaluation of the other people in the department. The meeting should be part disciplinary, because the employee should not be creating conflict within the office and should not be discussing compensation with others. You should make it clear that there will not be a change in compensation and that the compensation level or raise is not open for discussion. If you don't set that parameter in the beginning and stick to it, the employee will have unreasonable expectations and will always leave the meeting feeling wronged.

The other issue that causes jealousy and conflict is the one which involves a new person who is recruited to join the firm from another one. The new person will be doing the same function as an existing person, but because recruitment is involved, the new person may have been hired at the top end of the pay scale. This comes about because a company may have had a ceiling on pay increases due to poor earnings performance and existing employees with long experience may not have received increases for a period of time. Or they may have received very low increases and therefore may be well below the upper salary level for their position. Then a new person is hired at the top of the pay range, and naturally jealousy begins. It is understandable that the existing employee is offended, because it is difficult to accept that a new employee would be hired to do the same work for more money. Unfortunately, it happens in almost every company, and it typically is not something that local leaders can correct. Most companies perform occasional salary-level reviews to determine if the firm's pay levels are competitive with various local areas. At that time, if an employee's pay is below the norm for the given position, it will be adjusted. Once again, though, the leader must manage the expectations of the wounded employee and not get drawn into a comparative compensation discussion. Sometimes the only right answer is "It happens—and it is what it is."

The workload issue is a different story! Workload and working conditions are very easy for anyone to observe, and again you will find that life is not always fair in the business world. I have seen numerous situations where there are two people who have been hired to do essentially the same job at the same pay, but because they report to two different people, they have much different responsibilities and different work environments. By the luck of the draw, one person will have been assigned to a very demanding supervisor and the other to a laid back, relaxed supervisor. One may have too much work to do and the other a great deal of free time. You will almost never receive a complaint from the person with the relaxed supervisor, but you will hear from the one who reports to the demanding supervisor. Each person is at a similar career level with similar compensation, but each has a radically different experience. One can be treated as a true executive and the other an entry-level trainee. It all depends on the supervisor.

So the one employee comes to you to complain that his or her friend gets paid the same and has the same position but has a much easier work day. Do not think that this happens only to entry-level executives, because it can happen at any level. In every position I had, even when I was at the top of my career as a managing director and regional director, the work was vastly different depending on whom I reported to and in which division I worked. Even going back to my early experience with the two colonels in the army, I had a vastly different experience with each one. There, it was easy to see the difference, because I was the same person with two different supervisors. One was demanding and detail oriented, and the other was easy to work for and completely unstructured. Who do you think I learned the most from? Well, I already told you that it was the demanding colonel who taught me how to succeed, coach others, and appreciate excellence. The other colonel let me come and go as I pleased, and I can't remember anything in particular that he taught me. Who do you think I appreciated the most as I was progressing through my career? Obviously, it was the demanding person who pushed me to be the best I could be.

This brings me back to the two people who have very different work experiences. What do you do in each circumstance? There are several issues. First, you have to find out what is really going on and if there is really a different experience taking place. At first, you might think that the issue is with the supervisor of the person who has come to you to complain that he or she is overworked. Maybe it is! But possibly the biggest issue is with the supervisor of the other employee who seemingly has life so easy. If the work experience is appropriate with the supervisor we will call highly driven, then perhaps the other supervisor is inadequate and is not the right person for the job. In counseling the employee who is complaining about working too hard, it is important for you to keep in mind that we all appreciate those who have demanded the most of us, not the ones who have expected nothing of us. If you expect nothing from someone, you will get nothing. You will be a tremendous asset to the employee's career if you tell him or her why it is beneficial to work for the supervisor who expects the most. As for the conflict between the employee and the leader and the jealousy toward the other employee, it will all go away if you handle the conflicted employee properly. The situation should become a learning experience for the person who came to you.

> **If you expect nothing from someone, you will get nothing.**

Then, observe the easy supervisor very carefully, because there may be a problem that needs to be addressed. You may have missed poor work effort or missed reviewing the department's work output. Things may not be going well, or the department may be overstaffed. There is some reason why the work experience is seemingly so much easier.

CONFLICTS BETWEEN YOU AND OTHER LEADERS

This is an easy section to write about. The answer is simple—don't have any conflicts with other leaders. The reason is equally simple—there is no benefit to you or gain to be achieved from having conflicts with other leaders. The appropriate leaders for you to have conflict with are the ones at your competitors who you might want to outperform at every aspect of your business. Save your conflict for them. Here is a simple rule of thumb for internal conflicts. Handle all internal conflicts with other leaders on a one-on-one basis. That means that you should handle all conflicts directly between you and the other leader. **Never attempt to solve a conflict with another leader by going to the leader's supervisor.** All you will do is create an enemy within your own organization. The chance that the other leader's supervisor is going to take your side rather than the side of the person who works for him or her is slim. **At all times, try to work out your conflicts directly and quickly.** If you are a field leader, be prompt in resolving issues— particularly with home-office leaders. Home-office leaders, even those who are below you on an organizational chart, can do you great career harm if they choose. Here is how life is in home offices: The home-office leaders all talk to each other. They eat in the same cafeteria or go out to eat together. They see each other in the hallways or are together at the same meetings. The more conflict you have with home-office leaders, the more your name will be discussed among these leaders, and the discussion will not be pretty. **Make no home-office enemies. Do not have conflict with other leaders. Do not, in particular, have conflicts with home-office leaders.** Selfishly, you need the home-office leaders more than they need you, because you need them to get things done for you. Do everything possible to foster a group of home-office leaders who will assist you to solve a problem—hopefully ahead of some other leader's problem.

CONFLICTS BETWEEN EMPLOYEES AND CLIENTS

Conflicts can develop between employees and clients. Conflicts can develop between the salespeople who call the clients or between the clients and the service people who are required to deliver the product or service the salespeople promised. As bad as conflicts are within your company, they are infinitely worse when they involve your clients. As a leader, it is your obligation to represent your organization to the clients. You are responsible for the relationship with the clients of your business unit. We had a rule in the securities industry that was called the "know-your-customer" rule. It is one of the most important New York Stock Exchange rules, because it requires a representative of a member firm to know the essential elements of a client's financial needs and circumstances. This rule should be a part of every business and service organization in the country. Whether you produce steel or lead a hospital, you should know your customer. Most client conflicts develop because something did not happen as the client thought it would. That something can be anything. There is only one way for you to know if a problem is developing, and that is to know your customer.

An associate asked me to develop a plan that his sales managers could follow to become more involved in assisting their salespeople to develop more business. He felt that his salespeople did not see their managers as people who could help them grow their business. My first thought was to develop a program that would target new sources of business in the market areas his region served. I developed an elaborate plan based on an intense visitation program by his managers to every major corporation in their area. The more I thought about the plan, however, the more I realized it was the wrong one to present to him. I had fallen into the same trap most leaders fall into. His managers were missing the greatest opportunity to do more business by not meeting the most important current clients of the firm in person. Why worry about new clients if there is more business to be earned from the existing ones?

Leaders almost always first consider finding new clients when they are looking to grow revenues. They rarely see their existing clients as sources of new revenue. Yet the companies and people who already do business with them are the ones who are most likely to do even more business. Why go after someone else's client when your own client is receiving a level of service that can perhaps be improved, which in turn will assist in retaining the client and getting even more business? I ran my business with the belief that it was always possible to lose my best clients. I tried to take nothing for granted

So here is what I developed for my associate. Since his managers were not currently engaged in growing revenues, I felt that we had to start with small steps first. I told him to first require the local manager to meet any client who was visiting any branch location in his region. I wanted the sales or service people to inform the local manager when anyone was visiting so that the manager could be introduced to the clients. I felt that if I could not get the managers to meet everyone who came into their place of business, there was no point in asking them to go out someplace to meet clients. The program was simple. The salespeople, in advance, would provide the leader with the essential elements about the client (know your customer). The manager would take the time to review the current relationship so that he or she would be able to speak intelligently about any issues or problems the client faced. Then, when the client came into the office, the manager would be in a position to add value to the relationship.

By knowing the customer, the manager can grow business and aid in conflict resolution between the client and the firm. Think about it this way. If the first time an irate client meets the local leader is when he is already irate, what useful resolution will come about? How genuine will the client feel the manager is when he or she says, at that point, that he or she is interested in developing a better working relationship with the client? I think the client will think the sudden interest is no more than a knee-jerk reaction to the current problem. The client will think that the interest is shallow and based on fear of losing the client's business. Leaders resolve conflicts most easily when they know the clients.

The next thing I suggested was that once the managers had mastered meeting clients who visited their offices in person, it was time to go on the offensive and start meeting them at their places of business. In reality, the visits could take two forms. They could be in person or on the telephone. I found that if the first visit was in person, the telephone visits would be most efficient thereafter. Many clients appreciated a brief, *prearranged* telephone call to review the service they were receiving from our firm. In fact, the busier the client was, the more the brief telephone meeting was appreciated. In order to be sure that I called or visited with the most important clients, I set up a calling schedule at the beginning of each year. My experience was that our clients appreciated the calls and the opportunity to speak to a senior manager in our firm. There were times when I heard good news about the quality of our service, and there were times I heard bad news. But here is the important part of the story: all the news—good or bad—was important to hear. What started out as a discovery call became either a conflict-resolution experience or a business-improvement experience. Many times the calls were both.

> **But here is the important part of the story: all the news—good or bad—was important to hear.**

Perhaps you might think that *conflict* is too strong a word to describe the result of a service deficiency experience on the part of a client. But remember, it's only too strong a word to the service provider, not the client. The purchaser of a good or service sees any breakdown in delivery or performance as very serious and will act upon that experience quickly. Your calls to your top clients will uncover these breakdowns quickly. You will find that one of the most important functions of leadership is to have a close and knowledgeable relationship with your firm's clients. Knowing your client is good business in all ways and always!

CONFLICTS CREATE LEADERSHIP OPPORTUNITY

The way to look at all conflicts, big or small, is that they create leadership opportunities. Think about them this way. You are needed because issues and conflicts exist. Without them, the least qualified person could take your place. Whenever I found myself in the most difficult of situations, I would take a moment to remind myself that I got paid for my experience and ability to handle the tough decisions that those situations required. I didn't get paid for the good times. I got paid for the tough times.

> **It is in the resolution of conflicts that your employees see your value as their leader.**

The other way to look at conflicts is to remind yourself that it is in the resolution of conflicts that your employees see your value as their leader. I found that the people who worked in my region were the most appreciative when they realized that they could rely on me to solve an issue for them. Everything you do in leadership creates experiences for your employees that create either improved loyalty to you and the organization or ambivalence. People want to be able to rely on someone, and in today's high-turnover corporate employment environment, it is difficult for them to do. You have the greatest opportunity to lead in conflict. My open-door, open–cell phone policy created my leadership style. Some leaders would see being so openly available to over six hundred employees as being inefficient. Why not work through the six leaders who are in charge of the six hundred employees? That would be your first instinct—to go through the chain of command. But I said it earlier in the book, and I will repeat it here: people respect open leadership and will never take advantage of it. I can honestly say that in thirty-seven years, I never felt that anyone took advantage of my openness. The open communication was more an advantage for me than for any of the people I led, because it kept me informed. There was never a phone call or visit that did not have value. If you see openness and conflicts in this manner, you will be able to feel refreshed every day—even over four decades.

CHAPTER FIFTEEN SUMMARY:

1. Every conflict will appear to be a major crisis at the time it first occurs.
2. Dealing immediately with the conflict is not the best course of action, but your instinct will tell you it is.
3. There will be conflict between employees.
4. There will be conflict between you and other leaders.
5. There will be conflict between employees and clients.
6. Conflicts create leadership opportunities.

CHAPTER SIXTEEN

SUCCESSFUL LEADERS
NEVER STOP COACHING

One of the most important functions of a business leader is to motivate people to achieve the goals the leader has set for the organization. You might think that there are more important or equally important functions, but if you take the time to view every other function, you will find that they all support the achievement of the organization's goals. It should be obvious to even the newest of leaders that the goals cannot be met by the leader alone. Without the cooperation and success of the leader's team, nothing will be accomplished. Yet the one area that many business leaders fail to devote enough time to is the coaching of their teams. We discussed in prior chapters various parts of coaching, but here I want to specifically talk about coaching. There are different kinds and different levels of coaching, and each has its importance. Before discussing the specifics, I want to spend a little time on one of the most common comments I heard from leaders at all levels.

I'M TOO BUSY TO SPEND TIME COACHING

"I'm too busy to coach! I'll hire someone else to do it." You might as well say you are not going to work today! The day a leader stops coaching is the day the leader begins to fail. As soon as you think that a person is doing so well that he or she doesn't need you or your business is so great you can't make it any better, you might as well quit your job. I can't imagine or remember a day in my career when I did not coach someone in some way. Coaching is the essence of leadership. Almost everything we spoke about in prior chapters leads up to the need to lead by coaching. Of course the person who sits behind the computer handling those e-mails we spoke about is too busy to coach. He or she always has more pressing work to do, because there is always another e-mail to read. The person who handles action items over and over again rather than handling them once never has time to coach. The leader who sees him or herself as an administrator never has time to coach. In fact, coaching is the easiest aspect of leadership to put off, because it's like dieting—you can always start it tomorrow.

HOW TO FIND THE TIME TO COACH

Finding the time to coach is as simple as being structured in your approach to coaching. My method was simple and can be adapted to any kind of business. Again, I was in a sales management leadership position, so my example will be from that point of view.

- **It has to be scheduled**. The truth is that the only way to find the time to coach is to schedule it in advance so that it is a normal part of your day. If it's not scheduled, it won't happen. Every day, something will come up that takes up your time, and you will never coach.
- It can't just be generically scheduled—it has to be **specifically scheduled**. That is to say, at 2:00 p.m. on January 7, you are coaching person X for one hour. That means that X is preparing for the session, and more importantly, it means you are preparing for it.
- **First thing in the morning** before the day's issues started was the best time to schedule coaching sessions. I think that scheduling the session at seven thirty in the morning sends the message that the session is serious to you and the person being coached. People who have done this and have set specific coaching meeting times tell me that it is the most beneficial method to follow. The leader and the person being coached both understand the importance of

the meeting when it is scheduled formally in advance. Spur-of-the-moment coaching is nowhere near as valuable, and it never happens.

COACHING YOUR IMMEDIATE STAFF

Your first priority should be to train, develop, inspire, and coach your immediate staff. Certainly everyone in the reporting chain that ends with you is important, but no one is more important than those closest to you. The reason should be obvious, but here it is: The people on your immediate staff will be the ones who, if they are properly trained, will allow you the luxury of *free time* to concentrate on growing your business. If your staff is well trained, they will assist you in running the organization you are leading. This may sound too elementary to you, and you may be wondering why I would even mention this as an advantage in a book on leadership. But here is the reason! My observation is that leaders in general, and especially new leaders, do not know how to effectively utilize their immediate staff, and these leaders waste what should be their most important personal asset. If you do not see the people on your immediate staff as the most important people in your business life, you are missing out on the greatest personal efficiency expander at your disposal.

I have observed too many leaders who think they can do everything by themselves and have little confidence in anyone else doing anything as well as they do it. Then there are the leaders who trust no one with anything because they are afraid of sharing what they think is sensitive information. What happens in these circumstances is that the very people who should be assisting the leader to *lead* become clerical employees instead. Does this really happen? All the time! Why? There are two reasons. One reason applies to situations where the leader is new to a position and has inherited the previous leader's personal staff. In these cases, the new leader is not sure of their loyalty and looks with circumspection at the inherited staff. So the leader tends to keep many aspects of what he or she is doing to him or herself and therefore begins to perform many clerical functions. This is a real problem, and as anyone knows who has been in that position, there is no easy answer. It's obvious that you can't go in and replace everyone. You would never get the approval from your HR department. So what do you do? It depends!

I think it depends first on why the leadership position is available. Did the old leader fail, or did he or she get promoted to a new position in a new department or new location? If the old leader failed, has been demoted, and is still around, there may be a very good reason to proceed with caution with the staff you inherited. Maybe the old leader failed because his or her staff failed. It happens! The leader might have been too weak to make the difficult decision to replace ineffective people, and as they failed to perform up to the highest standards, the leader appeared weaker and weaker. Their failure became the leader's failure. You, as the leader, own the performance of those who directly report to you. Let me repeat—you own the performance of those who directly report to you. I repeated that for a reason. There are too many leaders who, when their performance is questioned, will explain that they could have done better if their direct reports had produced the results they expected of them. Then, to make it worse, they will give all the reasons why they knew their direct reports were not competent. I remember one leader who constantly used that excuse for poor performance in a particular aspect of his business. He would give me every reason why a particular person was not competent. Then, when I asked whether he had started the warning process for poor performance, he would say that it was too soon or that he was starting to see a change. Then I would talk to one of the people on my staff to see if the employee was really changing. They would say he wasn't, but the leader was afraid to make a change because he didn't have a replacement ready to step in. Don't ever pass the buck of poor performance to the shoulders of someone on your staff. It is not believable or ethical. So it is important to assess the staff you inherited and determine if they were one of the reasons for the replacement of the previous leader. You can easily find out. If they are not competent, reassign them as soon as possible. You will not do any better with them than your predecessor did.

If the leader you are replacing was promoted to a new position, your situation is much easier and can be easily managed. The best way to start to trust the previous staff is to start to treat them immediately as if they have been with you for years—but with one difference. You have to take the time to get to know them and train them on how you prefer to work with them. The obvious concern that leaders have in these situations is that they may start out using and trusting the existing staff and that trust may be violated in some way. Is this a realistic concern, and is it a big enough concern for you to keep too many functions private and thereby cause yourself to be inefficient and ineffective? Based on my years of experience, I will tell you that it should not be a concern if you follow the few simple rules below. These rules relate to how you speak about people. They are meant to protect you from the loose-lips syndrome of some personal staffers but also should be the basis of how you always speak about people. It is simple! Just as you should assume that anything you type in an e-mail will become public information, you should assume that anything you say about anyone or anything will become public information some day. With those assumptions in mind, remember this—most of us are not in the CIA and are not managing situations of such great secrecy that if anything slipped out to the public or to employees internally it would be damaging to us or our businesses. At least, it shouldn't be damaging if you follow these rules, which are excellent not just for your immediate staff but for everyone you lead:

1. Always be truthful.
2. Never say anything about anyone that would be embarrassing or harmful to them, your organization, or you, if repeated.
3. Never speculate about what you don't know to be fact.
4. Never gossip about other people or situations.
5. Keep your criticisms and comments professional at all times.
6. Be courteous to your immediate staff and all others.
7. Keep your sights on the business side of life when at work and don't let a person's private life influence how you speak of them.
8. Never make fun of anyone, whether it is good-natured fun or not. It will almost always be hurtful or offensive to the receiver—particularly if the remark is delivered in public.
9. Remember that you are the leader and anything you say will be taken seriously—as you should expect it to be.
10. If you want people to take you seriously most of the time, don't expect them to give you a pass when you want to

say something that you don't mean to be taken seriously. Remember—you're not Johnny Carson.

How to Develop Your Immediate Staff

The most important training technique for you to use with your personal direct reports is to spend as much time as possible with them. Of course, the most time will be spent in the beginning of your relationship, but I found that even after my personal team had been together for thirty years, there was absolutely no substitute for time spent together. What will happen over time is that you will spend less time on teaching your team what you expect from *them* and more time on asking them what they see and hear that needs to be addressed by *you*. In my position as a complex manager (prior to becoming a regional director), my immediate management team of three people was responsible for controlling a multi-million dollar sales organization. We didn't spend all day long together discussing what each of us was doing, but we always knew that we were available and supportive of one another at any time. Importantly, we each knew our own limitations, particularly me, and we never tried to reach into areas that were not our strengths.

You can only develop this kind of a relationship if you are personally willing to devote as much time as needed to your immediate leadership team. I found that treating them as equal partners in the business allowed the team to respond by truly being my partners and giving me the time and dedication that only a partner would give. I found that a collegial style of leadership worked best to develop the kind of management team I wanted. I believe that an imperious, aloof, dictatorial, cold leadership style will never produce a leadership partnership. It's easy to think that no one would be that kind of leader, but most leaders have at least some of these traits. In fact, every once in a while, one of my team members would remind me that I was wandering from my collegial leadership style by saying, "Oh—you're being the boss today!" I knew what they meant when they said it, and I could only smile and accept the criticism.

Now let me also be clear that there were times when I failed to communicate with my team by not telling them something I was doing or had instructed someone else to do. Whenever I didn't communicate something of importance, they were either embarrassed that they didn't know about it or were blindsided by the result, which they then had to manage through. It was always a negative and always caused strife within our little team.

Don't get caught up in the battle of the day!

It becomes too easy to make snap decisions without conferring with the people who will have to manage through those decisions. More often than not, you will make the wrong decision when you do not take the time to involve the people on your team. Trust the judgment of your team. They will be far less subjective than you and will normally give you good advice. It is far easier to take the time to get their opinions before you make a decision than to figure out how to fix a hasty decision later.

DEVELOP FIELD LEADERS

This was an important interest to me, because in my position as a regional director, I had twenty sales offices spread out in three states. The offices were divided into complexes and were managed by five leaders who were responsible for every aspect of business life in their locations. Each of the five leaders had local managers as well. They hired, fired, supervised, developed, set local goals, reviewed real-estate decisions, and were completely responsible for the profit-and-loss decisions in their markets. They had big jobs and operated semiautonomously on a daily basis. The important thing to keep in mind is that the people in these types of locations are as much your immediate staff as the ones who work in close proximity to you. The reason I want to highlight this is that very often your on-site immediate staff become a clique. It is natural that they do this, because they work together every day. Very often, they find themselves enforcing policy that you created with them that may not be appreciated by the field leaders. So as these little skirmishes progress over days, weeks, and months, a clique mentality begins to form in the home office location. As I mentioned earlier, I was a field leader because I managed a region of the country for my firm. Sometimes I was on the receiving end of the home-office-clique mentality.

Now just as I was a field leader, I was also a home-office leader to the five field leaders for the three states. It is very important for all of us in leadership to see that we are simultaneously outsiders in one reporting structure and insiders to those we lead. Everything we feel about the staff of the person above us others may feel about our staff. I think it is a very interesting dynamic and should give us empathy for those who report to us and influence how we treat them. Most importantly, it should be the basis for how we go about developing our teams and how we coach everyone on them whether in the field or the home office. If we are aware that a clique mentality exists, we will personally work harder to lead so that everyone on our teams feels the exact same entitlement whether they are in the field or sitting right next to us.

> **It is very important for all of us in leadership to see that we are simultaneously outsiders in one reporting structure and insiders to those we lead.**

For this reason, it is important to develop and coach field leaders in the context of a single team—field and home office together—and that field leaders and home-office leaders see one another as partners. You can achieve this partly by picking leaders for both sets of positions who are compatible. Your team selection skills will be the determining factor of your success in this regard. Because we put time and detail into this selection process, we were largely successful in creating a unified team. I say that with complete confidence, because the mark of a cohesive home office–field office team is when all members work as a cohesive team without the team leader directing the effort. I loved it when I heard one of my home-base team members say to a field person that they would "take care of the issue in question without telling Mr. Monastero." I was elated when I heard after the fact from one of my field-team leaders that he or she needed help on a particular issue that I normally would get involved in but one of my staff took care of it instead. When that kind of interaction—and more importantly, cooperation—takes place, you will know you have coached everyone on your personal team to be a true team player.

There is something else that needs to be said about coaching your team members. Being on the team does not mean everyone always is of exactly the same mind-set on a particular issue. There were plenty of occasions when one or more of the field leaders or home-office leaders did not agree with me or one another on a particular topic. Being of one mind means that we all approached the business we ran and the issues we faced with the same ethics, mission, goals, etc., but within that context, there was room for multiple views. Your job as the leader is to bring the various points of view together and, as the final decision maker, create an environment that allows those on your team to feel that they are a part of the decision process. Certainly you never want to stifle discussion or belittle a person's input. If you do, you will not be stifling just one person; you will be stifling everyone else too.

Leadership Team Coaching Ideas

1. **Quarterly reviews are for coaching.** During our quarterly reviews when the entire management team came together, it was my goal to be a listener in the group discussion and not the primary speaker. Leaders make a major mistake on these occasions if they think the quarterly-review-type meetings should be about passing down oracles of wisdom to their teams. First, let the team have their meeting so that your *listening* will provide you valuable information that will be useful when your time to speak comes. Your coaching topics will become obvious as you listen to the discussion. I started with my home-office staff reviewing their various fields of interest. Then each of the field managers reviewed all areas relating to business in their locations. We spent as much time as needed reviewing our business and our attainment of the year's critical objectives. I found that the small talk of everyone sharing what was going on in their respective areas of responsibility was more valuable than anything I could say. Then I would take what I had heard and weave it into a coaching session for the entire group. It worked because I was willing to be flexible and not predetermine what level of coaching was needed prior to the meeting.

2. **Make continuing education relevant.** The next thing that you need to do in coaching not just your field leaders but also

your home office leaders is to give them the tools they need to be independent leaders who feel empowered to perform in an excellent manner. It's not always an easy task! Much is made in business about the need for continuing education. I am sure there were times when my field leaders wanted to scream, "Enough with the training!" But I believed that the best thing I could do for them was give them the people skills, industry knowledge, business ethics, and goals skills that I learned from my leadership experiences. My coaching style was to impart as much of what I knew from experience as possible. It is comforting for new leaders to know that someone has already experienced the exact same type of issue that they are currently handling. Isn't it true that you have already faced the same kinds of issues, problems, opportunities, and other current events facing the leaders who report to you? I can't tell you how many times, when I was asked how to handle something, I found myself saying, "I was faced with a similar situation, and here is what happened." We spoke earlier about leaders who are definite maybes. I don't think there is a more important aspect of leadership than the mentoring we do with those who report to us. And there is no more important time to be decisive than when someone comes to you for advice. Of course you want to attempt to walk the leader through an analysis of the situation so that he or she arrives at the decision independently. But if the person is coming to you, his or her leader, for advice, it's because he or she really needs it. Think about it—would you go to your leader for advice if you could handle a situation on your own? No, you wouldn't, because you don't want to appear as though you are unable to solve the difficult decisions, and you care what your supervisor thinks about you. I formulated my continuing-education program from the issues that my field leaders and home-office leaders brought to me. As issues came up, I found the right person or persons, either within our firm or outside our firm, to speak to our leadership team and give us the tools to deal with what we were facing.

3. **Don't be judgmental.** Just today I spoke to one of my former leaders, and he mentioned that he missed the relationship we had, because we could talk about anything that was on his mind and in the end my support would still be there. He was saying that the support, encouragement, consistency, decisiveness, and inspiration traits that we spoke about earlier really do work. Considering the fact that I wrote an entire book about those traits, his comments were welcome. The message here for leaders is that you have to create an atmosphere that allows those who report to you the comfort of knowing that they can bring any situation to you. You have to create the environment for that to happen. If you are critical or even just impatient when someone asks for advice, the environment will not be productive. Your rule of thumb should be to assist each person in a way that is encouraging rather than critical. Even if the person has made a mistake and your blood is boiling, you have to offer just enough of a critique to educate the individual but not so much as to embarrass or cause there to be a lack of self-confidence. The worst thing you can do to one of your leaders—or anyone who reports to you—is to criticize her to the point she they can't make the next important decision for fear she will make a mistake. There are opportunities to coach in every circumstance. All you need to do is be open to the fact that even something negative can turn into a positive coaching opportunity.

4. **Find reasons to compliment people.** I call it the celebration mentality! Make coaching fun by finding reasons to compliment a person's efforts. Compliment in public as often as possible and critique only in private.

NECESSARY REQUIREMENTS FOR COACHING YOUR LEADERSHIP TEAM

1. **Start with a clear mission.**
   "We always knew what you expected." That's what one of my field leaders told me. It's impossible to coach anyone to accomplish anything if you have not developed a mission.

Your mission statement should direct all of your efforts, and your coaching should be specific to the organization's mission. Your mission should not change from week to week or even month to month. Your mission is a long-term plan and should encompass your aspirations for your business.

2. **The goals you set should specifically support the mission.**

It sounds almost too simple to say that all goals should support the mission. It's so simple that many of us forget to do it. For example, during one period in the bull market of the late nineties, I was given a goal to employ and train forty-five new salespeople in my area, which at the time consisted of only five sales offices. It was a quantity that exceeded the local business's ability to support while still maintaining a proper profit margin. The goal was set to show growth in headcount numbers so that security analysts would see that the quantity of salespeople was increasing. As the number of new salespeople increased beyond what the organization could support, both productivity and profits decreased. Our sales productivity numbers dropped below those of our peers, and we became known as an underachieving sales organization. In this case, the goal detracted from the mission of the firm to be profitable for the shareholders. **Leaders damage the morale of those they lead by giving goals that are not compatible with the mission.** You can't properly coach your leadership team if they don't see the value in the goals you set for them.

A TALE OF TWO LEADERS

I think it would be appropriate to mention again my experience as a junior officer working for the two colonels. It is important to contrast their leadership and coaching styles, because they were dramatically different and obviously made an impression on me that has lasted my entire career. The fact that both men made such a lasting impression on me should be the first lesson you take from my experience. If you are already a leader and a coach, stop and think about the work experience you are providing to those who are junior to you. You may be leading a young person who has just joined your organization. It may be his or her first job. The experience that you provide is going to be remembered for that person's entire work life. He or she is going to remember and speak about you, just as I am writing today about the two colonels. I hope that that thought alone will cause you to want to be a better leader and coach. It was the basis of how I wanted to lead and be remembered.

Since we have been brought up to know that an A is better than a B, I will use those designations for the leadership and coaching styles of the colonels.

LIKED OR RESPECTED

Colonel A never tried to be my friend, nor did I have any expectation as a twenty-two-year-old lieutenant that he would be my friend. Frankly, I was awed by his rank and position and held him in the highest respect. My prior military training was two months of basic training at the hands of various sergeants, and I had only observed a colonel from a distance. Now understand this: I wasn't afraid of the colonel; I was awed by him. There is a big difference. I had an expectation of what a colonel would be like, and he lived up to that expectation from the moment I met him. I tried never to forget the responsibility I had to my organization and those I led and took my role as a managing director seriously. There are people today who are looking up to you as their colonel, and as I said earlier, they see everything you are and do. They have an expectation of what you will be as their leader. They want to respect you. They may even be awed by you. Don't ever do anything to lose that high regard we all covet as leaders.

Colonel B was a kind, social person who treated me almost like a younger brother. He wanted me to think of him as a friend and did everything possible to help me relax in his presence. He was casual and did not expect me to salute every time I entered his office. He told me stories of the old days and enjoyed sports. I would see him at the officer's club, and he was always a gracious host. I may be overstating the case, but I hope not. He would have had my respect if he wanted it. He got my liking, because I really did like him. There was nothing not to like about him. But I wanted more from a leader and got it from Colonel A instead. I can remember everything A taught me, but I am sitting here writing this and I cannot remember one thing I learned from B that was of lasting value.

HOW TO GET BY VERSUS EXCELLENCE

Colonel B taught me how I could get by in the army and not be noticed. His thought was that if no one of higher rank noticed you, you wouldn't get called on to do anything. Keep your head down! Stay out of sight! Don't ruffle the covers! Never volunteer, because you don't know what you'll be asked to do! I know you have heard this advice from some well-meaning leader. The leader thinks he or she is doing you a favor, but it's the worst advice possible. Just the opposite is true if you want to advance your career.

I already told you what Colonel A did to develop my talents. He was just the opposite of B. He was a bird colonel just like B; he was at the top of his career and not far from retirement. The interesting thing that made him different was that he never acted like he was at the top of his career and near retirement. He was personally striving for excellence and wanted to do everything possible to merit the general's approval. He walked, talked, and delivered excellence. He could have coasted for the last few years of his career like B was doing, but he didn't. He inspired those of us who worked under him, because we knew he did not expect more from us than he was willing to give. His office light was on at night just like ours were.

NEGATIVE VERSUS POSITIVE

There were policies that Colonel B did not like, and he let it be known which ones they were. I did not start out with a personal opinion on any policies, because I didn't know one from another. Leaders need to be careful about showing their personal likes and dislikes for the various policies of the organization. As the saying goes, "That's more than I need to know." Those who report to you do not need to know who you like and dislike in the organization. It undermines the ability of the corporate system to work properly. If your leader constantly tells you that his leader, for example, is incompetent, then you will be concerned for the future of the organization. If you are a leader, keep your opinions to yourself. I don't know who Colonel A liked or disliked, but I knew who B disliked. It never came up with A. I also never knew which policies A disliked, because he always seemed to be positive and matter-of-fact about what we had to accomplish. Some leaders think that the people they lead will respect their objectivity if they let them know what they like and dislike about their organization. It's not the case. It undermines performance. By the way, Colonel B did not like Colonel A and showed it whenever he had the chance. Colonel A knew it but instructed me to ignore it. Who would you respect more?

I started this chapter by saying that coaching was one of the most important functions of a leader. I hope you agree!

CHAPTER SIXTEEN SUMMARY:

1. You are never too busy to coach.
2. Find time to coach.
3. Coach your immediate staff.
4. Develop field leaders.
5. Keep a list of team coaching ideas.
6. Remember the necessary requirements for coaching your leadership team.

CONCLUSION

In the final analysis, leadership is an art and not a technical function. I started the book by saying that leadership can be learned. However, I want to offer a small clarification here. You can learn the *things* of leadership, but it is the *heart* of your leadership that will determine your success. We are all different, and my style will not be your style. It doesn't mean anything about whether you will be successful or not, because there are many different styles of leadership. The most important thing for you to remember is that, in the long run, if you have the right motives for leading and treat people properly, your chances for success will increase dramatically. So I want to conclude with some final things that worked for me and formed the basis of my leadership style. I promise you that they will work for you too! They will be important aspects of your leadership style and will create an atmosphere where people want to follow your leadership.

Say please as often as possible. Say please as often as you can in as many situations as you can. People already know you are their leader, and they hopefully respect you. When you say *please,* though, they will not only respect you but also appreciate you. Say it to every single person every time you ask for anything.

Say thank you as often as possible. Our parents tried their best to drum thank you into our heads, and they were right! I said thank you in person and in notes. The notes were hand written and sometimes typed. People love getting notes at home. They would go up on refrigerators just like their children's report cards. They always said thank you for the notes. I said, "I appreciate you giving me your time." "I appreciate your advice." "I appreciate all you do for our office." "I appreciate how hard you are working." "I appreciate your help on that project." "I appreciate the business you do." You name it, and I appreciated it! Find reasons to say thank you. Say it to the mailroom clerks as well as your most senior executive officer.

Celebrate as often as possible. Find things to celebrate. I mentioned earlier that I called people to wish them happy birthday. I sent birthday cards to all our employees' homes. When someone had a baby, I sent a silver porridge dish engraved with the baby's name and birth date. When someone had a record sales month, we acknowledged it. For example, we had an old statue of a bull and bear in bronze. At the end of each production month, the statue would be moved from the office of the prior top producer to the new top producer. But it wouldn't be moved quietly. With great fanfare, I would go to the office where the statue currently resided and, holding it high where everyone could see it, take it to its new home. As I gave it to its new owner, others would often come to watch. It was great fun, and everyone came to look forward to the monthly movement of the bull. At the end of the year, I awarded a beautiful crystal bull and bear statue with an appropriate plaque to the person who won the bull the most often during the year. We naturally had a big celebration when it was awarded! We also celebrated anniversaries with the firm. In short, we looked for any reason possible to celebrate with our employees. Celebrations make business personal, and everyone wants to feel a personal connection to the place they work. You hear it all the time—people work for more than just money. Plus, celebrating is enjoyable, and it's an opportunity for you to be involved in the happy events in your employees' lives. There is one last thing to mention here, and it's not about a celebration; it's about sad events. A wise old Irish politician and businessman said this to me forty years ago, and I want to repeat it to you. He said, "You have to be invited to a wedding, but anyone can attend a wake." Be there for your people!

Be a visible leader. If you lead in one location, be visible as often as possible by walking around and speaking to people. Once, when business was particularly poor and it seemed as though people were letting down and coming to work late, I hung out at the receptionist's desk for a few mornings to greet people as they came to work. I didn't say they were late, but they got the message! If clients were waiting in the reception area, I stopped to greet them and asked if they were being helped. If you lead in multiple locations, get in the car and go. When you go, though, be relevant. Have something uplifting to say. Remember that you are the leader and the people and places you visit will be expecting to hear something important. Don't waste the moment! The worst thing you can do is to announce that you will be visiting a plant or a sales office on a particular date and then show up and have nothing new to tell the people gathered to hear you speak. Have an agenda for yourself. There is always something new and important to discuss. It makes the people who are gathered to meet with you feel important even if you just congratulate them on something their own department did well. Think about it this way. If your boss's boss was coming to town or to your department for a visit and a meeting for all employees was scheduled to hear her speak, what would your expectation be? That alone should inspire you to be relevant when you visit.

Have a short memory. This gets easier as you get older! I should say have a short memory about negatives and have a long memory about positives. You will experience insults, slights, arguments, and sometimes personal attacks delivered in the heat of the moment. Forget quickly! The person who confronted you will probably be embarrassed by the bad behavior and most likely will apologize. Now this is the hard one—whether they apologize or not, you need to forgive and forget. The worst thing you, the leader, can do is hold a grudge with someone you lead. It will hurt you more than them, and you will gain nothing from holding a grudge. You will be judged on the accomplishments of the people in the enterprise you lead. It's counter-productive to have lasting conflicts with anyone.

Say yes as often as possible. What a powerful word. Yes! People love to hear it. It usually costs you very little in dollars to say it, and it's usually good for business. I said yes as often as possible. I mentioned earlier that the business I managed had one of the best profit margins in our firm. Yet I said yes as often as possible. Many leaders possess an automatic no button. **Buy yourself a yes button.** The greatest satisfaction I got from being a leader was the simple statement, "I always knew I had your support." They knew they had support when I said yes!

Enjoy yourself. Leadership is the greatest honor anyone can bestow on you. Treat it with the trust and respect that it deserves.

Be a servant! Finally, be a servant to those you lead. The right to lead is based on the assumption that you will work for the benefit of those you lead—your constituents. Your constituents are the people you lead directly, all the people in your organization, your shareholders (if any), and those who are the ultimate users of your product or service. Have a servant mentality.

ENDNOTES

1. "Leadership," *Wikipedia,* last modified October 21, 2010, http:/en.wikipedia.org/wiki/leadership.
2. "Management," *The Business Dictionary,* accessed July 12,2009, http:/www.businessdictionary.com/definition/management.html.
3. Ferdinand F. Fournies, *Coaching for Improved Work Performance,* rev. ed. (New York: McGraw Hill, 1999).
4. "Management," *The Business Dictionary,* accessed July 12, 2009, http:/www.businessdictionary.com/definition/management.html.
5. "My Golden Rule: 49 Leaders, from Buffet to Spitzer, Share Their Secrets to Success," last updated November 28, 2005, http://money.cnn.com/2005/11/28/news/newsmakers/goldenrule_biz20_1205/index.htm.
6. Ibid.
7. Ferdinand F. Fournies, *Coaching for Improved Work Performance,* rev. ed. (New York: McGraw Hill, 1999).

Breinigsville, PA USA
14 March 2011
257612BV00001B/10/P

THEODORE
ROOSEVELT
THE NATURALIST

THEODORE ROOSEVELT
THE NATURALIST

By Paul Russell Cutright

FOREWORD BY FAIRFIELD OSBORN

HARPER & BROTHERS: NEW YORK

TO
AUNT BLANCHE
AND
UNCLE HOMER

Contents

Eight pages of photographs will be found following Page 112.

Foreword

by Fairfield Osborn

President of the New York Zoological Society
and of the Conservation Foundation

It is a fine thing indeed that this book has come into existence. At this time, especially, it has much significance for two reasons. First, here is the story of a man of amazingly broad interests, a person so vital that even during the great pressures upon him as President he found time, or rather made time, to actively pursue other interests. Theodore Roosevelt's life completely refutes the point of view so current today that success demands specialization.

The second great value of this book—again especially at this time—stems from the fact that Theodore Roosevelt, in his work and writings as a naturalist and conservationist, drives home the eternal truth that man is a part of the natural world around him. The growth of the physical and mathematical sciences within the last half century has resulted in the development of innumerable inventions which have, among other things, enabled man to master the air, to use radar and to release atomic power. As a result, we are apt to be tricked into believing that we are "the masters of the universe" and overlook our essentiality and one-ness with the natural world. Theodore Roosevelt was not so deceived. His was more than a sentimental love of the wilderness, of animal life, and of the other wonders of nature. He had as well a practical approach and because of this gave vital leadership to the cause of conservation.

The author deserves unbounded credit for the arduous work

he has done in gathering the material for this biography. He has put it together with talent and has produced a book so lively and readable that one may hope that it will exert the wide influence it deserves.

Preface

As LONG ago as 1923 George Bird Grinnell, long-time editor of *Forest and Stream* magazine, observed that the least-known side of Theodore Roosevelt's life "is that dealing with his devotion to outdoor life and what goes with that life." Grinnell went on to say that, "to many of his old friends it seems strange that this phase of his life, which meant so much to him, should have been so generally ignored, or should have been alluded to only casually by the many who have written of his different activities."

What Grinnell wrote over thirty years ago is equally true today. Roosevelt's biographers, concentrating on his political activities, have done little more than mention his confirmed love of nature. But as Lawrence F. Abbott has said, he was "more kinds of a man than biographical literature has heretofore attempted to embody in one man."

Perhaps Roosevelt's definitive biography might best be written as a collaboration with a soldier telling one side, a statesman another, a writer another side, a historian another, and a naturalist still another. Up to now only the political facet of his career has been reasonably lighted. The others are in shadow, with natural history in near darkness.

What are some of the more important features of Roosevelt's life as a naturalist that have been generally ignored or mentioned only incidentally?

One, of course, was Roosevelt's boyhood, when he made his decision to devote his life to natural history and initiated a vigorous program of self-education in biology. He practically

lived in the out-of-doors. His companions were the sun and the
wind, open meadows, tall timber, and birds. This was the period
when he amassed the fund of information about birds and other
vertebrate animals that was to astound the working naturalists.
This period, too, had much to do with shaping his character, and
fashioning patterns of thought and conduct that motivated many
important decisions in later life.

Not enough, either, has been said about Roosevelt's natural
history training at Harvard. Though in later years he was prone
to belittle it, the instruction received there from James, Shaler,
Mark, and others broadened immeasurably his knowledge of the
biological world, developed a recognition of the importance of
self-criticism and heightened his innate powers of perception,
reasoning, and creative thinking.

A good deal has been written about Roosevelt's role in promoting conservation in the United States, but not nearly enough.
In particular, not enough has been said about how he became
such an ardent advocate of conservation, about what led up to
his energetic espousal of conservation measures after he became
President. Only through knowledge of Roosevelt's years in the
West, where he personally witnessed the rapid destruction of
game animals, as well as the activities of the Boone and Crockett
Club, of which he was the first President and, for a number of
years, chief protagonist, can one fully understand his later championship of sound conservation policies.

Roosevelt's interest in conservation and natural history made
him many friends among both the amateur and working naturalists. The story of his association and close friendship with these
men—John Burroughs, Henry Fairfield Osborn, C. Hart Merriam,
Frank M. Chapman, and many others—and of his influence on
them, has not been fully presented to the public. To have the
President of the United States take a close personal interest in
them was something new, and gratifying, like Jupiter's befriend-
ing Philemon and Baucis. His attention warmed them and fired
them with unsuspected zeal. The period of Roosevelt's residence

in the White House, and the years immediately following, were marked by a definite upsurge in scientific thought, investigation, publication, and reevaluation of obsolescent ideas. According to David Fairchild, Roosevelt was "the first and last President of the United States to have a biological sense of proportions—to know the importance of everything from forests to birds, from hybridization to plant introduction."

How many Americans know that he was recognized by outstanding zoologists as one of the best field naturalists we have ever had in the United States? How many realize that he was acknowledged to be the foremost authority on the life histories of the big game of the United States? How many are aware that, because of his broad experience as a field naturalist, he was an authority on concealing and revealing coloration in animals? How many know that, in discussions of such topics as paleontology and evolution, reptiles, birds and mammals, he could hold his own with the authorities in these fields?

Roosevelt in his office, discussing his current budget with a cabinet officer, or laying down the law to a patronage seeker, was one kind of man. Roosevelt in the out-of-doors, seated by a campfire, with the wind in the trees, and the cries of night birds in the distance, was another kind of man.

Roosevelt began his life as a naturalist, and he ended it as a naturalist. Throughout a half century of strenuous activity his interest in wildlife, though subject to ebb and flow, was never abandoned at any time.

The material for this biography was gathered in large measure from the research library of the Theodore Roosevelt Association, 28 East 20th Street, New York City, before the library was moved in 1944 to Cambridge, Massachusetts, to become a part of the Harvard College Library. Additional research entailed visits to such places as the Harvard Biological Laboratories, the American Museum of Natural History, the Library of Congress, the Philadelphia Academy of Natural Sciences, and the Secretariat of the Boone and Crockett Club. Personal interviews have been entirely too numerous to mention.

In acknowledging my indebtedness to those who have been of help to me, I regret that I cannot name them all. I am deeply grateful to the late Mr. Leo E. Miller who read the chapters about the Roosevelt expedition to South America and offered valuable criticism and comment. I am indebted, too, to Mrs. R. W. Reasoner for allowing me to use letters written by her father, Abbot H. Thayer, to Theodore Roosevelt; to William Sheffield Cowles for permission to use letters from the Cowles collection; to Mrs. Joseph W. Alsop for permission to use letters from the Robinson collection; to Dr. St. George L. Sioussat, chief of Manuscript Division, Library of Congress, for permission to take excerpts from microfilm copies of Theodore Roosevelt letter-books; to Dean Sage, Jr., Secretary of the Boone and Crockett Club, for permission to examine material in the Secretariat of that organization; to the Theodore Roosevelt Estate; and to Charles Scribner's Sons who published many of the books from which quotations have been drawn here.

Unpayable debts of gratitude are due the following: the late Dr. L. M. Peairs, Department of Entomology, West Virginia University, for reading the entire manuscript and helping in the detection of errors and infelicities; Mr. Maurice E. Phillips, Philadelphia Academy of Natural Sciences, for reading critically the chapters on Roosevelt's early life; Professor C. A. Peairs, Jr., Boston University Law School, who gave unsparingly of his time in reading and criticizing the manuscript; Mr. Hermann Hagedorn, Executive Secretary of the Roosevelt Memorial Association, for reading the manuscript and offering suggestions of the utmost importance; and Miss Nora E. Cordingley, late librarian of the Roosevelt Library, for taking an active, personal interest in my research from beginning to end, and for more than fulfilling those duties expected of the competent librarian.

Jenkintown   P. R. C.
Pennsylvania

THEODORE ROOSEVELT
THE NATURALIST

1

The Student Naturalist

COLLEGE teachers often indulge in the pastime of trying to size up freshmen who enroll in their courses, wondering if fate has destined any for greatness. They may look about expectantly for certain signs. One teacher may be struck by a young man's bulge of forehead or coastline of jaw. Another by the use of a felicitous phrase or by some obvious mark of good breeding. And still another by apparent qualities of leadership.

The faculty who welcomed Harvard's freshman class of 1876 perhaps saw nothing in the new student body which would set it apart from previous ones. It is reasonably certain that his instructors did not spot Theodore Roosevelt as a man out of the ordinary. And none of them could have been blamed for that.

Roosevelt was seventeen (would be eighteen come October 27) when he arrived in Cambridge to begin his college education, and he bore practically no resemblance to the robust, wide-beamed figure he was to become in later years. Pictures taken of him in the mid-seventies show him to have been slender, underweight, frail. A pair of prominent sideburns did little to offset his generally anemic appearance. His teeth, so conspicuous a feature in maturity, had yet to do considerable sprouting, as did his entire frame. Anatomically speaking, Roosevelt under-

1

went almost complete metamorphosis between his Harvard days
and the later ones which saw him in high office.
Roosevelt entered Harvard with the avowed intention of devoting his life to natural history. He wanted to become, as he
said, "a scientific man of the Audubon, or Baird, or Coues
type." [1] He had not arrived at this decision hurriedly. Back of it
had been an active germination period of at least ten years. Beginning at the age of seven or eight, he had been one of the
most ardent juvenile naturalists who ever lost his heart to the
charm of woodland and glade. During this period he carried on
a vigorous program of self-education that explains not only
Roosevelt's decision to become a naturalist but also many of his
actions of later life.

As soon as the boy began to read he showed a marked preference for books about animals. One of the first he tackled was
Livingstone's *Missionary Travels and Researches in Africa,* a
volume so large and heavy for him then that he had difficulty in
carrying it from room to room. The celebrated missionary's en-
counters with rhinos, lions, elephants and other large African
animals may have formed the germ of the interest which grew
to have such a strong hold on him. His first book devoted solely
to animals was J. G. Wood's *Homes Without Hands,* a present
from his father. This volume became a cherished possession and
was read and reread until he knew its content by heart. As the
years slipped by, he turned the pages of increasingly larger,
more technical books about animals, books by Audubon, Wilson,
Baird, Nuttall, Coues, DeKay, Jordan, and other celebrated naturalists of the times. Even before he packed his belongings to
be off for Cambridge, he could probably have passed an examination in any, or all, of them.

The skull of a seal which came into his hands served as a
springboard to the founding of his own museum, the Roosevelt
Museum of Natural History. This museum was located first in

---

[1] The footnotes to this and all numbered references following will be
found at the back of the book, beginning on page 273.

Roosevelt's own room, but later, after the family maid lodged understandable complaints, in a case at the back of the upstairs hallway. Here the seal's skull was soon surrounded with shells, bird eggs and nests, insects, various minerals, and other odds and ends of juvenile industry.

Little more than this would be known about the Roosevelt Museum if it were not for a priceless document now carefully preserved in the Roosevelt Library at Harvard College entitled *Record of the Roosevelt Museum*.[2] This is an unpretentious record, consisting of only four or five pages of ordinary lined paper, on which was written in juvenile script on both sides, an account of the early history of the museum. The opening paragraph reads as follows:

At the commencement of the year 1867 Mr. T. Roosevelt, Jr. started the Museum with 12 specimins [sic]: at the close of the same year Mr. J. W. Roosevelt [West Roosevelt] joined him but each kept his own specimens, these amounting to hardly 100. During 1868 they accumulated 150 specimens, making a total of 250 specimens.

From this brief, much-to-the-point account, it can be seen that the museum, like most great institutions, had a modest beginning. As T. Roosevelt, Jr. overlooked no opportunities to add new specimens, it grew by leaps and bounds. At first he was a general collector, interested in everything from minnows and salamanders to ground hogs and blue jays. Later he tended toward specialization, devoting more and more of his energy to birds. When he entrained for Cambridge he left behind him a collection of bird skins which for size, variety, and skill of preparation was doubtless unequalled by any boy his age in the United States.

For a city boy, Roosevelt passed an uncommonly large amount of time in the woods and fields. He suffered from asthma, his attacks often being severe and of grave concern to his parents.

As a grown man, visiting the Bull Run battlefield, Roosevelt said to a companion: "When the Union and Confederate troops were fighting over these fields I was a little bit of a chap, and nobody seemed to think I would live." [3]

As a result Roosevelt's parents were at pains each year to plan their summer outings with strict attention to his welfare, usually deciding on places up the Hudson, such as Barrytown, Dobbs Ferry, and Spuyten Duyvil. Roosevelt liked these places. He found that he could breathe better here and he experienced, right from the start, an almost preternatural joy in the presence of wild animals.

Each day was full of the most fascinating events. In one of his first boyhood notebooks, *Notes on Natural History*, Roosevelt recorded many of his earliest experiences with animals, showing clearly his enthusiasm.

Mephitis chinga [skunk]. Common. One fell into our sistern, where it remained for three weeks, to the decided detriment of the water.

Hylodes pickeringi [tree frog]. One seen. It was captured and taken into the house. At night it afforded the entire family much amusement, being then let out, and put on the table, by the lamp, where it proved a remarkable flycatcher, leaping at any insect that was attracted near by the light.

A nest of the gray squirrel, procured August 8th, 1872, at Dobbs Ferry, N.Y. was situated in a chestnut tree . . . The nest contained three young, whose eyes were not yet open, and whom I took home and reared. I at first endeavored to persuade them to lap up some milk but they were too young to do so, so I purchased a syringe and tried them with that, squeezing a few drops of milk into each ones throat. One (a male) seized the syringe and sucked it on the second trial. I let him have as much as he wanted, and when he had finished, I felt how heavy he was and then pumped milk into the other two until they had attained his weight. In a day or two they all took to the syringe, and after that I had no more difficulty with them, giving each squirrel as much food as he wanted, three times a day. . . . One squirrel died soon, but the others lived happily on.

As he grew older, Roosevelt's parents took him and the other children (Anna, Elliott, and Corinne) to the Adirondacks and on two trips abroad, one to western Europe in 1869 and the other in 1872 to Egypt and the Holy Land. On their return from Egypt, Roosevelt's father bought a summer home in Oyster Bay, Long Island, and it was here that Roosevelt spent the summers of '74, '75 and '76 immediately preceding his Harvard residence. The Adirondack trip gave the boy his first taste of the north-woods, with its population of crossbills, three-toed woodpeckers and whiskey jacks, salamanders, frogs, and toads common to that region. Roosevelt kept a diary on this trip, showing careful concern for scientific names.

Lake George. August 3d/71
Before breakfast we boys indulged in a few shots on the airgun. After breakfast our party went off on a small steamboat but after an hour of this West, Ellie and I got tired of it and were put ashore to stay till the steam boat came back. We wandered about and I picked up a salamander (*Diemictylus irridescens*). I saw a mouse here which from its looks I should judge to be a hamster mouse (*Hesperomys myoides*). We saw a bald-headed eagle (*Halietus leucocephalus*) sailing over the lake.[4]

Martins. August 14/71
I observed while passing over here a wood frog (*Rana sylvitica*). I also observed several toads (*Bufo americanus*) and a singular creature which I think must be the toad frog (*Scaphiophus solitarus*). It was olive with two yellow stripes above, and yellowish white beneath.[5]

On this trip Roosevelt saw the Adirondacks before the lumbermen had taken their toll of the trees, before sportsmen had made inroads on the wildlife, and before tourists had crowded the lake fronts with cottages. It was a country of stillness and satisfying beauty. He was to return to it again and again.

From the standpoint of the naturalist, Roosevelt gained little or nothing from his first trip abroad. He was too young, and there were difficulties in collecting specimens in an environment of hotels, railway coaches, and populated thoroughfares. He did profit, though, from the subsequent trip to Egypt and the Holy Land. The high point to him was a trip up the Nile by *dahabeah*,

Typical page from the early notebook, "Notes on Natural History." These observations made at Dobbs Ferry in the summer of 1872 include Roosevelt's comment on the skunk (*Mephitis chinga*) which fell into the family cistern.

a light-draft, lateen-sailed houseboat common to the Nile in those days. The boat moved slowly and made frequent stops, thus allowing Roosevelt ample opportunity ashore to collect. Moreover he now had a weapon, a double-barreled shotgun, which his father had given him. With this he made decided inroads on the bird population along the Nile. At the end of the

Nile trip he wrote home that he had collected between one and two hundred birds. He added to this collection in the Holy Land and in Germany, where he spent a summer before returning to New York. He had with him as a constant companion a book on Egyptian birds, and with it in hand he seems to have had no difficulty whatever in identifying the species he encountered. Roosevelt, now thirteen, was a collector of information about birds as well as the birds themselves. When he next returned to Africa, forty years later, he could recall with no apparent effort many of his original observations on bulbuls, bee eaters, and other African birds.

The acquisition of the summer home at Oyster Bay was one of the most important events in the life of Roosevelt the young naturalist. For it was between tho time that he first moved to Oyster Bay until he entered Harvard more than two years later, more than at any other period that he learned about birds of the eastern United States and assembled the innumerable facts about bird flight and song, courtship and plumage, food habits and home life, which were later to astound many professional bird students.

Another important phase of the boy's training was the study of taxidermy, beginning when he was only eleven. His teacher was John G. Bell, who as a youth had accompanied the great Audubon on a collecting trip to the upper Missouri country. Roosevelt went regularly to Bell's shop (probably located at the northwest corner of Broadway and Worth Street) and there learned the fundamentals of successful preservation and mounting of animals, and the preparation of the conventional bird-skin, as practiced in the 1870's. This knowledge was a tremendous spur to his burgeoning ornithological enthusiasm. Without it he could not have assembled the large collection of Egyptian birds which he later brought home. No one knows how many bird-skins he prepared in his pre-Harvard days, but the number was easily in the hundreds. Four specimens which he mounted are now prominently displayed in the American Museum. According to Frank M. Chapman, one of America's outstanding ornithologists, he was, for his age, "a very promising taxidermist." [6]

Throughout these early years Roosevelt recorded his observations on animals. We find the evidence in his boyhood diary, in natural history essays, and, most particularly, in a series of notebooks he used for that purpose. He began this practice of jotting down observations when he was quite young and continued it most energetically until near the end of his Harvard residence. He crammed book after book with notes, especially while he was in Egypt and, later, at Oyster Bay. These boyhood notebooks, bulging with the fruits of his labors in the field, prove as convincingly as anything else he ever wrote how deeply rooted was his love of nature. [7]

Thus by the time he settled down for his four-year stay at Cambridge, he had developed into quite a naturalist. As a bird student, in his age group, he possibly had no peer. He had consciously neglected no phase of his training open to him. He had collected actively, had learned to preserve his own specimens, had founded a museum to house his specimens, had attempted animal portraiture, had read and assimilated the content of the books on natural history which seemed most important to him, and he had been so successful in becoming acquainted with birds—where his chief interest lay—that he could have identified on sight most of those common to the northeastern part of the United States. In addition, he had more than a passing knowledge of fish, amphibians, reptiles, and mammals of the same general region.

His schooling had been of the best possible kind, for he himself had been both teacher and pupil. At no time did he experience the counsel and companionship of an older naturalist initiating him into the wonders of the outdoor world. No one turned the boy's face to the countryside and to the open forest. He struck out for himself, took his own bearings, and was never so far diverted by other interests as to lose his course.

Roosevelt's companions in the outdoor world were boys of his own age, principally his younger brother, Elliott, and two of his first cousins, West and Emlen Roosevelt. After a time he met Frederic Osborn, a younger brother of Henry Fairfield Osborn. Together they collected in the woods of the Hudson River Highlands in the early 70's, briefly sharing a common interest in birds until the tragic accident in which Frederic was drowned.

Theodore Roosevelt's family background supplies no positive clue as to how he came by his love of natural history. His parents are known to have had an eye for the beauty of dogwood and azalea and an ear for the music of wren and thrush. And his father gave expression to these feelings in practical ways, being one of the founders of the American Museum of Natural History (1860) and a generous contributor to societies for the prevention of cruelty to animals.

Roosevelt's barrister uncle, Robert Barnhill Roosevelt, was a man of many parts whose interest in outdoor affairs followed a pattern surprisingly similar to that later followed by Roosevelt himself. This uncle had much to do with creating the cult of the hunter-naturalist; he wrote books on a variety of outdoor topics ranging from game fish and game birds to breech and muzzle loaders; and he foresaw the eventual destruction of many game animals unless they were protected by law.

In later life, when Roosevelt was asked how he came by his love of animals, he replied simply: "I can no more explain why I like 'natural history' than why I like California canned peaches; nor why I do not care for that enormous brand of natural history which deals with invertebrates any more than why I do not care for brandied peaches." [8]

II

Roosevelt was one of 230 freshmen who entered Harvard in the autumn of 1876, and one of a student body numbering 800. He engaged rooms at 16 Winthrop Street (now 38 Winthrop), situated between the College Yard and the Charles River. He did not take space in one of the college dormitories, because he had a choice only of ground-floor rooms, and it was considered unwise for him to occupy these because of his susceptibility to asthma. Probably, too, conditions in the dormitories had not changed much since the college days of Oliver Wendell Holmes, Jr. when students, in cold weather, poured water around the window frames so that it would freeze, seal the cracks, and thus keep out the cold air.

At 16 Winthrop, Roosevelt occupied a large, well-lighted study, with a mere alcove of a bedroom to the rear, and these he furnished in a manner unlike most other Harvard students' rooms. He adorned tables and bookracks with stuffed birds, he filled his shelves with books by Baird, Coues, Nuttall, and other naturalists, he brightened his walls with pictures of birds, and he filled niches here and there with the tools of the taxidermist. In one corner he set up an impromptu vivarium which contained, from time to time, such animals as salamanders, lizards, and snakes, the trophies of expeditions into the countryside adjoining Cambridge.

He had always been an untidy collector, and realized that he would have more latitude with his zoological activities in private rooms than in those subject to close dormitory supervision. In fact, he liked his rooms well enough to keep them for four years. That his landlady, Mrs. Richardson, accepted him and his specimens bespeaks considerable indulgence on her part, for she could hardly have regarded him as the ideal roomer. One night, for instance, she almost fell over a large turtle that had clambered out of its pen and was wandering through the halls in search of freedom.[9]

With one exception, Roosevelt had known nothing of classroom education until he entered college. Because of his uncertain health, he had been educated almost entirely by tutors. While quite young, for a brief period, he attended Professor McMullen's Academy, located near his home. His record there indicates that his mind, at least, was sound: grammar 89, arithmetic 92, geography 97, history 96, and spelling 88.[10] The validity of the spell-

Random sketches from a page of one of Roosevelt's
boyhood notebooks.

ing grade only should be questioned. Theodore then, and
afterward, jumbled his vowels and consonants in a manner
strictly Theodorian.

To prepare Roosevelt for his Harvard entrance exams, his
father engaged Arthur Cutler, a young, enterprising educator,
who was later to found the well-known Cutler School. Under his
tutoring, Roosevelt made rapid progress and had no difficulty in
passing his examinations.

Because he had been denied the usual elementary and high
school education, Roosevelt was unprepared for college in some

subjects: notably Latin, Greek, and Mathematics. He had learned a smattering of Latin from his taxonomic endeavors, but this had not led to any appreciable increase in vocabulary or to a familiarity with the grammar and syntax of that language. In Zoology, History, and Geography, subjects in which he was vitally interested and had read widely, he was far in advance of the average youth his own age. As a result of his study and residence abroad, he could hold his own in French and German.

Roosevelt began his college life only a few years after Charles W. Eliot had assumed the Presidency of Harvard. Eliot had plans for converting the College to a fresh outlook. One plan, already in effect when Roosevelt first appeared in Cambridge, was the shelving of the old traditional class system—all classes prescribed—in favor of one allowing certain electives.

Since this privilege, in 1876, extended only to upperclassmen, Roosevelt did not benefit from it immediately. His prescribed schedule, like that of the other freshmen, consisted of Greek, Latin, German, Greek and Latin Literature, Mathematics, Physics, and Chemistry. This represented the Harvard faculty's best judgment as to what constituted the ideal course of study for the young men of that day. Roosevelt accepted the requirements, just as today's freshmen accept those tossed at them. He did not even complain about the absence of natural history from the freshman curriculum.

He did refer, early in the year, to some trouble he was having with one or two of his subjects: "I think I am getting along all right in all of my studies except one, which is Prof. Purses' Theory of Determinants," he wrote his father. "I do not seem to make any headway at all in this. My Greek has also been pretty hard." [11]

These difficulties were temporary. His grades for the year show that he was quite able to hold his own: German 92, Greek and Latin literature 77, Greek 58, Latin 75, Mathematics 75, Physics 78, and Chemistry 75. He averaged 75 for the year and ranked 111th, which put him in the upper half of his class.

2

Some Tests of Strength

THEODORE ROOSEVELT's reputation as an ornithologist had preceded him to Harvard. The day after he arrived he was visited by Henry Davis Minot, another freshman, who had a like interest in birds. The two became inseparable. They frequented the shore in search of ducks and gulls, kept a weather-eye out for the rare or unusual fall migrant, enjoyed together the rustle of falling leaves, the ripening of late fruit, and the color in the trees. On week-ends they occasionally went to West Roxbury, Minot's home, where they compared notes and continued their outdoor observations. Minot was an exceptionally well-informed bird student for one so young, and his influence on Theodore Roosevelt was stimulating, as was Roosevelt's on him.

During the Christmas vacation of his freshman year, Roosevelt traveled to Maine. Here he met William Wingate Sewall and Wilmot Dow, two famous guides of the northwoods who were destined to play conspicuous roles in his life from here on. Arthur Cutler had met them the summer before while hunting in Maine, and he was so taken with Bill Sewall that he insisted Roosevelt meet this guide.

At that time Bill Sewall was 33, a large, raw-boned figure with tremendous physical strength, a kindly nature, and a long red-

13

dish-brown beard which added years and dignity to his counte-
nance. He was, everyone agreed, an admirable companion for the
wilderness trails, being versed in all aspects of hunting, tracking,
fishing, and wood-lore generally. He knew the language of the
out-of-doors as only few men did, and he could, if pressed, talk
it volubly, day or night, and in any season of the year. Roosevelt
had the good sense to listen to him.

Bill liked Roosevelt from the start. He admired the young
man's aggressiveness, his insistence on making his own decisions
and his strong convictions. "We hitched well, somehow or other,"
Bill said, "although he looked so pindlin' we thought we couldn't
raise him." [1]

Bill was kindly, humorous, and sensible. Moreover, he was a
good listener. Then, and later, Roosevelt liked a good listener.
Many years afterward John Burroughs wrote that Roosevelt was
not as enthusiastic about John Muir as he might have been. "I
think I could see where the rub was—both are great talkers, and
two talkers, you know, seldom get on well together. Now he finds
me an appreciative listener, and that suits him better." [2]

During his stay at Harvard, Roosevelt averaged two trips a
year to Sewall's home in Island Falls, Aroostook County, Maine,
having to make the last thirty or forty miles of the trip over
primitive country roads. He and Bill climbed Mt. Katahdin,
hauled dugouts up turbulent mountain streams, trailed caribou
through the deep snows of winter, and shared pork and hard-
tack. They did some fishing, but Roosevelt evinced no great interest in this sport. "Somehow he didn't like to sit still so long,"
Bill said. [3]

Arthur Cutler had warned Sewall that Roosevelt was inclined
to overestimate his strength, and that when ill or exhausted
would never admit it. But Bill was to find out to his complete
satisfaction that Roosevelt was not the weakling he had been
pictured. One day the two of them struck out into the woods and

did not end up until they had covered some twenty-five miles—
"a good fair walk for any common man," according to Bill.[4]

Under the shrewd, amiable direction of Bill, Roosevelt's familiarity with the northwoods grew by leaps and bounds. He became expert in the art of "roughing it." He learned the technique
of handling boats in rapid waters, he added greatly to his knowledge of northern birds and mammals, and he picked up much
useful information on how to hunt and trap. From these trips
Roosevelt, the slender-figured, under-developed boy, returned to
his studies physically stronger, each journey having contributed
its share to the development of muscle, bone, and sinew. Bill was
eminently good for Roosevelt and, as things turned out, Roosevelt was also good for Bill.

II

With the first signs of a New England spring, Roosevelt wrote
home:

By the way, as the time when the birds come back is approaching,
I wish you would send on my gun, with all the cartridges you can find
and my various apparatus for cleaning, loading it, etc. Also send on a
dozen glass jars, with their rubbers and stoppers (which you will find
in my museum) and a German dictionary if you have one.

As April warmed up into May, Roosevelt and Henry Minot
had their heads together more often. They talked of warblers
recently returned, of music in the marshes and of nesting vireos
and sparrows. More particularly, they talked about a trip together when the school year was ended, of vanishing into the
wilderness for a fortnight of diversion with only the birds to keep
them company.

Roosevelt had little difficulty in selling Minot on the Adirondacks. Arriving there on June 22, 1877, they spent one week together in the virgin forests skirting Lakes Spitfire and St. Regis,
and then, when Minot had to leave, Roosevelt stayed on for another week.

They had chosen an opportune time of the year—when the birds were in full song and each plume and feather was its brightest. The birds had been generally silent, and in poor feather, on Roosevelt's previous visits in late summer. Not so this time.

They heard the rose-breasted grosbeak "singing delightfully" from its home in the spruces, its cheery musical warble of single notes and short phrases reminding them of the robin. They listened to the red crossbill's "sweet, powerful and varied song, much like that of the purple finch." To Roosevelt, the crossbill was "one of the finest singers of the fringillidae." They loved the sweet plaintive song of the white-throated sparrow, and the short but rich melody of the mourning warbler. They listened admiringly to the winter wren, as with head cocked to one side and tail pointed to the sky, it poured forth its "gushing, ringing song, wonderfully loud for so small a creature." Roosevelt thought that no other songsters of the Adirondack woods, except the thrushes, sang so beautifully.

Nothing could equal the thrushes: the hermit, the olive-back, and the wood. For the first time in his life Roosevelt could listen to all three, could compare their songs. The olive-back, he wrote, had "a very sweet song, much like that of the wood thrush, but less rich and powerful, although equally liquid and varied." The song of the hermit thrush moved him more deeply than either of the others, and his description of it written when he was only eighteen should stand alongside other classic descriptions of bird music:

Its song, which is uttered until the middle of August, is very beautiful and peculiar to itself; it is more continuous than that of the olive-back and to my ear even sweeter, and fully equal to the song of the wood thrush; there is a weird, sad beauty in it which attracts the attention of the most unobserving, and once heard it can never be forgotten. It sings in the early dawn, at sunset, and if cloudy often through the entire day. I have even heard it at night. Perhaps the sweetest bird music I have ever listened to was uttered by a hermit thrush. It was while hunting deer on a small lake, in the heart of the wilderness; the night was dark, for the moon had not yet risen, but there were clouds, and as we moved over the surface of the water with the perfect silence so strange and almost oppressive to the novice in this sport, I could distinguish dimly the outlines of the gloomy and impenetrable pine forests by which we were surrounded. We had been out for two or three hours but had seen nothing; once we heard a tree fall with a dull, heavy crash, and two or three times the harsh hooting of an owl had been answered by the unholy laughter of a loon from the bosom of the lake, but otherwise nothing had occurred to break the death-like stillness of the night; not even a breath of air stirred among the tops of the tall pine trees. Wearied by our unsuccess we at last turned homeward when suddenly the quiet was broken by the song of a hermit thrush; louder and clearer it sang from the depths of the grim and rugged woods, until the sweet, sad music seemed to fill the very air and to conquer for the moment the gloom of the night; then it died away and ceased as suddenly as it had begun. Perhaps the song would have seemed less sweet in the daytime, but uttered as it was, with such surroundings, sounding so strange and so beautiful amid these grand but desolate wilds, I shall never forget it.

It was his devotion to the serene charm of northern woods that led him to describe this song with such depth of feeling. It was this same devotion that caused him to say in after years: "It is an incalculable added pleasure to anyone's sum of happiness if he or she grows to know, even slightly or imperfectly, how to read and enjoy the wonderbook of nature." [5]

Roosevelt had always been attentive to the melody of a bird. At times, judging from his voluminous notes, it appeared that he had lost all of his special senses except his auditory one. He was always making notes on the chirping and chattering that came out of the tree tops and the thickets bordering the roads. Only rarely did he refer to the gay plumage of a bird, like that of an oriole or tanager. Its music meant more to him than its color. In his serious effort to fix the bird's song firmly in his mind, he was aided by good hearing, excellent ear memory, a disposition to listen closely, and an inherent appreciation of melody and harmony.

An interesting and little-known outgrowth of Roosevelt's and Minot's Adirondack trip was their joint publication of *The Summer Birds of the Adirondacks in Franklin County, N. Y.*, a list of 97 species. This appeared in October, 1877, as a small leaflet of three or four sheets, without binding, title page, or wrapper. It was printed by the authors for private distribution and probably consisted of no more than a hundred copies. Of more importance, it was Roosevelt's first published contribution to zoology.

The authors were tremendously proud of the leaflet when it first appeared and, for a time at least, it was Exhibit A at 16 Winthrop Street.[6] They were even prouder when the zoologist, C. Hart Merriam, took note of it. Writing in the *Bulletin of the Nuttall Ornithological Society* for April 1878, Merriam said:

> By far the best of these recent lists which I have seen is that of The Summer Birds of the Adirondacks in Franklin County, N.Y. by Theodore Roosevelt and H. D. Minot. Though not redundant with information and mentioning but 97 species, it bears prima facie evidence of reliability—which seems to be a great desideratum in bird lists nowadays. Based on the sound principle of exclusion, it contains only those species which the authors have themselves observed there, and consequently furnishes that which was most needed, i.e. exact and thoroughly reliable information concerning the most characteristic birds of the limited region (Franklin County) of which they treat.

The Adirondack outing having proved such a success, Roosevelt and Minot discussed the practicability of more ambitious trips. They even considered going to England together. But before anything came of these plans, Minot withdrew from Harvard. Writing to his sister, Anna, in May of his sophomore year, Roosevelt said: "Old Hal Minot has left college! His father has taken him away and put him in his office to study law. I am awfully sorry and so is he." Some time later Roosevelt wrote Minot, telling of recent excursions into the country and of what he had seen. He concluded with these rather wistful words, "I have greatly felt the need of someone to talk to about my favorite pursuits and future prospects." During the remainder of his stay at Cambridge, Roosevelt found no one to take Minot's place.

In 1877 the *Naturalist's Directory*, a publication issued annually carrying the names of contemporary biologists, included a new one:

> Roosevelt, Theodore, 16 Winthrop Street, Cambridge, Mass.
> Vertebrates. Coll. Ex.

In this manner the young man informed the scientific fraternity of his day that he was interested in collecting and exchanging birds, mammals, and other vertebrate animals.

III

As a sophomore, Roosevelt had the privilege of electing certain courses. Harvard required Rhetoric, History, and Themes, but left the choice of others up to him. He chose two courses in German and two in Natural History. At last he was to receive formal education in the biological sciences.

Theodore Roosevelt arrived just a few years too late to sit at the feet of some of Harvard's most illustrious biologists. Louis Agassiz, European-born geologist and ichthyologist, no longer strolled through the College Yard "smoking his cigar in sublime disregard of law and order . . . every hair on his magnificent head bristling with energy, charm, genius." [7] No longer could he deny the evolution of man from some big-brained anthropoid. And Asa Gray, botanist extraordinary, though still living and still championing Darwin's natural selection theory, no longer entered the classroom. It is doubtful if Roosevelt knew him more than by sight. Other Cambridge greats, such as Jeffries Wyman, Charles T. Jackson, William B. Rodgers, William C. Bond, and Benjamin Peirce, who had rendered valuable service in the training of an earlier crop of Harvard scientists, had also faded from the picture.

The Natural History staff who taught Roosevelt consisted of Nathaniel Southgate Shaler and William Morris Davis, geologists; Edward Laurens Mark, William James, and Walter Faxon, zoologists; and George Lincoln Goodale and W. G. Farlow, botanists. Although these men were well-known among American scientists of their day—Shaler, for instance, for his brilliance as a teacher, Mark for his introduction of German research methods, and Goodale for bringing to Harvard the incomparable Blaschka collection of glass models of plants—they were not destined to wear such an aura of greatness as did Agassiz and Gray.

Neither in his autobiography, nor in any of his other writings, including the numerous letters he wrote home at the time, did Roosevelt do more than mention his professors by name. Perhaps one of Roosevelt's classmates supplied a partial answer when he wrote that most of the Harvard teachers of that day were stand-offish, "thought that the students were merely something to lecture to." [8] Roosevelt was certainly never on intimate terms with any of his Natural History teachers, with the possible exception of Shaler. Professor Shaler was liked generally by his students, and his Natural History IV (Geology) was one of the most popular courses then offered. Versatile, gregarious, Agassiz-trained, he was the sort to win admirers. Roosevelt visited in his home on occasion and was sometimes seen in the company of his daughters.

From several sources comes the information that Roosevelt talked out of turn in classes, was argumentative, voiced vigorous opinions. On one occasion as Shaler was lecturing, Roosevelt interrupted in the middle of a sentence to ask a question. Shaler stopped his flow of words, answered the query, and then continued. A few minutes later Roosevelt cut in with another question and once more Shaler answered with equanimity. A third time Roosevelt's curiosity could not be denied. At this last interruption, so report has it, Shaler drew himself up to his full stature of more than six feet, glared at Roosevelt and snapped, "See here, Roosevelt, let me talk, I'm running this course." [9]

Perhaps Roosevelt was more eager than argumentative. His Philosophy teacher, Professor Palmer, was to recall later that Roosevelt spoke rapidly, "sort of spluttered as if his thoughts came faster than his mouth could express them—something like water coming out of a thin-necked bottle. Thus it might be easily interpreted that he was more disputatious and vehement in his language than he really was." [10] And a classmate, in commenting on this near defect of speech, has said that he and others often started an argument just to rouse Roosevelt. Much to their delight, he would sometimes in his excitement lose altogether his power of articulation. [11]

Roosevelt's sophomore year brought him his first great sorrow. On February 9, 1878, his father died. It was a crumpling blow to the young man who had written in a letter soon after he entered Harvard, "I am sure that there is no one who has a father who is also his best and most intimate friend, as you are."

3

A Change of Course

THE February 23, 1878, issue of a short-lived periodical called *The Country*, carried a short account of a talk that had recently been delivered at a meeting of the Nuttall Ornithological Club by Theodore Roosevelt. A portion of the account went as follows:

Mr. Theodore Roosevelt, Jr. of New York said that some years ago English sparrows were apparently of service in New York City in destroying canker worms; but last year worms were very abundant in the gardens of that city, and not interfered with by the birds. In America he had never observed them molest grain but in Egypt he had seen them feeding in the fields in flocks of many hundreds, and on shooting them their crops were found to contain only grain. He had often watched them assault snow-birds, song and chipping sparrows, and had known them to kill a yellow-bellied woodpecker, actually mobbing it to death. Other birds, as purple martins, he knew they had driven away by occupying their boxes very early in the spring. This immigrant had spread into the surrounding country, and at West Point on the Hudson, land owners had been obliged to shoot them as they destroyed the buds of the fruit trees and drove away the song birds.

During the spring of his sophomore year Roosevelt started a scrapbook, the first of some 150 he compiled during his lifetime, and this paragraph adorns page one as a memento of what was known around Boston in 1877–78 as the Sparrow War. The conflict was bloodless but vehement and sometimes bitter. It arose over the question as to whether the English sparrow, which had been introduced into the United States about 1850, deserved plaudits or censure. On one side was a small group of articulate individuals who took the stand that this was not only an inoffensive bird but also one deserving protection. Did it not feed voraciously on a number of insects such as canker worms which everyone knew were harmful? A few of these well-meaning bird lovers even went so far as to supply the English sparrows with food and homes thus encouraging their multiplication. Outstanding among these was Dr. Thomas H. Brewer, a prominent physician and publisher of Boston and, incidentally, a member of the Nuttall Ornithological Club.

Opposing this group were many experienced ornithologists, who knew from personal observation that the English immigrant had multiplied to the point where it had become a serious enemy to many of the more-cherished songsters such as blue birds, wrens, and sparrows through killing them or driving them from their accustomed homes.

The facts of the case had been so unfairly presented to the public by the press, swayed by the influence of Brewer, that the Nuttall Ornithological Club of Cambridge finally called a meeting for the express purpose of determining what action they should take. The Nuttall Club at that time consisted of a group of young but serious-minded men who had founded the organization in Cambridge in 1874, just four years before the Sparrow War brought them into public prominence. Included among its founders and early members were scientists who were later to make ornithological history in the United States, men like William Brewster, Ruthven Deane, H. W. Henshaw, J. A. Allen, Charles F. Batchelder, H. B. Bailey, and Henry Minot.

Roosevelt became a member on November 26, 1877, probably on the recommendation of Minot who had joined earlier. In

Batchelder's memoir of the Club, written many years later, may be found this interesting comment:

Once in awhile—not often—there dropped in, together, two undergraduates, H. D. Minot and Theodore Roosevelt, Jr. . . . I am afraid some of us looked on the two a little askance. We recognized their ability, but both seemed a bit too cocksure and lacking in the self-criticism that, in our eyes, went with a truly scientific spirit. But they were young, and so were we! ¹

At the special meeting (January 28, 1878), with Brewer notably absent, several members, including Roosevelt, presented papers. All were similar in content in that they found the sparrow guilty of acts unbecoming a good bird citizen, a judgment not unexpected by those present. With the last paper read, the members drew up a report, incorporating the evidence that had been submitted. This they gave to the press, whence it found its way to newspapers and periodicals, including *The Country*, throughout the East.

Some of the Boston papers did not like the report. They said so at once. Articles and editorials appeared, some signed, some anonymous, all making much of the point that the Nuttall members were entirely too young for words of wisdom. One of the unsigned articles was attributed to Brewer, although he disclaimed authorship. It was full of barbs, some directed at Roosevelt:

A third, also sophomoric, draws upon an equally vivid imagination for his facts. He tells the world that when he was in Egypt—at what age he does not tell—he saw the house sparrow devouring grain & . . . How long has this species been known to be an Egyptian bird? He has also seen sparrows persecuting little *Chippies*, birds that on Boston Common live on the best of terms with these "ferocious foreigners," and has even known them to mob unto death big woodpeckers and so on. ²

Immediately, older and more experienced scientists, angered by the injustice of the criticism, rushed to the support of the youths of sophomoric rank. These supporters included men like J. A. Allen, of the Museum of Comparative Zoology, and Elliott Coues, then Secretary and naturalist to the United States Geological Survey of the Territories. The evidence they submitted, reinforced by the prestige of their names and positions, was difficult to controvert. The opposition languished and then expired.

At about the same time Roosevelt joined the Nuttall Club he affiliated himself also with the Harvard Natural History Society. Although the exact date of his admission is unknown, he played an active part in its affairs, at one time serving as its vice-president. On at least two occasions he presented papers, one entitled "Remarks on the Gills of Crustaceans" and another "Coloration of Birds."

To get material on Crustaceans, he traveled one day into Boston where he bought a large basketful of lobsters. As he was on his way back to Cambridge with them, on a crowded horsecar, several of the lobsters eased their way out of the basket onto the seats creating some excitement among the women passengers. This incident of his research was soon common knowledge, and according to one of Roosevelt's classmates, he liked to tell it on himself.[3]

In his autobiography Roosevelt wrote of an obscure ornithological publication which records information about the fish-crow and Ipswich sparrow.[4] This was a small pamphlet entitled *Notes on Some of the Birds of Oyster Bay*, which Roosevelt found time to write and have printed between club activities and laboratory dissections in his junior year. An even more modest contribution to science than his Adirondack paper, it consisted of brief notes on just seventeen birds he had collected and regarded as rare in the vicinity of Oyster Bay. The crow and the sparrow were among them. Though just a bird list, and an inconsequential one at that, it drew attention from J. A. Allen in the *Nuttall Bulletin:* "Several of the species are given as rare to the locality, while the observations respecting others are of interest." [5]

II

Roosevelt became a well-known figure on the Harvard "Yard." Students who drove dogcarts and wore mutton chops were not likely to be overlooked, and Roosevelt did both. Some said that he was admired by all. Others reported that he was a good deal of a joke. And still others said that he was "queer but eligible." [6] A fellow-student, Charles G. Washburn, declared that, "He was in a class by himself." [7]

Roosevelt readily attracted attention. He housed animals in his study. He asked the rector of a large Cambridge Episcopalian church for a Sunday School class, which he taught for more than three years. He went in for boxing and gained a local reputation for his aggressiveness and insistence on fair play. At 16 Winthrop he sought relaxation in Swinburne, Poe, and Tennyson. As a letter to his sister, Anna, attests, he even succeeded in interesting some of his classmates in poetry:

My respect for the qualities of my classmates has much increased lately, by the way, as they now no longer seem to think it necessary to confine their conversation exclusively to athletic subjects. I was especially struck by this the other night, when, after a couple hours spent in boxing and wrestling with Arthur Hooper and Ralph Ellis, it was proposed to finish that evening by reading aloud from Tennyson and we became so interested in "In Memoriam" that it was past one o'clock when we separated.

From an academic standpoint Theodore Roosevelt's third year at Harvard was his best. He really proved what he could do when he put his mind to it. Averaging slightly better than 87 and ranking 13th in his class, he had every reason to be proud of his record. Excellent grades in two Natural History courses had much to do with it.

Roosevelt's creditable showing as a junior might have been

even better if, early in that year, he had not met Alice Hathaway Lee of fashionable Chestnut Hill and fallen in love. He admitted as much when he wrote home: "I have done fairly; although perhaps not quite so well as I would have if Chestnut Hill had been a little farther from Cambridge."

III

Sometime near the end of Theodore Roosevelt's college residence he decided definitely to abandon natural history as a career. He may have been questioning the wisdom of his boyhood ambition as early as his sophomore year when he wrote home: "I must try and see Mr. Choate [presumably Joseph Hodges Choate]; it is time for me to think what I shall do when I leave college." But it was not until later, until the latter half of his junior year, that we have any proof of his change in plans. On February 7, 1879, for instance, he brought to a close that chapter of his life devoted to the keeping of boyhood field notes. And, about the same time, he severed connections with the Harvard Natural History Society, because of "a press of other duties (in my studies and in outside societies)."

In his junior year, too, Roosevelt began to evince more of an interest in other college subjects. In a letter to his mother he said: "Some of the studies are extremely interesting, especially Political Economy and Metaphysics. These are both rather hard, requiring a good deal of work, but they are even more interesting than my Natural History courses." Political Economy was taught by J. Laurence Laughlin. When interviewed at a later date, Laughlin said that Roosevelt once consulted him as to whether he should continue specializing in Biology or should turn to some other field, such as Economics. Laughlin told him that the country needed men who could think clearly on public questions.[8]

And then, on February 13, 1880, midway in his senior year,

Roosevelt wrote Henry Minot a letter that seems to admit of only one interpretation:

I write to you to announce my engagement to Miss Alice Lee; but do not speak of it till Monday. I have been in love with her for nearly two years now; and *have made everything subordinate to winning her; so you can perhaps understand a change in my ideas as regards science, etc.*[9]

What did Roosevelt mean, by his reference to subordinating everything to the winning of Alice Lee and to his changed ideas, except that Alice was cold to his idea of natural history? Would it be unreasonable to assume that the young lady, who carried the blood of the Lodges and Higginsons in her veins, had turned up her slightly tilted nose when Roosevelt, in proposing marriage, had offered the glamour of a career devoted to stuffed birds, pickled fish, and the peculiar assorted odors that go with a museum laboratory? Or did she, with uncanny prescience, sense his latent political ambitions and qualities of leadership, and persuade him that his life's work lay in broader fields?

It would be easy to conclude that Roosevelt abandoned natural history either because he became more interested in some other field, Political Economy for instance, or because Alice Lee put her foot down. But, according to Roosevelt himself, it was neither of these. He jettisoned earlier plans, he said, because Harvard utterly ignored the training of the outdoor naturalist, considered Biology to be a science only of the microscope and scalpel, and insisted that its students live in a world of tissues and embryos and embalmed specimens, all dead things, instead of in the woods and the fields and beside running streams where living things proclaimed their equal right to attention. This position, he declared, was traceable to the influence of the German universities, which Harvard was attempting to ape none too wisely or effectively. "The tendency," he wrote, "was to treat as not serious, as unscientific, any kind of work that was not carried on with laborious minuteness in the laboratory." His tastes, he

PORCELLIAN CLUB

Friday Feb 13th 1880

Dear Hal,

I write to you to
announce my engagement to
Miss Alice Lee; but do not speak of
it till Monday. I have been
in love with her for nearly two
years now; and have made everything
subordinate to winning her: so
you can perhaps understand a
change in my ideas as regards
science. &c.

Your Aff Friend
Theodore Roosevelt

The letter to Henry Minot announcing T. R.'s change in study plans.

then went on to say, were specialized in an entirely different direction.[10]

That was Theodore Roosevelt's explanation of why he abandoned natural history as a career, an explanation that loses some of its weight because it was not made until several years after he graduated from Harvard. The explanation came as a surprise to his former natural history teachers. According to Dr. Mark, Roosevelt while at Harvard never expressed any criticism to him about the way things were run, or to anyone else on the natural history staff so far as he knew.[11]

The young student's many letters from Cambridge to the various members of his family and to his friends (Minot for example) give no hint that he was dissatisfied about Harvard's policy of ignoring field work. In fact, from his letters one can build up a pretty fair case for the opposite point of view. Roosevelt was never inclined to be reticent about such matters in his correspondence, but was always frank and talkative about all his affairs and problems. In more than one letter, as we have already seen, he wrote of his enjoyment of this or that natural history course, or of how pleased he was with a particular mark.

Theodore Roosevelt perhaps abandoned natural history for a number of reasons but, as much as anything else, for lack of encouragement. No one in his own family urged him to devote his life to science. Apparently no member of the Harvard Natural History staff took a personal interest in him, as a teacher often does when attracted by a student's inherent enthusiasm or obvious ability. It seems certain, too, that Alice Lee took a dim view of Roosevelt's bent toward natural history. After Minot withdrew from college, Roosevelt had no companion who shared his enthusiasm for the outdoors. From what Batchelder has written, it is all too obvious that none of the Nuttall Club members befriended him.

When Roosevelt finally had to make a decision about a career his choice was made simpler by his recently developed interest in Political Economy. "I am going to try to help the cause of better government in New York City; I don't know exactly how," he told a friend shortly before graduation.[12]

IV

Theodore Roosevelt as a senior was a busy man. He had demands made on his time by his teachers, his clubs, the *Harvard Advocate,* of which he was an editor and, of course, by Alice Lee. Moreover he was waist deep in the writing of a book: *The Naval War of 1812.*

Busily engaged as he was, then, it is not surprising that his academic average fell below that of his junior year. It dropped from 87 to 81, and his rank from 13th to 45th, though he pulled down a healthy 91 in Natural History IV and a satisfactory 89 in Natural History VI.

Writing of his Harvard days in his *Autobiography,* Roosevelt said that he had been just a "reasonably good student." He was being modest—for a purpose. His record speaks for itself. He ranked 21st in a class of 161 and he received a diploma embellished *magna cum laude.* Roosevelt's rank, incidentally, was about the same as Grant's at West Point and Emerson's and Lowell's at Harvard. He was elected to Phi Beta Kappa and received "Honorable Mention" in Natural History.

Roosevelt was forever belittling his capacities as a student, hunter, naturalist, writer, and the like. He wished to leave the impression with the American citizen that he was just an average man who had been able to pull himself up by his own boot straps, as any other man of average ability, exercising the same industry and force of will, might do. It would have been an egregious political error, of course, for him to have become known to the public as something of a child prodigy.

Roosevelt terminated his residence at 16 Winthrop Street, Cambridge, on June 30, 1880. On that date he graduated from Harvard with a Bachelor of Arts degree and thereby automatically joined the great body of Harvard alumni. How he fitted into that group may be judged, perhaps, from an opinion expressed a few months later by a reporter for *The Pioneer Press*

of St. Paul who had just had a good look at him: "He is not at
all an ideal Harvard alumnus, for he lacks that ingrained con-
ceit and grace of manner that a residence at Harvard insures.
Although of the old Knickerbocker stock, his manner and car-
riage are awkward and not at all impressive" [13]

4

Ducks and Short-tailed Shrews

Soon after Theodore Roosevelt graduated from Harvard, he threw himself into a variety of activities, which made it appear that he would never again take more than the most casual interest in the inhabitants of the out-of-doors. He studied law under his uncle, Robert Barnhill Roosevelt, he completed *The Naval War of 1812*, he became active in the New York National Guard, assumed duties in the publishing house of G. P. Putnam's Sons, and ran successfully for the New York State Legislature. When he and Alice were in Europe on a belated honeymoon, he did not write home about the throstles and wagtails, but of his unbounded admiration for the genius of Rembrandt. In a letter from the Swiss Alps to Bill Sewall he made no mention of kestrel or chamois, but boasted instead of climbing the Matterhorn, after some Englishmen had scoffed at the notion that he could do it. The Roosevelts did visit the Paris Zoo, where he momentarily lost his power of speech when Alice asked him seriously who had shaved the lions, being unable to account otherwise for their manes.[1]

Roosevelt began to dispose of his bird collection. He had prepared his first skin in 1872, when he was fourteen, and he had energetically continued this labor of love until near the end of his college residence. In that time he stuffed at least two or three hundred birds. Some of these he mounted. This collection was one he could view with justifiable pride. It is highly unlikely that any other young man of his day had anything that would compare to it. He must have been well convinced that he would have no further use for it or he would not have considered parting with it.

In 1882, about the time he became a New York Assemblyman, Roosevelt presented the bulk of his collection, over 200 specimens, to the Smithsonian Institution. Five years later he gave what appears to have been the balance of it, some twenty specimens, to the American Museum. (Somewhere along the line he had weeded out many of his poorer skins.) I can find no explanation as to why he did not give it all in the first place to the American Museum, which his father had helped found and Theodore himself had consulted periodically in his youth. That the Smithsonian did not request the collection seems clear enough, for as soon as they had it they immediately gave several skins from it to the naturalist David Starr Jordan.

Roosevelt's decision to place his collection in Museum hands ensured its preservation. Even those specimens which went to David Starr Jordan are now safe, since this naturalist later gave them to the Indiana University Biological laboratories where they are today.[2]

Theodore Roosevelt's specimens, in whatever Museum, are highly prized today. At the American Museum, four of his mounted specimens are publicly displayed: a snowy owl, collected and mounted at Oyster Bay in 1876, and a group of three Egyptian birds (a spur-winged lapwing, a crocodile bird, and a white-tailed lapwing) mounted in 1872 or 1873. These are in good condition in spite of more than three quarters of a century of exposure, handling, and inevitable deterioration, the best possible proof of Roosevelt's sound methods of preservation.

With many of his skins may still be found his original specimen labels, with appropriate legend in Roosevelt's cramped, boyish handwriting. A few have pertinent collateral information on the reverse sides. For instance, we learn that a solitary vireo collected at St. Regis had a brown iris, slate-colored legs, and a crop crammed with beetles.

Politics, authorship, and other undertakings at first appeared to have driven from his mind the last vestiges of his boyhood interest in natural history. But at this very time he gave proof, by two acts, that he could no more turn his back forever on his original love than a sandpiper could renounce the seashore.

Under the euphonious title of *Sou'-Sou'-Southerly*, he wrote a graphic account of a trip that he and his brother Elliott made in a 21-foot, jib-and-mainsail boat on Long Island Sound one wintry day in late December. They were afloat from dawn till dusk, were nearly capsized two or three times on submerged rocks, and encountered everywhere great flocks of water birds: sheldrakes, loons, sea-coots, blue bills, and sou'-sou'-southerlies (long-tailed ducks), which periodically filled the air above them like huge zooming snowflakes. This essay could have been written only by one whose heart exulted at the sight of wings in action and warmed to the timbre and compass of mingled bird calls. Here is his opening paragraph:

Of all the waterfowl, that in the winter throng the half-frozen seas of Long Island Sound, the sou'-sou'-southerly is the most plentiful and most conspicuous. When the October weather begins to grow cool and sharp, and the northeast winds blow over the steel gray waters till they are tossed into long, foam-capped billows, then, for the first time small parties of these birds appear, their bold, varied coloring and harsh but not unmusical clangour at once attracting the attention of anyone who may be out sailing over the Autumn seas. On the clear fall days they can be seen a long distance off, and even before they can be seen, can be heard the loud "ha'-ha'-wee, ha'-ha'-wee," from the real or fancied resemblance of which calls to the words "sou'-sou'-southerly" they derive that one of their numerous titles with which I have headed this article.

At this time, too, he penned a letter to C. Hart Merriam (Chief of the U.S. Biological Survey from 1885 to 1910) about the carnivorous habits of the short-tailed shrew, a tiny insectivore about which Merriam had recently written in a monograph on the Adirondack mammals.

It is now apparent that Theodore Roosevelt was something of an authority on this animal. In fact, at an earlier date (perhaps in the pre-Harvard days when he had made several drawings of shrews), he had written an intriguing composition entitled *Blarina talpoides* (*Short Tailed Shrew*). After reading the Adirondack monograph, Roosevelt wrote Merriam to tell him how closely their observations on this shrew jibed—and to add a few thoughts of his own.

"In proportion to its size," Roosevelt wrote, "the male shrew is as formidable as any of our beasts of prey." He knew this to be true because at one time he had kept a male *Blarina* in a wire cage and had observed its behavior over a period of weeks. At first he fed it nothing but insects, which it devoured promptly and greedily, but later he introduced a full-grown pine mouse into the cage. The shrew, although conspicuously smaller than the mouse, attacked it without hesitation and succeeded in killing the mouse in short order in spite of the latter's struggles. Then Roosevelt tried it out on a seven-inch garter snake.

The little snake at first moved slowly about [Roosevelt wrote in his essay] and then coiled itself up on a piece of flannel. The shrew had come out from its nest, but did not seem to see the snake and returned to it. Soon afterwards it came out again and quartered across the cage; while doing so it evidently struck the scent (the snake all the time was in plain sight), raised its nose, turned sharply round and ran rapidly up to the flannel. It did not attack at once as with the mouse but cautiously smelt its foe; while the little snake moved its head uneasily and hissed slightly; then with a jump the shrew seized it, low down quite near the tail. The snake at once twisted itself right across the shrew's head and under one paw, upsetting him; but he recovered himself at once and before the snake could escape flung himself on it again and this time seized it by the back of the neck, placing one paw against the head and the other on the neck, and pushing the body from him while he tore it with his sharp teeth. The snake writhed and twisted, but it was of no use, for his neck was very soon more than half eaten through and during the next twenty four hours he was entirely devoured.

Roosevelt concluded with, "Certainly a more blood-thirsty animal of its size I never saw."

A comparison of Roosevelt's account with Merriam's reveals that Roosevelt—now a member of the New York State Legislature —was quite as conversant with the food habits of the short-tailed shrew as Merriam was, and as well qualified to discuss the subject. Roosevelt's observations, too, were made before Merriam's. But, as so often happened in his later years, Roosevelt assumed that the facts he had seen were already known, whereas if he had published them promptly, they would have stood as an original contribution to science.

Both the essay on the sou'-sou'-southerly and the letter to Merriam, not so important in themselves, show that the love of the outdoors, and of animals large and small, was still in his blood. And so was the urge to write about what he had experienced and observed in his outdoor ramblings. These two impelling proclivities had joined hands, and they would remain joined as long as Roosevelt lived.

5

First Taste of the West

ONE of the most fascinating and important chapters in Theodore Roosevelt's colorful, hyperkinetic life began on September, 1883, at three o'clock in the morning, when he stepped from a Northern Pacific train into the darkness enveloping the new-fledged cattle-town of Little Missouri, in the Bad Lands of Dakota Territory.

Roosevelt arrived in the Bad Lands in the last days of its wildness, while it was still "a land of vast silent places, of lonely rivers, and of plains where the wild game stared at the passing horsemen." [1] The old-timers could notice two important changes. The Indian villages, with their teepees and copper-colored inhabitants, had given way to the white man's towns, and the buffalo, once darkening prairie from the Red River to the Rio Grande, had dwindled from a multitude of 50,000,000 or more to a few scattered herds. In most other respects the Bad Lands looked as they had since the exuberant days of the Pleistocene.

This region, soon to become so familiar to Roosevelt, was located in what is now southwestern North Dakota. It was drained by the Little Missouri River, which here flows north before turning east to pour its waters into the Missouri. Numerous creeks fed the parent stream from both east and west, creeks bearing romantic names such as Prairie Dog, Black Tail, Little

Cannonball, Coyote, and Medicine Hat—all "sharp names that never get fat."

On either side of the Little Missouri arose steep, jagged buttes, on the slopes of which grew stunted pines and cedars, and sprawling sagebrush. These added touches of green to a colorful, stratified background made up of reds, blacks, purples, browns, and yellows, each of the different layers of sandstone, clay, and marl possessing its own distinctive hue. To Bill Sewall, the composition of the colors was like "a great rag rug such as the women make down in Maine, of all kinds and colors of rugs." [2]

Back from the Little Missouri on each side was the portion of the country referred to specifically as the Bad Lands, a region slashed and scored by the knives of the elements. For countless eons these weapons had been at work, dissecting the original landscape into all manner of fantastic-shaped ominences, with huge ragged, intervening fissures branching in all directions, their sides sometimes gentle slopes, other times sheer cliffs.

Beyond the Bad Lands was the prairie, level or undulating territory that stretched toward the horizon. In the spring this land was bright and green. In places, according to Roosevelt, a man could "gallop for miles at a stretch with his horse's hoofs sinking at every stride into the carpet of prairie roses, whose short stalks lift the beautiful blossoms but a few inches from the ground." [3] For the greater part of the year, however, the prairie land was dry and barren. In the more arid parts cacti and sagebrush dominated other plants.

The summers in this region could be extremely hot, and the winters equally cold. General Sully, after conducting a summer expedition into the Dakotas, was asked what the Bad Lands were like. He replied that he "didn't know they were like anything, unless it was Hell with the fire gone out." [4] After Bill Sewall had experienced temperatures as high as 125° F. in the shade he was convinced that a few of the fires still burned. Also, he experienced 65 below before he left that country.

II

Roosevelt had invaded the Bad Lands to hunt buffalo—while there were buffalo left to hunt. Following the fag end of a night spent in Little Missouri's only hotel, he inquired about a guide and was directed to a young man by the name of Joe Ferris. Ferris agreed to join him on a trip up the Little Missouri to the camp of a cattleman named Gregor Lang who would give them a base for daily forays into the surrounding country.

With these preliminaries out of the way, the two left Little Missouri for the Maltese Cross Ranch (also known as Chimney Butte), eight miles to the south, where Joe Ferris lived with his brother Sylvane and Bill Merrifield. The Ferrises and Merrifield were transplanted Canadians who had migrated to the Dakotas some two years before Roosevelt arrived. All three men were still in their twenties, quiet-mannered, rugged, self-reliant individuals, who had no inkling of the roles they were destined to play in the life of Theodore Roosevelt. Years afterward Roosevelt said to a biographer, "If you want to know what I was like when I had bark on you ought to talk to Bill Sewall and Merrifield and Sylvane Ferris and his brother Joe." [5]

Roosevelt spent the night at Chimney Butte and early the next morning left with Joe Ferris for Lang's camp, traveling by way of Big Ox Bow and the Fort Keogh Trail. They arrived in late afternoon and were welcomed by Lang and his son Lincoln. The elder Lang was a Scotchman, shrewd and well-informed, who liked to give expression to whatever was on his mind. He and Roosevelt got along well together. As a starter they sat up that night and talked till midnight. Lang had not previously been honored by a visit from a New York State Assemblyman.

Roosevelt's buffalo hunt was a combination of foul weather, ill luck, and indifferent shooting. For one solid week rain poured. Each morning Joe Ferris, who could take punishment as well as the next man but saw no reason for courting it, suggested that hunting would be difficult and it might be well to wait until the weather moderated; and on each occasion Roosevelt replied that he had come West to hunt and that was what he proposed to do, weather or no weather. Day after day they rode in drizzle and downpour, through rocky defiles, up slippery, winding mesa slopes, across rolling, sagebrush-covered prairie, without sighting a single buffalo. Each evening, plastered with the sticky gumbo mud characteristic of that region, they returned to Lang's modest quarters. Of the two it was Ferris who tired first and turned in. Roosevelt and Lang sat up till all hours discussing such manly topics as politics, literature, history, cattle, and conservation. At the conclusion of these talks Roosevelt would refuse Lang's offer of his bunk and roll up in his blankets on the hard clay floor.

Roosevelt did not get his buffalo until two weeks later. Not long afterwards he wrote:

No sight is more common on the plains than that of a bleached buffalo skull; and their countless numbers attest the abundance of the animal at a time not so very long past. On those portions where the herds made their last stand, the carcasses, dried in the clear, high air, or the mouldering skeletons, abound. Last year, in crossing the country around the heads of the Big Sandy, O'Fallon Creek, Little Beaver, and Box Alder, these skeletons or dried carcasses were in sight from every hillock, often lying over the ground so thickly that several score could be seen at once. A ranchman who at the same time had made a journey of a thousand miles across northern Montana, along the Milk River, told me that, to use his own expression, during the whole distance he was never out of sight of a dead buffalo, and never in sight of a live one.[6]

Before the two weeks were up, Joe Ferris had to alter his original opinion of Roosevelt. In that time Roosevelt had endured cold, hunger, and fatigue, he had shot badly, and he had been the victim of several unkindly accidents, such as being tossed over the head of his horse. Yet he was not only uncomplaining through it all; he was positively ebullient. Not once did he think of quitting. "It's dogged as does it,"[7] he kept saying to his companion. Ferris was as perplexed as he ever had been. Here was a man who courted misadventure, and whose determination increased in proportion to the difficulty of accomplishment. Joe mulled it over and eventually confided to Lincoln Lang that Roosevelt was "a plumb good sort." [8] From Joe Ferris, that was high praise.

III

Roosevelt not only got his buffalo, but he also got a good look at the Dakota land—and what he saw he liked. He talked more and more with Lang about it, and about the cattle business. One evening just before he left for the East he announced that he was going to invest money in cattle. He engaged Bill Merrifield and Sylvane Ferris as managers and gave them a check for $14,000 with which to buy stock. Later on, at his invitation, Bill Sewall and Wilmot Dow came West to join him.

In light of later events it seems clear enough that Roosevelt's sudden interest in ranching was secondary. Whether he would have admitted it or not, he wanted first and foremost a valid excuse to continue in the Bad Lands the very kind of intensive outdoor life he had just had a taste of: an excuse to use his gun, to ride through sagebrush and cactus, to watch the sundogs hanging in the red dawn, to observe the antics of the prairie wildlife, the pronghorn and blacktail, the skylark and sharptailed grouse.

When the arrangements for his ranching project had been completed, Roosevelt returned to New York to make his report to his family, some of whom thought he had lost his mind. Somewhat to the contrary, Gregor Lang was remarking to his son, "He is the most extraordinary man I have ever met. I shall be surprised if the world does not hear from him one of these days." [9]

6

Western Animals and Conservation

FROM 1883 to 1892, Theodore Roosevelt divided his time between the East and the West, traveling back and forth as many as two and three times each year. In the earlier part of that period, he was found much more often West than East. He came to know it at all hours of the day and in all seasons. The booming calls of the sharp-tailed grouse and the clamor of the sickle-billed curlew became as familiar to his ears as the wailings of the timber wolf and coyote. From his ranch house on the Little Missouri he rode in all directions: out onto the unending, pathless plains, through the dreary solitude of alkali desert, with its sagebrush and cactus, rattlers and prairie dogs, and over the naked, knifeblade ridges of the melancholy Bad Lands where the bighorn could be found.

Now and then he struck out on long journeys to the great mountain country of Wyoming, Montana, Idaho, and British Columbia. He made six such trips altogether: in 1884 to the Big Horn Mountains, in 1886 to the Coeur d'Alênes of Montana, in 1888 to the Selkirks of British Columbia, in 1889—the year he became U.S. Civil Service Commissioner—to the Bitter Root Mountains of Wyoming, in 1890 to Yellowstone National Park, and in 1891 to the Two-Ocean Pass country of Wyoming. The

43

following year, realizing that he had collected heads of all the larger game animals common to the United States except the collared peccary, he made still another ambitious excursion, a seventh. This was, of necessity, to an entirely different part of the country, to the Nueces River of Texas.

Roosevelt took these trips seriously. He even dressed up for them. One of his first acts after arriving in the Bad Lands was to engage a local seamstress to make him a buckskin suit. Probably no other acquisition ever gave him more pleasure. He had himself photographed in it, was continually boasting of its comfort and durability, wore it proudly on his hunting trips for years, and eventually passed it on to his children.

"It was the dress," Roosevelt said, "in which Daniel Boone was clad when he first passed through the trackless forests of the Alleghenies and penetrated into the heart of Kentucky; it was the dress worn by grim old Davy Crockett when he fell at the Alamo." [1] Roosevelt had coveted such a costume ever since he had read Mayne Reid, Cooper, and Parkman.

These years in the West were, of course, highly important ones to Roosevelt the naturalist. For instance, they made him familiar with Western animals, particularly large game. In the Dakotas, he learned what he could about white-tail and black-tail deer, pronghorn, buffalo, and bighorn sheep. On his trips to the Rockies he studied the elk, mountain goat, grizzly, and caribou. And what Roosevelt learned about these and other large quadrupeds was plenty. As a result he could speak with greater authority about their life histories than any other man then living. Professional scientists like C. Hart Merriam, chief of the United States Biological Survey, said so.

Roosevelt became familiar with Western birds, too. He made no effort to collect them, but he did identify each unknown species, having with him at all times for that purpose a wellworn copy of Coues' *Birds of the Northwest*.

The river which slowly flowed beside the ranch house was a

constant attraction to birds. In the hot summer mornings, Roosevelt could watch the prairie chickens and horned larks come down to drink, and in the fall the Canada geese, snow geese and pintail, mallard, widgeon, teal, and other southward-bound fowl, as they spiraled down to light on the river's surface. At other times he saw long strings of sandhill cranes flying by, following the winding course of the river, or large flocks of yellow-legs, as they interrupted their migration flights to congregate on the Little Missouri sandbars.

The river attracted vocalists. At times during the day, Roosevelt heard the ringing melody of the rock wren, the plaintive twittering of the horned lark, and the mourning dove's cooing, which always seemed faraway, and expressed, more than any other sound in nature, "the sadness of gentle, hopeless, never-ending grief." [2]

At night the poor-wills began "to utter their boding calls from the wooded ravines back in the hills." [3] One evening a poor-will lighted beside Roosevelt on his porch, and cried dolefully several times before flying away into the dusk. Some of the other birds, such as the owls and brown thrashers, sang continuously throughout the night, and were interrupted only by the snorting and stamping of deer that had come down to the edge of the open, or by the dismal wail of the coyote far out on the prairie.

To Roosevelt, the charm of a bird was in its song. He practically never exclaimed about the loveliness of its coat. It was as though, on hearing its melody, he shut his eyes tight, that no single note of the bird's music might be missed. Of all the Dakota bird songs, Roosevelt loved most that of the Missouri skylark (Sprague's pipit), a brown and gray-streaked bird of the interior plains whose music many bird lovers think compares favorably with that of the English skylark. He heard it first on the prairie:

Nothing was in sight in the way of game; but overhead a skylark was singing, soaring up above me so high that I could not make out its form in the gray morning light. I listened for some time, and the music never ceased for a moment, coming down clear, sweet and tender from the air above. Soon the strains of another answered from a little distance off, and the two kept singing and soaring as long as I stayed to listen; and when I walked away I could still hear their notes behind me. In some ways the skylark is the sweetest singer we have; only certain of the thrushes rival it, but though the songs of the latter have perhaps even more melody, they are far from being as uninterrupted and well sustained, being rather a succession of broken bursts of music.[4]

Although Roosevelt rated the song of the skylark as among the best, he recognized that other connoisseurs of bird music might disagree with him. So much depended upon the mood of the listener and upon the surroundings, he said. With him, the skylark's song was intimately associated "with the sight of dim hills reddening in the dawn, with the breath of cool morning winds, with the scent of flowers on the sunlit prairie, and with all the strong thrill of eager and buoyant life." [5]

Out on the plains dwelt everywhere the sharp-tailed grouse. Now and then Roosevelt was able to creep up on them, when they had gathered in their dancing rings. It was fun to watch them shuffling round each other, wings outspread, all the time keeping up a curious clucking and booming that accorded well with their strange gyrations. Of more interest to him was the great sage cock, the largest of American gallinaceous birds except the wild turkey. It was common then, although it is now rapidly being exterminated. Roosevelt frequently heard the deep, sonorous boomings of the cocks, in the morning before sunrise, as they challenged one another or called to their mates. These calls were uttered in a hollow bass tone which could be heard long distances in still weather; but they were hard to follow up because of a ventriloquial effect.

Other birds besides the sage cock that Roosevelt knew well in the Bad Lands are now extremely rare, and a few are no longer seen at all. The upland plover, for instance, which he found breeding along the Little Missouri, is nearing extinction, and the long-billed curlew, common in the Bad Lands in the eighties, is today rarely seen. According to Roosevelt, the curlews in springtime were one of the most conspicuous features of prairie life. He found them, in pairs and in small parties, scattered over the prairies and grassy uplands, where their loud, incessant clamor could be heard a mile away. During the nesting season, he once or twice enjoyed the delicacy of their eggs baked in hot ashes.

Roosevelt knew about Rocky Mountain birds, too, as revealed in a story told by Dr. Alexander Lambert, his personal physician at one time.

One day when we were at Glenwood Springs after the Colorado bear-hunt [early spring, 1905], he announced that he had that morning heard a Bullock's oriole. "Oh, no, Mr. President," replied his host. "Those birds do not come for a month yet; it is not possible, I think you are mistaken." "No," replied Roosevelt, "it cannot be; I heard him, I know the note well." His host was also a man of unusually wide knowledge of birds, and he expressed further doubt. Suddenly Roosevelt's face beamed with pleasure as looking out the window he exclaimed: "Turn round and look!" There, framed by the window, swinging on a branch of a flowering bush was a gorgeous Bullock's oriole, which as he swung sounded the disputed note.[6]

A full picture of the breadth of Roosevelt's knowledge of the wildlife of the West, gained during his several years residence there, can be obtained only by reading what he has written—about bighorn, blacktail, and caribou, about eagles, nutcrackers, and water ousels. It is clear, that in conversation about Western animals with the best-trained American ornithologists and mammalogists, even those who had themselves been a part of the West, he could hold his own. "He had," as one observer put it, "studied the habits of game while pursuing it; at the same time he had noted with interest and intelligence all the sights and sounds peculiar to the wilderness and, having the eye of a naturalist, had not allowed the smaller birds and mammals to escape unnoticed in his pursuit of a larger quarry."[7]

In later years when Theodore Roosevelt was asked to explain why he had had so many and varied experiences, his stock answer was that he had just put himself in the way of things happening and they happened. During his years in the West, he put himself in the way of a number of things, any one of which could have terminated on the spot a highly promising career.

On his trip to the Coeur d'Alênes after Rocky Mountain goat, for instance, he was pursuing his quarry along a shelving, slate-covered ledge just above a precipice when, to use his own words, he "nearly came to grief for good and all." [8] It happened very suddenly. One minute he was lunging forward over the uneven surface of the ledge, not too cautiously, and the next, as a piece of slate gave way beneath him, he was slipping over the face of the precipice. A moment later he landed in the top of a conveniently located pine, tumbled down through its branches, which slowed his speed, and halted finally in the lap of a balsam that stood just below the pine. He had held on to his rifle through it all, and his only loss was his glasses, which he found unbroken at the base of the balsam. "When I saw him fall I wouldn't have given two-bits for his life," said John Willis, his guide, "for it was easily a sixty foot fall." [9]

Shortly after his plunge over the precipice, Roosevelt and his companions—Willis and Merrifield—went out hunting goats. Toward mid-day, they unexpectedly came upon a magnificent waterfall which tumbled majestically over a precipice into a gorge, the walls of which rose on either side to a height of 300 feet. Roosevelt was so impressed with the beauty of the falls that he immediately broke open his camera to photograph it. He could locate no vantage point on the rim of the canyon that would include the entire scene in his viewfinder. Seemingly the only satisfactory place was a point between the rim and floor. Roosevelt told Merrifield and Willis to lower him into the gorge with a rope until he had reached that point. After he had his picture, he said, they could pull him up. Willis protested, but Roosevelt would not be deterred.

Merrifield and Willis followed instructions. They tied two hundred-foot lariats together, put one end around Roosevelt's mid-section, and wrapped the other around the base of a tree. They then lowered him with his camera into the gorge, letting him down as far as the lariats would allow. A few minutes later Roosevelt called to them to pull him up. At that moment the trouble began.

The two men heaved until they thought their arms would leave their sockets, but their combined strength was unequal to the task; they could not even get him started toward the top. Roosevelt was left dangling in mid-air like a giant, bifid plumb-bob, some 200 feet below the rim of the canyon, and at least 60 feet above the water which here rushed noisily and turbulently over the bed of the chasm.

Willis hurried to the bottom of the gorge to get the lay of the land. There he found Roosevelt still 00 feet in the air, but calm and possessed, and with an idea for a way out of his predicament. He thought it would be a perfectly simple matter for them to cut the lariat and let him plummet into the water beneath him. Willis told him that would be inviting suicide. He had a better idea; he remembered that he had a 50-foot lariat in camp, lighter than either of the two they had been using. He proposed to double it, tie it to the others, and thus let Roosevelt drop another 25 feet. This would reduce the distance to the water by almost half.

By the time Willis got back with the extra lariat Roosevelt had been dangling for all of two hours. The men hurriedly spliced the lariats, and then carefully lowered the future President of the United States another 25 feet. Willis now slid to the floor of the chasm again, while Merrifield remained above to cut the rope when all was ready. Willis had Roosevelt toss him his camera, and then studied the water to make sure that there were no boulders at the critical point. Finally he yelled to Merrifield to cut the lariat. Roosevelt hit the water with a splash, and then disappeared. A moment later he came up and Willis dragged him to safety. Except for some soreness, where the rope had bit into his chest, Roosevelt was none the worse for the experience.[10] Although Roosevelt subsequently wrote at considerable length about his trip to the Coeur d'Alênes, he understandably said nothing about this adventure.

It was on his trip to the Bitter Root Mountains, in 1889, that Roosevelt had one of the closest shaves of his entire hunting career. On this occasion he was by himself, and at the end of a long day of hunting. He had chosen a camp site, knee-haltered his horse, and was looking for grouse in the beautiful lodge-pole pine forest that surrounded his camp. Suddenly he saw the ungainly bulk of a large grizzly bear plodding along meditatively a stone's throw away. It was in plain view, and he immediately took aim and fired, his bullet entering the shoulder and ranging forward. Before he could shoot again, the bear reached the protection of a dense laurel thicket, into which it crashed and disappeared. Roosevelt had no intention of going into the thicket, nor did the bear have in mind to stay there. Suddenly it lunged into the open on the opposite side from Roosevelt, charged up the slope of a bank, and then stopped in plain view. What happened after that is best told in Roosevelt's own words:

He turned his head stiffly toward me; scarlet strings of froth hung from his lips; his eyes burned like embers in the gloom. I held true, aiming behind the shoulder, and my bullet shattered the point or lower end of his heart, taking out a big nick. Instantly the great bear turned with a harsh roar of fury and challenge, blowing the bloody foam from his mouth, so that I saw the gleam of his white fangs; and then he charged straight at me, crashing and bounding through the laurel bushes, so that it was hard to aim. I waited until he came to a fallen tree, raking him as he topped it with a ball which entered his chest and went through the cavity of his body, but he neither swerved nor flinched, and at the moment I did not know that I had struck him. He came steadily on, and in another second was almost upon me. I fired for his forehead, but my bullet went low, entering his open mouth, smashing his lower jaw and going into the neck. I leaped to one side almost as I pulled the trigger; and through the hanging smoke the first thing I saw was his paw as he made a vicious side blow at me. The rush of his charge carried him past. As he struck he lurched forward, leaving a pool of bright blood where his muzzle hit the ground; but he recovered himself and made two or three jumps onward, while I hurriedly jammed a couple of cartridges into the magazine, my rifle holding only four, all of which I had fired. Then he tried to pull up, but as he did so his muscles seemed suddenly to give way, his head dropped, and he rolled over and over like a shot rabbit. Each of my first three bullets had inflicted a mortal wound.[11]

The next morning Roosevelt returned to the scene of his triumph to remove the skull and the hide. The beauty of his trophy, and the memory of the circumstances under which it was obtained, led him to value it more highly than any other in his possession at that time. Ever afterwards he maintained that this was his narrowest escape from death by a wild beast during his entire lifetime.

Hunting trips may get a man into trouble in more ways than one; Roosevelt could vouch for that. In 1895 a Chicago lawyer, A. L. Trude, gave out an interview upon his return from a hunting trip to the West. He said that he had met two of Roosevelt's former guides, who told him that:

The only bear Roosevelt had ever shot was in a trap; that he had missed all of the white goats he had ever shot at, and that finally one of the guides killed one of the animals and then rigged it up to make it appear that Roosevelt had shot it, so he could get a photograph of it; and that all of the elk he had ever killed were cows and calves, which the pseudo guides had driven into pens, so he could shoot them without any trouble.[12]

The story was sensational and included circumstantial detail that added plausibility. Roosevelt was fit to be tied. To have both honor and sportsmanship called in question, in one and the same breath, was more than enough to make him raise his hackles. He immediately wrote Trude demanding a retraction and an apology. When he got no satisfaction he sent a letter to George Bird Grinnell, editor of *Forest and Stream,* who printed it. In this letter he vigorously denied each allegation and challenged Trude to supply the date and place where a single one of the incidents he recited had occurred. He concluded by saying, "Mr. Trude is unfit for membership in any club or association of gentlemen, and is unfit for the acquaintance of any men of honor." [13]

This letter was followed by another to *Forest and Stream,* by Jack Willis, who came to his defense.[14]

Then came the payoff. Roosevelt challenged Trude to a duel. According to Willis, Roosevelt wrote him of his challenge, asking him to serve as his second. In this letter he said: "My challenge gives Trude the choice of weapons, but that makes no difference. I will fight him with anything he names, and I am depending on you to see that there is no foolishness about it." [15]

Willis accepted the commission, and was somewhat mortified soon afterwards when he heard from Roosevelt that the incident was closed. Trude had apologized, throwing all the blame on the alleged guides.

7

A Natural History Trilogy

FOLLOWING his unsuccessful attempt in 1886 to become Mayor of New York City, Roosevelt spent most of his time during the next two years in writing. He prepared a biography of Gouverneur Morris (for the American Statesman Series) and he began his three-volume "magnum opus," *The Winning of the West*. In the fall of 1888, he supported vigorously Benjamin Harrison who defeated Grover Cleveland for President.

In May of the following year, President Harrison appointed Roosevelt a member of the United States Civil Service Commission. After Cleveland was reelected President in 1892, he retained Roosevelt as Commissioner. Roosevelt kept this position until May 5, 1895—a total of six years—when he resigned to become Police Commissioner of New York City, a post he held until April 19, 1897, when President McKinley appointed him Assistant Secretary of the Navy.

Roosevelt's residence in the West supplied him with the material for three books: *Hunting Trips of a Ranchman, Ranch Life and the Hunting Trail,* and *The Wilderness Hunter*. Together they constitute a natural history trilogy of the West. They met with such success that, for a time at least, Roosevelt seriously considered devoting all his time and energy to writing, of making it his life's work. "Mind you," he told Brander Matthews (October 5, 1888), "I'm a literary feller, not a politician, nowadays." [1]

These books about the pursuit of large game animals set a new style. They were far from being just a hunter's narrative of trophies bagged, as most of the hunting books of the time were. In addition to accounts of the chase, they included vivid pictures of windswept prairie and baldface mountain, of lovely, sweet-smelling flowers and endless virgin forests; thumbnail sketches of birds and small mammals; and fascinating biographies of large game animals, from buffalo to bighorn.

These faunal biographies held abundant detail that had not previously dignified books of this kind. For instance, nothing so thorough and satisfactory about the private life of the grizzly had yet appeared as that in the chapter on this animal in *The Wilderness Hunter*. And no essay on the bighorn could match Roosevelt's in *Ranch Life and the Hunting Trail*. In fact, none of the large beasts of the West had been treated so completely upon the basis of a single individual's personal knowledge.

No one up till then, either, seems to have combined so successfully the offices of the hunter with those of the naturalist and writer. Through Roosevelt's words the reader was able to see vividly the strange rough beauty of the Western landscapes and to hear meantime the notes and cries of their untamed inhabitants. He knew what he wanted to say. No one had to read his lines twice to find out what he meant. His books were, as Brander Matthews said, "Tinglingly alive, masculine and vascular." [2] No reviewer, however captious, ever insisted that his books were dull.

Yet none of Roosevelt's books on the West quite measured up to his expectations. *The Wilderness Hunter*, admittedly the best, did not turn out to be the *magnum opus* he had hoped for. In a letter to Owen Wister he wrote:

I wish I could make my writings touch a higher plane, but I don't well see how I can, and I am not sure that I could do much by devoting more time to them. I go over them a good deal and recast, supply or omit, sentences and even paragraphs, but I don't make the reconstruction complete in the way that you do.[3]

His chief liabilities in these days of apprenticeship were tendencies to repetition, perennial extravagance of statement ("He fairly lived in an atmosphere of superlatives," [4] one critic said), and occasional grammatical lapses. He invariably had his deer and antelopes jump "clean" over the hurdles in their path, and he split infinitives right and left, in those days a heinous grammatical offense. When he learned, after he had become President, that Professor Lounsbury of Yale approved of splitting infinitives, Roosevelt wrote him: "Good for the split infinitive! Here have I been laboriously trying to avoid using it in a vain desire to look cultured and now I shall give unbridled rein to my passion in the matter."

Although Roosevelt leaned heavily on the literature available to him, and on the experience of other men whom he considered trustworthy, he acquired most of his knowledge of Western animals through close, personal observation.

The literature available to him, that he had with him at his Elkhorn Ranch, included T. S. Van Dyke's *Still Hunter,* Colonel Richard Dodge's *Plains of the Great West,* Judge John Dean Caton's *The Antelope and Deer of America,* and Elliott Coues' *Birds of the Northwest.*[5] In his opinion, these books about Western animals spoke out with greatest authority. Anyone familiar with his unusual powers of memory and concentration can feel reasonably certain that he assimilated everything of value to him in these books. In addition, he took what he wanted from Burroughs and Thoreau, Audubon and Bendire, Catlin and Parkman, and Ruxton and Lewis and Clark, whose writings he knew chapter and verse. Commenting on Roosevelt's knowledge of animal literature, Stewart Edward White said, "He preferred to argue from experience rather than authority, though he seemed to have read and to possess on file in the front of his mind about everything that had been said on the subject." [6]

Roosevelt would talk with anyone about animals. He preferred the word of the naturalist, but gave close attention to that of trapper, hunter, cowboy, or Indian guide. At first, like W. H. Hudson, who at times gave easy credence to the Argentine gaucho, he was prone to accept seemingly credible report as truth. Later he learned to sift fact from fancy, and to put his trust only in those men he had found through experience to be reliable. "Above all things," wrote Henry Fairfield Osborn, "he desired to be truthful and strictly accurate, and he took infinite pains not to exaggerate but to present the real facts." [7]

Reviewers of the eighties and early nineties were generally enthusiastic about Roosevelt's books. They went so far as to compare them favorably with those of some of the most celebrated naturalists. The London *Spectator*, for instance, said that *Hunting Trips of a Ranchman* "could claim an honourable place on the same shelf with Waterton's *Wanderings* and Walton's *Compleat Angler*." [8] And the Chicago *Unity* thought that, "Among American writers who have attempted to describe nature, few save Thoreau and Burroughs, have been as successful as Mr. Roosevelt." [9] George Bird Grinnell said that it was the freshness and spirit of *Hunting Trips of a Ranchman* that made it so delightful. He was reminded of Parkman's *The Oregon Trail*. Grinnell was of the opinion, though, that Roosevelt had an inclination "to accept as fact some statements made in books, and others by men with whom he had talked, who were either bad observers or careless talkers." [10]

Speaking of the animal biographies in *Ranch Life and the Hunting Trail*, the New York *Tribune* said, "These are full of information about the habits of game, especially the mountain sheep, white goat and blacktail deer. There is not a dull line between the covers of this spendidly printed and made volume, and Mr. Remington's illustrations are full of spirit and fire." [11]

The Wilderness Hunter, the last of this Western trilogy to come from the press, was, from a zoological standpoint, a more mature, a more finished study than either of its notable predecessors. By now Roosevelt could count ten years in all (this was 1893, while he was still Civil Service Commissioner) since he had first looked upon the canyons and coulees of the Bad Lands. As the months and years had slipped by, he had not only increased his stockpile of information about the Western wildlife but also had sharpened his faculties of observation, reflection, and self-criticism. "It has seldom been our good fortune to read such an entertaining account of sport in the United States as that which is contained in *The Wilderness Hunter,* wrote the London *Field.*[12] "No song of bird or flower or the shyest plant which grows escapes his appreciative notice," added the Philadelphia *Telegram.*[13]

Roosevelt did not include in these books everything of importance that he might have. He had been of the opinion right along that many of the things he had seen had already been reported. "I vaguely supposed," he wrote later, "that the obvious facts were known, and I let most of the opportunities pass by." [14]

Fame lets down the bars to slander and abuse. When Roosevelt became President, some of his contemporaries familiar with his hunting books went out of their way to declare that he was just a hunter, thereby impugning him as a naturalist and implying that he would rather put a bullet in an animal than observe it alive. This question of whether Roosevelt was more hunter, or more naturalist, keeps cropping up, and it needs answering.

Actually, no hard and fast line separates the true hunter from the naturalist. Any good hunter is, by necessity, something of a naturalist; and any naturalist who uses a gun for collecting purposes, as Roosevelt did, whether he was after bird-skins or buffalo heads, is something of a hunter. More than that, any hunter worth his salt knows that to be successful he must acquire a respectable store of woodcraft and must possess some knowledge of the quarry he pursues. The carrying of a rifle does not preclude a keen interest in the everyday lives of animals, large and small, a joy in the music of birds and the color of flowering plants, and a spiritual uplift in the presence of towering pines and rugged mountain slopes.

Roosevelt hunted in that spirit. When he killed his first caribou, after days of arduous scrambling over the unfriendly ridges of the Selkirks, he said: "It was one of those moments that repay the hunter for days of toil and hardship; that is if one needs repayment, and does not find life in the wilderness pleasure enough in itself." [15] Jack Willis (one of his Western guides) could vouch for that. He said that Roosevelt was happy when game was around but when it was not he "turned to enjoyment of the scenery and the air." [16]

From the very first days of his residence in the West he inveighed against the hunter who shoots indiscriminately, whose chief thought is the size of his bag. As early as 1885 Theodore Roosevelt was saying that a true sportsman shoots only for the peculiarly fine trophy, or to supply the ranch table. Jack Willis had been too free with his ammunition until Roosevelt took hold of him. "There is no sportsmanship about that," he told him. "It is just plain murder and a good sportsman like you ought to be ashamed of it." [17] In only one instance that I can find did Roosevelt seem to overstep the self-imposed limits of his own rule. That was on the Two-Ocean Pass trip when he killed nine elk. This instance was later thrown in his face, with damaging results, and it would have done little good for him then to state the truth—that some of these had been killed for food and the others to fill promises he had made to friends to bring back heads for them. One, for instance, was for Henry Cabot Lodge.

Roosevelt had little patience with sentimentalists who opposed hunting in any form. To him the killing of a large game animal (provided the species was stable) was of no more significance than the killing of a baldface hornet or a crimson-spotted newt. All were living things, the difference being of degree rather than of kind.

He emphasized that the normal end of a wild animal is usually a tragic one, that death from old age is the exception. The ending of life by a bullet was more merciful, he argued, than death by fang, disease, or starvation. Moreover animals, especially those protected on reserves, often multiplied to the point where their food requirement exceeded the available supplies. In such instances, if they were not shot they starved or weakened, and thus fell easy victim to predators.

Theodore Roosevelt's years in the West gave him a broader knowledge of animals, but they gave him something else far more important—priceless lessons in the need for conservation. He was able to bear witness that several of the prairie animals, just in the few years he had known the West, had been greatly decreased in number by the game butchers. He had been spectator almost daily to the devastating force known as erosion. And he had long, meditative looks at the great Western forests. In the preservation of these forests, he came to realize, lay seeds of our future prosperity and growth as a nation. Many of his later acts, such as the creation of Western forest reserves, stemmed from his intimate knowledge of those timberlands gained while hunting elk and goat beneath their perpetual shade. Roosevelt might have been a conservationist under any circumstances, but he would not have been such an enthusiastic, indomitable, crusading one if he had not known the West.

II

When one of the worst winters in the memory of the oldest inhabitants of the Bad Lands struck the Dakotas (the winter of 1886–1887), killing off the cattle, not by the hundreds, but by the thousands, Roosevelt's experiment in ranching came to a sudden, decisive end. The $50,000 he had lost, though, was not all liability. To a friend in later years Roosevelt said: "Do you know what chapter or experience in all my life I would choose to remember, were the alternative forced upon me to recall one portion of it, and to have erased from my memory all the other experiences?" And he answered the question himself: "I would take the memory of my life on the ranch with its experiences close to Nature and among the men who lived nearest her."[18]

Theodore Roosevelt probably continued the experiment in ranching as he did because the land of prairie and tall mountains helped him forget a great personal loss. By a tragic coincidence, both his wife and his mother had died, on the same day, February 14, 1884, his wife after giving birth to a daughter, Alice.

Two years later, Roosevelt ran unsuccessfully for Mayor of New York City. Soon after the election, in December, he re-married. His bride was Edith Kermit Carow, whom he had known as long as he could remember. As children they had played games together in and around Gramercy Park and Union Square. While on his trips to Europe and Egypt Theodore had written long letters to her, addressing her as, "My own darling Edie."

After their honeymoon, Theodore brought Edith to Sagamore Hill, a home he had finished building about 1885, three miles east of Oyster Bay. The country here, originally owned by the Indian chief, Sagamore Mohannis, was familiar to Roosevelt. He knew every foot of it. He had often traveled over it in pre-Harvard days while hunting warblers, sparrows, and other birds to fatten his collection.

Then and thereafter, there was no place to Theodore and Edith quite like Sagamore Hill, not even the White House. It became the home of the five children born to them: Theodore, Jr., Kermit, Ethel, Archibald, and Quentin. Today, a National Monument, it is almost as well known to Americans as Monticello and The Hermitage.

8

"Field Work Also Is Necessary"

THIRTEEN years after Theodore Roosevelt received his *magna cum laude* at Cambridge, he was appointed by the Harvard Board of Overseers to a three man committee with instruction to report on the condition of the Zoology Department and to submit recommendations for its improvement. The inclusion of Roosevelt on the committee with Walter Faxon, still a teaching member of the Zoology staff, and Clarence J. Blake, a well-known ear specialist, was recognition of the name he had made for himself as a naturalist.

Roosevelt approached his task seriously, and with some relish. He revisited the College Yard and consulted with scientists of the Zoology Department and of the Museum of Comparative Zoology, among them the ornithologists W. E. D. Scott and William Brewster. Roosevelt had known the latter, it will be remembered, when the two participated in the "Sparrow war" and other activities of importance to the Nuttall Club. On this visit he learned that the general run of Zoology courses offered the undergraduate was substantially the same as when he had been a student at Harvard, and the Zoology teachers—Mark, James, and Faxon—were all still on the job. The only important change effected had been a separation of Zoology from the old Natural History Department, making of the former a department to itself.

William Brewster apparently talked freely to Roosevelt about changes that, in his opinion, would benefit the Zoology Department and, in turn, the Museum. At any rate, on April 6, 1893, Roosevelt wrote to Brewster from his office in Washington—he was still Civil Service Commissioner—saying: "You have given me the suggestions I need; and they shall all go in."

After he had mailed this letter, Roosevelt completed his report and sent it to Faxon to find out how it would sit with him. Faxon did not like it; this became perfectly clear when Roosevelt wrote again to Brewster:

> I found that Mr. Faxon radically disagreed with my report. He is evidently a great believer in the school which puts the biologist and embryologist at the head, and which are substituting for the old term "naturalist" the word "biologist"; whereas I think that at present we need to develop the old school naturalist much more than is being done. We will probably therefore have to put in two reports. He objected to my putting in the paragraphs which I did after consultation with yourself and Mr. Scott, on the ground that they were irrelevant. So they are, if the zoological courses are to be treated as he would wish them to be treated, but they are not in the least irrelevant if these courses are to be treated as I think they ought to be. If you see Mr. Faxon you might jog his mind about returning to me my report. He has had it about a month, and I now want to send it to Charles Francis Adams of the Board of Overseers.[1]

As previously pointed out, Roosevelt, so far as is known, said nothing derogatory about teaching practices or courses offered in the Natural History Department, either to the Harvard zoologists, or to his friends or family, while he was in residence at Cambridge. He first came out with such criticism now, in 1893, thirteen years after his graduation, when he filed his separate report (because of Faxon's dissent) with the secretary of the Board of Overseers.

Roosevelt's report was lengthy and repetitious. He broke it

into two parts: one, recommendations for the improvement of the Zoology Department, and two, suggestions for exhibiting to better effect the material in the Museum of Comparative Zoology.

In the first part, Theodore Roosevelt called to the attention of the Board the undue emphasis Harvard zoologists were placing on microscopic work. He thought this emphasis was misplaced because microscopic work was such a small part of Zoology. "The place of the microscope in biology by no means answers in importance to the telescope in astronomy," he insisted.[2] He admitted that the microscopist had an "honourable function" to fill in science, but, in his opinion, it was not nearly as important as that, "Of the systematist and the outdoor collector and observer of the stamp of Audubon or Bachman, Baird or Agassiz." [3]

This undue emphasis on microscopic work, Roosevelt said, was due to the effort made by Harvard zoologists (German-trained Dr. Mark in particular) to ape the Germans, who had taken the lead in the use of the microscope. He thought the faculty went entirely too far in this, accepting not only what was best in the German methods, but also the bad and indifferent as well.

Proper biological work, he went on to say, should include much more than microscopic anatomy and embryology. "Field work also is necessary," and if impracticable during the months of the regular school year it should be provided for in the summer months.[4] "The highest type of zoologist," he insisted, "is the naturalist . . . who can work both in the laboratory and afield." [5]

In the second part of his report, Roosevelt emphasized the need of arranging to better advantage the exhibit material in the Museum. He thought it should be organized to show such things as, for instance, the systematic position of different groups, the effect of environment on those animals which range uninterruptedly over large geographical areas, and the relation of mammals and birds to their breeding, feeding, and general life economics.

Theodore Roosevelt, of course, was quite within his rights in deploring a lack of field work at Harvard. The curriculum, when he was a student, did not include even one field course. If it had, he probably would not have been minded to abandon natural history as a specialty. He had entered Harvard with the avowed intention, as we know, of becoming a naturalist of the stamp of Audubon, Wilson, or Coues. One can imagine his distaste for the restraining walls of the laboratory, when he yearned for the freedom of the seashore or of the open valley.

At the same time, his disparagement of the microscope was shortsighted. He seems to have been unaware of the changes that had been taking place in biological instruction, changes which definitely were for the better. For a long time the progress of zoology and botany had been impeded by attaching undue importance to the collecting and classifying of animals and plants, and by ignoring the equally important problems of function, structure, and development, a full understanding of which depended upon the magnification afforded by the microscope.

The changes in instruction had begun before Roosevelt entered Harvard. They had, in fact, got their first legs in Germany, with the publication of texts by such eminent scientists as Schleiden and Sachs. Sachs' *Textbook of Botany*, for instance, translated into English in 1875 (the year before Roosevelt went to Cambridge), had a tremendous influence in the United States. For the first time, students were brought face to face with the existing status of biological research, were made aware of the infinite number of fields of inquiry, and were stimulated to give their lives to scientific investigation. For the first time, too, teachers realized that further progress in biology depended on the training of investigators. Thus the pendulum, in a few short years, moved rapidly in the opposite direction, away from field work to laboratory. At Harvard field work was abandoned almost completely.

It is surprising too, that Roosevelt did not recognize Harvard's ability to complement the self-training that he already possessed. This teaching had been sound, as far as it went, but its inadequacy should have been apparent even to him. It seems strange that he did not welcome the opportunity to inquire further into the anatomy, physiology, and embryology of animals, subjects which were prerequisite to a broader, clearer understanding and appreciation of his beloved birds. And one wonders why he had not been eager to enter the invertebrate world, if for no other reason than to learn its importance in the ornithological world.

Harvard not only gave him this highly important background material, but it also supplied him with a fund of information about such related things as plants, minerals, and fossils, which was of much value to him in later years. All of this was much more important to him, in his early twenties, than the advanced training in the field in ornithology he had looked forward to getting.

Theodore Roosevelt's criticism did not bring the results which he had desired. It had been unnecessarily harsh and blunt. "If you must grasp a nettle, grasp it firmly," he was wont to say. He followed this rule on occasion with success, but often his nettles were only buttercups to others.

To say that Harvard zoologists were disturbed by Roosevelt's report would be a conspicuous understatement. Justly or not, they felt like an indulgent father who had been kicked in the pants by an ungrateful son. They resented, too, his making recommendations for the Museum, when he had been instructed by the Overseers to report only on the Zoology Department. As one zoologist put it, "It was matters of this kind in which he seemed unable to keep his head clear that led to many disturbances at Harvard." [6]

As a matter of fact, the Harvard zoologists of 1893 were all in favor of adding field courses to the then limited curriculum. Right then, however, the Harvard Corporation was not in a financial position to increase the budget for that purpose. According to one Harvard teacher, the Corporation tried to raise funds from other sources, even asking Roosevelt himself to help. But Roosevelt "never so much as raised a finger." [7]

Theodore Roosevelt continued to dislike the emphasis on German microscopic methods. In the spring of 1912, George H. Parker, of the Harvard Biological Laboratories, introduced Roosevelt to a German exchange professor, Dr. Kükenthal, who had devoted several years of his life to microscopic studies of whale embryos. Roosevelt's first question was, "I suppose you work with the microscope?" When the professor answered that he did, Roosevelt then asked what animal he studied. To this question the German could make only one reply: "Whales!" In commenting on this incident, Dr. Parker said: "I had seen Mr. Roosevelt under many circumstances and had recognized his great ability to meet any emergency in which he found himself, but I never saw him so nonplused as he was at that moment by Dr. Kükenthal's reply, nor did he recover himself during the whole of the ensuing, brief conversation." [8]

Roosevelt was registering a valid criticism however, in his skirmish with the Board of Overseers about the teaching of field work at Harvard. On this point, C. Hart Merriam, long-time head of the United States Biological Survey, had this observation to make: "T.R. lived during the period of ultra-microscopic specialization in the study of animate nature—the sad period in which the good old term 'natural history' fell into disuse, actually disappearing from text-books and college curricula. Nevertheless he was not misled. The keenness of his observation coupled with his intimate first-hand knowledge of nature enabled him to recognize the necessity for field work and convinced him of the absolute need of museum specimens for exact studies of animals and plants." [9]

Merriam followed this observation with another: "If his [Roosevelt's] major interests had not been diverted into the time-consuming field of politics he would have been one of America's foremost naturalists." [10]

9

"I Must Have a B. and C. Dinner"

THEODORE ROOSEVELT's historians have almost completely over-looked the Boone and Crockett Club. Although they are inclined to agree that his greatest service to his nation while President of the United States was educating its people to the need for con-servation, none of his biographers seems to have grasped the in-fluences at work in his youth and young manhood which impelled him to crusade so energetically in behalf of our forests and wildlife. His boyhood self-schooling in natural history was one influence and his years in the West another. The Boone and Crockett Club was still another.

This Club was the outgrowth of long, serious talks, beginning in 1887, between Roosevelt and George Bird Grinnell, editor of *Forest and Stream* magazine. It was only natural that these two should get together. Roosevelt was by now a veteran of four years' experience in the West and Grinnell had been a naturalist to Colonel William Ludlow's reconnaissance to the Northwest. As a result, both had been spectator to the wanton killing of game for hides, and Grinnell's report to Colonel Ludlow was one of the earliest protests against mercenary game slaughter.

Vaguely at first, and then more clearly, Roosevelt and Grinnell foresaw the dangers threatening many of the large quadrupeds inhabiting the Rockies and the great Western plains. As Grinnell put it:

We regretted the unnecessary destruction of game animals, but we did not know all it meant, nor had we the vision to look forward and imagine what it portended. So though we discussed in a general way the preservation of game, it must be confessed—in the light of later events—that we were talking of things about which we knew very little. We wanted the game preserved, but chiefly with the idea that it should be protected in order that there might still be good hunting which should last for generations.[1]

Although they may not have envisioned at the moment just what the destruction of game animals foreshadowed, Roosevelt, for one, became more and more convinced that some action should be taken, as promptly as possible, to protect them. In the autumn of 1887 he proposed to Grinnell that they take the lead in forming a club to be composed of worthy sportsmen who were, at the same time, experienced big-game hunters. When Grinnell fell in with the idea, Roosevelt took the first step by inviting to his home on Madison Avenue these men: West Roosevelt, Elliott Roosevelt, Archibald Rogers, E. P. Rogers, J. Coleman Drayton, Thomas Paton, J. E. Jones, Rutherford Stuyvesant, and Grinnell.[2]

The meeting had been called, Roosevelt explained, to organize a club of worthy sportsmen who would be active in promoting: (1) manly sport with the rifle; (2) travel and exploration in the wild and unknown parts of the country; (3) measures for the preservation of the large game; (4) observations on the habits and natural history of the wild animals; and (5) interchange of ideas and opinions on hunting, travel, and exploration.[3]

When Roosevelt's proposals met with general approval, he set a date (January 1888) for the formal organization of the club. At that meeting the club received its name (The Boone and Crockett Club), Roosevelt was elected its first president, and

Archibald Rogers its first secretary. Twenty-three men attended this organizational session and they automatically became charter members.

The constitution of the Club, approved early in its history, provided that no one should be eligible for membership who had not killed with the rifle in fair chase at least one adult male of three of the following species of American big game: bear, buffalo, mountain sheep, caribou, cougar, musk-ox, white goat, elk, wolf, pronghorn, moose, and deer. Since Roosevelt had already shot an adult male of at least eight of these, there was no doubt as to his eligibility.

The Club grew rapidly. Within a short time it could boast of 70 regular members and twenty associates. It had quality, too, as some of the names gracing its roster bear witness: Henry Cabot Lodge, United States Senator from Massachusetts; Boies Penrose, political tycoon from Philadelphia; Caspar Whitney, editor of *Outing Magazine;* C. Hart Merriam, head of the United States Biological Survey; and others such as General A. W. Greely, Thomas B. Reed, Henry L. Stimson, and Elihu Root. There were shortly four honorary members: General William Tecumseh Sherman, Judge John Dean Caton, General Philip Sheridan, and Francis Parkman.

The Club immediately gave proof of its serious intent. At an early meeting it instructed its Committee on Parks to throw its weight behind proposed federal legislation for a zoological park in the nation's capital.[4] By an act of Congress, the National Zoological Park was established the very next year.

At about the same time, Roosevelt appointed a committee "to promote useful and proper legislation towards the enlargement and better government of the Yellowstone National Park." In taking this step, the Club was attacking a problem important to the entire nation.

Although Yellowstone, by act of Congress in 1872, became a National Park and was placed under the control of the Secretary of the Interior, Congress unfortunately did not include in the act a law enforcement provision. Ten years later, when the Northern Pacific Railroad extended its lines to the Park, making the entire Yellowstone region available to the public, there was still no such provision. Shortly afterwards a real threat to the Park developed when certain promoters realized its possibilities as a pleasure resort. Forming a syndicate, the promoters were soon successful in securing from the Department of the Interior a provisional lease for ten plots of ground, each of 640 acres, strategically located at points of greatest scenic interest. This syndicate, calling itself the Yellowstone Park Improvement Company, at once began to "improve" the Park by cutting timber for hotels and other buildings, while the imported labor further "improved" the region by defacing valuable geological formations and killing off wild game.

Fortunately, the efforts of the syndicate to secure these leases, which would have given them a monopoly in the Park, did not go unnoticed by the public. Immediately Grinnell, Archibald Rogers, and others of equal standing, all of whom later became members of the Boone and Crockett Club, took the lead in an effort to thwart the design of the syndicate. The agitation they stirred up resulted in the detailing, by the Secretary of War, of a force of troops under the command of Captain Moses Harris for duty in the Park. Harris, by protecting the game and preventing forest fires and defacement of geyser formations, put into operation most of the protective measures that have since been employed.

More years went by, and still Congress had made no provision as to how the 1872 law should be enforced. This was the situation in 1888 when the Boone and Crockett Club was organized. Roosevelt and others at once joined with Grinnell and Rogers to push Congressional action hitherto frustrated by a powerful House lobby. One of Roosevelt's reasons for visiting Yellowstone in 1890 was to make himself better acquainted with conditions in the Park.

The Club's influence made itself felt. In 1894 Congress passed the Park Protection Act, which was promptly signed by President Cleveland. This Act, by providing proper penalties and suitable enforcement, assured adequate protection for the animal life, geological formations, and the superb forests of hardwood and conifer in Yellowstone. In this way the Park was saved, and the Boone and Crockett Club, with Theodore Roosevelt as President, deserves much of the credit.[5]

This was important, but now to something even more so. While the Club was bringing pressure on Congress to pass the Park Protection Act, it was at the same time using its influence to have large forest regions of the West set aside as forest reserves. In this it joined with the American Forestry Association and other powerful organized groups. The result was a bill passed on March 3, 1891, "one of the most noteworthy measures," according to one historian, "ever passed in the history of the nation." [6] It contained this significant clause:

That the President of the United States may, from time to time, set apart and reserve in any State or Territory having public lands bearing forests, any part of the public lands wholly or in part covered with timber or undergrowth, whether of commercial value or not, as public reservations, and the President shall, by public proclamation, declare the establishment of such reservations and the limits thereof.

Taking advantage of this law, Presidents Harrison, Cleveland, and McKinley set aside almost 50,000,000 acres of forest land. Now Roosevelt had a finger in the passage of this Forest Reserve Act, and he followed closely all that his three predecessors in the White House did with it. Of even greater importance is, of course, what he himself did with it at a later date.

Roosevelt played an important role, too, in the bringing into being of the New York Zoological Gardens. Although Madison Grant, a fellow member of the Boone and Crockett Club, was chiefly responsible for getting the necessary measure through the State Legislature, it was Roosevelt who put Grant in a position to advance the measure. Writing to Grant late in 1894 Roosevelt, who was still Civil Service Commissioner, said:

I saw Grinnell, and he seemed to think your proposal [of founding a Zoo] was a very good one, but he also seemed a little doubtful as to whether I should appoint a committee when I have no explicit authority to do so. However, I think I'll go ahead and do it; I should like some advice from you as to the committee. Grinnell should be put on simply as an advisor, also Root, but neither of these can do much work. Now, besides yourself, what other two men ought I to put on?

This committee, with Grant as its chairman, soon drafted a bill which the State Legislature passed, with only minor modifications, early in April 1895. About one month later the New York Zoological Society was organized, with nine Boone and Crockett Club members on its first Board of Directors. A year and a half later, following a gift by the city to the Society of 261 acres in the southern extremity of Bronx Park, the Zoo was officially opened to the public. Roosevelt was delighted with Grant's success: "I congratulate you with all my heart upon your success with the Zoo bill," he wrote him. "Really, you have done more than I hoped. I always count myself lucky if I get one out of three or four measures through."

One other phase of Roosevelt's Boone and Crockett Club activities remains to be told. Few people now living have even heard of it. In 1889, at the Club's annual meeting, Roosevelt and Grinnell were asked to serve as a two-man editorial team to bring together in book form a series of articles by Club members on North American big game. These two men, working closely together over a period of years, published not just one, but three volumes: *American Big-Game Hunting, Hunting in Many Lands*, and *Trail and Camp Fire*. The first appeared while Roosevelt was Civil Service Commissioner, the second while he was head of the New York Police, and the third after he had gone to Washington as Assistant Secretary of the Navy.

Grinnell, as editor of *Forest and Stream*, was, of course, an old hand at this sort of thing. But Roosevelt, outside of his brief experience with the *Harvard Advocate* and a few perfunctory months with Putnam's, had had no special editorial training, although it was well known that he could dash off a good story on any familiar topic, using acceptable ideas and phraseology, in almost the time it takes to tell it. He had other qualifications, too, such as boundless energy and intense enthusiasm, which went a long way in offsetting his lack of experience.

Our information about this editorial venture derives largely from a succession of letters Roosevelt wrote during this period to Grinnell, Owen Wister, and Madison Grant, to mention just a few of his correspondents. One of the first letters he wrote as editor was to Owen Wister, about an article Wister had promised:

> To my delight I received your letter today . . . I could give you till the first of May, but I would much prefer to have the manuscript here by the 20th of the month. I have been very anxious to have you write the white goat piece for us. I have so far five first class articles for the Club book, by Chanler, Rogers, Grinnell, Col. Williams and Col. Pickett. I have three or four others with which I am less contented, and I have the promise of four more, which will be very good indeed, if they are written as they ought to be. In any event I think I can say the success of the volume is assured.[7]

Roosevelt read greedily all of Wister's stories on the West. He thought they took rank with Bret Harte's. It was in an earlier short story (*Hank's Woman*) that Wister described the antelope's "Twinkling white tailless rear," thereby eliciting a "bully for you" from Roosevelt. The latter took relish in passing along at once this "twinkling" phrase to Frederic Remington who, while illustrating one of Roosevelt's stories, had made the egregious error of drawing an antelope with a tail![8]

Wister, incidentally, dedicated *The Virginian* to Roosevelt. Their friendship had started at Harvard. After a hiatus of a decade, it had been renewed when Wister joined the Boone and Crockett Club. And it was at a meeting of the Club that Roosevelt lambasted the "sickening details" of a recent magazine story of Wister's, thereby beaming a strong light on one facet of Roosevelt's character—his purity of mind. What Wister had written had actually happened, he had seen it happen. He defended himself on that ground. Roosevelt replied "I think that *conscientious descriptions of the unspeakable* do not constitute an interpretation of life, but merely disgust all readers not afflicted with the hysteria of bad taste. There's nothing masculine in being revolting. Your details really weaken the effect of your story, because they distract the attention from the story as a *whole*, to the details as an offensive and shocking part." ⁹

In these Boone and Crockett Club letters, Roosevelt nearly always included some vigorous idea of his own, most often about big game or an allied natural history topic. For instance, in a letter to Madison Grant, he launched into a lively discussion of the relationship of American mammals to European:

Our species [Roosevelt wrote] are certainly distinct from those of Europe as a rule; but speaking scientifically, I think you will find I am correct in what I say of their close relationship. The best zoologists nowadays put North America in with North Asia and Europe as one arctogeal province, separate from the South American, Indian, Australasian, and South African provinces, which have equal rank. Our moose, wapiti, bear, beaver, wolf, etc., differ more or less from those of the Old World, but the difference sinks into insignificance when compared with the differences between all these forms, Old World and New, from the tropical forms south of them. The wapiti is undoubtedly entirely distinct from the European red deer, but I don't think the difference is as great as between the black-tail and white-tail deer. Its normal form of antler is, as you describe, six points, all on the same plan, without any cup on top, and the fourth or dagger point having a prominence which it does not have at all in the European red deer; but occasionally, especially in Oregon and

Washington, elk are found with this cup, and when a rather under-sized Oregon elk possessing this cup is compared with one of the big red deer of Asia Minor, which are considerably larger than those of Europe, the difference is less by a good deal than the difference be-tween the black-tail and white-tail. But all of these points can very interestingly be treated in the article to which you refer.

Such expositions support Burrough's contention that Roose-velt was "a naturalist on the broadest grounds, uniting much technical knowledge with knowledge of the daily lives and habits of all forms of wild life." [10]

Once Grinnell, in writing to Roosevelt, spoke in glowing terms of President Cleveland's act of creating, near the end of his administration, a number of new forest reserves. He spoke without mentioning President McKinley, Cleveland's successor, on whom fell the responsibility of execution. The omission drew from Roosevelt an interesting statement—in light of later events —about the politics involved in such an act.

The act of creating these reserves, Roosevelt said, was a touchy matter, because the majority of the people were opposed to it. Although it was something that had to be done and he was glad that it had been, nevertheless the act called for consider-able courage and a great deal of tact. He then went on to point out that whereas Cleveland had issued the order, none of the trouble fell on him, for he left office almost immediately after-wards, leaving the administration and enforcement to his suc-cessor, McKinley. This kind of practice, he said, was common enough; he had seen it done by every President since the law was passed. In fact, it was about the only way of making prog-ress along certain lines. Therefore, Cleveland deserved no more credit than McKinley—if as much—for the latter had to en-counter real difficulty before the act went into effect.

In this same letter to Grinnell, Roosevelt made the point that naturalists should pay more attention in their travels to the large game animals. The author of a recent book, he said, would have produced a much more valuable work if he had done this instead of collecting beetles and working over the geology of the country. "The geology and the beetles will remain unchanged for ages," he said, "but the big game will vanish, and only the pioneer hunters can tell about it."

Roosevelt told Grinnell, too, that all naturalists worthy of the name should bring their experiences and observations together, in book form, instead of doing them piecemeal and leaving them in pamphlet form in scientific journals.

Why in the name of heaven [he went on] have you never published more of your experiences in book form? They would be worth a hundred times as much as dry-as-dust pedantic descriptions by Shufeldt and a lot of other little half-baked scientists. I know these scientists pretty well, and their limitations are extraordinary, especially when they get to talking of science with a capital S. They do good work; but, after all, it is only the very best of them who are more than bricklayers, who laboriously get together bricks out of which other men must build houses, when they think they are architects they are simply a nuisance.

It is not clear what prompted this particular fulmination against the working biologists who, in Roosevelt's words, make bricks instead of houses. In his report to the Harvard Board of Overseers he had expressed himself in similar language. It is altogether likely, therefore, that the seeds of his pique germinated in the Harvard laboratories, where, as in other such laboratories, biologists commonly reported the progress of their research, in short papers, to the scientific periodicals of their choice. Roosevelt, himself, wrote innumerable short magazine articles, but he was always careful to see that they were published later in book form.

The correspondence between Roosevelt and his fellow members of the Boone and Crockett Club includes long letters and short letters. Explosive ones and engaging ones. Letters well splashed with interlineations. (It was a rare thing indeed when his letters did not contain some last-minute thought hurriedly scribbled down in his own handwriting.) Letters to new members, letters about the Club annual dinners, about committee affairs, illustrations, possible legislation, the sentimentalists who deplored the killing of large game. "The more I realize what a quantity of bad people we have around," he said, "the more I want to see the good people keep a little iron in their blood."

No one could have legitimately accused Roosevelt of not keeping iron in his blood during this period when he served first as Civil Service Commissioner in Washington and then as Police Commissioner of New York City. Although up to his ears in work, faced with all manner of difficulties in bringing out the three Club books, Theodore Roosevelt kept on the job and saw it through. He and Grinnell had every right to be proud of the three Boone and Crockett books. They received favorable comment from reviewers both at home and abroad. They reflected, too, a metamorphosis in the editors' thinking during the time which elapsed between the publishing of the first and last volumes. As the years went by they saw reason to devote more space in the books to the natural history and conservation of the larger game animals, and less to the actual details of hunting.

Little doubt exists that during the formative years of the Club Roosevelt was the mainspring that kept it moving. Writing to his sister, Anna, on October 20, 1892, while Civil Service Commissioner, he said:

I must have a B and C dinner when I am with you at the end of November; just Rogers, Chanler, Grinnell, etc., to talk it all over. You see I have had to do the whole thing myself so far, in order to get it started at all, and having many other irons in the fire, have only just been able to see that this one got hot.

Roosevelt was President of the Club from 1888 to 1894, a full six years, and continued extremely active in all of its affairs until the intervention of the Spanish–American War. He not only brought about its birth, but also coddled it in its infancy and helped it to develop into the powerful instrument which it became for the conservation of our wildlife and natural resources generally.

The Boone and Crockett Club, with Roosevelt at its helm, could point with pride to its accomplishments. It would be an obvious exaggeration to say that Roosevelt was primarily responsible for all its successes; he would have been the first to disclaim such credit. But by forming the Club and giving it competent and vigorous leadership, he was able to set in motion forces which advanced the cause of conservation in the United States. He became thoroughly convinced of the importance of this work; so much so, that a decade later when he was put in a position of high influence, he was ready to give the work a powerful impetus.

"Roosevelt's services to science and conservation were many," said Grinnell, "but perhaps no single thing that he did for conservation had so far-reaching an effect as the establishment of the Boone and Crockett Club." [11]

10

Coyotes and *Cervus Roosevelti*

IF ROOSEVELT admired any man in Washington scientific circles above another, it was the head of the United States Biological Survey, C. Hart Merriam. In the fall of 1896, while Police Commissioner of New York City, Roosevelt came to Merriam's defense vigorously when Lodge criticized certain monographs prepared by the Survey:

> Now, I was a little disturbed at what you said to me about Hart Merriam. On most matters I accept your judgment as much better than mine. On this will you for the time being accept mine. The only two men in the country who rank with Merriam are Agassiz and Jordan.[1]

Despite this high rating, Roosevelt did not hesitate a few months later to differ with Merriam. The conflict arose when Merriam revised the coyote genus, breaking it into eleven distinct species.[2] Now Roosevelt had lived among the coyotes for years, had frequently encountered them on his rambles across the wide prairie floor, had watched their furtive shapes disappearing in the moonlight. To him they all looked much alike. He positively did not believe they could be dissected into eleven distinct species no matter who held the scalpel. So he shoved other matters to the back of his desk and wrote a paper called

"A Layman's View of Specific Nomenclature." This was published in *Science* shortly after Roosevelt resigned as Police Commissioner of New York City. The initial paragraph reads as follows:

Anything that Dr. Hart Merriam writes is sure to be of great value. He is one of the leading mammalogists and he has laid all men interested in biology under a heavy debt by reviving the best traditions of the old-school faunal naturalists and showing that among the students of the science of life there is room for other men in addition to the section cutter, the microscopist and the histologist.[3]

With this agreeable introduction out of the way (which included another slap at Harvard teaching methods), Roosevelt got down to brass tacks. In his judgment, the division of coyotes suggested by Merriam was just as logical as the arbitrary division of Americans into four groups: New Englanders, Kentuckians, Indians, and Negroes, with the New Englanders differing as much from the Kentuckians as they do from the Indians or Negroes. The important point, though, he urged, was the "essential likeness of all the coyotes one to the other." Exorbitant splitting can serve no useful purpose, he went on, and may ultimately have the effect of impairing the good features in the Linnaean system of classification.

By taking this stand Roosevelt definitely aligned himself with the "lumpers," that recognized body of taxonomists who deprecate undue cleavage of the genus, as opposed to the "splitters," who take the contrary point of view.

Merriam, some two weeks later, replied to Roosevelt. He paid a return compliment: "He is a writer of the best accounts we have ever had of the habits of our larger mammals." He then went on to say that the rule then in vogue for validating or invalidating a species was a matter of intergradation: "Forms known to intergrade, no matter how different, must be treated as subspecies and bear trinomial names; forms not known to intergrade, no matter how closely related, must be treated as full species and bear binomial names." [4] It was on this basis, Merriam said, that he had seen fit to break the genus as he had.

Roosevelt was puzzled. He made this clear in a second article. He did not understand at all how great the differentiation, or intergradation, should be in order to establish specific rank. Moreover, he had "certain conservative instincts which are jarred when an old familiar friend is suddenly cut up into eleven brand new acquaintances." [5]

In the midst of these exchanges of taxonomic opinion between Roosevelt and Merriam, the venerable Biological Society of Washington focused a spotlight on the two men. In planning its 277th meeting, it hit on the idea of asking Merriam to defend his recent revision of the coyotes. Merriam agreed—on the condition that Roosevelt be on hand to present his side. This was soon arranged, with the meeting being held on the night of May 8, 1897, in the old Cosmos Club assembly hall. Roosevelt had now been Assistant Secretary of the Navy for one month.

Merriam, who was introduced first, read a carefully prepared paper. Roosevelt then spoke extemporaneously. According to L. O. Howard, a government entomologist, who presided:

He made a very forceful argument from his view point and from that obviously of other hunters, and rather staggered some of the really scientific men in the audience by the cogency of his reasoning. He talked at length, as was customary with him, and the hour of adjournment (10 o'clock) came before he had finished, but by unanimous vote he was allowed to proceed until he was satisfied. He sat down after having made a distinct impression on his scientific and rather critical audience. Merriam asked for five minutes in which to reply, in the course of which he completely demolished the Rooseveltian argument, and there was nothing more to be said. It was a memorable meeting, and no one who was there will ever forget it. Most of us saw Roosevelt for the first time then, and were greatly impressed by him. Among the taxonomists present there were of course, lumpers as well as splitters, and the lumpers got some satisfaction from the future President's arguments. [6]

The majority of those present, including Howard, knew little or nothing of Roosevelt's storehouse of information on animals. So they naturally felt that he was somewhat presumptuous to question the findings of the head of the Biological Survey. Their attitude may have made him feel, as he did on another occasion, "like an airedale that had walked in on a convention of tom-cats." [7]

But a sizable number of important scientists did not think Roosevelt had been presumptuous at all. They agreed whole-heartedly with him, were quite impressed with the "cogency of his reasoning." J. A. Allen, for instance, wrote that it was ex-tremely unwise in revising genera "to adopt so elastic and un-philosophic basis, and withal so open to the influence of the personal equation." [8] Richard Lydekker, the famous British zool-ogist, expressed the same vigorous opinion and went on to say that, "Roosevelt probably knows more about the big game of North America than any other man . . . is really a very accom-plished field naturalist." [9]

The question of whether to treat certain forms (requiring de-scriptions) as new species, or merely as new geographical races, is still difficult to answer, even by those engaged closely in taxonomic work. In the case of the coyote, however, thousands of specimens are now available in museums for study, and so much work has been done on them, that mammalogists no longer hold Merriam's conclusions valid. [10] The slight differences that Merriam saw in the skulls of coyotes, and the disparities in color between desert, mountain, and prairie forms which influenced him to create eleven new species, are now considered over-balanced by similarities, the same similarities to which Roosevelt pointed with such vigor from the beginning of the argument. "As often happens the instinct of a nature-lover comes closer to the truth than more logical thinking." [11]

One other feature of the argument deserves comment. Roo-sevelt was on his good behavior; he used only the mildest of words. He did not, for instance, accuse Merriam of "suffering from a species of moral myopia complicated with intellectual strabismus," as he did another adversary.[12] He had too much respect for Merriam. In fact, he was even afraid that he had hurt his feelings.

I almost broke the heart of my beloved friend Merriam [he wrote Henry Fairfield Osborn]. He felt as though he had been betrayed in the house of his friends; but he really goes altogether too far. He has just sent me a pamphlet announcing the discovery of two new species of mountain lion from Nevada. If he is right I will guarantee to produce fifty-seven new species of red fox from Long Island.

On the other hand, Merriam may have felt that he had broken the heart of his beloved friend Roosevelt. Not long after the coyote controversy had begun to wane, Merriam "discovered" a new species of elk which he named *Cervus Roosevelti*. There is nothing to indicate that he held his tongue lightly in his cheek in doing so; certainly Roosevelt did not think so.

Merriam had found this new species in the Olympic Mountains of Washington, and claimed that it differed in coloration and antler shape from the typical Rocky Mountain elk (*Cervus Canadensis*). In his description of it he included these words: "It is fitting that the noblest deer of America should perpetuate the name of one who, in the midst of a busy public career, has found time to study our larger mammals in their native haunts and has written the best accounts we have ever had of their habits and chase." [13]

This recognition may have posed a problem for Roosevelt. He had just made it clear what he thought about Merriam's creating supernumerary species of coyotes and mountain lions. Now Merriam had come up with a new species of elk and, so far as one could see, the only difference in the situations was that this latest form had been named after Roosevelt.

If Roosevelt entertained any idea of refusing the honor he discreetly hid it. To decline it would have been to destroy whatever feeling of cordiality the head of the Biological Survey held for him. Moreover he had never had an animal named after him before; *Cervus Roosevelti* sounded good to him.

I am more pleased than I can say at what you have done [he wrote Merriam]. No compliment could be paid me that I would appreciate as much as this—in the first place, because of the fact itself, and in the next place because it comes from you. To have the noblest game animal in America named after me by the foremost of living mammalogists is something that really makes me prouder than I can well say. I deeply appreciate the compliment and I am only sorry that it will never be in my power to do anything except to just merely appreciate it.

Roosevelt showed his delight in another way. Not long after writing Merriam he was asked by the editors of a British encyclopedia, *The Encyclopedia of Sport*, to contribute a number of articles on American game. In his article on the elk he wrote as follows:

There are several aberrant forms of wapiti, including one that dwells in the great Tule swamps of California. There is also an entirely distinct species with its centre of abundance in the Olympic Mountains of Washington and on Vancouver Island. This species Dr. Hart Merriam has recently done the present writer the honor of naming after him (*Cervus Roosevelti*).

Fifty years and more have passed since Merriam thus honored Roosevelt. Today, sad to relate, the Olympic elk is just another subspecies—*Cervus canadensis roosevelti*.

II

The mills of the gods ground rapidly for Theodore Roosevelt in 1898. Assistant Secretary of the Navy in Washington in April, Rough Rider in Texas in May, San Juan hero in July, Governor of New York in November.

In spite of his short term of office as Governor (two years) and interference from capricious political bosses, Roosevelt came through with considerable important legislation and an enhanced reputation for serving the people well. He was particularly successful in improving the conservation laws.

As soon as he took office in Albany he began investigating the efficiency of the Fisheries, Forestry, and Game Commission. In his Annual Message of 1900, he commended the Commission for the progress that it had made in such things as the propagation of fish and the increase of deer, but he warned that as railroads reached farther and farther into the wilderness, the Commission could expect more forest fires and more illegal hunting. He recommended that the number of game wardens be increased, that an intensive study be made of state forest reserves, that the laws governing forest fires and the dumping of wastes into streams be tightened, that it be made illegal to use bird feathers in wearing apparel, that the open season on game and fish be made uniform throughout the state, and that the Adirondacks and Catskills be kept in perpetuity as great parks for the benefit and enjoyment of the people.

Before Roosevelt's term of office expired the State Legislature had acted favorably on certain of these recommendations. If he had had a longer stay in Albany, he undoubtedly would have accomplished much more. The two years were valuable to him, though, if for no other reason than that they taught him much about the ropes that had to be rigged before laws could be passed. In that time, too, he wrote a letter of some consequence. It was to Frank M. Chapman, who was just then beginning to make a name for himself as an ornithologist at the American Museum of Natural History:

I need hardly say [Roosevelt wrote] how heartily I sympathize with the purposes of the Audubon Society. I would like to see all harmless wild things, but espcially all birds, protected in every way. I do not understand how any man or woman who really loves nature can fail to try to exert all influence in support of such objects as those of the Audubon Society.

Spring would not be spring without song birds, any more than it would be spring without birds and flowers, and I only wish that besides protecting the songsters, the birds of the grove, the orchard, the garden and the meadow, we could also protect the birds of the seashore and of the wilderness

The Loon ought to be, and, under wise legislation, could be a feature of every Adirondack lake, and Terns should be as plentiful along our shores as Swallows around our barns.

A Tanager or a Cardinal makes a point of glowing beauty in the green woods, and the Cardinal among the snows.

When the Bluebirds were so nearly destroyed by the severe winter a few seasons ago, the loss was like the loss of an old friend, or at least like the burning down of a familiar and dearly loved house. How immensely it would add to our forests if only the great Logcock were still found among them.

The destruction of the Wild Pigeon and the Carolina Paroquet has meant a loss as severe as if the Catskills and the Palisades were taken away. When I hear of the destruction of a species I feel as if all the works of some great writer had perished; as if we had lost all instead of only part of Polybius or Livy.

This letter made a tremendous impression on Chapman and, through him, on all others in the Museum and the Audubon Society who were closely associated with him. Chapman at once had it framed and hung on his office wall where countless scientists from then until his death, close to half a century later, had the opportunity and pleasure of reading it.

For the first time, Chapman was fully apprised of Roosevelt's great love for birds, whether of beach, open wood, or sun-bathed meadow, of his intense desire to have them protected, and of his profound sympathy with the aims of the Audubon Society. From that moment on Chapman and other members of the Society knew that they had in Roosevelt an influential friend, one who would come to their help—as he was shortly to do—when they needed it.

According to Chapman, "The growing demands of official life on Colonel Roosevelt's time and thoughts never drove the bird from his heart. Rather did he become increasingly dependent upon the friendship of nature for relief from the cares of office. Birds formed a part of his outdoor life. They were the vocal calendars of the hour, the month, the season." [14]

11

In the Clutches of the Press

ON ROOSEVELT's first trip to the Adirondacks, when he was just a youngster of twelve, his favorite guide, Mose Sawyer, had told him about a hunting experience he and a companion had one winter day when the snow lay deep through the white pine forests. Young Roosevelt was so impressed that he wrote his version of it in his diary that night:

Well, they had hunted a long time unsuccessfully when Mose noticed what he thought was the track of a large dog, leading up to a fallen tree. When he had reached there a large animal bounded away and he went after it, when it suddenly went slower and his companion cried out "stop, Mose, stop!" He stopped and saw to his horror a large panther going slowly off. It had been too astonished at first to think of resistance. He said that in another minute he would have been in the clutches of the beast.[1]

Just thirty years later Roosevelt went on a panther hunt himself, and was caught, not in the clutches of the panther, but in the imaginative claws of the press. This experience with the fourth estate occurred in the high latitudes of Colorado, where panthers bear such aliases as puma, mountain lion, and cougar. The time was early in 1901, immediately after Roosevelt had concluded his labors as Governor and had fallen heir to a happy

89

moment of leisure preceding his inauguration as Vice President of the United States.

Roosevelt arrived in Meeker, Colorado, on January 11, after a 45-mile drive from the railroad through eighteen-below-zero weather. He left the next morning on horseback with hunting companions for a ranch north of the White River owned by John B. Goff, who was to be his host and guide.

The town of Meeker, Rio Blanco County, in the northwest corner of Colorado, high in the Rockies, was a tiny place, remotely located. On the departure of Roosevelt for Goff's ranch it must have been even a lonelier place than before his arrival. That was particularly true for the small group of newsmen left behind. Huddled about stoves awaiting Roosevelt's return they could find little to do and, worst of all, nothing newsworthy to write. But commitments had to be met. So, for days after Roosevelt bestrode his mount and galloped off into the wilderness, the newsmen worked overtime concocting stories of the progress of his hunt, each and every one a product of the imagination. Words flowed as freely as the water under the ice in the White River, and clever minds worked them into whoppers which, the following day, appeared in papers large and small from Pawtuxet to San Diego. Paul Bunyan would have been glad to claim them for his own.

On the initial day of the hunt, according to the first yarn, Roosevelt succeeded in bagging a particularly large and vicious mountain lion, but only after a vigorous eight-mile chase through deep snow (in a four-horse tally-ho according to one version).[2] The next day he escaped from a monstrous grizzly only by a miracle,[3] and on the third he was treed by a pack of hungry wolves. The New York *Herald* announced the latter story with the caption: ROOSEVELT UP TREE FOUR HOURS. According to this sample of extravagant fancy, Roosevelt wandered out from camp at dusk, gun in hands, looking for varmints. When he started back he discovered he had lost his bearings. To make matters worse, he soon became aware of the shadowy forms of wolves—conservatively 100 of them—behind him on the trail. As they grew bolder, he was obliged to climb a tree. In so doing he dropped his rifle, leaving himself unarmed except for a pistol. This he fired at the wolves, but more in the hope that his companions would hear his shots and come to his rescue than that he would scatter the pack. The men in camp heard no gunfire, however, and did not become alarmed over his absence until about nine o'clock, when they went out to look for him. They found him, half frozen, up the tree, where he had been for four long, miserable hours.[4]

The public seemed ready to accept these stories at face value —even the fantastic report some newsmen concocted about Roosevelt's bag. In the first few days of the hunt, according to this apocryphal account, the Vice-President-elect had killed 303 animals: 46 lions, 16 kittens, 22 lynx cats, 19 catamounts, and 200 other varmints.[5]

Practically every paper in the country, even the most reliable, carried this piece and the others, thus calling nation-wide attention to Roosevelt's handiness with his rifle. Protests were a natural sequel. The Forum Literary Society of Phillips Andover Academy roundly condemned the spirit manifested by Roosevelt "in ruthlessly taking the lives of innocent and unoffending animals without provocation and with the sole aim of gratifying a desire for killing." [6]

To the reporters these tall stories were just good clean fun; but not to Roosevelt—after he found out about them. "It was exasperating to learn," he wrote Lodge, "not only that those ridiculous stories about my hunting trip had been published but that they had coolly attributed them to my 'press agent.' " [7] Roosevelt well knew the effect that these stories would have, planting ever deeper the already germinating seeds that he was a game-butcher.

The facts of Roosevelt's hunt were quite different. He did not even glimpse a grizzly—these animals hole up in the winter. He did not see any wolves, although at night he heard their eerie wailings. He spent his time hunting and studying mountain lions. As he pointed out, astonishingly little of a satisfactory nature was on record about this big American cat, and as it had steadily declined in number, so had opportunities for studying it.

How successful Roosevelt was in getting information on mountain lions may be judged from the account he later wrote of their appearance, distribution, and behavior. It was the most complete, most reliable biography that anyone had written about this animal up to that time. Scientists, impressed with it, were beginning to learn that, "while they knew more of their specialty than he, he knew a great deal of what they supposed only an expert knew, and he often knew more about other forms of creatures than they did." [8]

Roosevelt killed fourteen mountain lions all told on this trip. He carefully preserved the skulls and sent them to Merriam. "Your series of skulls from Colorado," Merriam wrote Roosevelt, "is incomparably the largest, most complete and most valuable series ever brought together from any single locality, and will be of inestimable value in determining the amount of individual variation." [9]

"Very few people are aware of Roosevelt's knowledge of mammals and their skulls," said Merriam on another occasion. "One evening at my house (where I then had in the neighborhood of 5,000 skulls of North American mammals) he astonished everyone—including several eminent naturalists—by picking up skull after skull and mentioning the scientific name of the genus to which each belonged." [10]

II

Theodore Roosevelt was inaugurated as Vice President on March 4, 1901. The Senate convened the following day and was in session until March 9, in which time Roosevelt had his first and last opportunity to preside over that body. When Congress reconvened in the fall he was President of the United States, having been elevated to that position by the simple pressure of an assassin's index finger.

If the country at large was still unaware that Theodore Roosevelt loved the forests and the animals which dwelt in their shade, and sought wholeheartedly their preservation, he did not leave them long in doubt. In his first message to Congress he said: "The preservation of our forests is an imperative business necessity. We have come to see clearly that whatever destroys the forests, except to make way for agriculture, threatens our well being." [11] He recommended that the forest preserves be enlarged, that the existing ones be better protected, and that some of these be made preserves for wild forest creatures. He foresaw greater uses for the forest reserves, and urged that additions be made whenever practicable. He asked for flood control, that waters now running to waste might be used for irrigation.

In this same message, Roosevelt commended the Department of Agriculture for introducing into the United States plants of economic importance, various fruits, grains, and grasses. He praised the Department, too, for its progress in soil surveys, applied chemical research, and plant and animal breeding. He told Congress that there should be no halt in the work of the Smithsonian Institution and the National Zoological Park, particularly in their plans for the preservation of the vanishing races of great North American animals.

No President of the United States had ever before given such recognition to the federally employed scientists. They were almost beside themselves with gratitude.

Further focusing the attention of the American people on wildlife preservation, Roosevelt soon published a book. This volume made history, of a sort. Bibliophiles of the nation's Capital who read their Washington *Times* on Sunday, June 22, 1902, were undoubtedly attracted to one review, and especially to a sentence it contained: "For the first time in the history of the country a book has appeared bearing the name of the President of the United States as that of the author."

Of the twenty-five Chief Executives who had preceded Roosevelt, not one had published a book while residing in the White House. The book which broke the hundred-year-old precedent had nothing to do with politics, history, or statesmanship. It was entitled *The Deer Family*, and was the first volume of the ten proposed for the "American Sportsman's Library," a series then being published by The Macmillan Company and edited by Caspar Whitney, editor of *Outing Magazine*. Roosevelt wrote it in collaboration with T. S. Van Dyke, D. G. Elliot, and A. J. Stone, and contributed chapters on elk, pronghorn, whitetail, and blacktail. These chapters contained little that he had not said before in one place or another, but what he did say, now that he was President, carried far greater weight than ever before and, because for once he omitted largely descriptions of the chase and concentrated on animal behavior, he proved more conclusively than ever the wide range of his knowledge of large game animals.

The President had an altercation with Caspar Whitney soon after a copy of *The Deer Family* reached his desk. On looking it over he immediately spotted two illustrations with incorrect titles. One was labeled "The Black-tail of Colorado" and the other "Whitetail in Flight." The former picture, Roosevelt wrote Whitney, "is of an animal with a head of the Colorado blacktail, but with a tail of the blacktail of the Columbia. There is not and never has been any kind of Rocky Mountain blacktail or mule deer, which has such a tail as that carefully and prominently pictured on this illustration." As to the other picture, "Whitetail in Flight," Roosevelt said, "both the head and the tail are those of the Colorado or Rocky Mountain blacktail, or mule deer. In both these pictures the titles are ridiculous. The first one does not look any more like a whitetail than a cow with a horse's tail would look like a genuine cow."

If the reviewers noted the "ridiculous" titles Roosevelt called to the attention of Whitney, they made no mention of them. The Washington *Times*, for instance, was more struck with the fact that the President "with so many other things on his hands should find the time to be a clever writer of natural history." [12] This editor might have been the more impressed had he known that Roosevelt was able to distinguish between the Colorado blacktail and the Columbia blacktail by a mere glance at their tails!

III

Never before had the White House known such activity, such joy of living. The President, of course, contributed his share to this sudden change, but he was not the only lively member of the Roosevelt family.

The First Lady was gentle and, to her friends, the fairest-minded person they knew. With no thought of occupying a position "behind the throne," she accepted the spousal duties of watching over her husband, and of smoothing out the many inevitable wrinkles of White House life in addition to the normal ones of caring for her children. She was a balancing influence in a world of strenuous action where equilibrium often deteriorated.

Contributing measurably to the excitement were the six Roosevelt children: Alice, now a young lady of sixteen, piquant and comely, who ruled a kingdom all her own and earned the title, "Princess Alice"; Theodore, Jr., Kermit, and Ethel, aged fourteen, twelve, and ten, respectively; and Archie and Quentin, the babies, aged seven and four.

At that time only a few of the stories relating to the activities of the children were allowed to go beyond the White House walls, the parents drawing a strict line between their official and social life. It was just as well. From the moment this juvenile sextet set foot inside their new home, there began probably the grandest scramble in the history of that historic edifice. The children pried into every niche and crevice, from attic to cellar, from front stoop to rear veranda. They sped from chamber to chamber on roller skates. They pock-marked the stairs with stilts, took dips in the fountains, and played leapfrog over the furniture. Once they took Archie's pony for a ride in the White House elevator, and ended up by introducing it to the second-floor bedrooms.

The President was not entirely oblivious to this activity; in fact, he sometimes participated. At least we know that he joined the children in pillow fights, obstacle races, hide-and-go-seek, blind-man's-buff, and other games. At times he thought of the blow to his dignity, but not often. Once, for instance, after a big romp with the children in the Sagamore Hill hay mow, he wrote Mrs. Roosevelt's sister, Emily Carow: "Of course I had not the heart to refuse; but really it seems, to put it mildly, rather odd for a stout, elderly President to be bouncing over hay-ricks in a wild effort to get to goal before an active midget of a competitor, aged nine years. However, it was really great fun." [13]

Roosevelt believed it a duty to play with his children. He believed, too, that he should treat them as equals, should take time to answer their questions, to give advice when asked for, to instill in them the manly virtues, to stimulate their curiosity, to add to their sum of knowledge.

Being a naturalist, Roosevelt saw to it that his children learned to love the out-of-doors. One of his pleasantest tasks was instilling in them something of his own enthusiasm for birds and mammals and trees and flowers. Anyone visiting Sagamore Hill or the White House in those days could not escape the fact, revealed by the assemblage of pets, that a naturalist lurked nearby. As a letter from the White House to Joel Chandler Harris shows,

Roosevelt was almost as interested in the pets as the children themselves:

All of the younger children are at present absorbed in various pets, perhaps the foremost of which is a puppy of the most orthodox puppy type. Then there is Jack, the terrier, and Sailor Boy, the Chesapeake Bay dog; and Eli, the most gorgeous macaw, with a bill that I think could bite through boiler plate, who crawls all over Ted, and whom I view with dark suspicion; and Jonathan, the piebald rat, of most friendly and affectionate nature, who also crawls all over everybody; and the flying squirrel, and two kangaroo rats; not to speak of Archie's pony, Algonquin, who is the most absolute pet of all.[14]

There were other pets, too. "Did I ever tell you," Roosevelt wrote a friend, "about my second boy's names for his Guinea pigs? They included Bishop Doane; Dr. Johnson, my Dutch Reformed pastor; Father G. Grady, the local priest with whom the children had scraped a speaking acquaintance; Fighting Bob Evans, and Admiral Dewey."

At one time, briefly, there was a bear. "Some of my Republican supporters in West Virginia have just sent me a small bear," he wrote the above-mentioned friend, "which the children of their own accord christened Jonathan Edwards, partly out of compliment to their mother's ancestor, and partly because they thought they detected Calvinistic tendencies."[15]

Returning from one of his trips to the West, Roosevelt brought with him for the children Bill the Lizard (a horned toad) and Josiah, a badger. In a letter to Senator Lodge upon his return, he said: "Josiah, the young badger, is hailed with the wildest enthusiasm by the children, and has passed an affectionate but passionate day with us. Fortunately his temper seems proof."[16]

One day the proprietor of an animal store gave Quentin three snakes, a large king snake and two smaller ones, identity unknown. Quentin hurried home and ran unannounced into his father's office. What happened thereafter the father told in a letter to Archie, who was then away at school:

I was discussing certain matters with the Attorney-General at the time, and the snakes were eagerly deposited in my lap. The king snake, although most friendly with Quentin, had just been making a resolute effort to devour one of the smaller snakes. As Quentin and his menagerie were an interruption to my interview with the Department of Justice, I suggested that he go into the next room, where four Congressmen were drearily waiting until I should be at leisure. I thought that he and his snakes would probably enliven their waiting time. He at once fell in with the suggestion and rushed up to the Congressmen with the assurance that he would there find kindred spirits. They at first thought the snakes were wooden ones, and there was some perceptible recoil when they realized they were alive. Then the king snake went up Quentin's sleeve—he was three to four feet long—and we hesitated to drag him back because his scales rendered that difficult. The last I saw of Quentin, one Congressman was gingerly helping him off with his jacket, so as to let the snake crawl out of the upper end of the sleeve.[17]

Theodore Roosevelt invited practically all of the celebrated naturalists and hunters to visit him at the White House, men like John Burroughs and Alfred Courtenay Selous. He often prevailed upon them to entertain the children. In a letter to Kermit, dated November 19, 1905, he said:

Last Monday when Mother had gone to New York I had Selous, the great African hunter, to spend the day and night. . . . Before we came down to dinner I got him to spend three-quarters of an hour in telling delightfully exciting lion and hyena stories to Ethel, Archie and Quentin. He told them most vividly and so enthralled the little boys that the next evening I had to tell them a large number myself.[18]

Time and occasion permitting, the President would often go hiking with his children, or take camping excursions with them. Other children besides his own often went along. In Washington, he was occasionally seen in Rock Creek Park with a small army of youngsters scurrying along behind him in a grim effort to keep up. At Sagamore Hill, where he might be found during the summer months, he now and then took the time for an overnight excursion with the children to some point along the Sound. On these outings, Roosevelt never missed an opportunity to point out to the children any interesting plant or animal, and to identify for them the songs of warblers, vireos, and thrushes.

He liked to cook, and on these camping-out trips he prepared the food. One of his specialties was frying-pan bread, which he had often prepared on his hunts in the Rockies. He referred often to this in his books, and when some youngster wrote to ask him how he made it, he replied:

The way I make frying-pan bread is to grease the bottom of the pan, then make a thin cake of dough with flour, water and baking-powder, and after it has been warmed enough to have some consistency, tip the pan in front of the coals, turning the cake over when necessary. I am a very poor cook, however, and only eat my own frying-pan bread from dire necessity.[19]

Roosevelt was modest about his cooking ability, for in a letter to Emily Carow, he wrote:

I took Kermit and Archie, with Philip, Oliver and Nicholas out for a night's camping in the two rowboats last week. They enjoyed themselves heartily, as usual, each sleeping rolled up in his blanket, and all getting up at an unearthly hour. Also, as usual, they displayed a touching and firm conviction that my cooking is unequalled. It was of a simple character, consisting of frying beefsteak first and then potatoes in bacon fat, over the camp fire; but they certainly ate in a way that showed their words were not uttered in a spirit of empty compliment.[20]

Theodore Roosevelt always wrote to his children, often at length, when they were away from home, or when he himself was away—on a trip to Colorado, to California, to the Canal Zone, or farther destinations. On such trips, he did not content himself with a single family letter; he wrote individual letters to each member. These letters were crowded with information on a wide range of topics, ranging in importance from a dinner engagement or a tennis match to the deepest state secrets. Apparently, though, he could trust his children with secrets. Once Quentin, aged eight, was overheard replying to a newsman who had

asked him some question about his father. "Yes, I see him sometimes," he said, "but I know nothing of his family life." [21]

With few exceptions, the letters that Roosevelt addressed to
his children contained some comment on the out-of-door world:
horses, dogs, deer, cougars, all kinds of birds, flowers, trees.
Wherever he happened to be, Sagamore Hill, Washington, the
Canal Zone, Louisiana, Mississippi, Grand Canyon, he found
some interesting natural history observations or episodes to pass
along to the children.

After the President and Mrs. Roosevelt had spent a particularly
pleasant April afternoon visiting Washington's birthplace, Roosevelt had to tell Kermit all about it:

> Every vestige of the house is destroyed, but a curious and rather
> pathetic thing is that, although it must be a hundred years since the
> place was deserted, there are still multitudes of flowers which must
> have come from those in the old garden. There are iris and narcissus
> and a little blue flower, with a neat, prim, clean smell that makes one
> feel as if it ought to be put with lavender into chests of fresh old
> linen. The narcissus in particular was growing around everywhere,
> together with real wild flowers like the painted columbine and star of
> bethlehem. It was on a lovely spot on a headland overlooking a broad
> inlet from the Potomac. There was also the old graveyard or grave
> plot in which were the gravestones of Washington's father and mother
> and grandmother, all pretty nearly ruined. It was lovely warm weather
> and Mother and I enjoyed our walk through the funny lonely old
> country. Mocking birds, meadow-larks, Carolina wrens, cardinals, and
> field sparrows were singing cheerfully.[22]

A letter to "Blessed Archie" from California contained observations made along the coast where Roosevelt had been riding
with Dr. Rixey, his personal physician:

> I wish you could have been with me today on Algonquin, for we
> had a perfectly lovely ride. Dr. Rixey and I were on two very hand-
> some horses, with Mexican saddles and bridles; the reins of very
> slender leather with silver rings. The road lead through pine and
> cypress forests and along the beach. The surf was beating on the rocks

in one place and right between two of the rocks where I really did not see how anything could swim a seal appeared and stood up on his tail out of the foaming water and flapped his flippers, and was as much at home as anything could be. Beautiful gulls flew close to us all around, and cormorants swam along the breakers or walked along the beach.[23]

In the fall of 1907, Roosevelt went bear hunting in Louisiana. From his camp at Bear Bayou, he reported to Archie:

We have had no luck with the bear; but we have killed as many deer as we needed for meat, and the hounds caught a wildcat. Our camp is as comfortable as possible, and we have great camp fires at night.

One of the bear-hunting planters with me told me he once saw a bear, when overtaken by the hounds, lie down flat on its back with all its legs stretched out, while the dogs barked furiously all around it.

Suddenly the bear sat up with a jump, and frightened all the dogs so that they nearly turned back somersaults.[24]

This particular letter was typical of many Theodore Roosevelt addressed to his children, especially the younger ones, in that it was illustrated—two pictures in this case. One showed the bear on its back with the encircling dogs, the other the bear sitting up and the dogs, with tails neatly tucked between their legs, running for dear life. The children always looked forward to these "picture letters," as they called them.

What could a President find of a zoological character to write about to Quentin while aboard the U.S.S. Louisiana on his way to Panama?

You would be amused at the pets they have aboard this ship. They have two young bulldogs, a cat, three raccoons, and a tiny Cuban goat. They seem to be very amicable with one another, although I think the cat has suspicions of all the rest. The coons clamber about everywhere, and the other afternoon while I was sitting reading, I suddenly felt my finger seized in a pair of soft black paws and found the coon sniffing at it, making me feel a little uncomfortable lest it might think the finger something good to eat.[25]

The information in some of these letters borders on the incredible. One of the most remarkable incidents related by the

President of the United States in a family letter is contained in a
note to his "Darling Ethel" after she had gone to Sagamore Hill
for the summer and he had had to stay on in the White House:

Today as I was marching to church, with Sloane some 25 yards behind, I suddenly saw two terriers racing to attack a kitten which was
walking down the sidewalk. I bounced forward with my umbrella,
and after some active work put to flight the dogs while Sloane captured the kitten, which was a friendly, helpless little thing, evidently
too well accustomed to being taken care of to know how to shift for
itself. I inquired of all the bystanders and of people on the neighbor-
ing porches to know if they knew who owned it; but as they all disclaimed, with many grins, any knowledge of it, I marched ahead with
it in my arms for about half a block. Then I saw a very nice colored
woman and little colored girl looking out of the window of a small
house with on the door a dressmaker's advertisement, and I turned
and walked up the steps and asked if they did not want the kitten.
They said they did, and the little girl welcomed it lovingly; so I felt
I had gotten it a home and continued toward church.[26]

Whether Theodore Roosevelt was reading to members of his
family, walking at their sides, camping-out with them, or writing
letters to them, he was constantly giving expression to his deep
and constant love of all living things, of nature in all its moods
and revelations.

IV

In early November, 1902, Theodore Roosevelt went on a bear
hunt to the Little Sunflower River country of Mississippi. He had
just ended the serious anthracite coal strike of that year, and he
was ready for a vacation. On the very first day of the hunt, some
other members of the party caught up with a small brown bear.
They stunned it with a blow over the head, tied it to a tree, and
then sent a messenger after the President. Roosevelt, of course,
refused to shoot it. Instead, he told them to let it go.

The newspaper dispatch released the next day, describing
Roosevelt's refusal to shoot the small bear, struck the eye of
Clifford K. Berryman, feature cartoonist for the Washington
Post. He saw possibilities in it. But he never dreamed that his

cartoon, "Drawing the Line in Mississippi," would almost overnight become a topic of conversation from coast to coast.

The Berryman cartoon which originated the Teddy-bear.

This pictorial caricature appealed to the public fancy as no
other had done before. It was printed and reprinted—literally
millions of times. It was talked about more than the weather.
Poets, satirists, actors, politicians all took notice of it. Then the
toy-makers knew their big moment had come. They produced
the Teddy-bear—which was soon accepted equipment in every
nursery. As time went on the Teddy-bear became the standard
decoration for all Republican meetings, big and small, was "more
in evidence than the eagle and only less usual than the Stars and
Stripes." [27]

12

With Burroughs in Yellowstone

DURING the spring of 1903, shortly after agreeing to arbitrate the Alaskan boundary dispute, the President of the United States revisited Yellowstone National Park and took with him as a traveling companion a celebrated naturalist, John Burroughs. Though the trip was attended with much publicity, the reporters left unmentioned Roosevelt's real reasons for visiting the Park, his most likely purpose in inviting Burroughs to go with him, and, in particular, Burroughs' on-the-spot estimate of Roosevelt as a naturalist.

Roosevelt began making his plans for this trip as early as the preceding December, shortly after returning from his bear hunt in Mississippi. He wanted to take a look at the large game animals in the Park that had become, through a decade of protection, so astonishingly tame, and he wanted to see for himself whether they were holding their own, how they were being protected, and whether poaching was a problem. He had still another incentive: the great lodestone of the West that drew him back recurrently, almost with the regularity of the seasons. At the same time, being a man of action, he wanted, if possible, to use his rifle again. With that in mind, he wrote the Superintendent of the Park, Major John Pitcher, asking him about the practice of killing mountain lions there, and adding that, if he got into the Park the following spring, he would like to hunt them, "That is, on the supposition that they are 'varmints' and are not protected."

The newspapers soon got wind of Roosevelt's desire to hunt in Yellowstone. Yellow journals printed one story after another of his alleged plans to exterminate the game animals in Yellowstone and nearby territory. The New York *World* stated flatly: "Folks on the inside here say Mr. Roosevelt does not care shucks about the Park. What he wants to see is game and lots of it." [1] Private citizens became distressed. A woman wrote John Burroughs pleading with him to teach the President to love the animals the way Burroughs did. [2]

By this time Roosevelt was distressed himself. This talk of his not loving the animals and of his being a game-butcher was getting out of hand. The spurious yarns that had originated in Meeker, Colorado, only a few short months before, had had a more prejudicial effect than anyone could have surmised.

Roosevelt made two moves in short order. He abandoned all plans to hunt, reconciling himself instead to two weeks of travel through the Park just for the fun of seeing it all, and he invited Burroughs to go with him. The first decision was imperative. Why he invited Burroughs is not so clear. But how better could he allay this newspaper talk about his blind, promiscuous killing of game than to have the gentle, nature-loving sage of the Catskills arm-in-arm with him day after day? Such a twosome would be as innocent as the town's prize burglar attended by the Methodist parson. If Roosevelt did not have such thoughts in mind when he asked him to accompany him, then he made unwittingly one of the cleverest moves of the year.

Less than a month before the date set for his departure, Roosevelt wrote Burroughs as follows:

If the Senate will permit, and unless it proves impossible to dodge the infernal yellow papers, I would like to visit the Yellowstone Park for a fortnight this spring. I want to see the elk, deer, sheep, and antelopes there, for the Superintendent of the Park, Major Pitcher, tells me that they are just as tame as domesticated animals. I wonder whether you could not come along? I would see that you endured neither fatigue nor hardship.

Burroughs, at that time a mellow sixty-six, was delighted. "I knew," he wrote later, "that there was no man in the country with whom I should so like to see it as Roosevelt." [3] The President was equally pleased: "Three cheers! I think I shall be able to go into Yellowstone without doubt, if only for a week or two." [4]

The President and John Burroughs had met before, perhaps first in 1889, when Roosevelt told him how homesick Burroughs' books had made him on one of his boyhood trips to Europe, and how he had enjoyed them since.

The two naturalists renewed their acquaintance in 1892 when Roosevelt wrote Burroughs, taking issue with his published assertion that European forms of animal life were, as a rule, larger and more hardy and prolific than the corresponding forms in the United States.

. . . it seems to me, looking at the mammals, [wrote Roosevelt] that it would be quite impossible to generalize as to whether those of the Old or New World are more fecund, are the fiercest, the hardiest, or the strongest. A great many cases could be cited on both sides. Our moose and caribou are, in certain of their varieties, rather larger than the Old World forms of the same species. If there is any difference between the beavers of the two countries, it is in the same direction. So with the great family of the field mice. The largest true arvicola seems to be the yellow-cheeked mouse of Hudson's Bay, and the biggest representative of the family on either continent is the muskrat. In most of its varieties the wolf of North America seems to be inferior in strength and courage to that of northern Europe and Asia; but the direct reverse is true with the grizzly bear, which is merely a somewhat larger and fiercer variety of the European brown bear. On the whole, the Old World bison, or so-called aurochs, appears to be somewhat more formidable than the American brother; but the difference against the latter is not anything like as great as the difference in favor of the American wapiti, which is nothing but a giant representative of the comparatively puny European stag. . . .[5]

In ensuing years the friendship of the two men grew as they met now and then in New York City and again at the Governor's mansion in Albany. If Roosevelt deemed it wise to have a naturalist accompany him to Yellowstone, one who could still the objectionable talk about his killing game indiscriminately, he could not have made a better choice.

II

With the arrival of the Presidential train at Gardiner, Montana, at the north entrance to the Park, Roosevelt and Burroughs began a fortnight of episodes to be recalled with pleasure as long as they lived.

In order to see as much of the Park as possible they traveled from place to place, spending only two or three days at each. The first week they had three different camp sites in the northeast corner of Yellowstone, in that portion drained by the Gardiner River. Since only a sprinkling of snow covered the ground here, they moved from one point to another on horseback. During the second week they visited the geyser regions, at a higher elevation, where snow still lay five to six feet deep, requiring sleighs for getting about.

One of Roosevelt's personal requirements was a periodical hitch in the open alone. A day or so after the first camp had been established he went off by himself, walking eighteen miles over rough country. That evening about the campfire he told Burroughs about a bird song he had heard—one entirely unfamiliar to him. From the description, Burroughs thought it might have been that of the Townsend's solitaire, a bird famed as one of the loveliest songsters of the West.

The next day they covered some of the same territory the President had been over the day before. As they reached a certain wild, rocky spot above a deep chasm, Roosevelt remarked that it had been here he had heard the strange bird song; and then, a moment later, "And there it is now." A few yards farther along the trail, they caught sight of the bird itself. It was a Townsend's solitaire. Said Burroughs, "The President was just as eager to see and hear it as I was." Both thought, however, that the song hardly deserved the praise that had been bestowed upon it.[6]

An hour or so later, the two men halted briefly at the foot of a grass-covered slope where their attention was attracted to a series of plaintive, bird-like notes that issued from the grass near them. Both men thought they were bird notes, although they had not the faintest idea as to what bird might make them. They began investigating at once, for there was no thought of going on until they had identified the animal responsible. Both were amazed to discover the notes were produced by a musically talented ground squirrel.[7]

Late that afternoon after reaching the second camp site, located on Cottonwood Creek near Hell Roaring Creek, they had a similar experience. Some distance away they heard another strange note, a sound such as a boy might make by blowing into the mouth of an empty bottle. "Let's go run that bird down," cried Roosevelt. Away went the stocky figure of the President of the United States, followed by the slender, white-bearded veteran of Slabsides, straddling logs and leaping rocks, until they stood beneath the tree from which the unfamiliar sound came. High in the top they could make out the indistinct form of a bird, but without the aid of binoculars they had thoughtlessly left behind, they could not name it. Roosevelt hastily returned to camp after the glasses and with their help they soon recognized the bird as a pigmy owl, not much larger than a bluebird. Neither had seen this species before. "I think," wrote Burroughs, "the President was as pleased as if he had bagged some big game."[8]

Following a short stay on Cottonwood Creek, the party headed for Tower Falls. On the way they arrived at the summit of an elevated plateau commanding an open area some three or four miles wide. Everywhere here were elk, an enormous herd, distributed unevenly over the rolling landscape. With the assistance of binoculars, Roosevelt and Burroughs made a careful tabulation of the number, estimating it at close to three thousand. It was one of the big moments of the trip for the President, who watched the herd intently for four hours.

Arrived at Tower Falls, Roosevelt quickly spotted a band of bighorn on the opposite side of the canyon at the top of a steep, shelving wall some five or six hundred feet high. The animals stood within easy rifle shot but showed no evidence of unrest. The question at once arose as to whether the animals could possibly descend the face of the canyon wall to reach water. The feat seemed impossible, but the men hoped they would attempt it.

Toward evening word was brought to Roosevelt and Burroughs that the bighorn were starting down. At the moment the President was shaving, but he exclaimed enthusiastically, "By Jove, I must see that," and rushed from his tent, his face covered with soap, and a towel around his neck.

He and Burroughs selected a point of vantage, where, with field glasses, they watched the sheep make a breathtaking descent down the almost vertical face of the canyon wall, saw them leap from ledge to ledge, zigzag back and forth, and finally plunge straight down to the bottom, without once making a misstep. "I think the President was the most pleased of us all," wrote Burroughs. "He laughed with the delight of it, and quite forgot the need of a hat and coat till I sent for them." [9]

With each succeeding day Burroughs became more and more amazed at Roosevelt's broad knowledge of animals, his ingrained enthusiasm for outdoor life and the length to which he would go to supplement his already capacious storehouse of natural history facts. One day, following their arrival in the lower geyser basin, the two were riding along in a sleigh (the snow was still lying several feet deep in this sector of the Park), when suddenly Roosevelt jumped out. He scrambled hurriedly over the frozen surface of the snow for a short distance and then, using his soft felt hat as a protection to his hand, made a successful lunge for a tiny dark-colored animal which was doing its best to elude him. He came back to the sled clutching his prey, and beamingly announced to Burroughs, whose astonishment knew no limits, that he had just caught a meadow mouse belonging to the genus *Microtus*. He hoped it might prove to be a new species.[10]

Later that day Roosevelt prepared the skin of the mouse—neatly as a professional taxidermist would have done it, Burroughs reported—and then, after making certain measurements, wrapped it up for shipment to C. Hart Merriam. A letter went with it:

I send you a small tribute in the shape of a skin, with the attached skull, of a microtus—a male, taken out of the lower geyser basin, National Park, Wyoming, April 18, 1903. Its length, head and body, was 4.5 inches; tail to tip, 1.3 inches, of which .2 were the final hairs. The hind foot was .7 of an inch long. I had nothing to put on the skin but salt. I believe it is of no value to you, but send it on the off chance.

I have thoroughly enjoyed having John Burroughs with me. Porcupines and seemingly also skunks have diminished in the Park during the last twelve years [Roosevelt's last visit had been in 1890]. Coyotes are numerous. Apparently there are no gray wolves. I have just found where a cougar killed a big bull elk . . . The water ousel stays here all winter. I have heard it sing beautifully this time, and also the solitaire.

Merriam subsequently informed the President that the mouse (*Microtus nanus*) was not new to science, although new to the Park. It was the only animal Roosevelt killed in Yellowstone.

When Burroughs related this incident to a reporter some days later, the thought came to him: "Suppose he changes that *u* to an *o,* and makes the President capture a moose, what a pickle I shall be in! Is it any more than ordinary newspaper enterprise to turn a mouse into a moose?" [11]

In addition to the solitaire and pigmy owl, Roosevelt and Burroughs saw many other birds. One afternoon in the Norris geyser basin, for instance, they identified a mountain blue bird—almost identical with the eastern variety in both voice and manner—the western purple finch, a junco, a western robin, and several kinds of sparrows. In addition to the larger game animals, such as deer, elk, and bighorn, now in a state of semi-domestication, they encountered Rocky Mountain woodchucks, snowshoe rabbits, a marten, numerous coyotes, and an occasional pine squirrel. There were no bears about yet, these animals not having quite finished their hibernal sleep. Roosevelt was disappointed, for he had heard a great deal from the soldiers of their tameness. Several months later he wrote Burroughs about an amusing report on the bears he had just received from one of the men in the Park:

I think that nothing is more amusing and interesting than the development of the changes made in wild beast character by the wholly unprecedented course of things in the Yellowstone Park. I have just had a letter from Buffalo Jones [a famous old plainsman then in charge of bison in Yellowstone], describing his experience in trying to get the cans off the feet of the bears in the Yellowstone Park. There are lots of tin cans in the garbage heaps which the bears muss over, and it has now become fairly common for a bear to get his paw so caught in a tin can that he can not get it off, and, of course, great pain and injury follow. Buffalo Jones was sent with another scout to capture, tie up, and cure these bears. He roped two and got the can off one, but the other tore himself loose, can and all, and escaped owing, as Jones bitterly insists, to the failure of duty on the part of one of his brother scouts, whom he sneers at as a foreigner. Think of the grizzly bear of the early Rocky Mountain hunters and explorers, and then think of the fact that part of the recognized duties of the scouts in the Yellowstone Park at this moment is to catch this same grizzly bear and remove tin cans from the same bear's paws in the bear's interests. . . .

Roosevelt and Burroughs spent the last days of their visit in the Park visiting Old Faithful, Yellowstone Falls, and Yellowstone Canyon, where the snow was so deep that they had to travel from one place to another on skis, a novel experience to Burroughs. On their final morning together, with faces reddened and noses peeling, they left at five o'clock for Mammoth Hot Springs, on their way out of the Park. From Yellowstone Burroughs returned home by way of Washington, Idaho, and Montana. Roosevelt went on to the Grand Canyon, and then to Yosemite, to meet John Muir.

III

Influenced by Burroughs, Roosevelt paid more attention to birds in Yellowstone than he might have otherwise. As his own account of the trip evidences, he was really more interested in the larger mammals. For example, he was tremendously pleased on the day he arrived to find, almost within the city limits of Gardiner, a band of at least one hundred prongbuck, so tame that he could ride within fair rifle range of them before they fled. He was even more delighted, as already related, when he was able to study mountain sheep at such close quarters. Blacktail deer were even tamer, many of them actually feeding on the parade grounds at the Fort. He enjoyed most, however, watching the elk. After leaving the Park, he wrote a long letter to Merriam, telling him that the game was certainly more plentiful than when he was last in the Park, that the elk far outnumbered other animals, there being at least 15,000, and that most of those he had found dead had succumbed to the deep snow, cold, or starvation.

John Burroughs did not find the large game, nor yet the birds, the most interesting feature of the Park. "The most interesting thing in that wonderful land," he asserted, "was, of course, the President himself." [12]

One evening, as though to prove his versatility, Roosevelt

Theodore Roosevelt
aged ten.

Snowy Owl collected and
mounted by Roosevelt in
1876. Now on display in
the American Museum of
Natural History.

Theodore Roosevelt about a year before he entered Harvard.

Roosevelt (right) with Bill Sewall and Wilmot Dow, on a hunting trip in Maine during his college years.

Theodore Roosevelt in the buckskin suit of which he was so proud. This picture furnished the frontispiece for his *Hunting Trips of a Ranchman*.

Camping with John Burroughs and guides in Yellowstone National Park (1903).

The President of the United States relaxing in the field with a friend.

Brown Bros.

Roosevelt with John Muir (at T.R.'s left) in Yosemite at the
base of a giant Sequoia (1903).

George Bird Grinnell

Henry Fairfield Osborn

LEADING FELLOW-NATURALISTS OF T.R.'S TIME

C. Hart Merriam

Frank M. Chapman

The Roosevelt family in 1903. From left to right: Quentin, the President, Theodore, j▮
Archie, Alice, Kermit, Mrs. Roosevelt, Ethel.

e Smithsonian scientific party in Africa (1910). Left to right: R. J. Cuninghame, Kermit, T.R., Edmund Heller, Hugh H. Heatley.

Riding in the children's train to visit the zoo in Buenos Aires, prior to the expedition into the South American jungle.

The starting point down the River of Doubt, showing Colonel Roosevelt in his cano (1914).

Returning from South America: Roosevelt, Leo E. Miller, and George K. Cherrie.

talked at length about paleontology, rapidly giving "the outlines of the science, and the main facts, as if he had been reading up on the subject that very day." [13] Burroughs, having no
previous knowledge of Roosevelt's studies under Shaler at
Harvard, was properly impressed. Not since Thomas Jefferson
had a President of the United States demonstrated an interest
in fossils.

Burroughs was much more impressed, though, with Roosevelt's knowledge of present-day animals. Ever since a day in
July, 1863 (Roosevelt was then a child aged four), when Burroughs walked into the Library of the United States Military
Academy at West Point and chanced upon a copy of Audubon's
Birds with its strikingly colored illustrations, he had been a
close student of nature. He was in a position to make a sound
appraisal of the President's capabilities as a naturalist:

I can not now recall that I have ever met a man with a keener and
a more comprehensive interest in the wild life about us—an interest
that is at once scientific and thoroughly human . . . When I first read
his "Wilderness Hunter," many years ago, I was impressed by his rare
combination of the sportsman and the naturalist. When I accompanied him on his trip to the Yellowstone Park . . . I got a fresh
impression of the extent of his natural history knowledge and of his
trained powers of observation. Nothing escaped him, from bears to
mice, from wild geese to chickadees, from elk to red squirrels; he
took it all in, and he took it in as only an alert, vigorous mind can
take it in. On that occasion I was able to help him identify only one
new bird. All the other birds he recognized as quickly as I did.[14]

Burroughs was sure that Roosevelt's hunting activities were
prompted, in large measure, by his interests as a naturalist and
that his hunting records contained more live natural history
than any similar writings, with the possible exception of those
of the Scottish naturalist-sportsman, Charles St. John. "I have
never been disturbed by the President's hunting trips. It is to
such men as he that the big game legitimately belongs," Bur-

roughs was to write. "Such a hunter as Roosevelt is as far removed from the game-butcher as day is from night." [15]

The most flattering tribute the American poet-naturalist paid to Roosevelt, however, was a published testimonial to his powers of observation:

> The President is a born nature lover, and he has what does not always go with this passion—remarkable powers of observation. He sees quickly and surely, not less so with the corporeal eye than with the mental. His exceptional vitality, his awareness all around, gives the clue to his powers of seeing. The chief qualification of a born observer is an alert, sensitive, objective type of mind, and this Roosevelt has in a preeminent degree.[16]

Burroughs went on to say that everyone sees the big things, but that the true observer is known by his skill in seeing the little things, in observing the presence of natural objects effortlessly, spontaneously, and without premeditation. "President Roosevelt," he asserted, "comes as near fulfilling this ideal as any man I have known. His mind moves with wonderful celerity, and yet as an observer he is very cautious, jumps to no hasty conclusions." [17] The Yellowstone trip ripened the existing friendship between the two naturalists, a friendship that was to last until Roosevelt's death.

IV

A few weeks before Roosevelt left the White House for the West, in company with John Burroughs, he addressed a letter to John Muir, the celebrated author, botanist, and glaciologist:

> I write to you personally to express the hope that you will be able to take me through the Yosemite. I do not want anyone with me but you, and I want to drop politics absolutely for four days and just be out in the open with you. John Burroughs is probably going through the Yellowstone Park with me and I want to go with you through the Yosemite.

Roosevelt's choice of a companion for the canyons and Sequoia groves of California's magnificent Paradise was a particularly happy one. John Muir, the Scottish-born naturalist, knew Yosemite as no man then or since has come to know it.) Since journeying West from his boyhood Wisconsin home in 1868, he had passed the ensuing thirty-five years in a systematic study of Sierra nature. He knew intimately the trees, flowers, rocks, glaciers, and streams. Of even more importance, he had, in later years, devoted himself increasingly to preaching conservation, stressing in particular the fact that commercial exploitation already threatened some of the more outstanding show-places of the West, the giant Sequoia forests among them.

Muir met Roosevelt at Raymond, California, on Friday, May 15, 1903. They immediately detached themselves from the throng assembled at the station, and disappeared until the following Monday. Report has it that Roosevelt's first question to Muir was, "How do you tell the Hammond from the Wright flycatcher?" [19]

Plans for this trip may have seemed elaborate to the Yosemite naturalist. It is said that when Muir was once asked what preparation he customarily made for a trip into the woods, he replied, "I put some bread and tea in an old sock and jump over the back fence." [19] For the trip with the "Influential man from Washington" he had had to provide mules, packer, cook, and all necessary camping paraphernalia.

Ordinarily such an experience as this visit to Yosemite would have proved sufficient incentive for both Roosevelt and Muir to write detailed, circumstantial accounts. That neither of them did so is cause for regret. As a result, one must draw upon scattered bits of material from different sources. From these it appears that both men enjoyed the days together to the full.

I trust I need not tell you, my dear sir [Roosevelt wrote Muir from Sacramento, May 19], how happy were the days in the Yosemite I owed to you, and how greatly I appreciated them. I shall never forget our three camps; the first in the solemn temple of the great sequoias; the next in the snow storm among the silver firs near the brink of the cliff; and the third on the floor of the Yosemite, in the open valley fronting the stupendous rocky mass of El Capitan with the falls thundering in the distance on either hand.

Enthusiasm was expressed, too, in a letter he sent "Oom John" (the familiar Dutch appellation Roosevelt gave Burroughs) the same day:

I have just come from a four days trip to and into the Yosemite with John Muir. Both the Yosemite and the big trees were all that any human being could desire. John Muir is a delightful man, and with the exception of yourself, the pleasantest possible companion on a trip of this kind. I was a little surprised to find that he knew nothing about any birds save a few of the most conspicuous; but he knows so much about rocks, trees, glaciers, flowers, etc., that it is simply captious to complain.

Muir, in turn, wrote at least two letters about the trip. To his wife, he said, "I had a perfectly glorious time with the President and the mountains. I never before had a more interesting, hearty, and manly companion." [20] And to C. Hart Merriam, "Camping with the President was a memorable experience. I fairly fell in love with him." [21]

From another source we learn that the chief topic of conversation between the two men was conservation. Muir dwelt at great length on the necessity for urgent action to save the great forests of that region. He spoke so forcefully that Roosevelt came away from the Yosemite "with a greatly quickened conviction that vigorous action must be taken speedily, ere it should be too late." [22] Soon after Roosevelt returned to Washington, he said:

Surely our people do not understand even yet the rich heritage that is theirs. There is nothing in the world more beautiful than the Yosemite, the groves of giant Sequoias and redwoods, the Canyon of the Colorado, the Canyon of the Yellowstone, the three Tetons; and the people should see to it that they are preserved for their children and their children's children forever, with their majestic beauty all unmarred.[23]

Roosevelt thought that Muir's books of the Sierras should be in the hands of every true lover of nature; he always recommended Muir's description of the water ousel. But Roosevelt appreciated most Muir's ability to influence contemporary thought, resulting in "the preservation of those great natural phenomena which make California a veritable Garden of the Lord." [24]

Yet the President did not warm to Muir in the way he did to Burroughs. Their interests did not wholly coincide. Roosevelt never did get over his surprise at Muir's indifferent knowledge of birds. One evening in Yellowstone, for instance, a thrush began to pour out a flood of melody. Roosevelt wanted Muir to verify his belief that it was the song of the Western hermit thrush, and was amazed that his companion had not been listening to it, in fact did not even know the song. Muir, Roosevelt contended, was not interested in the small things of nature; he liked only the big things, such as mountains, trees, and glaciers. For instance, he knew nothing of the wood-mice, Roosevelt said, although he could talk at length about the deer and bear.

Roosevelt apparently did not stop to think that Muir may have been disappointed to learn that the President did not speak the language of the glaciers and mountains so familiar to him. Burroughs' explanation, mentioned earlier, was that both men were great talkers, and that great talkers seldom get along together.

But when John Muir died, on Christmas Eve, 1914, Roosevelt's tribute was warm and generous:

Ordinarily, the man who loves the woods and the mountains, the trees, the flowers, and the wild things, has in him some indefinable quality of charm which appeals even to those sons of civilization who care for little outside of paved streets and brick walls. John Muir was a fine illustration of this rule. He was by birth a Scotchman, a tall and spare man, with the poise and ease natural to him who had lived much alone under conditions of labor and hazard. His was a dauntless soul, and also one brimming over with friendliness and kindliness.[25]

13

"I'll Back Up Gorgas"

FERDINAND DELESSEPS, who had built the Suez Canal, started work in the early 1880's to join the Atlantic and the Pacific, strong in the conviction that he had the money and the men to complete the job. By 1890 he had neither. All that was left was a partly completed ditch, heaps of rusting tools, and machinery almost obscured from sight by the growth of the jungle, and row upon row of white crosses to mark the graves of those who had toiled and lost. DeLesseps had thought the construction of the Canal was chiefly an engineering problem; it was too late when he discovered that it was also a medical problem. He had failed to take into account the corrosive forces of the jungle, principally malaria and yellow fever. Thus the French had to abandon their work.

The United States might have failed as well if it had not been for the labors and wisdom of men like Ronald Ross, Walter Reed, Carlos Finlay, William Gorgas, and Theodore Roosevelt.

It was not until the year 1897 that Major Ronald Ross concluded his researches on malaria, thus proving conclusively that that disease is transmitted by the female *Anopheles* mosquito. Three years later the Walter Reed Commission, ordered to Cuba at the end of the Spanish American War, when the death rate

among American soldiers was higher from malaria and yellow
fever than from all other causes, established beyond question—
with an indispensable assist from Dr. Carlos Finlay—that another mosquito (*Aedes aegypti*) transmits yellow fever.

The significance of these discoveries penetrated slowly the
minds of men, including some medical men. They hesitated to
accept the findings, even after William Gorgas, an army doctor,
had eradicated yellow fever from Cuba by killing mosquitoes,
leaving not even a pinpoint of virus on that island to foster
future epidemics.

There were others, however, scientists of vision. When work
began on the Panama Canal, they saw only too clearly what
might happen if the construction of the Canal was undertaken
without adequate provision for dealing with mosquitoes. As soon
as congress had authorized the formation of an Isthmian Commission, a delegation of five eminent American scientists called
upon Roosevelt at the White House. They were Drs. William
Henry Welch and William Osler of the Johns Hopkins Medical
School; Dr. John R. Musser, President of The American Medical
Association; Dr. Bryant, President of the New York Academy of
Medicine; and L. O. Howard, representing the American Association for the Advancement of Science. Dr. Welch, spokesman
for the committee, has told the story of the meeting with the
President in these words:

The visit to President Roosevelt relating to Panama Canal affairs
was to press upon him the importance of making Gorgas a member
of the commission . . . An appointment had been made with the
President at the White House at 12 noon. I was selected to be the
spokesman. We passed through a room crowded with persons waiting
to see the President, and I felt that he must begrudge every minute
we occupied, especially as what I had to say I had previously communicated to him by letter, and I knew that Leonard Wood had
already urged upon him all that I could say and more. . . . When
we finished presenting our argument, which altogether could not have
lasted more than fifteen minutes, President Roosevelt began talking

to us and continued for at least twenty minutes, in a very interesting, dramatic, and amazingly outspoken fashion. He told us that he did not frame the law enacted by Congress, and it did not meet his ideas of what the situation demanded. He would have preferred a single director, who should select engineers, sanitarians and other experts. Instead of that, he had to pick out seven members to make up a commission and the law provided that no less than five of these should be engineers, without one word about a doctor or a sanitarian. "How can I under these circumstances," he said, "put a doctor on the commission?" [1]

Roosevelt concluded by saying that he fully appreciated the importance of what they had told him, and that he would find the best man possible to take care of the health of the Zone. The upshot was that Gorgas was appointed; but he went as a subordinate officer, and not as a commissioner with powers of independent action.

Colonel William Crawford Gorgas arrived in Panama in June, 1904, with only a small group of trained assistants, and without adequate supplies and equipment necessary for fighting mosquitoes. He undertook the task with the confidence born of previous successful experience. He knew what had to be done and how to go about it. He knew that *Aedes* mosquitoes are peculiarly domesticated insects, preferring an environment in or about homes, where they breed only in clean water—in tin cans, broken bottles, flower vases, rain barrels, and the like. His job was to destroy these breeding places, and thereby the mosquitoes. That was all there was to it. In six months he had eliminated the "yellow jack" from Havana, a city that had known its presence continuously for 200 years; he felt confident he could do the same in Panama.

But it was not to be that simple. In Havana he had had full authority; on the Isthmus he had practically none; he took orders from above. When he asked for supplies—pyrethrum powder, crude oil, sulphur, wire-screening—he was informed by obstructive superiors that they were useless, that if he would rid the place of its filth, and unspeakable smells, he would eliminate disease in no time. What he needed was shovels, he was told, not oil and screens. It was all nonsense about mosquitoes carrying disease, anyway.

The attempts of Gorgas to convince the commissioners that one infected mosquito was more dangerous than a thousand cesspools were all in vain. Stupidity, red tape, and lack of sympathetic understanding hampered him at every turn. Gorgas knew, as did Welch, Osler, and others, that though the Isthmus was only forty miles wide, every one was a mile of dense, tropical jungle, swarming with mosquitoes, each and every one a potential carrier of malaria or yellow fever; he knew that the overcoming of these diseases, especially the latter, was the indispensable step without which the Canal project would fail. Time and again he went over the evidence in favor of the mosquito transmission of disease with the head of the commission. His arguments were futile. He was dead wrong, he was told. He took his story to General George W. Davis, first Governor of the Canal Zone and the man who had built the Washington Monument. He thought he might receive help from him. But Davis was also an engineer. "I'm your friend, Gorgas," he said, "and I'm trying to set you right. On the mosquito you are simply wild. Get the idea out of your head. Yellow fever, as we all know, is caused by filth." [2]

To make matters worse, yellow fever picked this moment to multiply its victims. When the Commission demanded that Gorgas be removed from his post, he was saved only by a report of The American Medical Association, which had been quietly investigating the sanitary work in the Zone. The report said, in substance: "Stupidity clothed with authority is an odious bedfellow, and Gorgas is in bed with the Panama Canal Commission." [3]

Soon afterwards, due in large measure to the investigation of the American Medical Association, Roosevelt fired the first Commission and appointed a second. But it was not long until it, too, was clamoring for the dismissal of Gorgas. It was the same old story. Its members, once again engineers, knowing little or nothing about the insect transmission of disease, insisted that the only way to clean up the Zone was to bury garbage and drain stagnant pools. Even after yellow fever began to subside, as a result of Gorgas' efforts, they said it would have subsided anyway.

The chairman of the new Commission was Theodore P. Shonts, a railroad builder, brusk, tactless, and domineering. The new Governor of the Canal Zone was Charles E. Magoon, a former lawyer and government official, polite and agreeable. About one thing they agreed. Gorgas had failed and must go. The sanitary department must be reorganized. Shonts seems to have been the more determined of the two, and he immediately let his plans be known. Gorgas was to go and be replaced by an Osteopath, an old friend of his whose only recommendation was that he had been in the South and had seen yellow fever.

Mr. Shonts was not joking. In spite of the fact that Gorgas had completely eliminated yellow fever from Cuba and had recently been the subject of the unqualified praise of the American Medical Association for making a conspicuous success, under unbelievable handicaps, the head of the Isthmian Commission proposed to throw him out and entrust the fate of the Canal to a man who had had no experience whatever with tropical diseases!

When this proposal met with an indifferent response, Shonts next suggested the name of a physician, well-known to the medical profession and familiar with yellow fever, but who was hostile to the idea of mosquito transmission and had every intention of ignoring the lessons learned in Cuba. That other candidates, more deserving of the position, were later proposed, in no way removed the stigma of utter incompetence from the members of the Commission.

In due time the Commission recommended to the Secretary of

War, William Howard Taft, that Gorgas be removed and that Dr. Hamilton Wright be named as his successor. Taft approved this recommendation and sent it to the President.

A historian of that time had expressed the opinion that, "Had any other man been President at that time it is almost certain that Gorgas would have been displaced." [4] What Taft proposed to do is clear. But Roosevelt was not to be stampeded.

He first put the matter up to Welch. Should he retain Gorgas? "I shall hold you responsible for every word you put in your letter," he said. [5]

Welch replied that since he would be held responsible for every word he would be obliged to say that he knew of no one so well qualified to carry on the work as Gorgas.

Still undecided, Roosevelt called in his old friend and personal physician, Dr. Alexander Lambert, and put the problem up to him. It was an epochal meeting. In the opinion of many well-informed scientists, that meeting decided the fate of the Panama Canal. Roosevelt began by saying that he was not satisfied with what he had heard about Gorgas. He had been informed by Shonts that Gorgas was not cleaning up the Zone, and smells and filth were just as prevalent as ever. The Secretary of War, he added, had reviewed the case and had joined with Shonts in recommending his dismissal.

Lambert chose his words carefully as he replied. He knew, even better than the President, the importance of this conference, and just how much was at stake. He was at pains to point out that odors and dirt have nothing to do with the spread of malaria and yellow fever, that these diseases are transmitted from one person to another in only one way, by the bites of infected mosquitoes. That being true, he went on, there is only one way to make war on these diseases and that is to make war on the insects that transmit them. The old way, he said, was to clean out the filth; the new way was to clean up the water puddles and other breeding places of *Anopheles* and *Aedes*. "If you fall back upon the old methods of sanitation, you will fail, just as the French failed. If you back up Gorgas and his ideas and let him make his campaign against mosquitoes, then you can get that Canal. I can only give you my advice; you must decide for yourself. There is only one way of controlling yellow fever and malaria, and that is by the eradication of the mosquitoes." [6]

The President listened attentively, saying nothing until Lambert had finished. He then reflected a few moments before speaking: "It is queer," he said finally, "I never appreciated before how essential it was. But I do now. By George, I'll back up Gorgas and we will see it through." [7]

Roosevelt immediately called Shonts to the White House. After a few preliminary remarks he shook his finger at Shonts and said, "Now I want you to get back of Gorgas." [8]

Lambert had reason to feel proud of his day's work. Thereafter he was to think of it as perhaps the most important in his life. The success or failure of the Canal had been in his hands.

The result of Roosevelt's decision is now history. The accomplishments of Gorgas went far beyond the most sanguine hopes of men like Welch, Osler, and Lambert. Yellow fever deaths became fewer and fewer. One day before long, Gorgas entered an operating room in the government hospital at Ancon. He was in a jovial mood. A number of surgeons were performing an autopsy on the latest yellow fever victim. "Take a good look at this man, boys," he said, "for it's the last case of yellow fever you will ever see. There will never be any more deaths from this cause in Panama." [9] In exactly fifteen months Gorgas had eliminated from the Isthmus a disease that had been endemic since the days of Balboa and Pizarro, and possibly for centuries before.

Gorgas stayed on to convert one of the world's most pestilential regions into the healthiest. The death rate in the United States in 1914, the year the Canal was completed, was 14.1 per thousand; in the Canal Zone it was 6 per thousand.

Roosevelt later paid a well-deserved tribute to Gorgas when he said to him in a letter, "If ever there was a man who won his position strictly on his merits, you are the one." [10]

II

In the Fall of 1905, at the time he was playing a conspicuous role in terminating the Russo-Japanese War, Roosevelt published *Outdoor Pastimes of an American Hunter*. The majority of his chapters, although reshaped, had previously appeared either in *The Deer Family* or in one or another of the Boone and Crockett Club volumes. "I find it very unsatisfactory to have any of my writings in a volume where they are combined with those of other men," he told a friend.

He dedicated *Outdoor Pastimes* to John Burroughs. "It is a good thing for our people that you should have lived; and surely no man can wish to have more said of him," Roosevelt wrote.

The Yorkshire *Post* was pleased to note that Roosevelt had not lost his early love for the wilds. On the contrary, it stated, "The work at the White House has deepened it, and it will be observed with pleasure by naturalists on this side that his interest increases in the purely scientific side of hunting, and that he is ready to do all that he can to preserve game from the indiscriminate slaughter which has now been going on for some years." [11]

The *Harvard Graduates Magazine* thought *Outdoor Pastimes of an American Hunter* was the most entertaining book Roosevelt had yet set before the public; that it put the reader "in a glow like a ten-mile walk against a brisk, health-giving northwester." [12]

14

The Nature Faker Controversy

THE opening gun in what was to be known as the "nature faker" controversy was fired early in the year 1903, by John Burroughs. From behind breastworks hastily prepared on the slopes of the Catskills, he took deliberate aim at a group of young nature writers who had recently founded a new style, a new school, of creative literature. Burroughs credited the artist-naturalist, Ernest Thompson Seton, with founding the style, and William J. Long, Charles G. D. Roberts, and others with copying it.

Seton went to the out-of-doors for his characters and atmosphere. He took birds and mammals, endowed them richly with human attributes, and wove about them exciting romances, in which they played the roles of hero, archvillain, and scapegoat. Children, in particular, liked the stories, and they sold widely. Seton's imitators, with their variations of the general theme, were almost a matter of course.

These writers, according to their accusers, had one thing in common. Although they declared each story to be based on personal observations, they yet drew upon their imaginations. Some went further than others, giving full rein to their fancies. Though their stories may have been delightfully written, and highly enjoyable to children, they misled their readers by making animals do things which animals never did.

Burroughs' attack, labeled "Real and Sham Natural History," appeared in *The Atlantic Monthly*. Ostensibly a broadside against all nature writers who had failed to distinguish successfully between fact and fiction, it was actually a two-barreled attack, one barrel being discharged at Seton and the other at William J. Long. With vigor belying his three score years and six, Burroughs blasted away at one of Seton's latest books, *Wild Animals I Have Known* (*Wild Animals I Alone Have Known*, Burroughs called it) and at one of Long's most recent called *School of the Woods*. With these books he would have no quarrel, he said, if the authors had admitted they were romancing, but when both had stated in prefaces that every word was based on fact, he had to take issue with them. He then went on to criticize Seton for "trifling with natural history" and Long for his theory that animals consciously teach their young, actually conduct schools for the purpose of instructing their young in the rudiments of how to fly and sing, capture their food, and protect themselves from their enemies.

"Now the idea was a false one before Mr. Long appropriated it [from Seton]," Burroughs declared, "and it has been pushed to such length that it becomes ridiculous. There is not a shadow of truth in it." He believed, instead, that the actions of lower animals are motivated almost entirely by instinct, that they are not taught fear of their enemies, man for instance, but are instinctively afraid.[1]

In due time Burroughs' article arrived at the White House, where Roosevelt read it. He lost no time in addressing its author:

I was delighted with your *Atlantic Monthly* article. I have long wished that something of the kind should be written. The fashion of the books you are criticising was of course set in Kipling's jungle stories, but equally of course the latter are frankly fairy tales, and so they can do only good—though Kipling makes one or two blunders as when he takes it for granted that the great wild beasts like the song birds mate in spring. But when the people like those you criticize solemnly assert that they are relating exact facts they do positive harm.

Roosevelt was not too sure, though, about the position Burroughs had taken on instinctive action, and he was especially concerned about his flat statement that animals are instinctively afraid of man.

Don't you think [Roosevelt went on] that you perhaps scarcely allow sufficiently for the extraordinary change made in the habits of the wild animals by experience with man, especially experience continued through generations? I do not believe that there is any instance whatever that teaches them to be afraid of him in regions where he is wholly unknown. On Pacific islands that have never been visited by ships the birds at first have not the slightest fear of man, nor do they fear either cats, dogs or pigs. Proverbially cute though the fox is, the Falkland Island fox and in most of the Arctic regions the Arctic fox were both found by the first explorer to be as bold, stupid and helplessly fearless as these Pacific islands birds.

Roosevelt was perturbed, too, about Burroughs' generalization that animals never teach their young. While he thought that the statement was substantially correct, he was of the opinion that on rare occasions animals do teach their young. He told Burroughs about a setter dog which thrashed its young when the latter stupidly flushed a bird. And he had every reason to believe that such intelligent mammals as wolves and foxes practiced both conscious and unconscious teaching of the young. Burroughs must be very careful, Roosevelt said, about making his assertions too sweeping, so that his opponents could not point to exceptional instances which they would claim vitiated all his criticisms.

Burroughs wrote back: "I shall never cease to marvel at the variety of your interests and the extent of your knowledge . . . You seem to be able to discipline and correct any one of us in his chosen field. My *Atlantic* paper has some hasty streaks in it." [2]

Not long after the above letter was written, Roosevelt and

Burroughs were together in Yellowstone National Park renewing their youth in the chase of field mice, singing gophers, and solitaires. They discussed all aspects of the nature-faker controversy, and reviewed thoroughly the subjects of animal pedagogy and instinctive action. Much of what happened later stemmed from these amiable interchanges of opinion. Burroughs did not again attack Seton. Roosevelt cautioned against it, stressing Seton's valuable and trustworthy work of recent years, although, he said, he did "confound fact and fiction."

II

The Reverend William J. Long, as the real storm center of the nature-faker controversy, needs proper introduction. Long was a graduate of Harvard (1892), Andover Theological Seminary, and held M. A. and Ph. D. degrees from Heidelberg University. He had studied, too, at the Universities of Paris and Rome. In 1903, when Burroughs first took up the cudgels against him, Long was pastor of the First Congregational Church in Stamford, Connecticut, and the author of such books as *Ways of Wood Folk*, *Fowls of the Air*, and *School of the Woods*, the last volume being the one which stirred up the tempest in his ecclesiastical teapot.

As he grew older, Long became more and more of a philosopher, his books containing frequent references to, and quotations from, Descartes, Hume, Kant, and others. He wrote well and interestingly. Contemporary critics spoke in flattering terms of his literary skill. For instance, William Lyons Phelps thought that from the point of view of natural history, as well as that of literary art, his books were masterpieces.[3]

According to Long himself, he was an intimate student of the outdoor world, having gained his experience of birds and mammals through more than twenty years of roughing it in the great northern forests. He had, he said, followed the animals in all seasons of the years, sometimes alone, and at other times in the company of trappers and Indians. The knowledge of trappers and Indians, he assured his readers, "is fatal in its accuracy," he had more than once "gone fifty miles out of his course" to interview them.[4]

Long replied to Burroughs' *Atlantic Monthly* article. He made a special effort to prove that animal behavior is so diversified that no man has a right to condemn the observations of another as false. Animals even perform in ways to tax human credulity, he said. By way of illustration he went on to recount the behavior of two Baltimore orioles, a behavior so incredible, he insisted, that he dared not print it until after he had verified the details for a second time.

According to Long the two orioles were constructing a nest in a buttonwood tree and encountered difficulties, not being able to find branches sufficiently stiff and straight to support the nest. Undismayed, they flew to the ground where they found three sticks of a size, and at once tied them together in a perfect triangle. The skill they demonstrated in doing this was remarkable, for "at each angle they fastened one end of a cord and carried the other end over making it fast to the middle of the opposite side. Then they gathered up the loops and fastened them by the middle all together, to a stout bit of marline." Their staging now completed, they flew with it into the buttonwood tree and suspended it about two feet below a stout limb, the marline being "tied once around the limb, and, to make it perfectly safe, the end being brought down and fastened to the supporting cord with a reversed double hitch, the kind that a man uses in cinching a saddle. Moreover the birds tied a single knot at the extreme end lest the marline should ravel in the wind." [5]

If Long had taxed human credulity only with the oriole story, he might never have incurred the wrath of Burroughs, Roosevelt, and other American naturalists. However he did so again and again. Not long afterwards he published a magazine article called "Animal Surgery." In this he insisted that animals undeniably "practice a rude kind of medicine and surgery upon themselves." To support this statement, he then went on to describe the behavior of a woodcock which, he claimed, had a broken leg and had "deliberately put it into a clay cast to hold the broken bones in place until they should knit together." [6]

Naturalists other than Burroughs now felt compelled to protest. William Morton Wheeler, Harvard's eminent entomologist, for instance, said:

Mr. Long virtually claims that a woodcock not only has an understanding of the theory of casts as adapted to fractured limbs but is able to apply this knowledge in practice. The bird is represented as knowing the qualities of clay and mud, their lack of cohesion unless mixed with fibrous substances, their tendency to harden on exposure to air, and to disintegrate in water . . . But the mental horizon of Mr. Long's woodcock is not bounded by the qualities of mud. He is familiar with the theories of bone formation and regeneration—in a word, with osteogenesis, which by the way, is never clearly grasped by some of our university juniors.[7]

Frank M. Chapman joined in with the thought that Long has placed on record, in spite of his youth, "more remarkable statements regarding the behavior of birds and mammals of New England than can be found in all the authoritative literature pertaining to the animals of this region." [8] And Roosevelt wrote Burroughs, "I never read such nonsense in my life."

III

Roosevelt's part in the initial skirmishes of the nature-faker controversy was limited almost entirely to exchanges of opinion with Burroughs. There were at least two exceptions: he wrote Lyman Abbott protesting publication of Long's articles in The Outlook and he told Seton, "Burroughs and the people at large don't know how many facts you have back of your stories. You must publish your facts."

Seton heeded this counsel and at once sat down with paper and pencil to prove his right to a naturalist's ranking—if proof were needed—and discontinued in large measure his quasi-factual stories of animal life. Three or four years later he published *Life Histories of Northern Animals,* and a decade afterwards a more comprehensive work, *Lives of Game Animals,* for which he, ironically enough, received the Burroughs' Medal, among other awards.

A behind-the-scenes figure at first, Roosevelt was very much on the stage in the second and concluding act of the controversy. But there was to be a time interval of three years before he was to take Burroughs' article as a text, in order, as he said, "to skin Long alive."

In 1905 Long published a book called *Wayeeses the White Wolf.* Briefly told, it was the story of a large wolf that killed caribou by biting through the body wall just behind the fore legs, its fangs piercing the heart. Roosevelt read this story and then talked it over with Edward B. Clark, a young newsman and naturalist who was a familiar figure at the White House. This feat was mechanically impossible, the President declared. More than that he did not believe that wolves attacked their prey in that manner. Such untruthfulness in reporting animal actions, he said, deserved the worst kind of censure. "Well," said Clark, "why don't you do something about it?" Roosevelt thought it over for a moment and then replied, "I think I will." [9]

Without more ado he gave Clark permission to write down in detail, in the form of a statement dictated to him, all that he had been telling him about the nature fakers. It was a story Clark had been waiting for, and he was ready to handle it. He put it together that evening and the next day showed it to Roosevelt. The President thought it did not go quite far enough, and so sat down and enlarged it by as much as a third, writing out on White House stationery in longhand his additional comment. Thus amended and enlarged, it was given to *Everybody's Magazine* by Clark.

Having made his decision to scalp the enemy, it was only natural that Roosevelt should break the news to Burroughs. He did this half apologetically:

You will be pleased to know that I finally proved unable to contain myself, and gave an interview or statement, to a very good fellow, in which I sailed into Long and Jack London and one or two others of the more preposterous writers of "unnatural" history. It will be coming out soon, but I do not know in what magazine.

I know that as President I ought not to do this; but I was having an awful time toward the end of the session and I felt I simply had to permit myself some diversion.

What Roosevelt had been spoiling to do for four years he had finally done. From 1903 through 1906, because he was President, he could not afford to get into an altercation; but in 1907 he could do so because he had to permit himself a diversion.

Clark's article, which appeared in the June issue of *Every-body's*, was entitled "Roosevelt on the Nature Fakirs."[10] After some introductory build-up, including a quotation from Merriam that Roosevelt was the world's authority on the big game animals of North America, Clark allowed the President to speak for himself:

I don't believe for a minute [said the President], that some of these men who are writing nature stories and putting the word 'truth' prominently in their prefaces know the heart of the wild things. . . . They don't know, or if they do know, they indulge in the wildest exaggerations under the mistaken notion that they are strengthening their stories.

As to the propriety of placing their books in the hands of children to teach them nature, that was an outrage, Roosevelt said. If they had been written as fiction, and given to the children as fiction, all would have been well and good, but there was "no more reason why the children of the country should be taught a false natural history than why they should be taught a false physical geography."

Like Burroughs, Roosevelt used most of his ammunition on Long. He took Long to task particularly for the story about the great white wolf. It was absurd from beginning to end, the President said. In the first place, animals, except sharks and alligators, did not attack others by seizing the shoulder region. They went for the throat or flank. In the second place, he had himself seen scores of animals killed by wolves, and not one of them had been killed in the manner described by Long. In the third place he had the testimony of an expert (George Shiras) who had seen hundreds of animals killed by wolves. Without exception, they had met their death by wounds inflicted in the throat or flank. In the fourth place, a bite by a wolf in the region just back of the shoulder would not reach to the heart; the fangs of the wolf were simply not long enough. He suggested that Long hang a grapefruit in the middle of a keg of flour and then see for himself whether a large dog could bite through the wall of the keg and reach the grapefruit.

Soon afterwards the mail arrived at Long's home in Stamford, Connecticut. Long, as described by a reporter who arrived with the postman, was then a man of forty, about six feet tall, and weighing in the neighborhood of 175 pounds. He had a "rather boyish face, both open and engaging, and he was nervous and swift of feet and hand. He talked with immense frankness and rapidity." [11]

Long's nervousness and rapidity of speech at the moment were undoubtedly manifestations of his general distress of mind. Not many private citizens had been singled out for attack before by a President of the United States, and certainly no one for writing stories about animals. The experience could not be described as a particularly happy one. No doubt Long did feel, as Mark Sullivan said, "like a dove shot at by an elephant gun." [12]

As reporters by the score besieged his home, and his name appeared in headlines and cartoons throughout the country, Long was at first a little incoherent, an obviously disconcerted protagonist uncertain of his role. He quickly pulled himself together, however, and prepared his first public statement—an open letter to the President.

Long accused Roosevelt of deliberately going out of his way to attack a man he did not know, of taking advantage of his high position, and of hiding behind another man in his alleged interview. "There are only two noticeable things about your article," he said, "its bad taste and its cowardice." Although he shrank from this controversy with all his soul, he went on, he was forced to reply, for the sake of truth and of the thousands who read his books and loved them. He implied that he would soon give Roosevelt his come-uppance.[13]

In his second open letter, which followed two weeks later, Long proved that he could be "as belligerent as one of his own wolves, and more effectively deadly because more coldly deliberate."[14] He began by characterizing Roosevelt as "a man who takes delight in whooping through the woods killing everything in sight. . . . He doesn't know what a square deal means, either for wild animals or men." He could see no resemblance between the chest of a caribou and a keg of flour with a grapefruit inside. He thought it ridiculous for Roosevelt to assume the role of a naturalist. He is a hunter, Long said. Then the author went to bat in earnest:

Who is he to write, "I don't believe for a minute that some of these nature writers know the heart of a wild thing." As to that I find after carefully reading two of his big books that every time Mr. Roosevelt gets near the heart of a wild thing he invariably puts a bullet through it. From his own records I have reckoned a full thousand hearts which he has thus known intimately. In one chapter alone I find that he violently gained knowledge of 11 noble elk hearts in a few days.[15]

Long had read Roosevelt's *Hunting Trips of a Ranchman* and *The Wilderness Hunter* with deadly purpose in mind. He had gone through them page by page, paragraph by paragraph, making note of every animal Roosevelt had killed, underscoring those hunts attended with the greatest bloodshed. The most gory incidents he now proceeded to quote verbatim, scrupulously laying emphasis on Roosevelt's jubilation at the kill. He was far from overlooking the Two-Ocean Pass trip, when the youthful Roosevelt, yielding to the lure of the trophy, killed eleven elk all told. Having conjured up before the eyes of his reader a series of gruesome pictures portraying the President as a heartless game-butcher, Long finished with these words: "If it is charged that I do not understand nature as Mr. Roosevelt does, I stand up and plead guilty; yes, guilty in every page, every paragraph, every sentence." [16]

To much of the public, Long's counterattack was convincing. They felt that Long, even if he had written false natural history, was less guilty of wrongdoing than Roosevelt, who had slaughtered so many wild game animals. They put themselves in Long's shoes, wondering how they would feel if singled out for attack by the man in the White House.

Roosevelt's enemies, of course, had a field day. They declared that, "Dr. Long is deserving of the Carnegie Medal, the Garter, the Cross, and every other mark and symbol of unusual and remarkable personal bravery." [17]

Even papers formerly friendly to the President went against him. One said, "It seems that there are many strange things going on in the woods of which the ordinary person had no idea; but the same ordinary person would prefer to see the President of the United States keep out of these personal controversies." [18] Lyman T. Abbott, editor of The Outlook, was plainly disgusted that the President should engage in controversies not affecting his political leadership. "The Outlook," he said, "hopes that Dr. Long and Mr. Thompson Seton will continue to write about animal life, and that the children will continue to read their books." [19]

Roosevelt took most of the criticism in his stride, but Abbott's comments (he counted Abbott among his friends) really set him back on his heels. He could not understand, he wrote Shiras, how such "honest people of more than average intelligence could swallow Long's stories hook, line, and sinker."

II

How the controversy would have ended, if it had not been for Edward W. Nelson, is a matter for speculation. Nelson, a field naturalist for the Biological Survey, and unheard of in the scrap until now, seems to have become slightly nauseated over the whole affair. Some time in June he wrote Clark that "the actual working naturalists whose lives have been spent mainly in the trained observation of animal life, have scarcely been heard from in this controversy." He proposed, "in view of the outrageous character of the claims set up by the fakers," that a "symposium of the opinions of the working naturalists on the subject of the Long style of natural history would be of some service in putting the matter on its proper basis." He had consulted various naturalist friends, he said, and they, agreeing with him, had volunteered to furnish material for such a symposium.[20]

Adversaries of Roosevelt were later to claim that he himself took the initiative in arranging the symposium. The truth is that he knew nothing of it until some time after Nelson had made his proposal to Clark. The completed article, which appeared in the September issue of *Everybody's Magazine*, was entitled "Real Naturalists on Nature Faking."

William T. Hornaday, Director of the New York Zoological Park, led off the symposium. "Whenever Mr. Long enters the woods," he said, "the most marvelous things begin to happen. There is a four-footed wonder-worker behind every bush and a miracle every hour. Only the Omnipotent eye could see all the things that Mr. Long claims to have seen."

J. A. Allen, Curator of Mammalogy and Ornithology at the American Museum of Natural History, struck at Long for his statement that naturalists who attacked him were jealous because his books were forcing theirs out of the market.

C. Hart Merriam used the influence of his high position as Chief of the United States Biological Survey to discredit Long by explaining how the latter endowed his animals with new cunning and new habits. "The Reverend Dr. Long," he asserted, "is possessed of that rare gift which Dr. Carroll D. Wright called the Creative Memory. . . . A nature writer blessed with the Creative Memory does not have to go about wasting valuable time waiting and watching for animals to appear and do something."

In the same issue of *Everybody's Magazine,* another article followed the one just summarized. This was entitled "Nature Fakers," and it was by Roosevelt himself. His chief protest in this piece was against the editors who had accepted Long's publications as suitable for school children to read. "We abhor deliberate or reckless untruth in this study of natural history as much as in any other," he wrote, "and therefore we feel that a grave wrong is committed by all who, holding a position that entitles them to respect, yet condone and encourage such untruth."

III

The Outlook had said that it regretted seeing the President attack a private citizen, because the private citizen stands on uneven terms in any discussion with a person occupying the President's position. *The Outlook* was not alone in that feeling; many others, including some of Roosevelt's best friends, regretted his taking this step while he was President. In truth, Roosevelt himself knew that he should not have taken it; he had previously told both Burroughs and Clark that he could not afford to engage in any such altercation as long as he was in the White House.

Then, too, in many people's minds, Roosevelt's attack had been unnecessarily harsh and blunt. There is no question but that it would have carried greater weight if he had followed one of his own most cherished bits of advice—to speak softly while carrying a big stick. But he did not always practice what he preached.

Whether any permanent good resulted from the controversy or not is a matter of opinion. Frank Chapman thought so. "We still have nature fakers with us," he said, "but today there is far less chance that the product of their pens will pass editorial censorship or deceive the public than there was when the former were keener for copy and the latter knew less about nature." [21]

Long's next book was entitled *History of English Literature*.

15

"Pleased as Punch"

WHEN friends came to see Theodore Roosevelt they went away feeling taller. His ability to heighten the mental and moral statures of men extended to all classes, but to no single group more fully than to the naturalists. His influence on them, the inspiration he gave them, was an important feature of his life and of theirs.

From Boone and Crockett Club days until his death, Roosevelt went out of his way to cultivate the friendship of his fellow naturalists. He enlisted their help in preserving American wildlife, he encouraged them in their natural history explorations. "It was to help along things like this that I took this job," he told David Starr Jordan after becoming President. He kept after other naturalists to write books about their field and laboratory research, their successes in the chase and their hazards of exploration, whether in the mountains of Montana, the unexplored jungle of the Amazon basin, or the open country of East Africa. One of the first tangible results of this amiable insistence on writing was Winthrop Chanler's *Through Jungle and Desert* (1896). "In giving this book to the press," wrote Chanler, "I gratefully acknowledge the help I have received in preparing it from numerous friends and especially from the Hon. Theodore

140

Roosevelt, to whose encouragement and advice its present appearance is largely due."

As soon as Roosevelt became President his influence immediately became a potent force. He made use of it unhesitatingly as opportunities presented themselves, and nothing pleased him more than the knowledge that he had talked a naturalist into doing something he considered worthwhile, such as writing a book about his adventures on a museum expedition to the wilds of Africa or South America.

Before Roosevelt was through being President, he knew personally practically all of the leading American naturalists of the day: Burroughs, Hornaday, Chapman, Merriam, Ditmars, Beebe, to mention a few. Being President made it easy for Roosevelt to meet these men. He invited them to the White House, or to Oyster Bay, where he talked with them by the hour, routine executive duties temporarily pushed aside. He was far happier with them than with a group of congressmen or governors; what the naturalists had to tell him about the behavior of a warbler, the discovery of a new species of trout, or a projected trip to the wilds of Peru was more exciting to him than anything politicians could say. If an explorer had a manuscript in preparation, Roosevelt discussed it with him and perhaps, as he did more than once, offered to read it critically. If another asked him to prepare a preface, he obliged. If, afterward, he became enthusiastic about the book, he wrote a glowing account of it for *The Outlook* or *The New York Times Book Review*. If for some reason he failed to meet a naturalist whose literary style pleased him, he did not hesitate to write him letters of praise and encouragement—but sooner or later most of these men got to the White House. The experience was really a thrilling one for them. They had been recognized by the President of the United States.

Many naturalists sent him complimentary copies of their books as they came off the press. They took it for granted that he would be pleased—and he was. He immediately acknowledged receipt with words both gracious and flattering. Grinnell received such a letter for a book on duck shooting, David Starr Jordan for one on fishes, William Beebe for one on birds, and Edgar A. Mearns for one about the mammals of the Mexican Boundary. Roosevelt read practically everything of importance that came along, but he never passed up a book on animals. What amazed the naturalists was how closely he kept tab on them; more often than not he had read their books before the authors could get copies to him.

Many naturalists, of course, dedicated their books to him, as had Winthrop Chanler. When Frank T. Bullen asked permission to dedicate one of his latest, Roosevelt replied that he would be more than pleased, that he thought his *Cruise of the Cachalot* better than anything of the kind since Herman Melville. "Why I think I could pass a competitive examination in *The Cruise of the Cachalot*, and in many of your other writings as well," he said. Although Bullen's books appealed only to a limited following, to those who were enamored of the open seas and their inhabitants, Roosevelt was one of that group.

Roosevelt wrote Hornaday that he was delighted with his *American Natural History*, and he sent word to Madison Grant that his piece on mammals was just the kind of thing that always struck his fancy. To the zoologist, Robert Ingersoll, he said:

I have long admired your writings and it would be a great pleasure if some time I could have the chance of seeing you, by preference at the White House, if not there, out here [at Oyster Bay] at lunch some day this summer.

By the way, in your "Life of Animals," which I gave to my son Archie, your quotation from Coues at the outset embodies just what I think is the goal which the best scientists and the best nature writers should always have before them. There is no use in having a book scientific in its accuracy if no one will read it, and it is worse than no use to have a book that is readable and at the same time false.

Coues' statement referred to was that it is possible to make natural history entertaining and attractive as well as instructive, with no loss in scientific accuracy. Roosevelt had long since taken this stand, and he never wavered from it. He often said that certain scientists seemed to feel that if they are interesting it somehow reflected unfavorably on their professional standing. To illustrate, he recalled a sentence he had run across as a boy in the works of a well-known scientist. What the author had wanted to say was that "Pigeons walk, and don't hop." It did not strike him as dignified to use such everyday words, so he said instead, "The terrestrial progression of the Columbidae is gradient but never saltatorial." [1]

Roosevelt believed, too, in popularization. He often referred to such men as Hornaday, Osborn, and Chapman as living examples of scientists who, without loss of accuracy or substance, had "made the present and past life history of this planet accessible in vivid and striking forms to our people generally." [2] When Raymond L. Ditmars published *The Reptile Book*, Roosevelt had more to say on this topic:

I have a very strong belief [he wrote Ditmars] in having books which shall be understood by the multitude, and which shall yet be true—in other words, scientific books written for laymen who have some appreciation for science—so that the books will be of value to all men who are interested in the subject. It seems to me that your volume exactly fulfills these requirements. Personally I have long wanted to have in my library some good book on reptiles.

In this same letter, Roosevelt gave young Ditmars (not yet thirty) an additional slap on the back. He said it was genuinely refreshing to come upon a book like his, but he wished that he had written as fully as he certainly could have about the great number of interesting experiences that he must have had. For instance, just how did the crocodile kill the big sea-turtle? Did the crocodile bite through the shell? Did the king snake ever kill diamond-back rattlesnakes, where the rattler was as big as the king snake? "It would be a great pleasure if I could see you some time," he concluded. The sequel to this correspondence was a succession of books which Ditmars later wrote about the great number of interesting experiences he had had: *Thrills of a Naturalist's Quest, Confessions of a Scientist, The Making of a Scientist,* and *Snake Hunter's Holiday,* to mention a few of his more popular works.

Roosevelt gave a similar boost to Frank Chapman's initial literary ventures. "I wonder how I ever got on without your 'Birds of the Eastern United States' and your book on warblers," he told him. And again, on Chapman's publication of *Camps and Cruises of an Ornithologist,* "Not only shall I enjoy the book, but what is more important, I feel the keenest pride in your having written it . . . I like to have an American do a piece of work really worth doing."

Is it any wonder that Ditmars, Chapman, and other American biologists reached for pen and ink with which to add new titles to a growing list of publications? Had they not been told by the President of the United States, a distinguished author and naturalist in his own right, that their books were second to none? The volumes that Chapman and Ditmars alone wrote would fill a sizable shelf. Would the list be so long if the great mentor in the nation's capital had not given special recognition to their beginning efforts?

In the same manner, Roosevelt applauded the authors of books on wildlife photography. "The pictures in your book [*Wild Wings*] are remarkable," he wrote Herbert K. Job, "and I am delighted that my letter should appear as an introduction. I know I shall enjoy to the full reading the book itself."

When he learned that Richard Kearton, British photographer-naturalist, was coming to the United States, the President immediately wrote him that he was looking forward to seeing Kearton and his bird pictures, and that he must come to the White House. "By the way," he said, "do you know the work of Mr. Job, an American photographer? I believe it to be good and genuine. Also, do you know the work of Mr. George Shiras, Jr.?

His photographs are mostly of mammals but he has photographed birds also. His work is really remarkable. I will be glad to have you meet him when you come to Washington."

After Roosevelt had read G. C. Shilling's *With Flashlight and Rifle*, a picture study of the wild, nocturnal animal life of equatorial Africa, he told Shilling: "I congratulate myself continually on what you have done, and I confess that I envy you your experiences. I wish I could have the good fortune of meeting you some time in America."

Roosevelt was so impressed with George Shiras' unusually successful flashlight pictures of wild animals that the President told the photographer he would be derelict in his duty if he did not write a book in which his wonderful pictures and his almost equally wonderful observations would be recorded in permanent form. "Pamphlets disappear and photographs vanish completely," Roosevelt warned. Some time later when he learned that Shiras was actually at work on the book the President was delighted. "Do you remember, my dear fellow," he wrote, "what I have so insisted upon to you, even at the cost of seeming to be rude; viz., that to have the capacity to do a monumental piece of work, and then not do it leaves the net result just exactly as if you had no capacity at all."

Shiras finally completed his "monumental piece of work," but unfortunately not until some years after Roosevelt's death. *Hunting Wild Life with Camera and Flashlight*, a two-volume record of sixty-five years of observation and photography in the woods and waters of North America, is today a mute tribute, not only to the rare photographic skill of a talented American naturalist, but also to the friendly, persistent prodding of Theodore Roosevelt.

Roosevelt was directly responsible for another book, one by Frederick Courtenay Selous. During his years in Africa the celebrated big-game hunter had collected a sizable stack of notes on the behavior of African animals, but thinking them of little importance had consigned them to a study drawer. There they would have remained if, on Selous' visit to the White House in 1903, Roosevelt had not found out about them and insisted that Selous use them as the foundation for another book. "You have the most extraordinary power of seeing things with minute accuracy of detail, and then the equally necessary power to describe vividly and accurately what you have seen," he told Selous.

As Selous finished his chapters he sent them in installments to the President of the United States to criticize, the President having offered to do this. With a final batch, the author asked Roosevelt if he would write a foreword, which the President willingly did.

Selous brought out *African Nature Notes* early the next year (1908). He dedicated it to the President of the United States, "not only because it was entirely owing to his inspiration and kindly encouragement that it was ever written but also because both in private and public life he has always won the sincere admiration and esteem of the author."

Roosevelt was delighted with the book, and with the dedication. He wrote that he was "pleased as Punch." He liked, too, a line in the preface which said that the President's knowledge of animals was not limited to the big game of the United States or North America, but that he had an unbelievable familiarity with the fauna of the entire world, gained through a careful study of practically every book that had been devoted to the subject.

Roosevelt had great luck in inducing Selous, Shiras, and others to write about their work. In only one instance did he come a cropper—with C. Hart Merriam. As early as 1903, when Roosevelt and Burroughs were in Yellowstone, the President wrote:

John Burroughs and I agree that it is very lamentable that you will not produce a really big book . . . when one meets a genuine master in his profession—and such I think you—it is a loss to the world if he fails to put his discoveries in durable, in abiding, form. This is exactly what I fear will be the case with you. To publish quantities of little pamphlets is merely to take rank with the thousands of small and industrious German specialists. You have it in your power to write the great monumental work on the mammals of North America, *including their life histories.*

The months went by and Merriam continued to collect facts without making any attempt to generalize, apparently perfectly agreeable to the idea of taking rank with the thousands of small German specialists. Roosevelt, on the other hand, was still at his self-appointed task of trying to persuade Merriam that if the latter waited until he had exhausted the resources of trinomial nomenclature on every obscure shrew or field mouse from Florida to Oregon, he would postpone his great work until it was too late. The President was still at this task five years later, when he wrote: "Oh Heavens! how I wish I could make you really appreciate what I said the other day, and sit down in good faith and all solemnity and write the great formal natural history of the mammals of North America, life histories and all, which you alone can write."

But Merriam never wrote the great formal natural history of the mammals of North America. He may have been opposed in principle, as some scientists are, to any form of popularization; he may have been piqued at Roosevelt's constant hammering on the theme that pamphlets are inconsequential in themselves; or he may have been unable on his salary to get the needed clerical assistance.

The period of Roosevelt's residence in the White House was marked by a resurgence of vigorous and enthusiastic activity in the working places of many naturalists. Some of them liked to call it the golden era of America science. They had been made to feel "taller."

16

A Bird Lover in the White House

THE story of Theodore Roosevelt's companionship with birds during the years of his Presidency is without parallel—no other President, before or since, or the head of any other government for that matter, has ever taken such an interest in the avian folk of the world.

The White House grounds are, of course, spacious—like a small city park. They are liberally planted with shrubs and trees—redbud, dogwood and crabapple, maple and magnolia—and with a wide variety of colorful annuals and perennials, all of which attract birds. At any time of the year, but particularly in late April or early May, Roosevelt liked to stroll through the White House grounds, to glimpse the crimson of cardinal or tanager or to catch the clear, bold song of thrush or wren. His favorite hour was the one just after breakfast, before the morning chorus had subsided. Often, after returning to his office, he would dictate a letter to one or another of his children, who were away at school, telling them what he had seen or heard. One day late in March he wrote Kermit: "The birds have come back, not only song sparrows and robins, but a winter wren, purple finches and tufted titmice are singing in the gardens; and the other morning early Mother and I were waked up by the

148

loud singing of a cardinal in the magnolia tree just outside our window."

On other days he wrote the children about the "creaking, gurgling blackbirds," the crows "cawing in their queer spring voices," the warbling vireos that had built a nest in the linden, the cardinal which "glowed like a live coal" among the white blossoms of the catalpa, the Carolina wren that sang such a merry roundelay, the handsome sapsucker that had spent a week with them, and the warblers that were trooping to the north in full force. There was hardly a letter that did not contain some nature comment, if not about birds, then about fall colors or spring flowers. "I think I get more fond of flowers every year," he said in one letter.

Roosevelt found time while President to write magazine articles about the White House birds. In one he wrote of the warblers that crowded the trees at the height of the spring migration:

. . . myrtle, magnolia, chestnut-sided, bay-breasted, blackburnian, black-throated blue, Canadian, and many others, with at the very end of the season the blackpolls; exquisite little birds, but not conspicuous as a rule, except perhaps the blackburnian, whose brilliant orange throat and breast flame when they catch the sunlight as he flits among the trees.[1]

In this same article Roosevelt said that he had never before seen purple finches in such numbers in the White House grounds as during the previous spring. When he sat by the south fountain under an apple tree, then in full bloom, sometimes as many as three or four would be singing in the fragrant bloom overhead.

One day Roosevelt saw his first Cape May warbler. He wrote Burroughs that he had spotted it in a pine, where he was able to get a good look at it with his field glasses. "It was a male in the brilliant spring plumage; and the orange-brown cheeks, the brilliant yellow sides of the neck just behind the cheeks, and the brilliant underparts with thick black streaks on the breast made the bird unmistakable."

He was not so lucky in identifying other warblers. He told Burroughs that he had been trying with only moderate success to obey Emerson's injunction to name the birds without a gun. Even with the best binoculars, he found it extremely difficult to establish the identity of those warblers that insisted on sticking to the tree tops. He was often disgusted, he said, when, after listening for a full half hour to a fine, wiry little song, and catching only glimpses of a small, agile bird fluttering behind a spray of leaves, the elusive, little musician would fly away without his having the slightest idea what it was. And he could not tell the dull-colored females apart at all, he added.

Roosevelt's exciting discovery of the Cape May warbler was soon followed by another. One hot June night, while roaming the grounds for a breath of air, he found two owls: "little bits of fellows, with round heads, and no head tufts, or 'ears.'" [2] He immediately put in a call for Edward B. Clark, who on his arrival, found the President out on the White House lawn gazing fixedly at the owls, perched obligingly a few feet above his head on top of the porch pillars.

"What are they?" Roosevelt demanded.

"Saw-whet owls," Clark replied.

"I know it," he said, "but I wanted an ornithologist to corroborate my identification so that the bird sharps of the Biological Survey won't elect me to the Ananias Club when I report to them." [3]

Roosevelt, as a part of his program to keep fit, made innumerable walks from the White House to the less frequented places in and around Washington, to Rock Creek Park, for instance, or some promontory along the Potomac above or below Chain Bridge. In this way he discovered bogs, briar patches, or second growth where, at the right season, he could count on finding particular species of birds. There was a brush-grown, swampy plot of ground along the north bank of the Potomac, for instance, where, in the spring, he always found the ground-loving Kentucky warblers and the largest of all the warblers, the yellow-breasted chats. And in Rock Creek Park there was another locality invariably inhabited by the little blue-gray gnatcatchers.

Early one spring John Burroughs visited at the White House. He had lunch with the family and afterwards went with Roose velt on a walk through Rock Creek Park. "We saw no birds," Burroughs said, "they could not keep up with us. I haven't walked at such a pace in years." [4]

Roosevelt's young niece, Corinne, (named for her mother), attended the same luncheon. Roosevelt thoughtfully placed her next to Burroughs. As soon as all were seated the President, according to Corinne, turned to Burroughs and said: "John, this morning I heard a chippy sparrow and he sang 'twee, twee,' right in my ear." Burroughs came back: "Mr. President, you must be mistaken. It was not a chippy sparrow if it sang, 'twoo, twee.' The note of the chippy sparrow is 'twee, twee, twee.'" [5]

From that moment, if Corinne is to be believed, the President of the United States and the celebrated naturalist ignored all others at the luncheon, as they launched into an argument, loud and prolonged, as to whether the chipping sparrow's song consisted of two notes, "twee, twee," or of three, "twee, twee, twee."

Near the end of his second term as President, Roosevelt made a list for Mrs. L. W. Maynard, of the birds that he had seen in and around Washington. Mrs. Maynard later included this list in her Birds of Washington and Vicinity. It contained the names of 93 birds, 57 of which Roosevelt had identified on the White House grounds. Nine of the 57, red-headed woodpeckers, flickers, orchard orioles, purple grackles, redstarts, catbirds, tufted titmice, wood thrushes, and robins, he had found nesting there.

This list was incomplete, Roosevelt said. He had seen others he had forgotten.

Roosevelt was rarely so busy that he could not find time for the birds. More than once, while in the middle of an important conversation with a distinguished public figure, he would jump from his chair and run to the window, at the same time motioning to his caller to follow him. In a tree, just outside his window, a bird would be singing. Roosevelt would move excitedly from one side of the window to the other, seeking a glimpse of the tiny, feathered songster, and then point to a branch near the top of the tree.

II

In order to have a secluded retreat, not far from Washington, where he could go for a few days at a time and have the birds around him, Roosevelt built a country home south of Charlottesville in Albemarle County, Virginia. It was an unpretentious, four-room frame structure, which cost him less than five hundred dollars. He called it Pine Knot.

From time to time, after a particularly strenuous week in Washington, the President with Mrs. Roosevelt and an occasional guest or two, would hurry to Pine Knot. Here, on May 18, 1907 (at almost exactly the time his nature faker article appeared in *Everybody's*), Roosevelt made a discovery as exciting to him as the shooting of his first grizzly. He immediately wrote two letters. In one, to Burroughs, he said: "I have just been in Albemarle County, Virginia, where there were a great many birds, and where to my utter astonishment, I saw a small party of wild pigeons, the first I have seen in twenty-five years."

In the other, to Hart Merriam (May 23, 1907), he wrote more fully:

On May 18th near Keene, Albemarle County, Virginia, I saw a flock of a dozen passenger pigeons. I have not seen any for twenty-five years and never dreamed I should see any again; but I could not have been mistaken (tho I did not kill any for I did not have a gun, and in any event nothing could have persuaded me to shoot them). I saw them flying to and fro a couple of times and then they all lit in a tall dead pine by an old field. There were doves in the field for me to compare them with, and I do not see how I could have been mistaken.

For some time now ornithologists had considered the passenger pigeon extinct in the wild. It is not at all surprising, therefore, that both Merriam and Burroughs doubted the validity of Roosevelt's observation. After receiving Burroughs' opinion, Roosevelt replied as follows:

Your letter makes me a little doubtful whether I ought to speak about having seen those pigeons without some corroborative evidence. I do not think it possible I could have been mistaken, not only because there was a flock of about a dozen of them and because I saw them two or three times on the wing, but because they lit on the dead tree in such a characteristically pigeon-like attitude. The only other birds they could possibly have been were doves, but they were larger and there were plenty of doves in the neighborhood which I continually saw, and the pigeons were in a flock. I shall write down and see if I can get any information as to anyone else having seen them.

This was fast becoming an increasingly important matter to Roosevelt. On the same day, May 27, he addressed himself to a Mr. Joseph Wilmer, Rapidan, Virginia. On his latest visit to Pine Knot, he said, he had talked briefly with Dick, his [Mr. Wilmer's] colored foreman, who had told him about seeing a flock of what he called "carrier pigeons." He then made this request:

Would you mind asking him just where he saw them; whether they were flying or lit; if they were in a flock, and if so, how many of them? Ask him to describe their appearance—whether they had pointed tails, and in other words whether they lookt [sic] like large doves, and if not, what they did look like. What made him think they were wild pigeons? Had he ever seen any before or heard of them? I have some ornithological friends who are very much interested in this matter.

While waiting for a reply, his mind reverting constantly to passenger pigeons, Roosevelt got off another note to Burroughs:

I have written down to see if I can get information about those passenger pigeons. It doesn't seem to me possible that I was mistaken. Nevertheless, I have had one or two curious experiences of the fallibility of human vision (once a cowpuncher and I firmly believed we had discovered a village of *black* prairie dogs, thanks purely to the peculiar angle at which the sunlight struck them) and just at the moment I don't want to get into any kind of controversy as to a personal observation of mine on natural history.

What Roosevelt probably meant was that he did not want to become involved just then in *another* controversy, since at this moment he had his hands full with the nature fakers.

One week later, Roosevelt heard from Mr. Wilmer and immediately reported to Burroughs:

I have corroborative evidence about the wild pigeons. My close friend, Mr. Joseph Wilmer, whose farm, Plain Dealing, is a mile from Pine Knot, our little house, writes me as follows:

"On May 12th last Dick saw a flock of about 30, followed at a short distance by about half as many, flying in a circle very rapidly between the Plain Dealing house and the woods, where they disappeared. They had pointed tails and resembled somewhat large doves—the breasts and sides rather a brownish red. He had seen them before, but many years ago. I think it is unquestionably the 'Passenger Pigeon'—Ectopistes migratoria—described on page 25 of the 5th volume of Audubon. I remember these pigeon roosts, as he describes them, on a smaller scale, but large flocks have not been seen in this part of Virginia for many years."

The Dick to whom he refers is his colored foreman, the man whom I have shot turkeys with and whom I have rambled around with in the woods a great deal. He knows nothing of birds from books but he is a singularly close observer. I found that whatever he told me about birds I could count upon absolutely, and he is much interested in them. It seems to me that with this bit of corroborative evidence I can be very sure I was not mistaken—indeed I can hardly see how it would be possible for me to be mistaken.

That settled the matter for the President. He was so far convinced that he included his discovery in an article which appeared in *Scribner's Magazine* that fall. But Burroughs, Merriam, and other naturalists had good reasons for thinking that he had been wrong. For one thing, there was no unquestioned record of a passenger pigeon having been seen in the wild since 1898, nine years before Roosevelt had made his observation. For that year there were five accepted records: one each for Kentucky, Michigan, Pennsylvania, New York, and Manitoba.

On the other hand, reliable observers had made claims of seeing passenger pigeons here and there since 1898, but for one reason or another their claims had not been accepted. Roosevelt now joined this group. Whether he actually saw them or not no one can say positively. Ornithologists at the American Museum of Natural History, however, are inclined to think that he did. As they point out, he knew the bird well from his earlier years and his statement that mourning doves were present for comparison would seem to take the observation out of the realm of the dubious.[6] If so, a President of the United States may have been the last to see passenger pigeons in the wild.

Pine Knot was an inspiration to Roosevelt, both botanically and ornithologically. His visits there developed in him a greater love of trees and flowers, as well as of birds. He enjoyed more than ever before in his life the stately charm of the clean-boled tulip trees, which grew larger here than on Long Island, the frothy, greenish-yellow blossoming of the chestnuts, and the lively beauty of flowering redbud, dogwood, laurel, and azalea. He had never been quite so enthusiastic about wake robins, moccasin flowers, the demure little Quaker ladies, the china-blue Virginia cowslips, the blood-red Indian pink, and the painted columbine, all of which brightened the forest floor at Pine Knot.

The birds were, of course, much the same as on Long Island, but with some interesting differences. For instance, he found chipping, vesper, field and grasshopper sparrows common enough, but song sparrows rare, and there were no Savannah sparrows at all. Moreover, indigo buntings and bluebirds, which he had seen at Sagamore Hill only during the migrating seasons, were breeding here in numbers, were exceedingly common. He could not understand why they did not nest at Oyster Bay. Wood thrushes were rarely seen or heard, but meadowlarks abounded, the reverse being true on Long Island. He could account for some of these differences, but not all.[7]

The Virginia birds were a musical lot. "The clucking, whistling, whooping and calling" of the yellow-breasted chats seemed never to stop for a minute. The white-eyed vireos, which occupied the same thick undergrowth as the chat, sang their emphatic, voluble notes all the day long, and the mockingbirds, whose song invariably sent Roosevelt into raptures, gave daily demonstrations of their imitative genius. In spring and summer Roosevelt often breakfasted on his Pine Knot porch, where he could enjoy to the utmost the music of the cardinals, Carolina wrens, mocking birds, and other common choristers; and at night he often walked out to the small clearing about the place to listen to the familiar notes of the whippoorwills, the eerie, tremulous whistles of the screech owls, and the hoots and screams of bigger owls.

Roosevelt thought that he should share Pine Knot with other naturalists. The spring before he left the White House, he invited Burroughs down to join him on his Virginia rambles. "We would show you many birds, some of them new; and we *might* see passenger pigeons," he wrote, by way of inducement. Burroughs immediately accepted the invitation.

Although it was late afternoon when the two naturalists reached Pine Knot, Roosevelt thought they should do some birding. They started out, with the President in the lead, setting a brisk pace that took them rapidly along country lanes and through fields and hardwood forests. At the end of a mile or more they stopped, wiped the sweat from their faces, and then returned at the same rapid pace. That evening Roosevelt said to Burroughs: "Oom John, that was no way to go after birds; we were in too much of a hurry." When Burroughs quickly agreed, Roosevelt said that they would have to moderate their pace the next time.

The following morning they drove leisurely along some of the Virginia roads, stopping from time to time to make side excursions into the woods on foot. One of the first songs they heard was new to Burroughs. Roosevelt told him it was the song of the Bewick's wren. Burroughs then wanted to know if he had found here the little, blue-gray gnatcatcher, a bird he had not seen or heard for thirty years. Roosevelt replied that the last time he had seen one was in a patch of woods only a short distance away. They walked to the place and almost at once, as a thin wisp of song, exquisitely modulated, drifted down from the overhead foliage, Roosevelt cried out, "There it is now!" It was as though the gnatcatcher had been anticipating their visit, and was giving vent to its joy by bursting into full song.[8]

Later in the course of their walk Roosevelt showed Burroughs where he had seen what he took to be passenger pigeons. He pointed out to him the tree in which they had lit and described what they looked like and how they flew. Burroughs remained unconvinced.

Still later, in an open field, they encountered a flock of birds that Burroughs could not name. Roosevelt was puzzled, too, at first, but as he got closer and had a better look at them, he recognized them as female blue grosbeaks. This was one of the birds he had most wanted to show Burroughs.

In their cross-country rambles, the two naturalists recognized many late spring flowers: Indian pinks, moccasin flowers and the beautiful blue and white bird's-foot violets. "Roosevelt seemed to know the flowers as well as the birds," Burroughs said.[9]

Before the end of Burroughs' stay at Pine Knot, he and Roosevelt had identified more than 75 species of birds. Burroughs knew all but two, and Roosevelt all but two. "He taught me Bewick's wren and the prairie warbler," Burroughs said, "and I taught him the swamp sparrow and one of the rarer warblers; I think it was a pine warbler. If he had found the Lincoln sparrow he would have been ahead of me." [10]

Apparently there had been some doubt in Roosevelt's mind about his identification of the blue grosbeak, enough to cause him to write Chapman. On June 7, 1908, he replied to a letter:

. . . As regards the blue grosbeak, your description of the habits was exactly borne out by the conduct of the individuals we saw. They did not behave at all like indigo buntings or rosebreasted grosbeaks, but stayed by preference along the bushy sides of a ditch in the middle of an open pasture, frequently going out into the open grass. Both males and females would sit solemnly on the tops of some thick stalk or small twig a couple of feet high beside the ditch. The Bewick's wrens were very tame and confiding. To our ears not only their song but their subdued conversational chirping had a marked ventriloquial effect, seeming to be much farther away than it was. It had no resemblance to the song of the house wren, and none whatever to that of the Carolina wren.

I do not understand the principles upon which the sparrows are generically divided. The swamp sparrow seems to me in color scheme and even in voice to be more like a spitzella than a zonotrichia.

When Burroughs left for home Roosevelt gave him a complete list of the birds they had found at Pine Knot, with the suggestion that he write an account of their walks together through woods and fields. For years afterwards, whenever Roosevelt met Burroughs he would ask about this piece. At one time he prodded him by mail:

I do hope that you will include in your coming volume of sketches a little account of the time you visited us at Pine Knot, our little Virginia camp, while I was President. I am very proud of you, Oom John, and I want the fact that you were my guest when I was President, and that you and I looked at birds together, recorded there—and don't forget that I showed you the blue grosbeak and the Bewick's wren, and almost all the other birds I said I would.

Many years went by before Burroughs got around to writing about the Pine Knot experiences. By that time it was too late for

Roosevelt to read them. But he did not forget to record that Roosevelt had shown him the Bewick's wren and the blue grosbeaks.

III

The President spent parts of each summer at Oyster Bay, where the birds were as familiar to him as the landmarks along the beaches which front the Sound. Sagamore Hill, surrounded by wide open fields and stretches of woodland, was a natural bird refuge. Sooner or later the Long Island birds visited there, many to settle down and raise their families. Roosevelt knew what birds nested on his place and where they nested: the Baltimore oriole in the elm near the porch corner; towhees and Maryland yellowthroats in the hedges bordering the garden; robins over the transom of the north hall door; song sparrows, catbirds, and kingbirds in the lawn shrubbery; grasshopper sparrows in the meadow beyond the garden; barn swallows in the stable; flickers in the orchard; and prairie warblers in the cedar-grown field beyond.

He knew, too, which birds returned year after year to the same location, which ones were more abundant than the year before, and which were not so common as in his youth. He gave proof of this during the summer of 1904 in a letter to the ornithologist, Edward Howe Forbush:

Around my home here on Long Island, and also in Washington, I have been unable to see any differences in the number of birds. Around my house, for instance, the robins, wood thrushes, catbirds, meadow larks, song sparrows, chipping sparrows, grasshopper finches and Baltimore orioles are as plentiful as ever. So with the barn swallows at the stable. I never saw bluebirds more common than this year at Washington. Here at Oyster Bay my observations have gone over some thirty-one years. During that time I do not believe there has been any diminution in the number of birds as a whole. Quail and woodcock are not as plentiful as they were. I am inclined to think that last winter may have been hard on the quail round about here.

But on the other hand there are one or two other wild birds that I think have increased in numbers. The great mass of the species, I should say, are just about as numerous as they were.

Roosevelt furnished other examples of how well he kept track of the birds over the years. For instance, when he returned to Oyster Bay for the summer of 1906, he found purple finches nesting there, two pairs of them. He had never known them to make their homes there before. One pair had built right by the house and the other by the stable. His attention was drawn to them by "the bold, cheerful singing of the males, who were spurred to rivalry by one another's voices." [11]

Later the same year, while sitting on his porch in his favorite rocking chair, he heard the familiar "ank-ank" of nuthatches coming down from a young elm at the corner of the house. He walked out onto the lawn, expecting to find white-bellied nuthatches, which had always been fairly common at Sagamore Hill. Instead, however, he found that the "ank-anks" had been made by a pair of red-bellied nuthatches, birds that he had known well in the Adirondacks and Aroostook County, Maine, but which he had never seen before in all his years at Oyster Bay. They showed no fear of him, running up and down the trunk, and scrambling around the limbs, even though he stood only ten feet away. He called Archie and Quentin out to see them, and then they all went inside to look up their pictures in Wilson.[12] (Roosevelt thought that Wilson's and Audubon's were still the most satisfactory large ornithologies for the amateur bird student.)

During the following summer (1907), Roosevelt noted that only one of the two pairs of purple finches returned, and that the Baltimore orioles, for the first time in many years, failed to hang their nests in the elm by the house; they began one, but for some reason did not finish it. The red-winged blackbirds, however, were more plentiful than they had been for several years, two pairs nesting in the tall grass near the old barn. This was the first time, he said, that they had nested nearer than the wood-pile pond. He thought it might have been due to the season being so wet and cold.

Perhaps the season had something to do with the black-throated green warblers being present that summer. Roosevelt was sure that they had been nesting in the neighborhood, although he had seen only males and found no nests. Each male inhabited a particular area of woodland, flitting about in the tops of the tallest trees. Throughout June they sang all day long "a drawling, cadenced little warble of five or six notes, usually uttered at intervals of a few seconds." [13] When Roosevelt learned that other Long Island ornithologists had been seeing black-throated green warblers, he concluded that they had extended their range southward, had become regular summer residents. He wrote Chapman to find out if he were right:

This June [he wrote] there have been some black-throated green warblers out on my place here. I have only seen males, but I am sorry to say that I either have to be very familiar with a bird or else it has to possess very marked and striking characteristics or else I am apt to fail to recognize it, and therefore the females may be here also. I am inclined to think that they are, for each male has its own little locality and stays there day after day. Do you know if they breed in the neighborhood of New York City or on Long Island?

I wish it were possible for you to come down here for a day. I should much like to walk about this place and have a really big ornithologist tell me what some of the bird songs are.

Whether Chapman visited him at this time or not we do not know, but Burroughs did. He and the President spent an entire day rambling through the meadow where Roosevelt had been cutting hay, and the grove where he had found the black-throated greens. The warblers were still singing their cadenced little tunes. In the meadow they found grasshopper sparrows and in the orchard purple finches, orchard orioles, and many other birds. Roosevelt was able to show him most of the birds that he had wanted him to see.

Not long afterwards, the President made another discovery, this one indicating that a southern species of warbler was extending its range northward. A bird-loving neighbor told him that she had found a Dominican or yellow-throated warbler inhabiting the trees near her home, that both she and her husband had seen it several times. Roosevelt, knowing that this warbler rarely came farther north than Virginia, was inclined to think that they had mistaken it for a Maryland yellow-throat. A few days later his neighbor sent word that she had been hearing the warbler again, and asked if he would not like to come over. Only a few minutes after he arrived, they both heard a "loud, ringing, sharply accented" song which Roosevelt had never heard before. The singer kept to the tops of some tall pines, but soon it came down to the lower branches where they could see it distinctly. Roosevelt needed only a glance to convince him. He could see distinctly the characteristic olive-gray back, yellow throat and breast, and the white line above the eye. There was no doubt about it; it was a yellow-throated warbler, and not a Maryland yellowthroat.[14]

Thinking that his identification might be disputed (perhaps having the passenger pigeon incident in mind), he shot the warbler and sent it to the bird men in the American Museum. He shortly wrote Burroughs about it:

Three days ago I shot a yellow-throated or Dominican warbler here —the first I had ever seen. I was able to identify it with absolute certainty, but as the record might be deemed of importance I reluctantly shot the bird, a male, and gave the mutilated skin to the American Museum of Natural History people so that they might be sure of the identification. The breeding season was past, and no damage came to the species from shooting the specimen; but I must say I care less and less for the pure "collecting" as I grow older.

While looking at Fuertes' drawing of the Dominican warbler in Chapman's warbler book, Roosevelt thought he detected an error. He believed that the famous bird illustrator had made the bill too short. Some time later he told Frank Chapman about it. Chapman investigated. The bill *was* too short—by about half a millimeter! [15]

The years of a President are soon passed and gone. Before Roosevelt knew it, he was at Oyster Bay for the last summer he would spend there while still President of the United States. But he was content; he was back home with his birds. What could be more natural than that he should write Burroughs about them:

Here all the birds were back just as they had been last summer. The black-throated green was not in the grove where I showed him to you, but either he or another was in a grove some three or four hundred yards off, and there have been several of his kind around the place. The purple finches have nested near the house, and the Baltimore oriole in the same drooping elm that I showed you. They skipped nesting there last year. The orchard orioles, cuckoos, and the grasshopper sparrows, and all the others are here as usual, but I haven't seen anything new this summer, excepting at this very time a song sparrow is preparing to rear a second brood and is getting some of the material (of all things!) by plucking out loose bristles from the door mat of our door.

17

"For the People Unborn"

THE story is told of a Congressman who, when pressed to aid in the conservation of his country's natural resources for posterity's sake, retorted, "What has posterity ever done for me?"

This was the prevailing attitude of the public toward conservation prior to the twentieth century. Ever since John Smith felled the first trees at Jamestown in 1607, America's steadily increasing population had considered its water, soil, forests, game, and minerals as inexhaustible; each generation thought only in terms of the present, never of the future; public welfare yielded to private interests. Not until 1873, when the Association for the Advancement of Science petitioned Congress to enact legislation, was there any concerted action to preserve our natural resources. And it was not until 1891, after the Association had repeated its petition, that the federal government finally took its first steps: establishing a Bureau of Forestry and giving the President of the United States authority to set aside forest reserves from public timberlands.

When Theodore Roosevelt took office as President in 1901, our natural resources had been shamefully, irreparably depleted. Roughly one half of all the timber in the United States had been cut, an unestimable amount of precious topsoil had been washed away, minerals had been wasted at a shocking rate, and many birds and mammals approached extinction.

In the light of these facts, the United States should be forever grateful that at this time a man came to the White House who, by instinct and training, was a conservationist. No other President, before or since, has been so well prepared for the task of inaugurating and implementing a national conservation program. His preparation, covering some thirty years, had begun in the woods and fields of Long Island and along Maine and Adirondack wilderness trails. It had been continued in the Bad Lands of the Dakotas, in the forests of the Rockies, in the meeting places of the Boone and Crockett Club, and in the Governor's office at Albany.

Roosevelt's active life in the out-of-doors had made him thoroughly alive to the value of timberland, and its vital relation to soil and water conservation. His years in the West had given him abundant opportunity to observe first hand the rapid destruction of buffalo and antelope and other game animals and, in the more arid regions, the crying need for reclamation of land through irrigation and reforestation. His association with the Boone and Crockett Club had brought him into close contact with men who, like himself, were becoming more and more concerned over the waste of our national heritage. And his years as Governor of New York had taught him the ropes which had to be rigged before laws could be passed. Without this background Roosevelt's accomplishments in conservation could not have been so far-reaching, nor so certain of success.

He possessed other qualifications for the job, too: his intense Americanism, sincerity of purpose, effectiveness as a public speaker, popularity with the people, and skillful use of the pen.

Theodore Roosevelt was only one of many who understood the necessity of conservation. He gave full credit to such men as Major John Wesley Powell, founder of the Geological Survey; Senator Francis G. Newlands, sponsor of the Reclamation Act of 1902; Frederick H. Newell, founder of the United States Reclamation Service; and Gifford Pinchot, founder of the Forest Service. Pinchot, of course, was to become Roosevelt's right-hand man—young, aggressive, he was deeply concerned about the rate at which the United States was depleting its soil, water, trees and minerals, and conscious of what all this meant to the problem of national welfare and efficiency.

The President, therefore, was not alone in formulating the conservation program. Perhaps most of the ideas did originate in the minds of Pinchot, Newell, and others. But, as one historian has well said, "Originality in a statesman is rarely the discovery of an idea, but the power to secure its application. The public man has to persuade the vast and indifferent aggregates who compose a modern democracy to adopt the opinions of a few till they believe these to be the expression of their own wishes." [1] Only after Theodore Roosevelt got behind the conservation program, did it receive the vigor and publicity it needed. More than any other man, he was responsible for awakening in the American people the desire to make effective and continuing use of existing natural resources for the benefit of both present and future generations.

Roosevelt's program, broadly speaking, was three-fold: (1) reclaiming of land through irrigation, (2) preservation of forests through use, and (3) protection of wildlife. Minerals received comparatively little attention, soil practically none. Their big innings came considerably later.

II

The President tackled reclamation first. Even before he had moved his family and belongings into the White House, he met with Pinchot and Newell to discuss plans whereby the national government would assume a more active role in the irrigation of Western arid regions. In his first message to Congress, on December 3, 1901, he said: "The western half of the United States would sustain a population greater than that of our whole country today if the waters that now run to waste were saved and used for irrigation. Great storage works are necessary to equalize the flow of streams and to save the flood waters. Their construction has been conclusively shown to be an undertaking too vast for private enterprise." [2]

The artificial watering of farm lands in the United States had had its inception centuries ago among the cliff-dwelling Indians (ancient canals may still be found in the Southwest) and was continued by the early Spanish missionaries. The earliest Anglo-Saxon attempts to irrigate were made by the Mormons, in Salt Lake valley in 1847 and, somewhat later, by the Union Colony (an early experiment in socialism) at Greeley, Colorado. Of course these attempts were on a small scale so that, as late as 1870, no more than 20,000 acres had been irrigated in all of the United States. [3]

When Roosevelt took office in 1901, not much more of the irrigable West had received water than in 1870. This was due in large measure to the fact, as Roosevelt had said, that many highly-needed undertakings were too big for private enterprise. The construction of huge reservoirs, for instance, demanded federal aid.

On the day Roosevelt sent his message to Congress, a group of Western Senators and Representatives, headed by Newlands, were all set to draft a bill in line with Roosevelt's recommendations. Due to the vigor with which Roosevelt pushed this bill, it became law on June 17, 1902. This measure (the Reclamation Act) made it possible to reclaim arid public lands for agricultural purposes, with water from federally constructed projects. The settlers paid a fee to the government for the water supplied them, thus creating a revolving fund continuously available for the work.

Within twenty-four hours after Roosevelt signed the bill, the Secretary of the Interior began putting it to work. Red tape was slashed without mercy, and the whole program expedited in a manner heretofore unknown in Washington. By 1904 sixteen reclamation projects were under way in as many Western states, and by 1908 the number had increased to thirty, involving the irrigation of over 3,000,000 acres of land. Some of these projects were of tremendous magnitude. For instance, there was the engineering feat of leading the waters of Colorado's Gunnison River to the Uncompahgre Valley, requiring a tunnel ten feet high, ten feet wide, and five miles long, through the intervening mountain. Then there was the Roosevelt Dam, 260 feet high, impounding the waters of Arizona's Salt River. When this was completed it had created one of the largest artificial bodies of water in the world. It now irrigates close to a million acres of land, given over mostly to the growing of alfalfa, sugar beets, and semi-tropical fruits. When Roosevelt dedicated this dam in 1911, "he was looking upon what was largely a product of his idealism." [4]

When Roosevelt left office in 1909, the reclaiming of waste lands was a complete success and the government enthusiastically behind it. Thousands upon thousands of acres, once arid, sterile land, were abundantly green with vegetation, as water with the aid of sunlight gave them life, while numerous small towns, peopled with enthusiastic home owners, had sprung into being. The Roosevelt-Pinchot-Newell vision, of millions of desert acres in bloom, was well on its way to reality.

III

The great hardwood and softwood forests which originally covered much of the United States had no equal in any other country in the world. They overlay an estimated billion acres, roughly one half of the entire land surface. They were particularly valuable because of the large stands of pine, spruce, fir, and other conifer which have always been much in demand for building purposes. By the end of the twentieth century approximately half of this magnificent original heritage was gone, with four-fifths of what survived in private hands. No longer ago than the close of the Civil War—to illustrate how rapidly the federal government was disposing of the public domain—only one fourth of the standing timber had been privately owned.

The only significant move that Congress had made toward protecting the forests, before Roosevelt came to office, was the passage, in 1891, of the Forest Reserve Act giving the President authority to set aside forest reserves from the public domain. By virtue of this power, Presidents Harrison, Cleveland, and McKinley had established reserves totaling almost 50,000,000 acres. Although this was a promising beginning (insuring that these timberlands would be safe from exploitation), it was only a beginning, for the United States continued to cut its forest trees far more rapidly than it planted them. Conditions had not changed much since pioneer days when, as Roosevelt said, "the American had but one thought about a tree, and that was to cut it down." [5]

One of Theodore Roosevelt's first moves was to strengthen the existing federal agencies devoted to forest study and control, of which there were two. The Bureau of Forestry, under Pinchot, contained all the trained foresters in the government service, but had nothing to do with supervision of public timberlands. The bureau administering these timberlands, a division of the General Land Office, had no trained foresters; a few of its personnel, consisting mainly of clerks, had never even seen a forest reserve. In his first message to Congress, Roosevelt urged the consolidation of the forest work in the hands of the trained men of the Bureau of Forestry.

Pending consolidation of these two agencies into the United States Forest Service (not effected till three years later), the Bureau of Forestry, with Roosevelt's vigorous support, accelerated its program. Among other things, it enlarged its corps of foresters; it began laying plans for forest reserves in the East (hitherto entirely in the West); it made a careful study of the Western timberlands to determine their condition and needs, thereby laying the groundwork for future expansion; it began experimental planting on the preserves; and it examined public lands for new reserves.

Of even more importance was the Bureau's program of education. In this they were aided tremendously by the newspapers, who gave space without cost to every page of copy supplied them. At the close of Roosevelt's second term, information about the forests appeared monthly in some fifty million copies of newspapers. As new and significant forest facts were collected, the Bureau printed additional bulletins. In 1907, for instance, 61 bulletins were issued, totaling over a million copies, as opposed to 3 bulletins in 1901, totaling some eighty thousand copies. In these and other ways the people were informed, as never before, of the needs and purposes of practical forestry. "Without this publicity," according to Roosevelt, "the Forest Service could not have survived the attacks made upon it by the representatives of the great special interests in Congress; nor could forestry in America have made the rapid progress that it has." [6]

Roosevelt knew from the beginning that the fate of the forests —and other natural resources—depended upon intelligent education of the people. Most Americans knew little or nothing about the rate at which the trees were being destroyed, and what this meant to future generations. What Roosevelt himself did to bring this message into the homes of farmers and merchants, factory workers and professional men, was as important as anything else he did while President.

Over and over again he said, "Every lover of nature, every man who appreciates the majesty and beauty of the wilderness, should strike hands with the far-sighted men who wish to preserve our forests." [7]

In an address to the Society of American Foresters (March 1903), he told them that they must play a major role in educating the people, in convincing them that the future success of the home makers depended upon the wisdom with which the nation took care of its forests.[8]

To the people of Sacramento, after his visit to Yosemite with John Muir, he said:

Lying out at night under those giant Sequoias was like lying in a temple built by no hand of man, a temple grander than any human architect could by any possibility build, and I hope for the preservation of the groves of giant trees simply because it would be a shame to our civilization to let them disappear. They are monuments in themselves . . . in California I am impressed by how great your state is, but I am even more impressed by the immensely greater greatness that lies in the future, and I ask that your marvelous natural resources be handed on unimpaired to your posterity. We are not building this country of ours for a day. It is to last through the ages.[9]

If Roosevelt hammered home one thought more than any other—and how important that is all too many Americans fail to realize even today—it was that the forests are not alone for the current generation. The expression, "For the people," he emphasized, "must always include the people unborn as well as the people now alive, or the democratic ideal is not realized."[10]

The President continually emphasized, too, the importance of the forests in conserving soil and water, that the cutting of timber meant erosion and floods. He gave space to it in all his messages to Congress. In his 1908 message—unique in that it was illustrated—he treated his audience to a lecture on the havoc wrought by deforestation in Asia. In this he stressed a report recently brought back from the Wu Tain Shan Mountains of North China containing proof of the damage to denuded mountain country. To open the eyes of Congressmen more widely to this devastation, he attached to his message enlarged photographs showing barren mountainsides, sand-covered plains, and other treeless expanses where, in the days of Marco Polo, had flourished one of the most productive and heavily forested regions in all Asia. They showed bottom lands devoid of the mulberry trees that once had been centers of the silkworm industry; they showed hillsides, once fertile and abundantly cultivated, now barren and cut by erosive forces into innumerable sterile gullies; they showed rivers, at one time deep and wide, now shallow currents between shrunken banks.

In concluding his illustrated lecture, Roosevelt said: "The lesson of deforestation in China is a lesson which mankind should have learned many times already from what has occurred in other places. Denudation leaves naked soil, then gullying cuts down to bare rock; and meanwhile the rock waste buries the bottom lands. When the soil is gone, men must go; and the process does not take long." [11] Were these words prophetic? Who in the United States does not know of what has already taken place in our midwestern Dust Bowl?

Roosevelt's use of photographs to point up his message impressed David Fairchild, then one of the younger members of the Bureau of Plant Industry. "I have always felt that this incident," he said, "showed an alertness in matters of a biological character which it would be hard to duplicate in the careers of other Presidents. He was a great biologist and those of us who were believers in the world as a biological one, not one of merely men and women, were keenly affected." [12]

But Roosevelt was doing much more than talking about forests. While the Forest Service was being rounded into a highly efficient organization, and the people were being taught their obligations to conserve their trees and other natural resources, he was taking advantage of the authority given to the President by Congress in 1891 to set aside forest reserves. During the seven years of his administration he added almost 150 million acres of timberland to the reserves, thereby more than trebling the acreage set aside by all preceding Presidents. This acreage equaled in area all the states touching the Atlantic from Maine to Virginia, with the addition of Vermont, Pennsylvania, and West Virginia, and was greater than that of France, Belgium, and the Netherlands combined. Those familiar with the roles Roosevelt had played as President of the Boone and Crockett Club, and Governor of New York, saw nothing surprising in this action; they expected nothing else.

Roosevelt added a large slice of this territory in 1907, after a group of Senators, representatives of the great special interests, had made a clever move to block further reserves in the Northwest. This group tacked an amendment onto an Agricultural Appropriations Bill, an amendment forbidding the President to exercise his authority in the states involved. They did this knowing full well that Roosevelt could not afford to veto the entire bill because that would hamstring not only the work of the Agriculture Department but also the Forest Service, too.

What Roosevelt did to evade the rider is today a tale told in almost every textbook of American history. Knowing that Pinchot had made a careful study of the Western forests that should be set aside as reserves, he was in a position to act immediately. He ordered Pinchot to give him a plan for incorporating these forests into the National Forests system, this to be in his hands before the deadline for his signature on the Agricultural Appropriations Bill. Without any hesitation, and with a clear conscience, he approved the plan and signed the necessary papers, beating the deadline by two days. It was a *tour de force* of which he was justly proud, for when the Senators woke up to what had happened, they discovered that sixteen more million acres of timberland had gained sanctuary, out of reach of land grabbers.

The nationalization of these forests had been accomplished in the face of bitter opposition. The term Forest Reserve (later happily changed to National Forest) was unfortunate, many people interpreting it to mean that timber could not be cut and game could not be killed; that the Reserves, like National Parks, were to be kept virgin as mighty playgrounds for the people. The friends of special interest, knowing well that this was not the case, took every advantage of the misinterpretation. It took time to educate the people to the fact that the National Forests were for the public benefit, that every stick of timber fit to cut was there for cutting, every acre of pasturage was there for grazing, every natural advantage of any kind was there to be utilized. The only restrictions were those to safeguard waste and to prevent permanent injury to the forest cover.

As Roosevelt neared the end of his stay in the White House, he knew as well as anyone that the fight for the American forests had just begun, that the main battles lay ahead. He gave vigorous expression to this thought to an Arbor Day audience of school children in the spring of 1907:

It is well that you should celebrate your Arbor Day thoughtfully, for within your lifetime the Nation's need of trees will become serious. We of an older generation can get along with what we have, though with growing hardship; but in your full manhood and womanhood you will want what nature once so bountifully supplied and man so thoughtlessly destroyed; and because of that want you will reproach us, not for what we have used, but for what we have wasted . . . So any nation which in its youth lives only for the day, reaps without sowing, and consumes without husbanding, must expect the penalty of the prodigal whose labor could with difficulty find him the bare means of life.[13]

Roosevelt left office with the assurance that he had done much to educate the people to a growing need of forest conservation. As one editorial comment of the time put it: "Many years of agitation have brought a general disposition on the part of both National and State authorities to deal with forests in accordance with a consistent and foresighted policy." [14]

IV

As Theodore Roosevelt took office in 1901, there were only five National Parks in the whole of the United States: Yellowstone, Yosemite, Sequoia, General Grant, and Mt. Rainier. Congress added five more during his administration: Oregon's Crater Lake, a six-mile wide lake of exceptional beauty situated in the crater of an extinct volcano; Oklahoma's Platt National Park, the scene of unusual mineral springs; South Dakota's Wind Cave, noted for its limestone caverns; North Dakota's Sully Hill, a wooded, hilly tract around Devil's Lake; and Colorado's Mesa Verde, containing the best-preserved prehistoric cliff dwellings anywhere in the United States.

Roosevelt summarized his views on the National Parks when he laid the cornerstone of the gateway to Yellowstone Park on April 24, 1903:

> I cannot too often repeat that the essential feature in the present management of the Yellowstone Park, as in all similar places, is its essential democracy—it is the preservation of the scenery, of the forests, of the wilderness life and the wilderness game for the people as a whole, instead of leaving the enjoyment thereof to be confined to the very rich who can control private reserves.[15]

On June 8, 1906, Congress passed the National Monuments Act. This measure authorized the President in his discretion to "declare by public proclamation historic landmarks, historic and prehistoric structures, and other objects of historic and scientific interest that are situated upon lands owned or controlled by the Government of the United States to be National Monuments."[16] While giving the President power to create National Monuments Congress, of course, kept the right to itself to create National Parks.

In the years from 1906 to 1909, the President established sixteen National Monuments, the first of some one hundred now scattered over the United States. The best known of those he himself created are: Wyoming's Devil's Tower, an 865 foot tower of volcanic rock, perhaps the plug of an ancient volcano; California's Muir Woods, with its magnificent grove of redwoods; New Mexico's Petrified Forest, known everywhere for its exceptional collection of petrified conifers; and Arizona's Grand Canyon, one of the world's greatest natural wonders, with its mile-deep chasm.

At the site of the latter monument, in 1903, Roosevelt said:

In the Grand Canyon, Arizona has a natural wonder which, so far as I know, is in kind absolutely unparalleled throughout the rest of the world. I want to ask you to do one thing in connection with it in your own interest and in the interest of the country—to keep this great wonder of nature as it is. I hope you will not have a building of any kind, not a summer cottage, a hotel, or anything else, to mar the wonderful grandeur, the sublimity, the great loneliness and beauty of the Canyon. You can not improve it. The ages have been at work on it, and man can only mar it.[17]

During his administration Roosevelt battled unsuccessfully to have the Grand Canyon made a National Park. First a game preserve (1906), then a National Monument (1908), the Grand Canyon did not achieve the status of a National Park until 1919.

In 1910 an estimated 200,000 people visited the National Parks, and in 1916 approximately 350,000. Today visitors to the Parks and Monuments are counted by the millions. It is increasingly evident, as Roosevelt once wrote, that the Parks and the Monuments represent "one of the best bits of National achievement which our people have to their credit in recent years."[18]

v

In 1894 Congress had made it illegal to kill wildlife in Yellowstone National Park, thus establishing the first federal sanctuary, where ousel and nutcracker, bighorn and elk, could live out their lives unmolested by rifle or shotgun. When Roosevelt became President this was the only federal wildlife refuge in all of the United States.

The idea developed slowly that our wildlife would have to be protected if many important species were not to suffer serious reduction in number if not actual extermination. Just as many people thought of the trees only as something to cut down, so did they think of the animals only as something to shoot down. They might have continued such thinking for a longer time if it had not been for what happened to the buffalo and the passenger pigeon. Early in the present century they awoke to the fact that these two animals, among the most valuable and most distinctive of all American animals, were so near extinction that it was doubtful if either could be saved. Through thoughtless, unremitting slaughter, man had reduced the original buffalo herd, estimated at 60,000,000, to a few small groups containing not more than 800 individuals all told. Man alone had done that. In the same way, he had cut down the passenger pigeons, originally darkening the heavens by the billions, to the point where any report of seeing one, even by such a reputable observer as Theodore Roosevelt himself, was considered highly doubtful.

And now, as Roosevelt came to office, still other species of birds and mammals were rapidly approaching a similar vanishing point.

He had always protested against those who shot wildlife wantonly, and this criticism extended to the plume hunters, who annually slaughtered countless beautifully feathered birds to further the ends of the costume designers. As Governor of New York, it will be recalled, Theodore Roosevelt had insisted that the state forbid factories to make bird-skins into articles of apparel. Birds in the trees and on the beaches were much more beautiful than on women's hats, he had insisted. After he became President, he was in a position to do even more about it. He took his first important step on March 14, 1903.

For some time ornithologists had been making a determined effort to get protection for the birds on Pelican Island, a pinpoint of land in Florida's Indian River, where the plume hunters had been making such inroads on the egrets and other birds of lively plumage that it was feared they would soon be exterminated. When all other efforts failed they appealed directly to Roosevelt. In considering this appeal Roosevelt asked: "Is there any law that will prevent me from declaring Pelican Island a Federal Bird Reservation?" When told that there was none, the island being federal property, he replied, "Very well, then I so declare it." [19]

— In this manner, quickly, without fanfare, Roosevelt established the first Federal Wildlife Refuge. Pelican Island was only a speck of land, less than four acres in extent, but from that time on its birds and other innocuous animals were able to mate and raise their young without fear of human molestation.

Having made this start toward protecting our wildlife, Roosevelt, between March 14, 1903 and March 4, 1909, created fifty more reservations, making fifty-one in all. They were scattered from the Gulf of Mexico to California and Oregon, even to Porto Rico, Alaska, and Hawaii. He gave protection to the colonies of laughing gulls, black skimmers, and brown pelicans on the Breton Island Reservation, Louisiana; he provided safe nesting grounds for migratory waterfowl on Klamath Lake and Malheur Lake Reservations in Oregon; he gave sanctuary to the sooty and noddy terns on the Dry Tortugas Reservation in the Gulf of Mexico; and he supplied protected homes for the petrels, cormorants, puffins, and murres on the Three Arch Rocks Reservation off the coast of Oregon.

Of course, others also deserve credit for this accomplishment. Individual crusaders like William T. Hornaday, George Bird Grinnell, Frank M. Chapman, William L. Finley, and T. Gilbert Pearson, and such powerful organizations as the National Audubon Society, the American Ornithologist's Union, and the Biological Survey supported the movement. But the question might reasonably be asked: "What would have been the result if someone else had been President of the United States when these friends of the birds visited the White House to intercede for the birds on Pelican Island?"

The mere recapitulation of the various steps Roosevelt took to protect "all the delicate beauty of the lesser and all the burly majesty of the mightier forms," [20] does not begin to tell the wildlife story. He gave the refuge movement such momentum that today birds and other animals are protected on almost 300 federal sanctuaries embracing more than 17,000,000 acres. Even this is far from the complete story, for many states, communities, and private citizens, taking their cue from the federal efforts originated by Roosevelt, have created hundreds of additional refuges where wildlife, both plant and animal, are protected as effectively as on any of the federal refuges. The simple truths that Roosevelt taught have sunk deep into the national consciousness, even to the extent that a swelling host of public-spirited American citizens are convinced, with Roosevelt, that "wild flowers should be enjoyed unplucked where they grow, and that it is barbarism to ravage the woods and fields, rooting out the mayflower and breaking branches of dogwood as ornaments for automobiles filled with jovial but ignorant picnickers from cities." [21]

During the seven and a half years ending on March 4, 1909, Theodore Roosevelt accomplished more for the protection of wildlife in the United States than all the twenty-four Presidents who had preceded him.

VI

The natural resources of a nation include not only water, forests, and wildlife, but also soil, phosphates, coal, oil, iron, zinc, copper, lead, and numerous other substances, both organic and inorganic. Over-all conservation was advocated as early as 1873, but nothing of consequence was done about it until near the end of Roosevelt's second term as President.

In 1907, while the Inland Waterways Commission was investigating the question of water development on the lower Mississippi, it suggested to Roosevelt that a conference be held that fall to consider *all* aspects of conservation.

Roosevelt was so enthusiastic about the proposal that he agreed to call the meeting himself. He made public his decision in Memphis, October 1907, in these words:

As I have said elsewhere, the conservation of natural resources is the fundamental problem. To solve it the whole nation must undertake the task through the men whom they have made specifically responsible for the welfare of the several states, and finally through Congress and the Executive. As a preliminary step, the Inland Waterways Commission has asked me to call a conference on the conservation of natural resources, including, of course, the streams, to meet in Washington the coming winter. I shall accordingly call such a conference. It ought to be among the most important gatherings in our history, for none had a more vital question to consider.[22]

It turned out to be an important gathering indeed. Roosevelt, throwing the full power of his office behind it, invited not only the Governors of all forty-eight states, but also Supreme Court Justices, Congressmen, representatives of learned societies, foreign dignitaries, and any number of scientists, including of course the recognized authorities on the natural resources of the nation. It was the first time that scientists had met on such an occasion on an equal footing with statesmen.

The President gave the opening address and spoke for fifty minutes. According to one observer, he "pointed the way to a more extended use of governmental powers, not only for the national government but for municipal and state governments, yet there was universal assent to every proposition that was presented. Those present felt they were witnessing an important historical event. In its earnestness and its restraint and suggestiveness it was perhaps the best speech Roosevelt ever made." [23]

An incident reflecting Roosevelt's friendship for his fellow-naturalists occurred at the close of the first session, when the guests filed by him to be greeted individually. L. O. Howard (who presided it will be recalled, at the meeting where Roosevelt and Merriam argued over the revision of the coyote genus) had reason to remember the incident.

I found myself in line immediately behind Dr. C. Hart Merriam, the animal and bird man. Immediately in front of him was William J. Bryan. As we reached the President, Mr. Bryan, in a pompous and somewhat condescending way (at least it seemed so to me), said, "Mr. President, I congratulate you, sir, on having started this conservation movement, which, in my opinion, has tremendous possibilities of good for the future of the country. I assure you, sir, that it meets my entire approval and will receive my hearty support." The President, with a trace of a humorous gleam in his eye, as he looked over Mr. Bryan's shoulder and saw Merriam and myself, said simply, "Mr. Bryan, I am pleased. 'Praise from Sir Hubert is praise indeed.'" Then, turning instantly to Merriam, he said, "How are you, Hart? What do you suppose John" (meaning John Burroughs) "and I saw on the twenty-fifth of March at Pine Knot? A Yellow Warbler, by George!" And then, turning to me, said, "Hello, Doctor! How are the bugs?" 24

The results of the conference were immediate and far-reaching. The Governors drew up a unanimous declaration supporting conservation, thirty-six state conservation commissions sprang into being, scientific bodies appointed numerous conservation committees and the National Conservation Association was organized. In sum, these actions gave the conservation movement a prestige and momentum previously unknown, and raised it to a plane enabling it to survive the various reverses it suffered later with periodic shifts in the political horizon.

Roosevelt was praised on all sides. According to one observer, "He has never appeared more statesmanlike than in looking anxiously to the physical future of the country; and in so easily and naturally obtaining the assistance of the Governors." 25 Another said:

President Roosevelt does new things, and usually good things, with an audacity that commends and only occasionally condemns him; and one of the most remarkable, even unparalleled, is that by which he invited the Governors of all the states and territories in the Union to come to Washington to consult as to the preservation of the natural resources of the country.26

The National Conservation Commission rolled up its sleeves almost at once and plunged into the near herculean task of inventorying the natural resources of the nation. It was the first time any country had ever attempted such a job. The Commission, headed by Pinchot, had its report ready in six months. "It laid squarely before the American people the essential facts regarding our natural resources, when facts were greatly needed as the basis for constructive action." [27]

This conference of Governors met with such enthusiasm that shortly Roosevelt determined to hold a North American Conference. In his invitations to Canada, Newfoundland, and Mexico he said: "It is evident that natural resources are not limited by the boundary lines which separate nations, and that the need for conserving them upon this continent is as wide as the area upon which they exist." [28]

The North American Conference convened in the White House on February 18, 1909, just two weeks before Roosevelt's term of office expired. This, too, was a success. The delegates not only agreed upon a declaration of principles but also urged that "all nations should be invited to join together in conference on the subject of world resources, and their inventory, conservation and wise utilization." [29] Roosevelt was so delighted with this idea, that he forthwith instructed the Secretary of State to extend invitations to forty-five nations to attend such a conference, to be held in The Hague at a date to be determined. Since he was to leave the White House in a matter of days, he was in no position to take further action personally, and the project died aborning.

The comprehensive conservation movement did not die aborning, however. Many of the state conservation commissions created in 1908 continue to function today, and the National Conservation Commission lived on until 1923. By that time hundreds of people were talking conservation for every one who had talked it when Roosevelt called the first general conservation conference in 1908 just fifteen years earlier.

So, from a meeting of three men (Roosevelt, Pinchot, and Newell) in 1903, in which they talked about what federal action could be taken to reclaim some of the arid wastelands of the West, evolved, within a few short years, the comprehensive conservation movement sharply focusing the attention of the American people upon the urgent need of a long-range policy to conserve all natural resources.

VII

Roosevelt himself did not consider his services in conservation as important as some others. His outstanding achievements, he once wrote in a letter to a London publicist, were his roles in building the Panama Canal, in terminating the war between Russia and Japan, and in doubling the size of the United States Navy. He did not mention conservation.[30]

The men most familiar with his record heartily disagree with him. As early as 1911 Senator Robert LaFollette made a prediction: "When the historian of the future shall speak of Theodore Roosevelt, he is likely to say that he did many notable things, but that his greatest work was inspiring and actually beginning a world movement for staying territorial waste and saving for the human race the things on which alone a peaceful, progressive, and happy life can be founded."[31]

One historian writing in 1937 of Roosevelt's conservation work, called it "his greatest service to the nation."[32] Another, in 1940, said that it was, "unquestionably the most important achievement" of his administration; and added, "Alone of our Presidents up to his time Theodore Roosevelt had grasped the problem of conservation as a unit and comprehended the basic relationship to national affairs."[33]

It was only natural that the conservationists themselves, Roosevelt's lieutenants in this fight for the forests and wildlife, should most enthusiastically endorse his labors. According to Gifford Pinchot: "The greatest work that Theodore Roosevelt did for the United States, the great fact which will give his influence vitality and power long after we shall all have gone to our reward . . . is the fact that he changed the attitude of the American people toward conserving the natural resources." [34] William T. Hornaday thought Roosevelt's conservation record "indeed enough to make a reign illustrious. He aided every wild-life cause that lay within the bounds of possibility, and he gave the vanishing birds and mammals the benefit of every doubt." [35] And Charles R. Van Hise, pioneer in the field of conservation, said that what Roosevelt did to bring this movement into the foreground of the consciousness of the people, "will place him not only as one of the greatest statesmen of this nation but one of the greatest statesmen of any nation of any time." [36]

Roosevelt himself gave the credit for this work to Pinchot, Newell, and others. "They actually did the job that I and the others talked about," he said.[37] For Pinchot he had a warm personal regard. Two days before he left the White House (1909) he wrote him as follows:

I have written you about others; I have written you about many public matters; now, just a line about yourself. As long as I live I shall feel for you a mixture of respect and admiration and of affectionate regard. I am a better man for having known you. I feel that to have been with you will make my children better men and women in after life; and I cannot think of a man in the country whose loss would be a more real misfortune to the Nation than yours would be. For seven and a half years we have worked together, and now and then played together—and have been altogether better able to work because we have played; and I owe to you a peculiar debt of obligation for a very large part of the achievement of this administration.

An occasional historian tends to belittle Roosevelt's share in the fight for conservation by implying that Pinchot was the mainspring. One such has even gone so far as to say that Roosevelt caught his enthusiasm for conservation from Pinchot.[38] That conclusion was based on inadequate knowledge, as anyone familiar with Roosevelt's background as a naturalist and conservationist could testify. If anything, it was Pinchot who caught fire from Roosevelt, and who succeeded where others might have failed because of the Chief Executive's perennial, contagious enthusiasm and aggressive leadership. There was credit enough for all in this fight for the woods, the water, and the vanishing wildlife, but the lion's share rightfully belongs to T.R. himself. Others may have originated ideas, but it was Roosevelt, who, by using the full power of his office, saw to it that they burgeoned and bore fruit abundantly.

Roosevelt did not cease to preach conservation after he left the White House. He supported the movement with undiminished fervor as long as he lived. Speaking to a group of Kansas farmers at Osawatomie on August 31, 1910, he said:

Conservation means development as much as it does protection. I recognize the right and duty of this generation to develop and use the natural resources of our land; but I do not recognize the right to waste them, or to rob, by wasteful use, the generations that come after us. I ask nothing of the nation except that it so behave as each farmer here behaves with reference to his own children. That farmer is a poor creature who skins the land and leaves it worthless to his children. The farmer is a good farmer who, having enabled the land to support himself and to provide for the education of his children, leaves it to them a little better than he found it himself. I believe the same thing of a nation.[39]

In 1916, in the last book he wrote devoted to his life in the out-of-doors, A Book-Lover's Holidays in the Open, Roosevelt included these lines:

A grove of giant redwoods or sequoias should be kept just as we keep a great and beautiful cathedral. The extermination of the passenger-pigeon meant that mankind was just so much poorer; exactly as in the case of the destruction of the cathedral at Rheims. And to lose the chance to see frigate-birds soaring in circles above the storm, or a file of pelicans winging their way homeward across the crimson afterglow of the sunset, or a myriad terns flashing in the bright light of midday as they hover in a shifting maze above the beach—why, the loss is like the loss of a gallery of the masterpieces of the artists of old time.[40]

18

Readying for Africa

LONG before his African trip became a reality, Theodore Roosevelt had had in the back of his mind the possibility of such a venture. In 1897, when Selous was in this country on a hunting trip, Roosevelt told him that such a trip was one of his greatest ambitions. But at that time, and for several years afterwards, he had little idea that he would ever be able to go.

It was not until the spring of 1908 that the President began to think seriously of an African expedition. The time seemed propitious. He knew that his duties as Chief Executive would terminate within a year, and that Taft probably would be his successor. In that event Roosevelt thought it might be wise to be out of the country, to avert any charge of interference with Taft's administration, such as would likely be made if he stayed at home. Moreover, he was still sound physically and wanted this trip more than anything else he could think of at the moment. On March 20, 1908, he wrote Selous who, at that time, was in England:

A year hence I shall stop being President, and while I can not be certain of what I shall do, it may be that I can afford to devote a year to a trip in Africa, trying to get into a really good game country. How would it do for me to try to go in somewhere from Zanzibar and come out down the Nile, or vice versa? What time ought I to go? That is, what time ought I to make my entry into the country? Is there anyone I could write to about an outfit? Is there anyone who could give me an idea of how much the trip would cost; and, finally, could you tell me whether there are people to whom I could write to ask about engaging porters, or whatever it is I would travel with? I hope I am not asking too many questions.

At about the same time Roosevelt wrote a similar letter to Edward North Buxton (another English big game hunter who had visited at the White House). The President said that he might go to British East Africa first, shoot around Uganda next, and then move north to Khartoum. He was willing to spend a year if necessary, he said, to achieve his objectives.

From then on, a steady stream of letters left the White House addressed to Selous and Buxton. These men were of inestimable aid to Roosevelt in the months ahead during which plans, elaborate in their scope, were gradually formulated and completed. They, more than anyone else, helped him to assemble his outfit, hire porters and other personnel, and work out his itinerary. He leaned upon them heavily for advice concerning a multitude of problems, both major and minor, that kept arising from day to day during the planning period. The ultimate success of the trip was due in good measure to their enthusiastic cooperation.

Although Roosevelt received most of his help from Selous and Buxton, he consulted many others, including Major General Sir Reginald Wingate, a Sudan official; Sir Alfred Pease, at whose home in British East Africa Roosevelt was to be a guest; Colonel J. H. Patterson, author of *The Man-eaters of Tsavo;* and Henry Fairfield Osborn. Charles Scribner's Sons, by guaranteeing Roosevelt $50,000 for magazine articles, thereby ensured the necessary means to cover expenses.

The early exchange of letters between Roosevelt and his British friends proved that he had in mind at first nothing more ambitious than a hunting trip to be made solely by himself and Kermit, who at that time was a nineteen-year-old freshman at

Harvard. But in June, three months after he had first written Selous, Roosevelt conceived a more ambitious plan: sponsorship by the National Museum. He gave a rough outline of it in a letter to Charles D. Walcott, Secretary of the Smithsonian Institution:

Now it seems to me that this opens up the best chance for the National Museum to get a fine collection, not only of the big game beasts, but of the smaller animals and birds of Africa; and looking at it dispassionately, it seems to me that the chance ought not to be neglected. I shall make arrangements in connection with publishing a book which will enable me to pay for the expenses of myself and my son. But what I would like to do would be to get one or two professional field taxidermists, field naturalists, to go with us, who should prepare and send back the specimens we collect. The collections which would thus go to the National Museum would be of unique value.

Roosevelt made it plain in this letter that he did not have the means to pay for the field naturalists or for the curing and transport of specimens for the Museum. He hoped, he said, to get rhinoceros, giraffe, hippopotamus, many of the big antelope, and possibly elephant, buffalo, and lion, together with a number of smaller mammals and birds, all of which would go to the National Museum if they would supply him with the men to care for these specimens. "I doubt if the National Museum would ever again have the chance to get a collection which would be from every standpoint as interesting," he added.

Because Walcott knew that the African zoological and botanical collections in the National Museum were decidedly below par for such an institution, he was immediately enthusiastic about the President's proposal. It was an eminently satisfactory arrangement all around: Roosevelt savoring the idea of Smithsonian sponsorship, and Walcott enthusiastic about Roosevelt's leadership. Roosevelt's only stipulations were that he and Kermit alone should do the actual shooting, and that no other member of the party should write anything about the expedition until after his articles had been published. It was only on those conditions that he could arrange a contract with Scribner's which would enable him to go.

With these details settled, Roosevelt's attitude toward the trip changed. He began to think of it as a natural history expedition instead of a hunting one. This viewpoint he made clear in a letter to Selous:

I used to be quite a taxidermist myself and I should like to make this trip essentially a naturalist trip. . . . I should expect the chief value of my trip to consist of the observations I was able to make upon the habits of the game, and, to a lesser extent, on the habits of the birds, smaller mammals, and the like. . . . I am much more pleased at making the trip a scientific one with a real object than merely a holiday after big game.

To Kaiser Wilhelm (January 2, 1909) he expressed the same viewpoint, "My trip to Africa will be taken partly as a big game hunter, but primarily as a naturalist."

Although Roosevelt no doubt meant exactly what he said, he would have been a discontented man if he had been obliged to make the trip solely for the purpose of studying the habits of African animals. The lodestone that originally attracted him to Africa, and continued to attract him, was the prospect of emulating the achievements of men like Selous, Baldwin, Cumming, and other celebrated African big-game hunters. He spoke the truth, though when he asserted over and over again that he wanted to shoot only one head of each species, with Kermit doing the same, and that under no circumstances would he do more except for additional specimens which might be needed to round out an exhibit for the Museum, or to supply the expedition with food. He disliked exceedingly the almost foregone conclusion that he would once again be accused of being a game-butcher.

Months before he embarked for Africa, Roosevelt was already giving serious thought to those animals he was most eager to shoot.

The animals I most wish to get, in their order [he wrote Buxton], are as follows: lion, elephant, rhino, buffalo, giraffe, hippo, eland, sable, koodoo, oryx, roan, wildebeeste, hartebeeste, water buck, wart hog, zebra, pallah, Grant's gazelle, bush buck, reed buck, topi.

In preparing this list of twenty-one animals the President was thinking only about those of British East Africa. He went on to say in this same letter that if he should be able to reach the Lado (in the southern Sudan), he wanted to make a hard try for the extremely rare white rhinoceros; that he was infinitely more anxious to get this animal than any other.

II

Now that the National Museum had taken a hand, Roosevelt found the scope of the planning for the trip greatly expanded, with the bulk of the responsibility still on his shoulders, however. It was up to the Museum to select the naturalists and decide what paraphernalia they would need in the field, but it was Roosevelt's expedition. He found it increasingly difficult to run the government and prepare for the trip at the same time. Nevertheless he went about his preparations methodically and painstakingly, ignoring no detail, however small, even though the ironing out of his problems was largely accomplished by transoceanic correspondence.

Roosevelt was delighted with the naturalists finally chosen: Edgar A. Mearns, Edmund Heller, and J. Alden Loring. They were seasoned collectors, and each in his own field a specialist. Mearns, a physician by training, had been one of the founders of the American Ornithologists' Union and had had broad field experience with both birds and mammals. Edmund Heller was a graduate of Stanford University, and, like Mearns, a man of rich field experience; it was Heller who subsequently prepared most of the skins of the large game animals that fell to Roosevelt's guns. The third naturalist, J. Alden Loring, was included for his skill in trapping small animals and preparing their skins.

It was Selous who first suggested to Roosevelt that he should hire a white man with safari experience to take charge of the expedition in the field. On first thought the President did not take to the idea. He did not want to feel as if he were "being conducted on a kind of Cook's tourist party." After more thought, however, he could see the wisdom of having a man familiar with the country who could relieve him of many responsibilities, and allow him more time for hunting and observation. The choice for this spot ultimately fell on R. J. Cuninghame, a hunter-naturalist and long-time resident of Africa.

Roosevelt had to provide provisions and equipment for more than two hundred men, who would be in the field for the better part of a year. Although it was to be expected that the party would subsist in good measure on the flesh of animals killed in the wild, Roosevelt knew from long experience that it would be impossible to live off the country alone, and that supplementary foods would have to be carried in on the backs of porters. He knew, too, the morale-boosting value of a few carefully selected delicacies. About this matter Roosevelt wrote Selous:

I want to take your advice as to what delicacies in the way of food to take. I entirely agree with you about jams. I hope it will be mainly strawberry, raspberry and blackberry jams, by the way, as I don't like most of the marmalades. Ought I to take some dried milk? They say it is very good; and they say that dried eggs are good. If they are mere luxuries I do not want either. How would it do for me to bring on from here some canned tomatoes and some canned Boston baked beans?

It was Selous who raised the question as to how much liquor Roosevelt would like to take with him. The reply was forthright: "I do not believe in drinking while on a trip of this kind, and I would wish to take only the minimum amount of whisky and champagne which would be necessary in the event of sickness." In an ensuing letter he was more specific. He had eliminated all the whisky, he said, except three flasks, but he had thought it wise to retain a case of champagne in case of fever. "Like you," he agreed, "I drink tea. I never take beer at all and spirits only for medicinal reasons."

There was much correspondence about the proper clothing to be included in the equipment, including frequent reference to such unwonted articles as spine pads, leather stockings, mosquito boots, wool socks, pith helmets, and abdominal pads. Roosevelt asked Selous if it was necessary for him to take a helmet, a kind of headgear which he loathed. He protested, too, about the abdominal pads, since they never did him any good. He asked Bill Sewall if the latter's womenfolk could knit him four pairs of wool socks, his experience having been that this kind of foot covering was best fitted for heavy work in the field.

Roosevelt finally chose for his own personal outfit heavy hobnailed shoes, khaki trousers with leather-faced knees, tan army shirts, and sun helmet. The latter he took, instead of his beloved and far more comfortable slouch hat, in deference to local advice.

Equally important was the matter of field and camping equipment. How many tents and what kind, how much mosquito netting, and how many plates and cups and cooking vessels, and how many, if any, portable bathtubs? Decisions had to be reached, too, about the number of porters and horses needed, about boats for the trip down the Nile, and about binoculars and photographic equipment. Kermit, after some instruction by men at the American Museum, was made head photographer. Roosevelt decided against taking moving picture cameras.

A personal problem not to be ignored was the number of spectacles to carry. With the passing of the years Roosevelt had had more and more trouble with his eyes. The climax had come in 1904, as a result of a sparring bout with a friend, when a blow produced a retinal hemorrhage in his left eye. An oculist warned him that if he did not discontinue his boxing he would lose his sight in that eye. He followed the specialist's advice, but lost his sight anyway. From 1908 on he was blind in his left eye. He was extremely sensitive about the loss, and confided the knowledge only to his immediate family and closest friends.[1] Since glasses were an absolute requisite, and easily broken, Roosevelt settled on nine pairs for the African trip. He had taken twelve pairs with him to Cuba.[2]

As Selous said, Roosevelt had a global knowledge of animals. Even before he decided to go to Africa he had read and absorbed everything of value to him in the books of such celebrated African hunters and explorers as Speke, Grant, Baker, Harris, Millais, Schilling, Selous, and many others. The first large book he ever read, it will be remembered, was Livingstone's *Missionary Travels and Researches in South Africa.* But he had not exhausted the literature on African animals, and as official duties eased during his summer vacation at Sagamore Hill, he grasped eagerly at this opportunity to enlarge his knowledge. In this pursuit he was greatly helped by Henry Fairfield Osborn, who sent him books from the American Museum Library. In mid-summer of 1908 Roosevelt wrote Osborn as follows:

I reenclose you those really helpful pamphlets and card catalog you so kindly sent me. Have you got that book by Findlay on "Big Game Shooting and Travels in Southeast Africa?" I should like to look at what it says. Also have you got the work of Sclater on the "Fauna of South Africa," both volumes I and II?

Osborn subsequently wrote that Roosevelt digested on an average five books a week—some of them thick and technical—sitting up late at night until he had completed them.

As news got around of his impending trip, men who had written of their adventures in Africa sent Roosevelt their books. One of particular interest was *My African Journal* by Winston Churchill. In acknowledging its receipt Roosevelt said:

Through Mr. Reid I have just received the beautiful copy of your book, and I wish to thank you for it. I had read all the chapters as they came out, with a great deal of interest; not only the chapters upon the very important and difficult problems of the Government itself, but also the hunting chapters and especially the one describing how you got that rare and valuable trophy, a white rhinoceros head. Everyone has been most kind to me about my proposed trip to Africa.

It was customary with Roosevelt when going on any kind of journey to take with him a few selected books for his personal

"Teddy at home in Africa"—from the Pittsburgh *Press*, 1909.

pleasure and relaxation. Since the African trip was to be protracted, he assembled more than usual; moreover, he had them bound alike in pigskin and stowed away in a specially made aluminum and oilcloth case. He selected them several months in advance, some sixty titles all told, not one of which had the slightest bearing on natural history. Roosevelt headed the list with *The Bible* and followed it with the best from such literary giants as Shakespeare, Poe, Scott, and Mark Twain. Each volume was conveniently small, so that it could be shoved into a pocket of Roosevelt's hunting coat when he was on safari. Thus, at the noon-hour siesta and other odd moments, he always had at hand a book in which he could lose himself. This collection of books became known as the "Pigskin Library," and later received much publicity.

After he had been in Africa about six months, Roosevelt wrote Henry Cabot Lodge and Mrs. Lodge:

You will both be amused to hear that at last, when fifty years old, I have come into my inheritance in Shakespeare. I never before really cared for more than one or two of his plays; but for some inexplicable reason the sealed book was suddenly opened to me on this trip. I suppose that when a man fond of reading is for long periods in the wilderness with but few books he inevitably grows into a true appreciation of the books that are good.[3]

In order further to buttress his storehouse of African zoological information, Roosevelt invited to the White House on every possible occasion men who had hunted and traveled on the "Dark Continent." In this way he met and talked with such well-known African explorers and hunters as the Earl of Warwick, Sir Harry H. Johnston, Sir John Harrington, Carl Akeley, and Colonel J. H. Patterson.

It was at one of these White House meetings that Carl Akeley told of seeing sixteen lions emerge from an African cave. Roosevelt could not let that observation pass. He turned to a Congressman present and exclaimed that he wished he had those sixteen lions to turn loose in Congress.

"But, Mr. President," protested the lawmaker, "aren't you afraid they might make a mistake?"

"Not if they stayed long enough," replied the President amid general laughter.[4]

In planning for the trip Roosevelt was aware of the dangers to life and limb. To Kermit he wrote, "I am pursuing my usual plan of taking all the precautions in advance." He had no fears for himself, but at times he had doubts as to the wisdom of taking Kermit with him. In his letters to the latter at Cambridge he warned him again and again that it was no child's play going after lions, elephants, and other such beasts.

As was to be expected, many well-meaning friends protested against his making the trip. Some of them based their arguments on the ever-present threat to life from African sleeping sickness. As a consequence, Roosevelt consulted the most eminent medical authorities about this disease, among them William Osler.

One of the friends who protested most strenuously was Cecil Spring-Rice, British Ambassador to the United States.

Mr. Spring-Rice has been writing some real Mrs. Gummidge letters to Mother about the trip [Roosevelt informed Kermit], saying how much he disapproves of it, and expatiating upon the dangers from wild beasts, from sleeping sickness, the black fever, and the like. I was immensely amused the other day to see an article in the Philadelphia Ledger in which the writer stated that as I had had a very picturesque career, and as it was probably now at an end, it would really be a fitting, and on the whole, a happy conclusion if I came to my death in some striking way on the African trip! I do not think Mother thought it quite as humorous as I did.

Roosevelt's invariable reply to those who tried to dissuade him from going to Africa was that he had lived longer already than the average man of eighty, and that he would feel this full consolation if he were seized with a fatal attack of sleeping sickness or struck down by some beast of ravin. "Certainly the fear of dying would not deter me from doing what I wanted to do," he asserted.[5]

The day before Roosevelt left the White House to make way for his successor, the heads of the government bureaus, among them L. O. Howard, came to say goodbye. When Howard shook hands with the President he told him to take especially good care of himself in Africa, and by all means to avoid sleeping sickness. Roosevelt's face broke into a broad grin as he replied: "Good idea, Doctor! That disease wouldn't comport with the popular idea of my character, would it?"[6]

One man who lost no sleep over the chance of Roosevelt's contracting sleeping sickness was Colonel Cecil Lyon, one of his former Western hunting companions. Said he:

They don't know the Colonel. He may be in danger of wildebeests, rhinoceri, dik-diks, lions or snakes, but no one who ever saw him would believe that sleeping sickness would ever catch up with him. That man's immune from that disease.[7]

There were other reasons than sleeping sickness to cause concern. Roosevelt was fifty years old, and as he said in a letter to Selous, he was in poor condition, and continued to have trouble with his left leg which had been hurt in a trolley accident six years before. Moreover, he was running somewhat to stomach (he weighed two hundred pounds) and was a little gouty. His description of himself as an "elderly man with a varied past which includes rheumatism," contained an element of truth.

But none of these things worried Roosevelt. He was not even much concerned about being followed by newspapermen, although he did tell Archie Butt that if one caught up with him in Africa his expense account to the National Museum would read: "Five hundred dollars for furnishing wine to cannibal chiefs with which to wash down a reporter of the New York Evening Post." [8] On the contrary, as time slipped by and the date of embarkation neared, it seemed that he could not contain his exuberance. Again and again the spirit of youth, forever an intrinsic part of his being, came spontaneously to the surface. In a letter to Sir Alfred Pease he exclaimed, "Really I can hardly believe that the game is what you describe. I am hot to be on the ground!" And then to Buxton a little later: "I have just had another awfully nice letter from Pease. . . . He gives the most alluring description of a place where he thinks I can get a lion and probably elephant, and certainly eland and oryx. By George, I am red hot to be out now!"

Just before sailing he received from Carl Akeley a plaster cast of an elephant's head, properly marked, as a guide in shooting this animal. His final gift, though, was a rabbit's foot from John L. Sullivan.

19

A Field Naturalist at Work

CARL AKELEY once said: "Few men could get so much out of a trip to Africa as Roosevelt could, because few men could take so much to it." [1] Roosevelt took to it a number of things. Some of these, those contributing importantly to his conduct as a naturalist, and to the success of the expedition, deserve to be examined in detail.

Roosevelt took with him to Africa, for one thing, an amazing fund of information about the animals of that abundant continent. This consisted chiefly of facts pertaining to the large game animals, although it was not limited to this group by any means. What was drawing Roosevelt to Africa was the prospect of collecting lions, elephants, and other monarchs of jungle and plain and the opportunities to study these animals in their native environments before they joined in oblivion such forms as the urus and the Irish elk. It behooved him to know about them. More than once he had had his critical say about naturalists who, while in Africa, had ignored its large mammals, favoring instead its insects, or shells, or minerals. The big game was vanishing, he remonstrated, but the beetles and the rocks would remain unchanged through the ages. Roosevelt had his own

198

sound reasons, therefore, for fixing his attention more particularly upon the game animals.

Of necessity, Roosevelt's studies of African game laid particular stress on antelopes. Africa is a land of antelopes. From the Sahara to the Cape they abound. There are numerous species and races. The word "antelope" actually has no zoological significance, being simply a term widely used to include all the cattle family which are not oxen, sheep, or goat. They differ from one another greatly, even more widely than some of them do from oxen, but all are cud-chewers, have two toes on each foot, and all males at least have horns. The hartebeest, sable, oryx, topi, koodoo, bongo, wildebeest (gnu), kob, duiker, oribi, gazelle, impala, and a goodly complement of other African animals, with names equally unfamiliar and outlandish, are all antelopes. They range in size from the diminutive dik-dik, no larger than a cottontail, to the large, cattle-like eland. The story of the Smithsonian-African expedition was much more a story of this strange, diversified group of animals, than of any other group or groups. Even Roosevelt was surprised at the number of antelopes he encountered and was able to collect for the National Museum.

Although Roosevelt himself saw great herds of antelopes, he knew as well as anyone that they represented only fragments of the great hordes that once covered the extensive plains country of East and South Africa, when Speke, Grant, Harris, Cumming, and other early hunters and explorers first visited the continent.

Shortly before he left for Africa, Roosevelt invited to Sagamore Hill "a group of the very best naturalists familiar with African life whom he could get together." [2] On that occasion, according to Osborn, who was one of the men present, he "displayed a knowledge of the genera and species of African game animals and of the precise localities where each might be found which was equal or superior to that of anyone else present." [3] Once a question arose, for instance, as to where Grevy's zebra, a subspecies with a limited distribution, might be found. Without hesitation, Roosevelt went to a map and put his finger on the one and only spot in Africa it was known to inhabit.[4]

Heller, though, was in a much better position, and better qualified, to pass judgment on Roosevelt's knowledge of African zoology than Osborn, or any other professional naturalist for that matter. Heller lived in the field with Roosevelt for months on end. He camped, bunked, ate, and trekked with him. He sat about the campfires with him at night when the conversation flowed freely and he followed him both day and night across plain and through jungle.

He had at his command [Heller wrote] the entire published literature concerning the game mammals and birds of the world, a feat of memory that few naturalists possess. I constantly felt while with him that I was in the presence of the foremost field naturalist of our time, as indeed I was. . . . Whatever I might say regarding my experiences in collecting animals in foreign lands, or as to my knowledge of animal behavior, Roosevelt always understood every detail.[5]

To give emphasis to this statement, Heller liked to tell about an incident that occurred one day in British East Africa. He referred in Roosevelt's presence to an obscure species of mouse that had been discovered a number of years before in British Columbia. He supposed that no one outside the large museums knew anything about it. Heller was literally astounded when Roosevelt proceeded to give him a complete biography of this humble rodent.[6]

Ornithologists, too, were amazed at Roosevelt's knowledge of African birds, not being familiar at all with his escapades as a stripling of fourteen when he had stuffed plovers, cormorants, bee-eaters, and numerous other birds that had fallen to his gun along either side of the Nile from Cairo to Aswan. What he had learned then he had not forgotten and, more recently, he had supplemented that information through the reading of many books about African birds.

Ornithologically speaking, Roosevelt was no stranger when he arrived in British East Africa. He had been on the grounds only a few days when he wrote that birds abounded, that he saw them wherever he looked: tiny birds and large birds, dull-jacketed and smartly colored. The wealth was bewildering; he *had* to give them his attention.

There were many kinds of shrikes, some of them big, parti-colored birds, almost like magpies, and with a kestrel-like habit of hovering in the air over one spot; others very small and prettily colored. There was a little red-billed finch with its outer tail feathers several times the length of its head and body. There was a little emerald cuckoo, and a tiny thing, a barbet, that looked exactly like a kingfisher four inches long. Eared owls flew up from the reeds and grass. There were big, restless, wonderfully colored plantain-eaters in the woods; and hornbills, with strange swollen beaks. A true lark, colored like our meadow-lark (to which it is in no way related) sang from bushes; but the clapper-lark made its curious clapping sounds (apparently with its wings like a ruffed grouse) while it zigzagged in the air. Little pipits sang overhead like our Missouri skylarks. There were night-jars; and doves of various kinds, one of which uttered a series of notes slightly resembling the call of our whippoorwill or chuckwills widow. The beautiful little sunbirds were the most gorgeous of all.[7]

Throughout his stay in Africa, Theodore Roosevelt continued to write about the birds he encountered. His records leave the impression that, space permitting, he would have liked nothing better than to go on and on about these songsters of rolling grasslands, thorn thickets, equatorial forests, and broad swamps of tall papyrus. The African birds disappointed him in only one respect. They by no means measured up in their singing to those of the United States. "At any rate," he wrote, "there is nothing that quite corresponds to the chorus that during May and June moves northward from the Gulf states and southern California to Maine, Minnesota and Oregon, to Ontario and Saskatchewan; when there comes the great vernal burst of bloom and song." [8]

In addition to his knowledge of animals, Roosevelt took with him to the "Dark Continent" a tremendous curiosity, one of the permanent and certain characteristics, according to Samuel

Johnson, of a vigorous mind. He sought in every possible way to gain first-hand information about the African animals: their distribution, the conditions under which they lived, their physical and mental behavior. Each day in Africa, as he came in from the field, he brought with him a whole parcel of observations. He pummeled Heller, Mearns, and Loring with questions—about bustard and francolin, leopard and warthog, roan and klipspringer, all of them to the point, many probing channels of thought previously unexplored, even by these professional naturalists. Some they could help him with, others he found the answers to himself, but still others stayed with him throughout the trip, annoying him, like the mosquitoes that sang about his ears the night through on the White Nile.

One puzzle he solved quickly—once he had the chance. Even before leaving the United States he had heard of the honey bird, an African bird that allegedly led human beings to bee trees. This was a matter he would have to look into. John Burroughs, for one, thought it was just another old wives' tale. "Go in the opposite direction from that which it seems inclined to take and see if it will follow you," Burroughs cautioned him.[9]

Roosevelt needed no prompting. From the moment he saw the flat-topped acacias and the aloe and olive trees of British East Africa, he began searching their foliage for a glimpse of this singular bird. He did not learn the truth about it, however, until weeks later, in the 'Nzoi River country near Mt. Elgan. It was a small bird, with a bill like a grosbeak's and toes like a woodpecker. He saw it fly to a nearby tree, where it chattered harshly as it hopped about among the branches. He followed, and it led him straight to a bee tree.

While camped on the 'Nzoi [he wrote] the honey birds were almost a nuisance; they were very common, and were continually accompanying us as we hunted, flying from tree to tree, and never ceasing their harsh chatter. Several times we followed birds, which in each case led us to bee trees, and then perched quietly by until the gun-bearers and porters got out the honey—which we found excellent eating by the way.[10]

To his mind, this experience with the honey bird was the most interesting one that occurred at this camp. Just a few days later his path crossed that of Carl Akeley's, who was on safari in this particular country at the same time. "He was much more excited," Akeley wrote, "over a honey bird he had been watching than over the elephant trail he had just crossed." [11]

Roosevelt did not solve other problems so readily—if at all. He had no answer as to why Grevy's zebra, which associates with the smaller zebra, never breeds with it. Similarly, he could not understand why most waterbucks, living right under the equator, have coats as long and shaggy as those of northern deer when most other antelopes have thin coats. And he was greatly puzzled as to why a lone individual of one species will consort with an individual of an utterly different species. He was witness to several such alliances: an oryx and a zebra that took to each other, a male giraffe that teamed up with two bull elephants, and of an old bull hartebeest that attached itself to, of all things, a big male rhino. Roosevelt felt that the element of safety possibly entered into any explanation of these extraordinary partnerships but, at the same time, he wondered if a genuine physical need for fellowship was not nearer the answer.

Roosevelt's curiosity probed another question. According to him, "It is absolutely certain that in portions of Africa giraffes and certain antelopes—oryx, eland, hartebeest, and others—pass long periods of time, probably months, without drinking, and where other antelopes, such as gerenuk, never drink at all." [12] To him this was an impossible nut to crack. He simply could not understand why any animal subject to the terrible heat and dryness prevailing in that equatorial climate would not die of thirst within a very few days. He knew that man could not endure such conditions for more than forty-eight hours.

Scientists today know, or think they know, the answer to that question. They believe the gerenuk and other African antelope obtain the water they need through eating succulent plants, including their fruits, in which water is stored.

From his earliest days, Roosevelt had felt obliged to look at the stomach content of each animal he collected. In Africa he continued this practice. In this way he learned some strange facts: that one antelope, the gerenuk, liked the leaves of the toothbrush tree, while another preferred those of the wait-a-bit thorn. The rhino, on the other hand, doted on the thick, thorny leaves of one of the euphorbias, the juice of which is acrid enough to blister. "This suffices to show," said Roosevelt with an attempt at humor, "what a rhino's palate regards as agreeably stimulating." [13]

Roosevelt left Africa with his curiosity unsatisfied on innumerable points. Some of these were so important to him that he thought competent field men should be given the opportunity to look into them. He thought, too, that field naturalists would make an extremely important contribution to science by "living with" one or another of the more abundant species of antelope over a considerable period of time. He mentioned Thomson's gazelle as a likely candidate.

Any man or any woman interested in natural history [he wrote] could easily make an invaluable life study of these pretty and interesting little gazelles, because their tameness, their accessibility, and the nature of their haunts render it possible to study all their actions continuously and minutely from day to day throughout the season. Such a study, if serious and prolonged, and by a competent and interested observer, would throw much light on many problems of animal psychology.[14]

Oddly enough, at times, the African animals appeared to be as curious about Roosevelt as he was about them. In a land where the naturalists encountered dangerous animals daily as a matter of course, their experiences ran the gamut from suppressed excitement to near tragedy, from touches of melodrama to abundant humor. But no experience was more curious, or more amusing, to

Roosevelt than to find himself, as he did on occasion, the center of an all-African audience composed of attentive, inquisitive game animals. He might be in some natural concavity of the land, with isolated hills surrounding, each topped with animals of various kinds, all with their heads pointed in his direction, all apparently bent on determining what peculiar new form of beast had invaded their backyard. A lone rhino might be a half mile away in one direction trying to make him out through myopic eyes, a herd of wildebeest on an opposite eminence studying him in ruminative leisure, and hartebeest, topis, zebras, and Tommies occupying other segments of the perimeter, all standing quietly or maneuvering restlessly as though to obtain the best possible locations for satisfying their collective animal curiosity.

Roosevelt realized that the discovery of new species of large game animals, in any part of the world, was a thing of the past. For that reason, he saw no future for the big-game hunter unless he turned faunal naturalist, became a trustworthy observer and faithful recorder of what he saw. There was every incentive for doing this, he said, because the life histories of the large quadrupeds afforded an almost virgin field for investigation. So little was known, in fact, about these animals—their psychology, distribution, concealing coloration, adjustment to environment, and a host of other problems—that the naturalists had yet to find the answers to some of the simplest questions about them.

For such studies Roosevelt himself was, of course, eminently qualified. His years of field experience in the West had provided him with a grasp of the fundamental problems to be attacked. He knew what to look for. For instance, when he first encountered the Grant's gazelle, the questions about it that came to his mind were almost as numerous as the gazelles themselves: What is the preferred habitat of this animal? Do these gazelles graze or browse, and what is their main article of diet? Why is it of advantage for this animal to run in herds of a score or more? Do they mingle with herds of other animals? Do the bucks fight for mastery of the herds? Is there a fixed mating season? Does the mother leave the herd at the time of the fawn's birth? Are the senses of sight and smell of this species well developed? Are these gazelles more alert at night or during the day? Do they hide themselves or otherwise attempt to escape observation? Do they remain in the same general locale from year's end to year's end?

Observing closely, he discovered the answers to a number of these particular questions about the Grant's gazelle. And before he completed his stay in Africa he found the answers to long strings of questions about a small host of other African animals. As an aid in keeping track of what he saw, he carried with him in the field at all times a small notebook. Its pages were soon liberally covered with scribblings about all manner of animals and plants: impala and topi, nightjars and sunbirds, sweet-smelling jessamine and yellow-flowered mimosa, and many more.

From reading *African Game Trails* one gets the impression that Roosevelt's eyes missed very little. He saw scores of animals that had been killed by lions, but noted that the great majority had died out on the plains and not at the drinking places. He observed with interest how the white herons accompanied the buffalo while the latter were in the open, but when they entered the papyrus swamps the birds did not follow, apparently finding the dark cover uncongenial. He was quick to observe that a concealed animal becomes revealed with only a slight movement of the body, such as the twitching of a tail. He found that on moonlight nights the grayish, counter-shaded animals, like the eland and the oryx, were more difficult to see than the striped forms, such as the zebra. He noticed how, at a distance, the sunlight plays pranks with the coloring of animals so that, for instance, the cock ostrich shows up jet black and is far more conspicuous than the neutral colored hen.

Long before Theodore Roosevelt began combing the thorn thickets and reed-covered marshes of Africa for animals to fill empty niches in the Smithsonian, he had heard it said by certain concealing coloration theorists (to use Roosevelt's own term for them), that the spots and stripes of such animals as the giraffe, leopard, and zebra were of benefit in concealing them from their enemies, that in the long struggle for existence in times past the striped animals had been more successful than the uniformly colored ones because they were better concealed. In other words natural selection had been more kind to the fitter of the two types, the striped and spotted ones.

Almost at once, upon arrival in British East Africa, Roosevelt was struck with the fact that the great majority of the African big-game animals, whether forest, marsh or open-plains animals, were neither striped nor spotted but monochrome. More than that, of those that did wear stripes, certain ones, the bushbuck and eland for example, were in the process of losing them. To Roosevelt that meant one of two things: "either that stripes are not concealing or, that if they are concealing then natural selection has only been able to develop them in one-twentieth of the animals to which they would have been of benefit." [15]

As time went on, Roosevelt paid more and more attention to the color patterns of the striped and spotted forms, giving each its fair share. What he found to be true of one was substantially true of all. His observations on the giraffe, for instance, pointed out that it was an animal of the dry, treeless country or of the open forests where the trees were scattered or habitually stunted. It never invaded the dense forests. Because it lived in the open, and because it was so tall (as much as 17 feet or more) and had such an absurd shape, it was, to Roosevelt, one of the most conspicuous animals in nature. Any beast of the plains could see it, even at great distances; the native hunter could see it, and even Roosevelt himself, with his imperfect vision, could see it.

Its coloration is of no consequence whatever in enabling it to escape from its foes [he said]. When feeding, when coming to drink, when resting, it never seeks to escape observation, and trusts entirely to its own wariness, to its keen senses, especially to its sight, and its speed, for protection.[16]

Roosevelt's observations on African wildlife could be multiplied—almost endlessly. As Heller put it, "he demonstrated in his African expedition what a marvelous faunal naturalist he was by acquiring a great mass of new observations on the life histories of the animals with which he met." [17]

Finally, Roosevelt took with him to Africa the ability to command the respect and admiration of his men. The naturalists had been told that he would be a hard man to get along with. He got off to a good start with them when he insisted on eating at the same mess with them and on having the same kind of sleeping tent. In no time at all, they discovered that the Roosevelt they knew from personal experience, and the one that they had had pictured to them, were two entirely different individuals. They liked his unconventionality, his courage, and his concern about their physical well-being. "His chief thought," Loring wrote, "was for the welfare of the party." [18] Now and then, for instance, one or another of the naturalists brought in an animal that might be new to science. Roosevelt always made it possible for them to continue their collecting long enough, regardless of where they might happen to be at the time, to settle the matter to their satisfaction.

Nothing won the friendship of his companions as much as his insistence that they be given full credit for the contributions each had made toward the success of the expedition. Heller, for instance, upon returning from a previous trip to Africa, with a large collection of animals, was not allowed to have anything to do with his own material. When Roosevelt heard about this, he wrote Walcott that both the preliminary and final studies on the collection of large game animals should be entrusted to Heller. "After the way he has worked, it would be an injustice to let someone else get the credit and reap where he has sown. In the next place, no one else is as fit to make the report as it should be made." Roosevelt's request was granted. According to Akeley, "In natural history circles his influence in this direction marked a new era." [19]

The naturalists, too, liked Roosevelt's abundant humor. One night, at Lake Naivasha, several of the party went out to hunt springhaas (a nocturnal rodent). Roosevelt carried a shotgun, Mearns a burlap sack, and Loring a bicycle lamp. When Loring said that the preparations reminded him of a chicken-stealing outfit, Roosevelt spoke up: "For goodness sake, Loring, don't speak of such a thing before newspaper men; that's the only crime they haven't thought to accuse me of!" [20]

On another occasion, Roosevelt agreed to divert the attention of a rhino ("a large beast whose long suit is courage and short suit brains," according to T.R.) while the others in the party stalked buffalo. When he had finished this job successfully he said: "So you see, there's an occupation that settles the question as to what shall we do with our ex-Presidents. They can be used to scare rhinos away." [21]

II

When Roosevelt reached Khartoum, where the expedition was disbanded, he found awaiting him a letter from Walcott:

We are more and more pleased and delighted with the results of the expedition in your charge. The whole enterprise, and its achievements, are so thoroughly characteristic of yourself and of what we have known of your three associates, that nothing less was expected, were the fates kindly and if no untoward incident interfered with the execution of your well matured plans.

The Smithsonian-African Expedition enriched the National Museum to the extent of 5,013 mammals, 4,453 birds, 2,322 reptiles and amphibians, not to mention thousands of fish, insects, shells, plants, and a quantity of anthropological material. Many of the species and subspecies were new to science. Roosevelt contributed some of them himself. A new race of Grant's gazelle

(*Gazella granti roosevelti*) was described by Heller from specimens shot by Roosevelt on the Athi plains, as was the Lado kob shot by him at Rhino Camp on the Nile.

The collection, especially of large mammals, was the largest that had ever been brought out of Africa by a single party. It placed the African section of the National Museum in the forefront of zoological collections. No longer was there any need to apologize to the London or Berlin Museums. The series of skins of such animals as the white rhino, giant eland, reticulated giraffe, northern sable antelope, and Vaughan's kob were unrivaled in any other Museum. "I wanted to have Uncle Sam have a first-class collection, possibly a little better than anybody else," Roosevelt commented upon his return to the United States.[22]

The expedition had not only been the most successful one ever to penetrate Africa but it had also been a scientific one with a real objective, just as he had planned. Moreover he had made innumerable observations on the life histories of African animals, as he had looked forward to doing, and he had shot the animals he most wanted to shoot—all twenty-one of them, including the white rhino, which he had been more eager to get than any other.

When he was again surrounded by the peace and quiet of his beloved Sagamore Hill he said many times that he had never taken a trip so well worth taking, nor one so full of interest and solid satisfaction. In the evenings he would join Kermit in a cup of coffee on the front porch, seat himself in his favorite rocking chair, and look out over the tree tops toward the Sound. "For awhile he would drink his coffee in silence, and then his rocking chair would start creaking and he would say: 'Do you remember that night in the Sotik when the gunbearers were skinning the big lion?' or 'What a lovely camp that was under the big tree in the Lado when we were hunting the giant eland.'"[23]

20

In the Valley of the Itchen

SEVERAL months before Theodore Roosevelt left the United States for the abundant game country of British East Africa, he had received an invitation from Lord Curzon, Chancellor of Oxford University, to deliver the Romanes lecture at Oxford and to receive an honorary degree, these events to take place concurrently at such time as would be agreeable to him.

Although Roosevelt had not intended originally to include Europe in his itinerary, either going or coming, upon receipt of Lord Curzon's invitation he hurriedly changed his plans. "I can think of few things," he replied, "which I would rather do than to deliver the Romanes lecture. I accept with pleasure, and if Oxford desires to give me a degree I shall be much pleased to accept it."

This opportunity actually delighted Roosevelt more than his reply indicated. He knew it to be an honor that came to few men, that the series, now almost twenty years old, had been inaugurated by the learned master of science and intimate of Charles Darwin, George John Romanes, and that he would succeed on the platform such eminent men of science and letters as Gladstone (who gave the first lecture in the series in 1892), Thomas Huxley, Viscount Morley, Viscount Bryce, Sir Oliver

Lodge, and Lord Curzon. Moreover, the lecture was, as he said to Lodge, "something right in my line."

He began work on it at once, recognizing that he would have to complete it before setting out for Africa. He chose as his subject *Biological Analogies in History*, a topic which could conceivably have been suggested by Romanes' own earlier, comparable study tracing the parallel development of intelligence in the animal world and in man. When he completed it he asked Henry Fairfield Osborn to read it. He wanted to know, in particular, if, in any of his several references to titanotheres, one-toed horses, sabre-toothed tigers, mastodons, ground sloths, and other extinct beasts that had warred against each other in the long ago, he had strayed from the truth.

Osborn read the lecture carefully. He found it packed with parallelisms of the birth, growth, and death of species in the animal world and the birth, growth, and death of societies in the world of man. Among these he noted two or three that, in his judgment, went altogether too far. For instance, Roosevelt, taking the bit between his teeth, had compared one obsolete European government to the giant, extinct ground sloth, *Megatherium*, and another, that had shown little or no progress for some three centuries, to the great departed armadillo, *Glyptodon*. Osborn felt compelled to blue-pencil these analogies, giving as his reason that he was simply trying to avert open conflict between the United States and the nations alluded to.[1]

After toning down the parts with which Osborn had quarreled, Roosevelt considered his work on the lecture done; he steadfastly refused to touch it again. Eighteen months later, on June 7, 1910, he delivered it at Oxford without the further alteration of a single word or sentence.

After Roosevelt had made up his mind to deliver the Romanes lecture, he got in touch with Lord Bryce, British Ambassador to the United States. He told him that when he had ended his African trip for the Smithsonian, and had come to England, he would like the opportunity of passing a day or two in the country with someone familiar with the songs of British birds. Bryce communicated Roosevelt's pleasure to Britain's Foreign Secretary, Sir Edward Grey. Having been an energetic student of birds from youth, Sir Edward was only too glad to perform this service himself.[2]

Roosevelt already knew a great deal about British birds because he had read about them in books. As he himself said: "I know the lark of Shakespeare and Shelley and the Ettrick Shepherd; I know the nightingale of Milton and Keats; I know Wordsworth's cuckoo; I know mavis and merle singing in the merry wood of the old ballads; I know Jenny Wren and Cock Robin of the nursery books." [3] He knew the birds by name, and something of their appearance and habit, but not their songs. While in England, as a youngster of fourteen, he had skinned partridges, starlings, and snipe, but of course the first-hand information gained at that time did not include bird music.

When Roosevelt finally reached England, Sir Edward noted with misgiving the tremendous demands on Roosevelt's time, and wondered whether they would be able to hear the birds together after all. Before long, however, Grey received word that Roosevelt would like a date set. With many commitments already made there was difficulty in finding time, but in the end they settled on June 9, the last day Roosevelt was to spend in England before sailing for the United States.

All went as planned, and Roosevelt passed no pleasanter day during his entire European visit than that with Sir Edward. The two met at Waterloo Station, journeyed by train to Basingstoke, and from there by automobile to the pretty, smiling valley of the Itchen, in Hampshire, some fifty miles to the southwest of London. It was a part of the English countryside made celebrated by other great naturalists, Gilbert White and W. H. Hudson among them.

Sir Edward had been a little apprehensive as to how the walk would turn out. Not having met Roosevelt before, he did not know whether his distinguished companion would display much genuine enthusiasm for birds. "I found," said Sir Edward, "not only that he had remarkable and abiding interest in birds, but a wonderful knowledge of them. Though I know something of British birds, I should have been lost and confused among American birds, of which unhappily I know little or nothing. Colonel Roosevelt not only knew more about American birds than I did about British birds, but he knew about British birds also." [4]

Sir Edward discovered, too, that his companion had a well-trained ear for bird music. This surprised him, because he knew that this ability could not have been come by without much time spent in the open listening to birds, and it was difficult for him to understand how Roosevelt could have found the time in a busy life to do this. Said Sir Edward: "He had one of the most perfectly trained ears for bird songs that I have ever known, so that if three or four birds were singing together he would pick out their songs, distinguish each, and ask to be told each separate name; and when, farther on, we heard any bird for a second time, he would remember the song from the first telling and be able to name the bird himself." [5]

The Foreign Secretary was intrigued by the fact that Roosevelt had not only a well-trained ear, but also a discriminating one, being quick to express preferences among bird songs and logical reasons for his likes or dislikes. For instance, of all the songs he heard he definitely liked that of the blackbird (the merle) best, and he was almost indignant that its mellow, leisurely voice had received so little praise.

The song of another bird that drew his attention was that of the golden-crested wren (*Regulus cristatus*), the smallest of all British birds. "I think that is exactly the same song as that of a bird we have in America," he said, after he had listened a moment and Sir Edward had identified it for him. Some time later Grey relayed Roosevelt's comment to Ogilvie Grant, a professional ornithologist in the Natural Museum in London, who told him that the song of this bird was probably the only one that the two countries had in common.[6] The "bird we have in America" was the golden-crowned kinglet (*Regulus satrapa*), often considered a subspecies of the golden-crested wren which, of course, is no wren at all.

Sir Edward was much impressed with this demonstration of Roosevelt's alertness to the similarity in the two songs. "It was the business of the bird expert in London to know about birds," he said. "Colonel Roosevelt's knowledge was a mere incident acquired, not as the part of the work of his life, but entirely outside it." [7]

After enjoying for some hours the avian lyrics and choruses common to the valley of the Itchen, Roosevelt and Grey took a motor to the New Forest, a nearby wild, uninhabited stretch of woodland and heath in which grew many gnarled and ancient oaks. They heard only a few birds here, but among them was the familiar redbreast or robin. Roosevelt had no idea that it sang so well; he reveled in its gushing, careless strain. He heard here, too, for the first time the fine, clear, high-pitched notes and trills of the wren and found himself comparing its beautiful and finished performance with that of our winter wren. He noted that the two were somewhat alike, but that of the British species was not quite so musical to his ear.

Of all the birds that were seen or heard, Grey later recorded, there was not one of which Roosevelt did not know the general character and classification. Sir Edward made a list of them, at the end of the day, starring those that they had heard. They had seen forty-two and heard twenty-three.

The list did not include the nightingale. Because Roosevelt had previously heard its melody at Lake Como, he expressed no disappointment at not hearing it in the valley of the Itchen.

Furthermore, he agreed with those naturalists, such as W. H. Hudson, who thought that its song had been overrated.

. . . though it is indeed a notable and admirable singer [Roosevelt wrote], it is an exaggeration to say that it is unequaled. In melody, and above all in that finer, higher melody where the chords vibrate with the touch of eternal sorrow, it cannot rank with such singers as the wood thrush and hermit thrush. The serene, ethereal beauty of the hermit's song, rising and falling through the still evening, under the archways of hoary mountain forests that have endured from time everlasting; the golden leisurely chiming of the wood thrush, sounding on June afternoons, stanza by stanza, through sun-flecked groves of tall hickories, oaks and chestnuts; with these there is nothing in the nightingale's song to compare.[8]

Before he met Roosevelt, Grey was of the opinion that the former President of the United States was chiefly a man of action, an opinion held by many others. He was pleasantly surprised to find that he was also a man of books and wide learning. For instance, during the day, as they encountered this or that bird, Roosevelt recited appropriate lines from the poets.

One other discovery Grey made about Roosevelt, perhaps the pleasantest of all, "I saw enough of him," he said, "to know that to be with him was to be stimulated in the best sense of the word for the work of life." [9]

III

Ten days slipped rapidly by, and Roosevelt was again in the land of his birth. As his ship tied up to the east bank of the Hudson, he was accorded the most tumultuous reception of his entire life. That evening he was at home, at Sagamore Hill, with his family and among the birds of his own country.

I thoroughly enjoyed my stay in England [Roosevelt wrote a friend]. The men I met were delightful, and I felt at home with them. As a whole, they had my ideals and ways of looking at life. But the twenty-four hours I really most enjoyed not only in England but in all Europe were those I spent with Edward Grey the last twenty-four hours I was in England.[10]

21

T. R. Writes of Africa

FEW books have been written under conditions so adverse as Roosevelt's *African Game Trails*. He did most of his writing in the evening at the close of the day's hunt when the burden of fatigue was added to the enervating heat and the irritating presence of mosquitoes and other insects. He usually wrote in the gloom of his tent, sitting on a camp stool with a feeble lamp lighting his paper, and with hands and forearms covered with gauntlets and face protected by an improvised mosquito-netting shield. "Father was invariably good-humored about it," Kermit wrote, "saying that he was paying for his fun." [1]

Roosevelt made three copies, using an indelible pencil and carbon paper. As quickly as he had completed them, he wrapped two separately and sent them off by different routes. For instance, when he reached Uganda he sent one copy by runner to Nairobi, and thence to Mombasa, and the other down the Nile to Cairo. He sent them in blue-canvas envelopes. Although they often reached his publishers in a worse-for wear condition, they always arrived.

Along with the chapters Roosevelt often mailed letters. In these (to Robert Bridges, editor of *Scribner's* magazine) he discussed the chapters both as magazine articles and as parts of his forthcoming book. In one of his earlier letters (from British East Africa) he said:

I doubt if chapter 11 will be very thrilling—But chapter 12 ought to be good. It will deal with utterly new conditions. However, the country I there traverse is very unhealthy, and of course there is always the remote chance that I will be laid up; or that the conditions will prevent our getting game. If all goes well, I suppose you will publish the book a year from this fall? I agree with you that the best title is "African Wanderings of a Hunter-Naturalist." [2]

The first of Roosevelt's magazine articles appeared in *Scribner's*, October 1909, and his book—*African Game Trails*, not *African Wanderings of a Hunter-Naturalist*—came off the press about one year later, early in the fall.

None of Roosevelt's books, either before or afterward, sold as many copies as did *African Game Trails*. It immediately became a best seller, as Roosevelt admirers rushed to bookstands to get their copies, and then to lose themselves with their favorite ex-President in the chase of lions, hippos, kobs, bongos, koodoos, and other beasts of the veldt and forest. It was, according to the New York *Tribune*, "Of course, the book of the year." [3]

In some respects *African Game Trails* was the *magnum opus* he had always yearned to produce. Portions of it were beautifully written, especially the foreword. He wrote this as the trip was drawing to a close and was dated, Khartoum, March 15, 1910. The author was in a happy frame of mind and could say with unalloyed relish: " 'I speak of Africa and golden joys'; the joy of wandering through lonely lands; the joy of hunting the mighty and terrible lords of the wilderness, the cunning, the wary, and the grim." [4]

This foreword was actually a song of triumph in having tasted and found savory a land "radiant with bright-hued flowers, birds and butterflies, odorous with sweet and heavy scents"; in having successfully coped with "the lower things, that crawl, and fly, and sting and bite"; in having subdued "the fiercest beasts of ravin," and in having found in remote haunts "the fleetest and most timid of those beings that live in undying fear of talon and fang." [5]

The reviews, except those manifestly by political enemies, were cordial, if not always enthusiastic. The New York *Sun*, proverbially hostile, said that "the closed book would be an ornament to any drawing table." [6] *The Galaxy*, a periodical of that day, went even further, engaged in good old-fashioned swashbuckling abuse: "If there ever was a work which in the interest of humanity should be suppressed it is this . . . Roosevelt itches to flood the country with the weak and miserable studies of which he himself is the vaunting hero." [7]

Among unbiased reviewers, the Chicago *Record-Herald* placed *African Game Trails* in the first rank of outdoor literature: "It has action, adventure, the excitement of the chase, and, what is much more, it has the picture-making phrase that stirs the imagination on every page." [8] *The Independent* was loudly enthusiastic: "Take it any way you please, read it up or down, forwards or backwards, and even the most captious critic must admit that *African Game Trails* is a 'bully book.'" [9] These reviewers objected only to a lack of humor, thought it incredible that, from Nairobi to Gondokoro, Roosevelt found nothing at which to laugh, nothing at all with a humorous twist.

The National Geographic Magazine did not object to the serious-minded presentation: "No one can read the volume without being impressed by the serious purpose of the leader and of every member of his staff. To the writer of this review, 'African Game Trails' appeals as the strongest and best work of literature Mr. Roosevelt has yet written." [10]

When William Brewster wrote Roosevelt, telling him what he liked about *African Game Trails*, Roosevelt replied (May 8, 1911) as follows:

I am naturally very much pleased at what you say of my "Game Trails." But I am really more pleased because you praise it for what I regard as most important in it, that is, for the natural history—to use an old term of which I am fond. It is not that I showed any unusual powers in making the observations on big game; it is simply that they are usually seen only by hunters, and hunters as a rule seem to have their minds encased in horn so far as any observation is concerned that does not relate purely to killing the animal. Do you know that even on such a simple point as the actions of the honey guide I could not find one instance of a man writing at length just what the bird did as he himself saw it?

II

Roosevelt, as we know, had wanted Heller to write a book about African mammals, to be published by the Smithsonian Institution. Although Heller made a start on this, assembling notes for two or three chapters, he was unable to get much further with it due to the pressure of routine museum work.

In the meantime Roosevelt played with the idea of a book of his own on the African big game. After mulling it over, he had another thought. He expressed it (April 21, 1911) in a letter to Walcott:

When you come to make the big volume on mammals which Heller is to write, I wonder whether you and Heller would like me to write the life histories of at least the large mammals? I think that for the big game I could probably do it well, and I of course had better chances to observe than even Heller, although I would go carefully over each article with him. I want that volume to be the very best thing of its kind that can be written. There is a great deal I could put in that I did not care to put into my own volume.

Roosevelt's eagerness to share in this book on mammals, and to make of it "the very best thing of its kind that can be written," is patent in each word of this letter.

More than a year went by, in which time both Roosevelt and Heller prepared articles on the white rhinoceros. Of the correspondence which passed between them, if any, we have no record. Finally, on December 18, 1912, one month after he had been defeated as the Progressive Party candidate for President, Roosevelt wrote Heller as follows:

. . . I am glad the White Rhino paper will be published anyhow. I do not suppose you care to have my piece on the White Rhino's habits to be published in it. It is all ready. I will also be able to give you the one on the giant eland whenever you get that ready, if you want it, but I do not suppose you will. I am glad you are preparing the insectivora just on the plan you mention. You are quite right, the work at the Smithsonian will only be done while you are there in person to do it.

This letter was, of course, equivalent to a second plea to be allowed to collaborate. Heller may have had some bad moments; to become co-author with an ex-President of the United States, especially one of Roosevelt's stature, carried with it responsibilities which he no doubt foresaw. We know nothing of his thoughts on the matter, only that, soon after he had received the above letter, he submitted a proposal to Roosevelt that they pool their efforts. In his reply Roosevelt came as near whooping for joy as it was possible for a Knickerbocker ex-President to do without actually losing all dignity:

Your letter contains a suggestion which I think wonderful. I had been talking with people about producing a book on the life histories of African Big Game which we encountered. But it would be infinitely better to publish a book on the big game of East and Middle Africa, authors Roosevelt and Heller. Would that suit you, or would you want it "Heller and Roosevelt"? I should be perfectly content with the latter. You could furnish the scientific descriptions and then you would look over and correct my life histories. Will you let me know at once whether this suits your views and I will take it up and find out if we can get such a book published by Scribners or Macmillans . . . I think we could make a mighty good book together.

Apparently Heller thought that "Roosevelt and Heller" sounded all right, for in about a month Roosevelt wrote that he had made arrangements with Scribner's for the publication of the book. The two of them were to have all their material in not later than January 1 next, and each was to contribute approximately fifty thousand words. Roosevelt said that he would have his fifty to sixty thousand ready by about July 1 and that Scribner's had agreed to a royalty of twenty per cent, which he thought quite generous for a scientific work.

In the weeks that followed, Roosevelt and Heller wrote back and forth, as they traded chapters and read critically what each had written. On April 21, for instance, Roosevelt wrote:

Those sixty pages have come. Meanwhile I retaliate by sending you my chapter on concealing and revealing coloration. Now when you have gone over this, will you also go over it with Hart Merriam? All of my other chapters are pure narrative, but this represents some scientific thought. I hope that it will add a little to the value of the book. When you and Merriam are through with it, return it to me. I will send you some of the other chapters very shortly, and I will also write you in full about your chapters. I am absolutely certain, however, that they will be all right. We must not sacrifice too much in the desire to make the book popular. I think it would be first-class to put such a bibliography in. I hope you will do so. I will help you in any way I can.

More letters followed. They were full of talk about animal illustrations, and about such matters as preserving big-game skins and the validity of species.

Between the middle of January and the middle of May, no more than four months, Roosevelt had completed his share of the manuscript, some sixty thousand words or more. In that same period he had put the finishing touches to two other books: *History of Literature and Other Essays* and *Theodore Roosevelt an Autobiography*. On June 30 (1913) he wrote Kermit: "All three of my books are finished, thank heavens! I have never had more work than during the last eighteen months. The volume of essays will appear next October, the autobiography in November, the life histories of African game will be out in the early spring of next year."

III

Life Histories of African Game Animals was published early in 1914. It was a comprehensive work of two volumes and some eight hundred pages, with its content limited to a discussion of those game animals collected in East and Middle Africa by the Smithsonian-African Expedition, and to five introductory chapters covering such topics as game preserves, concealing coloration, flora of East and Middle Africa, and derivation of African fauna. Roosevelt contributed the life history of each species, and chapters on game preserves and concealing coloration. Heller wrote the technical descriptions and the other introductory chapters. Responsibility for the work was joint. The volumes were excellently illustrated with photographs, and with drawings by the artist, Philip R. Goodwin. Forty faunal maps, showing the distribution of the species under discussion, added value to the work.

One of the first comments on the work to arrive in Roosevelt's hands was a letter from Walcott, to whom the volumes were dedicated:

I have looked over the "Life Histories of African Game Animals," by Theodore Roosevelt and Edmund Heller, and am impressed with the thorough manner in which both the descriptive and technical work has been presented to the reader. It is a superb contribution, and all interested in natural history and in hunting large game must feel a debt of gratitude to you and Mr. Heller. Personally it is a source of great gratitude to have these volumes appear, as they fully answer so many questions asked, often in a not too friendly way, when the expedition was in your charge. . . .

If not out of place, may I say that I think you have done more to arouse the national conscience and to stimulate higher ideals among the young men of America than any one individual of our time, and that as the years go on this will be appreciated more and more.

Press notices were equally enthusiastic. Charles C. Adams, writing for the *Bulletin of the American Geographic Society*, said: ". . . the work is a very valuable contribution both to geography and zoology and no other book covers the same field. On account of their exceptional facilities and experience, the authors have given us a work which will long be standard in its field." [11]

Roosevelt was disappointed in the sale of the book, an eventuality he perhaps should have foreseen considering its technical language and the fact that it sold for ten dollars. He had hoped that many sportsmen and naturalists, in addition to professional scientists, would be eager to include these volumes in their personal libraries. Roosevelt was disappointed, too, that Merriam had failed to review the book as promised.

Merriam's review appeared tardily. *"Life Histories of African Game Animals,"* he wrote, "is a book which for all time will stand as a treasure house of information on the geography and general natural history of that region. In comprehensiveness, thoroughness, popular interest, and in the scientific value of its contributions to knowledge, it is far and away the best book ever written on the big-game animals of any part of the world." [12]

22

The Concealing Coloration
Controversy

ABRAHAM LINCOLN once said of a contemporary politician that
he was "a good man to raise a breeze." A number of people
thought Roosevelt was a good hand at that sort of thing. They
pointed, for instance, to the dispute he had with the New Hampshire artist and concealing-coloration theorist, Abbott H. Thayer.

This affair, which rivaled in intensity the nature-faker controversy, did not arrive in full bloom until 1910, although its seeds
were planted in 1896 when Thayer published an article called
"The Law Which Underlies Protective Coloration." This law
called attention to the discovery of an optic principle known as
counter-shading, which both artists and scientists seemed to have
previously overlooked. Simply stated, counter-shading was a
distribution of color in animals—dark above in light and pale
below in shadow—which resulted in an animal's concealment.

Thayer soon gave demonstrations of this principle, using
wooden decoys, half of which were painted dark over the entire
body and the other half dark above and white beneath. When
these were placed against a suitable background an approaching
observer could see only those decoys that were uniformly dark,

the others were invisible to him. Biologists immediately recognized the importance of counter-shading. As Frank M. Chapman said, one had only to see a demonstration to become convinced of its truth and application to the coloration of animals, since animals generally are dark above and light beneath.[1]

Thayer was an artist of great ability. He had studied for four years under Gêrome at the École de Beaux Arts. He was intensely vital, and at least a measure of his later success in convincing some scientists of the soundness of his theories, was due to this animation and force of personality. He was intensely interested in wild animals, too, although one of his shortcomings (later to become apparent) was inadequate field experience with animals.

As time went on, Thayer extended his demonstrations to include all color patterns. With artifically constructed backgrounds, or with natural ones of his own chooosing, he attempted to prove that all color is primarily protective. And in 1909 he published (in collaboration with his son, Gerald Thayer) *Concealing Coloration in the Animal Kingdom,* an elaborate treatise, richly illustrated, which brought together under one cover all of his theories about revealing and concealing coloration.

Both text and illustrations were open to criticism. The colored plates, in particular, lent themselves to it, because the animals portrayed were often placed against fictitious backgrounds. For instance, Thayer painted flamingos against a backdrop of red sunset and red matching clouds, his explanation being that this is nature's way of protecting these birds from "their enemies, such as anacondas, alligators, sharks, etc." [2] To demonstrate the obliterative pattern worn by the blue jay, he drew the bird against a bluish shadow on snow. "In such a situation," Thayer maintained, the jay's representation of sunlit snow, tree shadow, and tree stems is perfect." [3] In like fashion, he depicted the male wood duck against a background of green water, green trees, white clouds, and orange-colored water lilies.

Another theory of Thayer's, also open to criticism, was that many of the animals which appear conspicuous to man are not at all conspicuous to their natural enemies. This was so, he said, because man looks down upon them and not up at them against the sky, as do the beasts which prey upon them. For example, the large, white rump-patches of the pronghorn are not conspicuous to its foes, because the eyes of the latter are on a lower level than the rump and "their brightly displayed sky-lit white sterns blot out their foreshortened bodies against the sky." [4] He claimed, too, that the stripes and spots peculiar to such animals as zebras and giraffes are concealing.

Roosevelt did not enter the argument until Thayer's book was called to the former's attention—after his return from Africa. Up to that time most of the reviews of *Concealing Coloration in the Animal Kingdom* had been favorably worded. Louis Agassiz Fuertes, for instance, was loud in his praise of it,[5] and Chapman found fault only with a few of the illustrations.[6] But both Fuertes and Chapman were close friends of Thayer's and, as J. A. Allen afterwards pointed out, personal friendship had deterred more than one scientist from speaking his mind.[7]

With Roosevelt's ability to assimilate quickly the content of any book, he was not long in sifting the chaff from the grain. His diagnosis, based upon his many years of field experience, was that the book suffered from a spate of overstatement; that its author, like other enthusiasts in fields inadequately known, had wandered too far and seen too little. He discussed his conclusions with a few of his scientific friends and decided it was his duty to make appropriate response.

Roosevelt's first contribution to concealing and revealing coloration was an article published as Appendix E in *African Game Trails*. Others followed, notably a lengthy piece in the journal of the American Museum, and an introductory chapter to *Life Histories of African Game Animals*. In these articles he made it clear that, in his opinion, concealing coloration was of real value in the struggle for existence to some animals but, he said, "the theory is pushed to fantastic extremes." [8]

One extreme was Thayer's colored illustrations, the flamingo, wood duck and blue jay in particular. They stood on a par, Roosevelt said, "with putting a raven into a coal scuttle in order to show that its coloration is concealing." [9] Only a minute's reflection was sufficient, he went on—referring specifically to the wood duck—to show "that if the gaudily colored males of these birds are really protectively colored, then the females are not, and *vice versa;* for the males and females inhabit similar places." [10]

As to the obliterative effect of white rump patches and white tails of pronghorn and deer, Roosevelt felt that he was on solid ground, for he had been a student of these animals for thirty years. From his experience, the white rump of the pronghorn was at night often the only cause of the animal's being seen at all. Moreover, he had seen prongbuck against the skyline hundreds of times by daylight, and at least a score of times by night, and the only occasion the white rear could ever have such obliterative effect as that claimed by Thayer "would be at the precise moment when the animal happened to be standing stern-on in such a position that the rump was above the sky-line and all the rest of the body below it." [11] Such moments, he was confident, were rare indeed.

Roosevelt directed much of his attack at Thayer's pronouncements on the protective value of stripes and spots on such African animals as the leopard, zebra, and giraffe. Having just returned from a year with these animals in East and Middle Africa, where he had had every opportunity to watch them closely, Roosevelt had a distinct advantage over Thayer, who had not seen one of these animals in their natural environment. Roosevelt was convinced that these forms were among the most conspicuous of animals, that their coats had no concealing value whatever, and that they depended almost entirely upon their alertness, speed, and other individual habit to escape their enemies.

Roosevelt, in his various articles on coloration, took issue with Thayer on many other scores. He even questioned the importance of counter-shading, which had found so much favor with Chapman and other biologists. Thayer had made much of the point that such birds as whippoorwills and partridges owe their concealment, not so much to the inconspicuous coloration of their bodies, as to their being colored dark above and light below. But these particular birds when threatened by enemies, Roosevelt said, habitually crouched low on the ground, which action concealed the white of the underside and eliminated entirely any effects of counter-shading.

Roosevelt's contributions to the coloration issues would fill a small book. His views in general, however, may be summed up in a few short sentences. He had no doubt but that certain birds and mammals possess concealing coloration. On the other hand he believed that at least three-fourths or more of the birds and mammals of temperate North America have color patterns which, to a greater or lesser degree, advertise their wearers and thus do not conceal. Counter-shading in his opinion was of minor importance in concealing the majority of both birds and mammals. The principal factors in insuring the safety of most mammals and birds were speed, alertness, and other individual habit. Coloration was a minor and often negligible factor.

II

Two minor wrangles, related to, but somewhat apart from the main controversy, were known only to a few people. One was an out-and-out attack on Roosevelt's reliability as a reporter, by Francis H. Allen, an editor of Houghton Mifflin and member of the Nuttall Ornithological Club. Allen, writing in *The Auk*, declared that in a recent article by Roosevelt on concealing coloration, he had detected "upwards of fifty instances of misquotations, misrepresentations and perversions of Thayer's statements." [12]

Roosevelt was furious—not so much at Allen, for what he had said, as at *The Auk*, for publishing what he considered to be a thoroughly dishonest, untruthful, and mendacious assault. While still in a white heat of indignation he wrote a letter to the editor of *The Auk*, at that time Witmer Stone, of the Philadelphia Academy of Natural Sciences. It clearly reflected the state of his mind. He was not only indignant, but outraged, he told Stone, that a reputable magazine like *The Auk* would include such an article in its pages. Allen's attack was full of untruths, he said, and *The Auk* had a solemn obligation to correct them.

Roosevelt had stirred up a high east wind. It was quickly to subside, however, when Stone replied acknowledging an editorial oversight. He had been, he said, so strongly in sympathy with Roosevelt's opinions on the coloration issues that he had hesitated to exercise his duty as an editor with Allen's article for fear of being unfair to the other side. He concluded by saying that he would correct the oversight in the next issue of *The Auk*.

Roosevelt was still further mollified when he learned that Thomas Barbour, Harvard zoologist, was going to reply to Allen's article. As his next letter to Stone attests, his ire had quickly melted.

That is a very nice letter of yours and I appreciate it and thank you. I had just learned of Barbour's proposal through a letter he wrote me. I sent him a copy of the letter I wrote you and also a letter of which I enclose you a copy. It appears that Allen is a strong political opponent of mine and this was his way of getting at me. As I said in my other letter, I shall be delighted to answer any criticism of my views as such. But it is not possible for me to go into a controversy with a man who deliberately misquotes what I said and is deliberately untruthful about me.

The other minor wrangle involved Thayer's long-drawn-out, persistent attempt to induce Roosevelt to witness his demonstrations. This began late in the summer of 1911 (one year before the Bull-Moose Convention), when he sent Roosevelt a cordial invitation to come to his home in Monadnock, New Hampshire. One had only to see his demonstrations to be convinced, Thayer said.

In his reply, Roosevelt acknowledged the invitation as "a most attractive one," but then proceeded to ignore it in the remainder of his letter which he devoted to a re-statement of views previously set down in Appendix F and elsewhere.

Thayer was willing to endure rebuffs in the sake of his cause. He wrote again to Roosevelt, saying: "I can hardly bring myself to believe that you and a large number of our naturalists are in the extraordinary position of trying to write down and blacken a thing that *they will not consent to investigate*. What more flaming wrong can a man do his neighbor than to judge him untried?"

During the next few weeks, letters went back and forth. Roosevelt kept telling Thayer that he [Thayer] was an out-of-door man, an intense lover of nature, an artist of high ability, and that he could do exceedingly valuable work if he would only acknowledge to himself the limitations of his theory.

Thayer, having failed in his efforts to bring Roosevelt to New Hampshire, pondered his next move. Eventually he decided that if the mountain would not come to Mahomet, Mahomet would go to the mountain. Late in November, 1911, he sent word to Roosevelt that he would give his demonstrations in New York City during the first fortnight in December. He then made an error, a rather egregious one. He asked Roosevelt to advise if he could attend on short notice, since "the weather is such a factor in many of my things."

Theodore Roosevelt did not overlook Thayer's admission that the exhibitions depended on the weather. In his reply (Nov. 24, 1911) Roosevelt said:

I wish I could persuade you to look at those experiments from what I am sure is the only standpoint which will make them of practical

value, that is, realizing, if you have to take into account the weather
in making them, that you are taking into account just precisely what
animals can *not* take into account. It reminds me a little of an experiment with a peculiar kind of explosive powder which Congress once,
when I was President, forced the Navy Department to undertake. In
accordance with the direction of Congress, we tested shells loaded
with this explosive, with the result that one of them blew up inside a
twelve-inch gun and wrecked it. Thereupon the friends of the invention at once came down to me and indignantly protested that I
had tested the shell in cold weather, whereas it was only worth anything in hot weather! I had to explain that we could not count upon
having foes so gentle that they would only attack during summer.

When Thayer restated his views on the white "flags" of deer
and prongbuck concealing these animals by harmonizing with the
skyline, Roosevelt's imagination came up with a reply to end all
replies:

There is in Africa a blue rump babboon. It is also true that the
Mediterranean Sea bounds one side of Africa. If you could make a
series of experiments tending to show that if the blue rump babboon
stood on its head by the Mediterranean you would mix up its rump
and the Mediterranean, you might be illustrating something in optics,
but you would not be illustrating anything that had any bearing
whatsoever on the part played by the coloration of the animal in
actual life.

Thayer tried, almost desperately, to get Roosevelt to witness
his demonstrations. Roosevelt, in turn, tried to get Thayer to
face the facts. Neither yielded as much as an inch to the other.

III

The controversy, boiled down, was essentially a conflict on the
universality of concealing coloration. Both contestants were
partly in the right, and partly in the wrong. Thayer made his
biggest mistake in constructing theories, and then trying to force
the facts to fit them. Roosevelt, many scientists now feel, under-
rated the importance of the part played by color, and particularly counter-shading, in concealing an animal from its foes.

Roosevelt's greatest error, however, as in the nature-faker controversy, was his head-in-the-air assurance, and his harshness. It was seemingly impossible for him, ever, when tangling with an opponent, to use the delicate weapon. The reaction of the general public was natural: They wanted to know, in short, why Roosevelt didn't pick on someone his own size.

There will be little argument today against the proposition that the modern study of concealment and disguise in nature dates from Thayer's original contribution (in 1896), and that he deserves full credit for discovering the important principle of counter-shading. Authorities are of the opinion, too, that Thayer's *Concealing Coloration in the Animal Kingdom*, in spite of errors and subsequent data, still serves as a good introduction to the subject. In World War I, devices and formulas taken from it were put to practical use in disguising war and merchant vessels, and Thayer was hailed in some circles as the "Father of Camouflage."

Roosevelt, also, made important contributions. As Heller has said, "It was a great boon to the study of protective coloration to have a field naturalist of the wide experience of Roosevelt call attention to the numerous errors of application as well as to the defective reasoning in many color theories." [13]

It seems clear as William Beebe has said, that Roosevelt's main goal in the controversy "was that solitary point in mental space—the truth." [14]

23

"To the Land of the Quangley Wee"

DURING the waning months of Roosevelt's second term as President, the White House had played host to Father John Augustine Zahm, "a delightful little priest who was fond of Dante," [1] and equally fond of chasing about over various parts of the South American continent in the vanishing footsteps of the early Spanish conquerors. In fact, when he called at the White House, he had just returned from a journey up the Orinoco and down the Magdalena, in the course of which he had visited many out of the way localities and seen many strange sights.

Father Zahm (who often wrote under the pen name of H. J. Mozans) had come to the Executive Mansion to persuade Roosevelt to go with him on his next trip to South America. He wanted a companion who would be interested in the animals and plants of the equatorial forests, who could direct public attention to the lesser-known parts of the continent, and who would be capable of doing a "certain much-needed missionary work there . . . to dissipate prejudices." [2] He felt that Roosevelt, with his boundless energy and enthusiasm, was just the man for these purposes.

The little Catholic priest spoke so enthusiastically of his travels, and drew such entertaining pictures of the countries he had visited, that Roosevelt was tremendously impressed. His plans having been already well under way for the African expedition made it impossible for him to consider the suggestion at the moment; but he did not completely abandon it.

It was not until mid-1913, shortly after the "Bull Moose" had been shorn of its antlers, that the opportunity for such a trip presented itself. At that time Roosevelt was invited by the Brazilian, Chilean, and Argentine governments to address certain learned societies in those countries. Having no pressing commitments, he determined at once to accept, his decision being influenced partly by the growing urge for another fillip of excitement in the outdoor world, partly by Father Zahm's erstwhile entreaties, and partly by the circumstance that Kermit was now in Brazil, employed as a construction engineer.

Roosevelt soon invited Father Zahm to Oyster Bay, where they discussed the likely duration of the trip, probable expense, and the most propitious time of the year to start. They got in touch with the American Museum, which agreed to supply them with two naturalists and volunteered to aid in any other way practicable. They decided, too, on a tentative itinerary. As soon as Roosevelt had fulfilled his speaking commitments in the ABC countries, they would ascend the Paraguay River to its headwaters, and then, after crossing the divide, would go down one of the larger, southern tributaries of the Amazon, probably the Tapajos. From that point on they were undecided, although Roosevelt favored the Rio Negro, Casiquiare, and Orinoco way out, rather than the leisurely, less interesting Amazon-to-Para route.[3]

If Roosevelt had made a deliberate attempt to choose the most perilous route anywhere on the face of the earth he could not have done much better. It included some of the choicest pest holes in the world, and some of the most isolated regions of the continent. It was a much more difficult road, and a more perilous one, than the one he had chosen to follow through Africa. Yet Roosevelt was seriously considering it, in spite of his fifty-five years and his expanding waistline. It was not until later that he wrote, from added experience, that "the man should have youth and strength who seeks adventure in the wide, waste spaces of the earth." [4]

From the beginning it was doubtful that they could make the more hazardous part of the trip, the Rio Negro-Orinoco leg. But Roosevelt was hopeful to the very last. On July 30 he wrote Chapman asking him to inquire of the Brazilian Ambassador if they could be sure of finding a steam launch at Manaos to take them up the Rio Negro. And, on November 4, after he had reached Brazil, he wrote Chapman again, saying that if time permitted they might still attempt the long journey from Manaos by way of the Casiquiare to the Orinoco.

Roosevelt left most of the planning to Frank Chapman and Father Zahm. He did not personally assume responsibility for each and every detail himself as he had in preparing for the African trip. For instance, he corresponded with no one in South America familiar with the roads he would travel. He did not ask Osborn to supply him with books about the Amazon wilderness so that he might increase his knowledge of the geography, climate, and animal life of that part of the continent. In short, he did not even begin to plan as carefully for this trip as he did for the African one.

Not only did he fail to prepare carefully for the trip, but also, which was worse, he did not take it seriously. The general tone of his letters to Kermit, Chapman, Father Zahm, and others left the impression that he fully expected a minimum of discomfort and inconvenience, that he thought of the trip as being about on the same carefree level as Boswell's tour of the Hebrides. For instance, on June 23 he wrote Kermit, "I am going to see if it is possible to work across from the Plata into the valley of the Amazon. . . . It won't be anything like the African trip. There will be no hunting and no adventure."

And, in a letter to Father Zahm, he said, that it looked as if they were going to have "a delightful holiday from the time we leave Asuncion until we reach Caracas, with just the right amount of adventure."

He expressed himself in even lighter vein to Lodge:

I think I wrote you that October 4th was the date of my sailing. I hope I shall be able to make my trip northward into the Amazonian forest, and come out by the Amazon. Of course, however, it is possible we may not be able to do it, and so I don't want to announce in advance just where we are going, for if we find it impossible to get through, then we shall try some other plan . . . Altogether I think it one of the finest voyages ever undertaken since "The Jumbleys went to sea in a sieve," and since the voyage so feelingly portrayed by Lear undertaken by Slingsby, Guy, Ethel and somebody else to the land of the Quangley Wee.

It goes without saying that Roosevelt knew he might encounter hostile Indians, that his boats might be smashed in treacherous rapids, and that he would not be immune to the feeding habits of local insects. It is plain, however, that he did not expect any of these things to happen to him. If any maggots of concern worked in his brain during the summer of 1913, he has left no evidence of their activity.

The reasons for his lack of concern and general indifference seem fairly obvious. For one thing, he did not look forward to the hunting with enthusiasm; the South American wilderness had little to offer in the way of big game. Although he wanted to shoot at least one jaguar and one tapir, these beasts held out little promise of excitement to one who had felled lions, elephants, rhinos, and grizzlies. He would encounter, of course, many smaller animals of great interest to the zoologist, but these creatures did not excite his curiosity immediately. Also, since he had successfully completed the African trip, represented in advance as highly perilous, he found it difficult to become alarmed about purported dangers in South America. Moreover, the previous journey had taken the keen edge off his appetite for large-scale expeditions. Another probable factor was Father Zahm's holiday attitude, his two journeys into the interior of the southern continent having been made with no more incident or mishap than that generally associated with tourist travel in Arizona or Montana.

Roosevelt's inadequate preparation was offset in some measure by the caliber of the men who accompanied him. In addition to Kermit, Father Zahm, and Roosevelt himself, the party included Anthony Fiala, a former Arctic explorer, and the two naturalists supplied by the American Museum: George K. Cherrie and Leo E. Miller.

Cherrie, the senior of the two naturalists and the more experienced, had spent already twenty-two years collecting animals in various parts of Central and South America. Miller, though much younger than Cherrie, was well trained in tropical exploration, having demonstrated his efficiency as a field naturalist in the hinterland of Colombia, Venezuela, and British Guiana. He combined literary with scientific ability, a fact that pleased Roosevelt.

Fiala was an excellent choice for the job of assembling equipment and supervising its handling and shipment. It was he who brought together the tents, mosquito netting, cots, hammocks, ropes, pulleys, fly dope, quinine, food, and many other supplies deemed necessary for the trip. Although Roosevelt had little to do with this phase of the planning, he held himself responsible for his personal effects. He took with him his highly regarded Springfield rifle, two shotguns, and two revolvers. His clothing was left over from Africa: khaki coat and trousers, flannel shirts, hobnail shoes, wool socks, gauntlets to protect against mosquitoes, sun helmet for the open country, and slouch hat for the jungle shade. There is no record of his requesting raspberry preserves, canned tomatoes, or Boston baked beans.

II

The expedition sailed from New York on October 4, 1913. This was a year, almost to the day, after a would-be assassin, John Schrank, had come close to ending Roosevelt's life in Milwaukee with a pistol bullet.

The voyage was a pleasant one. There were serious moments, when Roosevelt talked alone with members of the party about the descent of the Tapajos, and there were lighter ones when, much to the delight of the passengers, he took to the floor to dance a hornpipe, or lent his avoirdupois to a tug-of-war. Much of the time he was alone with a book. He read two or three daily, generally in as many fields. Much to the amazement of Father Zahm, he read immediately after a meal. "His brain and stomach do not seem to be correlated as in ordinary mortals," the priest reflected.[5]

In any discussion of books Roosevelt played a prominent role. "It was then that we were often amazed," wrote Father Zahm, "by his broad and exact knowledge not only of the fauna of the countries we were about to visit, but also of the political and social histories of their peoples as well."[6]

After picking up Miller in the Barbados and Kermit in Bahia, the boat proceeded to Rio where it dropped anchor on October 21. Almost immediately Roosevelt was closeted with the Brazilian Minister of Foreign Affairs, Lauro Müller, who proceeded to tell him of a recent discovery on the central Brazilian plateau (the Plan Alto) by Colonel Candido Mariano da Silva Rondon and his colleagues of the Brazilian Telegraphic Commission. Colonel Rondon, Müller said, had located the headwaters of a large, unmapped river, which flowed northward toward the Amazon, but to an unknown destination. Müller wondered if Roosevelt might not want to meet Colonel Rondon to talk over the possibility of exploring this river.

There was no need for such a meeting so far as Roosevelt was concerned. He said immediately, "We will go down that unknown river!" [7] He was drawn toward the idea like Columbus toward the Indies. Here was something into which he could put his teeth. He at once wrote Chapman, his letter being characterized by an overflow of spirit which he had not demonstrated since shortly before his departure for Africa, when he had been "red hot to be out."

He told Chapman that this was "a feat worth doing," and that the rest of the party was as eager to go as he was, even after he had made it clear to them that this was probably a more hazardous undertaking than the one originally mapped out for them. Cherrie and Miller, he said, were more enthusiastic than the others; they believed that in this unexplored portion of the continent they might get collections for the Museum which would be really worth-while.

Thus was born the Expedicão Scientifica Roosevelt-Rondon, that would attempt a descent of the stream christened by Colonel Rondon: Rio da Duvida—the River of Doubt.

As soon as this news reached the United States, Roosevelt's friends deluged him with protests. Lodge wrote that he felt more anxiety about this expedition than any he had taken, simply because he had "a general belief that the untrodden parts of South America are probably more unhealthy than any other regions on the face of the earth." [8] And Osborn hurriedly sent word that he "would never consent to his going to this particular region under the American Museum flag; that he would not assume even part of the responsibility for what might happen in case he did not return." [9]

Roosevelt's reply was typical: "I have already lived and enjoyed as much of life as any other nine men I know; I have had my full share, and if it is necessary for me to leave my remains in South America, I am quite ready to do so." [10] It was not until afterwards that he said, "Genuine wilderness exploration is as dangerous as warfare." [11]

24

The Expedicão Roosevelt-Rondon

BEFORE the year 1913, which saw Roosevelt traveling the Brazilian wilderness, South America had been visited by many naturalists, including such eminent ones as Alexander von Humboldt, Charles Waterton, Richard Schomburgh, Alfred Russell Wallace, Richard Spruce, Henry Walter Bates, Louis Agassiz, and Charles Darwin. In their search for knowledge, Humboldt, Waterton, and Schomburgh covered chiefly the northern rim of the continent; Wallace, Bates, Spruce and Agassiz the tropical rain forest of the Amazon basin; and Darwin the eastern and western coasts south of the equator. But no naturalist until now had penetrated deep into that great central region of Brazil, the far off divide between the mighty Amazon and La Plata systems, where Roosevelt was now prepared to go.

The Expedicão Scientifica Roosevelt-Rondon, the name given it by the Brazilian government, got under way on December 9 when Roosevelt and his party boarded a small river steamer at Asuncion and began the ascent of the Paraguay. Three days later they reached the Brazilian border where they found awaiting them Colonel Rondon and several associates.

The river course at first ran through a vast, level plain, unrelieved by any elevation as far as the eye could see. To the east lay a well-settled country, and to the west the great indeterminate region known as the Chaco where Cherrie and Miller, while Roosevelt lectured, had made a fine collection of birds and mammals in spite of hungry hordes of flies and mosquitoes. Farther on the river ran through the *pantanal,* marshy country, where the whole region was a vast swamp, varied only occasionally by stretches of higher ground. Although birds and mammals abounded, collecting here was difficult to an extreme. As they left the *pantanal,* gradually reaching higher elevations, they entered forest.

Except for two or three side trips, enabling Roosevelt to satisfy a personal ambition to kill two of South America's largest game animals, the jaguar and tapir, the expedition moved steadily upstream, arriving after five weeks, on January 16, at a remote place called Tapirapoan where Colonel Rondon's Telegraphic Commission headquarters was located. From this outpost they were to begin a trip of 44 days' duration across the Paraguay-Amazon divide to the headwaters of the River of Doubt.

Before they could move, however, Rondon had to assemble some 200 mules, oxen, and horses to transport their food and equipment, Cherrie and Miller had to pack their specimens already collected and arrange for their shipment down the Paraguay, and Fiala had to reassemble and repack all supplies that had been transported upriver by boat.

The moment that Roosevelt made the decision in Rio de Janeiro to descend "that unknown river," the whole character of the expedition changed. From a strictly zoological one, it became quickly geographic—particularly from Tapirapoan on. Roosevelt called it, aptly enough, a zoogeographic reconnaissance.

On January 20 the party moved again, gradually escaping from the dense, almost impenetrable forest, as they unconsciously climbed to higher ground. Suddenly they emerged into open country. They had reached the Parecís plateau, the high tableland of Matto Grasso, at an elevation of 2000 feet. Here was a dry, sandy region, covered only with grass, stunted bushes, and man-sized ant-hills. The change from a lush, tropical forest to xerophytic plateau had been an abrupt through-the-looking-glass experience. One hour the party had been riding beneath a verdant canopy of foliage, in perpetual shade, the next they were in open country, with the horizon in the distance. Rheas, red wolves, and pampas deer supplanted monkeys, toucans, and parrots.

For a number of days the men enjoyed the sun and the sky, as they rapidly left behind them the romantic country of La Plata, crossed the divide between the two river systems, and approached the threshold of boundless, incalculable Amazonia. On February 23 they reached the Papagaio River, whose waters ultimately flow into the Tapajos. They were definitely over the hump. Here the party broke into three groups: Father Zahm turned back to Tapirapoan and the Paraguay; Fiala set off down the Papagaio and Tapajos; and the remainder went on along the route originally projected by Colonel Rondon.

Three weeks later, after beating their way farther to the west, Roosevelt's party reached a small stream that fed into the River of Doubt. Just six miles from there they would embark on their dash into the unknown. At this place the party divided again. Miller, with several Brazilian companions, was to descend the Gy-Paraná and Madeira to Manaos. Roosevelt, Kermit, Rondon, Cherrie, and eighteen others, all experienced in forest and river travel, were to undertake the exploration of the nameless river. Each party would carry only bare necessities, such as food, bedding, guns, ammunition, and surveying instruments. Roosevelt's contingent had assembled food for fifty days, enough to last them, they thought, with what fish and game they should be able to find along the way. The twenty-two men, with supplies and equipment, were to occupy seven dugout canoes, some of them ancient and waterlogged.

All was now in readiness for the descent of this river, which might take them in one week to the Gy-Paraná, in six weeks to the Madeira, or in eight—to a destination beyond the ken of cartographers. They shoved off shortly after mid-day on the 27th of February. Roosevelt was in high spirits, even though he had come up with a mild attack of malaria on the eve of departure. He was experiencing just the proper mingling of anticipation and derring-do to excite his spirit. "No white man had ever gone down or up this river or seen the country through which we were passing," he wrote.[1] Almost at once he found his world reduced to a ribbon of rushing water between two high walls of tropical verdure.

Just before pushing off, Roosevelt sent a letter to his editor, Robert Bridges. In this he said that the trip thus far had been both pleasant and interesting, with no real hardship. From here on it was to be different.

Toward the close of the fourth day they came to a series of rapids and waterfalls where they had to cut a trail around to the quiet water below, and make a corduroy road for the dugouts. It took them three days to complete the portage—a mild foretaste of what lay ahead. To make matters worse, annoying insects now suddenly became abundant. There were large horseflies the size of bumblebees, sand flies, piums, and worst of all, boroshuda flies, exasperating creatures that brought blood at once with their bites, and left marks that lasted for weeks.

Not only did they have to protect their bodies from flies and mosquitoes, but also they had to exercise every precaution to keep their clothing from being carried away by them. In this they were only partially successful. One morning Roosevelt reached for his underwear, only to discover that during the night parasol ants had almost excised one entire leg. According to Cherrie, "When the Colonel held them up for our inspection there was a shout of laughter, but I don't believe he relished our mirth." [2]

The next few days they made progress slowly, as they alternately ran rapids, made short portages and picked up speed on intervening tranquil reaches of the river. They encountered parties of monkeys, heard the now familiar notes of the false bell-bird, and discovered signs of the paca, agouti, peccary and tapir. The *camaradas* tapped a milk tree, from which oozed a thick, lactescent juice. Roosevelt found that the taste was not unpleasant, in spite of a stickiness which clung to his mouth.

In running the boats through the rapids the men labored in the water much of the time, often in touch with bushes and vines along the banks. Throngs of biting and stinging ants tumbled onto them, leaving their skins almost solid welts of inflammation. Among the ants were large ones over an inch in length, with a sting equal to that of a small scorpion.

The expedition experienced its first serious mishap on the night of March 11, the thirteenth day on the river. The river rose while the men slept, and tore two of the boats from their moorings. They found only fragments. Since the five remaining boats could not possibly carry all the men and equipment, it was imperative they stop long enough to build a new one. This delay was serious, especially from the food standpoint. They had been unable as expected to supplement their diet appreciably from the surrounding forest. The Brazil nuts on which they had counted had had an off year. These could have been roasted, or ground into flour, or prepared in various other ways, and in abundance would have been an extremely important item. And the river yielded only a few fish; the party had counted on these, too. The delay was serious for another reason: thus far they had traveled, in a straight line, not more than 35 miles of an estimated 400. The three days required to cut and dig out a boat represented a waste of time they could ill afford. According to Rondon, "These developments caused a great deal of annoyance to Mr. Roosevelt who feared lest all this should result in delaying still more the termination of the journey." [3] Roosevelt went over the plans of each day's march again and again with Rondon in an effort to speed up their progress and to anticipate future difficulties. He allowed nothing, however, to interfere with the preparation of his articles for Scribner's.

The new boat was launched on the morning of the 14th, after which they were on their way again. But the gods did not look upon them kindly. They soon entered a new series of rapids, where Kermit's boat was capsized and one of the *camaradas* with him drowned. Kermit escaped a like fate only by a miracle. After being tossed about in the rushing water and swept over a falls, he was saved when the current of the stream carried him within reach of overhanging branches. The search for the missing boatman was fruitless, but so far as the ultimate success of the expedition was concerned, the worst feature of the accident was the loss of the boat with a week's supply of boxed provisions, and tools for boat building.

After the enforced delay of searching for the boatman and the erection of a marker inscribed, "In these Rapids died Simplicio," they soberly took their places in the canoes and once more gave themselves up to the whims of the river. As they camped that night at the foot of another series of rapids, they realized more than ever the necessity for making greater speed. There was ample cause for the gloom which pervaded the camp; there would have been even more cause if they could have foreseen what lay ahead.

The morning of the 16th was dark and dispiriting, an omen of mishap yet unborn. Soon after embarking they once more found dangerous rapids barring their way. Colonel Rondon beached his canoe and walked ahead to explore the terrain, preceded by one of three dogs they had with them. Within a few minutes he heard the dog give a yelp of pain, followed shortly by another cry of distress, as it came into view and dropped dead at his feet, impaled by two long Indian arrows. To the dread of rapids and possible starvation was now added the threat of hostile savages.

Roosevelt immediately issued instructions for defending the expedition. While the boats were being lowered through the rapids he stood at the head of the portage, and Cherrie at the foot, gun in hand. They were ready to give a good account of themselves if attacked. But misfortune came from another direction. After they had lowered one boat successfully, and started another (the dugout just built), the cable broke and it sank, along with rope and pulleys. Affairs had rapidly gone from bad to worse: they now had only four boats, entirely inadequate to carry both men and supplies; they had consumed one third of their food, while possibly five-sixths of the distance remained to be traveled; they were surrounded by Indians of unknown number and intention which made it highly unwise to stop to build more boats; and they faced obstacles ahead that, although a matter of conjecture, were undoubtedly formidable. The only bright spot in the picture was the general good health of the party; even that was marred slightly by Roosevelt's continuing malarial chills.

After a lengthy conference they decided to go ahead as rapidly as possible, with thirteen of the men cutting their way through the rank tropical growth bordering the river, and the remainder handling the canoes; if all went well they would stop farther along to build additional boats. Roosevelt did not agree fully with this plan—it appeared risky to him to follow it in the Indian zone—but it was adopted. To facilitate progress they hurriedly discarded every dispensable item of equipment, retaining only food supplies and other actual necessities. That night Cherrie wrote in his diary, "It is doubtful if all our party ever reaches Manaos." [4]

The next day, the 17th of March, they made a good run, and that evening were cheered when one of the men caught a large fish for their supper. "How little it took to cheer us up," wrote Cherrie.[5] They camped just below the mouth of a stream that entered the Duvida from the west. This camp assumed more than usual importance the following morning, when Colonel Rondon assembled the members of the expedition to announce that, as a representative of the Brazilian Government, he was naming the tributary *Rio Kermit,* and the main stream *Rio Roosevelt.* By now it was apparent to all that the river they had been descending was not just a tributary of the Gy-Paraná, but a large stream hitherto unknown to the map makers.

During the next two days they came upon several Indian houses and shelters, but saw no Indians, and experienced no further sign of hostility. They therefore deemed it both wise and expedient to halt long enough to construct two new boats. These they built of lighter wood, with the result that they rode higher in the water, and were more satisfactory in every way than the dugout lost in the rapids. In the construction, however, the party lost four valuable days. As they prepared to embark they took stock once again of their rapidly dwindling rations. They had consumed half of their original supply, and the situation was only slightly alleviated by the discovery of some Brazil nuts and wild pineapples, and the capture of a few birds and fish. These items did not go far among twenty famished men. At this time, not through choice but necessity, they reduced themselves to two meals a day.

From March 22 to 26 the progress they made was dishearteningly slow, as they encountered one series of rapids after another, with the intervening stretches of smooth water good at best for only thirty or forty minutes each of easy paddling. The men toiled from dawn to dusk, dragging the heavy boats around rapids and waterfalls.

It was Cherrie's opinion that none of them would have come out alive if Roosevelt had not been with them. One example of his leadership occurred on March 27, when they had reached the foot of a long rapids and the canoemen were bringing down the empty boats, their contents having been removed and carried earlier to the bottom of the portage. Suddenly two of the boats, which had been lashed together to form a balsa, were caught in the angry rush of waters and capsized. Instead of being carried away and crushed, they were pulled downward by a peculiar action of the current and held tightly against the rocks. Cherrie, who saw what had happened, realized at once that if the boats should become disengaged they would be thrown against the boulders and smashed to tinder. As quickly as possible, he ran to the foot of the rapids to report what had taken place. It was Roosevelt who first rushed into the water, and who played the major role in raising the canoes and saving them. When Roosevelt subsequently wrote about this incident he said little about it, and nothing at all about the fact that he slipped and struck his weak leg against a stone, inflicting an ugly wound which became infected and did not heal until after he was out of the jungle. This injury was responsible for much of the suffering Roosevelt was to endure throughout the remainder of the journey. According to Cherrie: "His rushing into the water to assist was entirely characteristic of him. And he did this after many days of a fever which had weakened his vitality." [6]

Roosevelt could not stand idly by watching others at a time when action was required. From the very start of the trip Cherrie and Kermit had taken turns washing their clothes and those of Roosevelt. One day during this period Cherrie had taken their dirty clothes down to the river's edge to start cleaning them when Roosevelt, who had been watching Kermit's efforts to get the boats through some difficult rapids, called to Cherrie: "Kermit would like you to give him a hand with the boats." When Cherrie returned to camp that evening he found that the laundry had been done and hung up to dry. "It is the only time I have ever had my clothes washed by an ex-President of the United States!" the naturalist said. [7]

II

Succeeding days brought only more rough water and more portages. The plight of the party daily grew more critical and its gloom deepened correspondingly. On the morning of the 31st they dragged their canoes around still another chain of water-capped terraces and brought them to rest in a stretch of quiet water. Their spirits rose as they envisaged a day of rapid, uninterrupted progress, but the misfortunes which had beset them from the very beginning were to plague them again. Just one hour after embarking they struck a series of rapids which, in some respects, was the most difficult they had encountered on the entire journey. The water of the *Rio Roosevelt* converged to rush through a narrow gorge, where it leapt wildly down a boulder-studded channel. Mountains rose abruptly from the water's edge on either side. The question uppermost here was not, how long will it take to make the portage, but, will it be possible to make it at all?

Rondon and Kermit fought their way through the tangle of undergrowth bordering the river for a mile or more to ascertain what lay ahead. When they returned Rondon gave it as his opinion that they would have to abandon the canoes and each man fight for himself through the forest. The fate of the expedition rested upon a decision which now must be made, and made quickly. Should they accept Rondon's verdict, or should they renew their month-old struggle with the river in a last determined effort to get the boats to the foot of the rapids? Both Cherrie and Kermit refused to consider Rondon's suggestion; they thought it equivalent to a death sentence, and insisted that they fight their way down the gorge. Their final success was a tribute to their judgment.

The serious position in which the men found themselves had affected the health of all, but Roosevelt's most of all, because of his feeling of responsibility for the group. The attack of malaria which he now experienced was particularly severe, and Cherrie and Kermit took turns watching beside him through the night. Toward morning he called Cherrie to his side and said: "I want you and Kermit to go on. You can get out. I will stop here." [8]

Even before this, he had made up his mind that if the time ever came when he held up the expedition, he would arrange for the others to go on without him.

The next day Roosevelt's fever went down, but from that time on he was a very sick man. He had not only malaria to contend with, but also dysentery and deep abscesses. There were times when he was able to walk slowly over the portages, stopping to rest at intervals. When Kermit finished bringing down the canoes he would find his father sitting against a tree reading a volume of Gibbon or the Oxford Book of English Verse. He even kept up with his writing. On one of the manuscripts he later sent to Bridges appeared this marginal note, "This is not written very clearly; my temperature is 105°." [9]

The next few days were a succession of nightmares. The heart-breaking task of portage with its attendant griefs, and Roosevelt's alarming illness, were not the only crosses they had to bear. Other members of the party, including Cherrie, came down with malaria, another boat was lost to the voracity of the river and, finally, one of the *camaradas* went berserk and killed a companion.

That night Roosevelt's fever bounded again and he was out of his head. Once more they feared that he might not live. Kermit recorded the setting of those events:

. . . For a few moments the stars would be shining, and then the sky would cloud over and the rain would fall in torrents, shutting out sky and trees and river. Father first began with poetry; over and over again he repeated "In Xanadu did Kubla Khan a stately pleasure dome decree," then he started talking at random, but gradually he centered down to the question of supplies, which was, of course, occupying everyone's mind. Part of the time he knew that I was there, and he would then ask me if I thought Cherrie had had enough to eat to keep going. Then he would forget my presence and keep saying to himself: "I can't work now, so I don't need much food, but he and Cherrie have worked all day with the canoes, they must have part of mine." Then he would again realize my presence and question me as to just how much Cherrie had had. How good faithful Cajazeira waked I do not know, but when his watch was due I felt him tap me on the shoulder, and I crawled into my soggy hammock to sleep the sleep of the dead.[10]

The following day, Roosevelt's fever having gone down toward morning, they made a record run of 36 kilometres, the river running smoothly once again and the mountains falling away on either hand; but the day afterward so many of the men were sick that it was considered wise to stay in camp. Kermit had malaria, with a temperature of 104°, and Cherrie was laid up with dysentery. The few who were not sick were so weakened by lack of food and overwork that they had to have rest.

The next day, the 8th of April, they ran more rapids and made more portages. That evening Cherrie brought in three monkeys and Lyra got two piranhas, which the party promptly ate. Monkeys, more than any other animal, saved the expedition, but the piranha ran a close second. When studying the blood-thirsty habits of these fish along the lower reaches of the Paraguay, Roosevelt had had no thought that they might save human lives at a later date. They were bony but did not lack flavor, and they supplied energy.

There now followed a week in which the spirits of the men alternately rose and fell. As they heard the ominous sound of waterfalls ahead their hearts filled with foreboding; as these were passed and placid water ran beneath their boats hopes revived.

After such a series of unhappy episodes, they had little thought that the 15th of April would differ materially from preceding days. Two hours after climbing into the boats one of the men chanced to see on the left bank of the river a board on a post, inscribed with the two letters, "J.A." There was only one explanation. An adventurous rubber-gatherer had come up the river this far, and had marked the spot. They plied their paddles with renewed energy, and an hour later came on a recently-built *baraca*, a rubber-man's shack, located in a small clearing. They found no one at home, but the presence of household furnishings and two dogs proved that the owner was not far away. A short distance farther downstream they found another jungle habitation, occupied by an old black man, the first human being the party had seen for forty-seven interminable days. In the late afternoon they reached still another wilderness abode, where they passed the night. The owners informed them that they were fifteen days by canoe from the confluence of the *Rio Roosevelt* (known to them as the Castanho) and the Aripuanan, and that just beyond this junction there was a small river village called São João, where rubber steamers arrived periodically from Manaos, 36 hours away.

The expedition did not reach Manaos until April 30, two months after embarking on the waters of the River of Doubt (now shown on maps as the *Rio Roosevelt*), and five months after leaving Asuncion. In that time they had completed a journey of some 1500 miles, much of it through unknown, unexplored wilderness.

II

From both the geographical and zoological standpoints, the Expedicão Scientifica Roosevelt Rondon was successful. It had placed a new river on the maps of the world. In 1912 the large-scale maps of South America showed a great blank space in the very heart of the Continent, equivalent in size to the state of Nevada. This *terra incognita* was bordered on the west by the Gy-Paraná and the Madeira, and on the east by the Tapajos. It was this huge, unknown area that Roosevelt had traversed, and it was here that he had explored a new river the size of the Hudson.

Zoologically the results were gratifying, even though not up to original expectations. Cherrie and Miller had collected 2,500 birds and 500 mammals, not to mention a large number of reptiles, amphibians, fish, and insects. Moreover, the majority of these animals were from virgin territory, from areas previously unvisited by naturalists. They thus added enviable riches to the resources of the American Museum of Natural History. Among them were a considerable number of species entirely new to science, while practically all of the material was new to the Museum.

From another standpoint the South American trip was a calamity. Roosevelt's health was permanently impaired. He was never again effortlessly to display the energy and the ebullience of spirit that the American people had come to expect of him. Just one year after he started down the River of Doubt he wrote Surgeon-General Rixey:

. . . As for me, my dear doctor, I am practically through. I am not a man like you who keeps his youth almost to the end; and I am now pretty nearly done out. I would not say this except to my old friend, who was also my old physical adviser, because it is rather poor business to speak about one's physical ailments; but the trouble is I have rheumatism or gout and things of that kind to a degree that makes it impossible for me to take very much exercise; and then in turn the fact that I cannot take exercise prevents my keeping in good condition. I am more pleased than I can say that I was able to take the South American trip. I knew it would be my last thing of the kind.

But Roosevelt still stood by what he had said thirty years before: "I am always willing to pay the piper when I have a good dance; and every now and then I like to drink the wine of life with brandy in it." [11]

Roosevelt's account of his South American trip, entitled *Through the Brazilian Wilderness,* was published in book form in the fall of 1914. The elements were all present to make it of interest both to the layman and scientist. As J. A. Allen of the American Museum said:

The pages teem with information about the country, its natural history, its economic resources and its human inhabitants, whether wild, unclad Indians or European colonists, and is written with the inspiration that only the fresh impressions of daily events and experiences, jotted down in the field can impart.[12]

The predominant note in the book, wrote *The Geographical Journal*, was Roosevelt's "active interest in the myriad forms of plant or animal existence" he encountered.[13] *The Spectator*, carrying this line of thought even further, asserted: "Mr. Roosevelt's narrative is as fascinating as the famous pages of Bates." [14]

The comparison of Roosevelt's *Through the Brazilian Wilderness* with Bates' *The Naturalist on the Amazons* is flattering. The latter is one of the all-time classics of biological exploration, taking rank with Darwin's *Voyage of H.M.S. Beagle* and Wallace's *Malay Archipelago*. Actually, the two books have little in common. *The Naturalist on the Amazons* made its mark in the world because of Bates' painstaking researches on the small animal life of the Amazon basin and his innumerable important original observations culled from eleven years of residence. *Through the Brazilian Wilderness*, on the other hand, although a fascinating account of a five months' journey across central Brazil, with a series of clear-cut impressions of the animals and plants observed along the way, added little to what was already known about the South American biota.

It is possible, though, that *Through the Brazilian Wilderness* will be read as long as Bates' classic, because it contains the spirit-stirring account of Roosevelt's descent of the River of Doubt. A better record of adventure by rapids and cataracts, through impenetrable and unknown forests, it would be hard to find.

25

Organizing a Bird Club

THE years 1915, 1916, and 1917 slowly, grimly presented their troubled days to history. They were war years. Roosevelt had told his old personal physician, Dr. Rixey, that he was about through, but later events proved that he was still very much alive and kicking. Though physically unsound, he had lost nothing of his mental vigor. He made a tremendous contribution to the war effort at home. The only noticeable difference in his pattern of existence was a more careful blending of his political activities with the literary and scientific ones. The latter represented his leisure and took many forms. He reviewed books about animals and wrote articles on natural history topics for *The Outlook* and other periodicals. He visited a wildlife refuge he had himself created while President. He went all the way to British Guiana to see a tropical laboratory (William Beebe's) in which he had a personal interest. He reduced the population of devil-fish in the Gulf of Mexico. He gave the public *A Book-Lover's Holidays in the Open*. And he organized one of the first bird clubs formed in the United States.

Early in 1915 the naturalist, Ernest Harold Baynes, gave a talk at Sagamore Hill on how to attract birds. His audience consisted of Colonel and Mrs. Roosevelt and a number of their Long

Island neighbors. At the conclusion of his lecture Baynes asked the audience, as he had done at other places, if they would not like to support the growing bird club movement, then in its infancy. Roosevelt was enthusiastic about the idea, and in this way the Long Island Bird Club was born, with Roosevelt as its first president.

By lending his prestige and his sympathetic oversight to this club, Roosevelt in no time at all saw it develop into an influential organ in the conservation of American bird life. His first move was an appeal to the public:

I earnestly hope that all our fellow-citizens of Long Island will endeavor to forward the objects of the Bird Club. I wish to make the appeal especially to my fellow-Long-Islanders, who like myself, are permanent residents of the Island and have their homes and do their work on the Island. The preservation of birds is of great economic importance to all of us and especially to the farmers, because of the war they make upon the insect foes which are the most dangerous enemies of the farm, garden and woodland.

Our aim should be three-fold: First, to put a stop to all molestation of beautiful and useful birds by man or by the domestic creatures which man can control; Second, to encourage these birds by making existence easier for them; Third, to war against their natural foes.

Roosevelt went on to say that everyone should receive the same pleasure from having birds about the premises and observing their habits and listening to their songs, as from looking at beautiful pictures or listening to good music. He thought that it should be a matter of honorable responsibility on the part of every man and boy never to destroy birds wantonly, and to take action against those who did. "To kill our small birds is wicked," he said, since "nothing adds as much to the attractiveness of a house as to see a score or two of birds nesting about it." To encourage their presence, he suggested that every effort be made to provide food, drinking water, and artificial nesting places.[1]

Not one of these suggestions for encouraging birds was new to Roosevelt, who had protected and encouraged the birds about his Oyster Bay home for many years. As early as 1910 he had written Frank Chapman: "I would like to feed the birds round my house this winter. I suppose crumbs for the sparrows (*not* English sparrows) are all right. What kind of bones or other things ought I to hang up for the chickadees and other birds?"

Due in large measure to his enthusiastic leadership, the Bird Club of Long Island quickly extended its influence to other parts of the Island. Fifty or more communities organized branches of the parent club, so that hundreds of individuals all over the Island were soon giving the birds suet and nuts in winter, putting up nesting boxes in the spring, supplying water in summer, and discussing bird problems at regular scheduled meetings at all seasons of the year. From time to time, to inform more fully their members, the Club issued leaflets with advice on the kinds of food to give the birds, the kinds of trees, shrubs, and climbers most likely to attract birds, and how to construct suitable bird houses and water baths. Many Long Islanders with large farms or estates established private bird sanctuaries, and erected signs forbidding trespassing and the shooting of birds.

The Club soon extended its work into the schools. It engaged a field secretary to talk about birds to school children. "All over Long Island, in the little rural schools remote from large communities, as well as in the larger centers, the children listened with enthusiasm, became members of Junior Audubon groups, competed for prizes for the best pictures of birds and feeding stations." [2] Efforts in this direction met with such success that today only a few states have more Junior Audubon Clubs than Long Island itself.

The most valuable work of this club was not done on Long Island, however. "It was done indirectly," as Baynes has pointed out, "in scores of towns and villages throughout the country, where the people heard of the interesting work being done around Oyster Bay by Colonel Roosevelt and his splendid bird club, and determined to follow his good example by organizing clubs of their own." Baynes thought, and with good reason, that Roosevelt was "the greatest factor in America in the matter of preservation of bird and animal life." [3]

II

The following year (1916), Roosevelt published his last book devoted to the outdoors and to the creatures of plain and forest which had enriched his life so generously over so many years: *A Book-Lover's Holidays in the Open.* The lengthening years had brought no diminution in Roosevelt's ability to produce the rugged and glowing phrase. In fact, some of his readers thought *A Book-Lover's Holidays in the Open,* a miscellany of chapters on topics ranging from "Primeval Man" to "A Naturalists' Tropical Laboratory," surpassed in excellence of expression anything that he had previously done.

"If I could possess only a single volume of Colonel Roosevelt's," William Beebe once wrote, "1 should choose 'A Book-Lover's Holidays in the Open,' for in it are some of his most relaxed, his richest, literary moments. Once when we were walking Indian file down a steep wood trail headed away from Sagamore Hill, he suddenly turned and said:

" 'What book of mine do you like best?'

"And I answered without hesitation, for it had been running through my mind that very instant: 'The Foreword of your "Book-Lover's Holidays." '

"Then I quoted [from the Foreword], as I often have in lectures:

"The grandest scenery of the world is his to look at if he chooses; and he can witness the strange ways of tribes who have survived into an alien age from an immemorial past, tribes whose priests dance in honor of the serpent and worship the spirit of the wolf and the bear. Far and wide, all the continents are open to him as they never were to any of his forefathers; the Nile and the Paraguay are easy of access, and the border-land between savagery and civilization; and the veil of the past has been lifted so that he can dimly see how, in time immeasurably remote, his ancestors—no less remote—led furtive lives among uncouth and terrible beasts, whose kind has perished utterly from the face of the earth. He will take books with him as he journeys; for the keenest enjoyment of the wilderness is reserved for him who enjoys also the garnered wisdom of the present and the past." [4]

26

"Only Those Are Fit to Live Who Do Not Fear to Die"

On April 2, 1917, President Wilson announced that a state of war existed between the United States and Germany. Theodore Roosevelt immediately asked Wilson to allow him to form a Division of fighting men. When this request was refused Roosevelt threw himself with great energy into the winning of the war through vigorously worded speeches and magazine articles that helped to lift the spirit of the American people.

The year 1918 was the sixtieth for Theodore Roosevelt. It was to be his last. He made no more trips into the wilderness. He hunted no more the wild game of the mountains or the large animals of the sea. He filled no more volumes with his richly colored accounts of life in the out-of-doors.

In the months left to him, in spite of ill health and the drain of energy contributed to the war effort, he proved again and again that the birds and the beasts, the trees and the flowers, were among his deepest interests, those to which he would cling closest to the very end.

For many years Roosevelt had been interested in the twin problems of domestication and hybridization. As early as 1903 he had expressed the hope that a Government experimental

261

breeding station might be established where the buffalo and common cattle could be cross-bred. "If those cross breeds could be
successfully perpetuated," he said, "we could have animals which
would produce a robe quite as good as the old buffalo robe . . .
and animals which would be so hardy that I think they would
have a distinct commercial importance." [1]

At about the same time he was saying that he believed the
eland, the largest of the African antelopes, could be domesticated, even in the arid American West.[2] After his stay in Africa,
where he became acquainted with the eland in its native environment, he was more convinced than ever of this possibility.[3]

In the spring of 1918, Roosevelt was willing to support a project that Vilhjalmur Stefansson, the famous Arctic explorer,
wrote to him about—the desirability of domesticating that shaggy-
haired beast of the Northern steppes, the musk ox.

Now, as regards the musk-ox [Roosevelt replied to Stefansson]. I
most emphatically wish your project well, not merely as regards this
war but as regards the future of the country. Our domestic animals
are merely those of Asia, because it was in Asia that civilization arose,
and in consequence, as it penetrated in other continents, men found
it easier to use the animals already tamed, than to tame new ones.
The llama of the Andes is almost the only exception. It is a capital
misfortune that the African eland has not been tamed. It is a capital
misfortune that the musk-ox has not been tamed. To tame it would
mean possibilities of civilization in northernmost America, which are
now utterly lacking.[4]

Roosevelt never for an instant lost his interest in the big game
animals of our West. In April, 1918, after reading an article by
Grinnell describing the current status of the elk in Yellowstone
National Park, his thoughts went winging to the West, to the
high mountains and rolling rivers where, almost thirty-five years
before, he had first heard the bugling of the elk, to him one of
the most singular and beautiful sounds in nature. The elk, because of the protection afforded them, Grinnell had written, had
multiplied far beyond the limits of their natural food supply. As

a result, they were dying in ever larger numbers of disease and starvation.

Roosevelt wrote to Grinnell at once:

That's a most interesting article. You sum the whole thing up in your final paragraph. I have said the same thing much less forcibly two or three times at Boone and Crockett meetings, and was regarded as rather hardhearted for saying so. The simple fact is that if we get additional winter grazing grounds for the elk, or fed them alfalfa, in four years they would have multiplied beyond the limit again, and we should be faced by exactly the same difficulty that we are now. There is winter ground for a few thousand of elk in the Park but not much more than a fraction of the present number. As their natural enemies have been removed their numbers must be kept down by disease or starvation, or else by shooting. It is a mere question of mathematics, to show that if protected as they have been in the Park, they would, inside of a century, fill the whole United States; so that they would *then* die of starvation.

In the twilight of his life, Roosevelt made a final contribution to the coloration argument. This was a magazine article by him entitled "Common Sense and Animal Coloration," which took exception to some conclusions of W. H. Longley, a Goucher College scientist, who had been studying coloration of fishes in the waters surrounding the Dry Tortugas Islands off the west coast of Florida. He attacked in particular Longley's generalization, based solely on his observation of coral-reef fishes, that no protectively colored animal is betrayed by motion. "Because in a very small field he believes he has found a rule to obtain," wrote Roosevelt, "he believes it must obtain everywhere. To use his own words, it would be impossible to take a more 'wholly illogical' and therefore a more utterly unscientific position than this." [5]

Roosevelt's hackles had been raised, in the beginning, because Longley accepted the "essential truth" of Thayer's hypotheses on coloration. Before ending his criticism, he could not resist taking one final jab at his one-time adversary:

Mr. Thayer's book is delightfully written and contains valuable artistic truths; just as Milton's account of the creation of life in "Paradise Lost" contains noble poetry; and as regards mammals and birds Thayer's book contains just about as much new scientific truth as does "Paradise Lost." To treat his book as in this respect superior to such a book as Dewar and Finn's, stands on a par with ranking the noble Miltonic poem of the creation as scientifically above Darwin's "Descent of Man." [6]

In his extremely active, buoyant life, Roosevelt rarely looked back upon his past; he did not give himself time. Though now in his sixtieth year, there was not even a glimmer that he approached that age of mental and physical atrophy when men often insensibly turn from future prospects to ponder past events. However, in early summer, 1918, Roosevelt did glance back for a moment—to write a short piece about his life as a naturalist. It was an excellent example of compression, for Roosevelt covered this important phase of his life in less than 3,000 words. At the same time, it was a first-class specimen of self-deprecation.

His modesty occasioned such references to his boyhood natural history efforts as: "my wooden methods of mounting birds," "my clumsy industry in skinning specimens," and "my collections showed nothing but enthusiasm on my part." [7] He was proud, he said, of just three biological contributions: (1) his Western books, which he thought contained a good deal of information not found elsewhere, (2) his collaboration with Heller on the life histories of African game animals, which he considered "a serious and worthwhile contribution to science," and (3) his observations on revealing and concealing coloration.

How odd that Roosevelt did not include his contribution to conservation! Not once did he allude to the tremendously important role he had played in furthering the protection of the wild animals and the great hardwood and coniferous forests which gave home to these animals, and the momentum he gave to the conservation program as a whole. The only explanation is that he must have regarded conservation as somehow apart from natural history which, of course, it is not.

Roosevelt brought his paper on his life as a naturalist to a close with these words:

I do not think there is much else for me to say about my anything but important work as a naturalist. But perhaps I may say further that while my interest in natural history has added very little to my sum of achievement, it has added immeasurably to my sum of enjoyment in life.[8]

He continued to read everything with a biological slant that came from the press. And when he discovered a book that struck his fancy he often, as we know, reviewed it. During the waning months of his life, he reviewed at least three books on natural history that he was ready to recommend to his readers: one by Leo Miller on his travels in South America, one by E. W. Nelson on the wild animals of North America, and another by Osborn on the origin and evolution of life. Roosevelt's review of the last is particularly worthy of attention, because it reveals not only his wide knowledge of geology, paleontology, and organic evolution, but also his ability to follow the highly technical ramifications of Osborn's abstract theory of evolution involving physiochemical details of action, reaction, and interaction of energy.

According to Dr. Alexander Lambert, Roosevelt's interest in paleontology, in animals long extinct, was as intense as his interest in living creatures. He then went on to tell this story:

One morning at Oyster Bay, as we sat at breakfast, we loitered at table to listen to an interesting description of hunting in the Ural Mountains which his friend the ambassador from Germany, Baron Speck von Sternberg, was giving. The question arose of the difference between the aurochs and our own bison, and whence had come all the ancestors of the modern bovine animals, and Roosevelt spoke of the glorious hunting that the old kings of Babylon and Assyria had had in the chase of the huge wild bulls of their day, a royal and dangerous sport.

As we further discussed the ancient forms of life of our Western plains, Roosevelt described, in a connected way, the development of the great mammals on the North American continent, and how they differed from those which had grown up on the South American continent . . . His depiction of the varying waves of life was a vivid picture, and we listened, charmed and amazed.

"Where in the world did you find that knowledge?" asked Sternberg. "That is extraordinarily interesting."

Roosevelt, with a whimsical wit, replied: "It is all the fault of the Fourth-Class Postmasters. When I can't sleep, and have been struggling all day with intricate problems in all the States of the Union, and the appointments that must be made of the Fourth-Class Postmasters, I go up-stairs, and in order to get to sleep, I sit and study out how the empire of Alexander the Great broke to pieces, and into what other empires it developed, and also how all the strange creatures of former days developed, and seemed to have lived. After changing the subject in my mind, I can go to sleep.[9]

Roosevelt did not become involved in the debates on evolution that raged during the later years of his life. Since he was a firm believer in evolution, accepting it as fact rather than theory, it would not have been surprising if he had taken up the cudgels where Huxley laid them down, and offered to tangle with William Jennings Bryan who, at this time, with oratory untinged by basic fact, was questioning man's descent from "monkeys." However, in his evaluation of Osborn's book, Roosevelt did strike out at the anti-evolutionists: "Disbelievers in this great natural law," he said, "are of exactly the same stamp as those who a century ago challenged the law of gravitation." [10]

In July, news reached Sagamore Hill that Quentin had been killed in combat over the German lines. The four boys had enlisted early. Kermit was at first with the British in Mesopotamia and the three others with the Allies in Europe. Roosevelt had been writing each of them at least once each week. He complained bitterly about the uselessness of what he was doing at home—deeds not words were what counted—"Slacker-in-spite-of-himself," he signed his letters. In a letter to John Burroughs he said that it was almost more than he could bear at times to sit at home in ease and comfort, while his sons were facing dreadful danger.[11]

As time went on, Archie was wounded, Ted gassed. Kermit was awarded the British Military Cross for gallantry in action and Archie the *Croix de Guerre*. Ted was promoted to Lieutenant Colonel. Roosevelt's pride in them knew no bounds. In a letter to Archie he said:

> The people I most respect here now feel that what I did as President, or in any other way, does not reflect nearly so much credit on me as the fact that Mother and I were able to bring up four boys who have done as you have done. . . . You are having your crowded hours of glorious life; you have seized the great chance, as it was seized by those who fought at Gettysburg, and Waterloo, and Agincourt, and Arbela and Marathon.[12]

As January and February gave way to March and April, Roosevelt as he had done for more than half a century, redis covered the miracle of spring; he welcomed back the birds that had been away for the winter. He wrote the boys about these things so close to his heart: "Spring has fairly begun. The frogs are noisy in the ponds, the robins and song sparrows and redwing blackbirds are in song; the maple buds are red and the willow tips green; the first mayflowers and bloodroot have appeared."

As summer came on he wrote, "The country is beautiful beyond description. It is the high tide of the year, with tree and flower and bird." [13]

Then, Roosevelt received the news about Quentin. He bore his grief with fortitude but, as one observer said, "The old side of him was gone . . . the boy in him had died." [14] In "The Great Adventure," an editorial prompted by Quentin's death, Roosevelt gave expression to the high dignity of his sorrow: "Only those are fit to live who do not fear to die, and none are fit to die who have shrunk from the joy of life and the duty of life. Both life and death are parts of the same Great Adventure." [15]

When John Muir's wife died Roosevelt advised him: "Get out among the mountains and trees, friend, they will do more for you than either man or woman could." Roosevelt could not reach the mountains, but he did get out among the trees—the oaks and beeches and maples and tulips—and among the sweet-voiced birds. More often than ever before, he left his study to stroll alone through the woods and open fields.

The summer days gave way to autumn. The birds had fallen silent. Bobolinks and grackles, joining others of their kind to form large swirling masses, visited fields, orchards, and gardens. Goldenrod and aster colored the roadsides. The trees turned red and yellow and gold.

On Armistice Day, Roosevelt suffered an attack of inflammatory rheumatism. While in a hospital bed, though in great pain much of the time, he reviewed Leo Miller's *In the Wilds of South America* for the *American Museum Journal*. The editor of the Journal, fully recognizing the handicaps under which Roosevelt had worked, was much impressed. In introducing the review to his readers he made this comment: "Colonel Roosevelt prepared this article during his recent stay at a New York hospital, showing his vast interest in natural history, his great energy even under trying conditions of ill health, and his loyalty to the men whose work he had come to know personally on his expeditions." [16]

Roosevelt returned to Sagamore Hill on the morning of Christmas Day. It was a happy homecoming, not only because he was able to join his family on this significant holiday, but also because his physicians had encouraged him to believe that he would enjoy a measure of good health again. That he thought so himself was evident from the plans he began to make at once for the near future. Archie was home, convalescing from battle wounds, and Roosevelt wanted to take him devil-fishing with the deep-sea fisherman Russell Coles. On New Year's Day he wrote Coles:

My doctors tell me that in all probability I shall be able to go with you on March 1st. There is, of course, however, the probability that my convalescence may be slower than they suppose. At present I am utterly worthless. I hope you understand how deeply I appreciate your taking Archie along. My great desire is that he shall get a devil fish.

In the days immediately following, Roosevelt turned to a monograph on pheasants which William Beebe had just completed. He was so pleased with its content, and its language, which had all the charm of an essay by Robert Louis Stevenson, that he knew at once he must review it. On the evening of January 5, 1919, he wrote Beebe, telling him of his enthusiasm for the monograph, and asking him to explain a taxonomic point not clear to him before he proceeded with his review. This was the last letter Theodore Roosevelt wrote—the last of an estimated 150,000. The first had been about birds, and the last was about birds.

As the final contribution of a distinguished naturalist to the subject which he loved above all others, this letter is here reproduced verbatim:

I have read through your really wonderful volume and I am writing Colonel Kuzer about it. I cannot speak too highly of the work. Now one question: on page xxiii, final paragraph, there is an obviously incorrect sentence about which I formerly spoke to you. Ought you not call attention to it and correct it in the second volume? In it you say, by inference, that the grouse of the old world and the grouse of the new world are in separate families, although I believe that three of the genera and one of the species are identical. Moreover, you say that the family of pheasants includes not only the pheasants but the partridges and quail of the old and the grouse of the new world, and furthermore red-legged partridges and francolins, which of course you have already included in the term of partridges and quail of the old world. Obviously someone has made a mistake and I cannot even form a guess of what was originally intended. Do you mind telling me and I can say in my review that this slip of the printer will be corrected in some subsequent edition.

Roosevelt died the next morning at four o'clock, in his sleep, of a thrombus in the artery which feeds blood to the heart.

Within a few hours the entire world knew that Theodore Roosevelt had joined the "innumerable caravan."

Leo Miller, on a cross-country flight from Camp Jackson, South Carolina, to Langley Field, Virginia, had put his plane down at Fayetteville. He was walking along a street when newsboys began to shout that Roosevelt was dead. "For a long time," Miller said, "it seemed that it could not be possible that a man like that could ever die. The shock was very great and lasted for days." [17] The news reached Frank Chapman in Valparaiso, Chile, where he had gone in the interests of the Red Cross. "He had been my inspiration for nearly twenty years," he said. "Suddenly life seemed to lose its flavor." [18] John Burroughs, still enjoying the poetry of life at eighty-two, was by his fireside in the Catskills when the news was brought to him. "The old man's tears come easily, and I can hardly speak his name without tears in my voice," he said. "I have known him since his ranch days in Montana; and to know him was to love him. . . . The world seems more bleak and cold since he is no longer in it." [19]

But, of course, John Burroughs was wrong in one particular. Theodore Roosevelt *is* still in the world. He is alive, many times, and in many different places. He is seen, through his books, in all the vigor of his youth, as he watched the prairie fowl or the bighorn or the antelope in the Bad Lands, or, as a mature man, seeking to separate the threads of mystery surrounding the lives of leopard, oryx, or gazelle in that land "where the wanderer sees the awful glory of sunrise and sunset in the wide waste spaces of the earth." [20] He is seen in the books of others—Chapman, Seton, Ditmars, Akeley—that were written because he believed in them, and they in him. Young naturalists, many of them, have seen him in the snowy owl, which stands alone, in a special case, in the American Museum, and thousands of those who visit the National Museum have seen him in the eland, topi, kongoni, and numerous other African animals at the Smithsonian. Travelers to out-of-the-way places have seen him on the Dry Tortugas Islands, or any one of scores of other wildlife refuges, where birds today, in the thousands, raise their families unmolested by man or other enemies. Others see him daily in huge reservoirs, in blooming lands once arid, in rivers that run clearer, in great forests untouched by fire, in covered watersheds, in tree farms, in trout-filled streams, in bird sanctuaries. Millions of Americans see him each year in national parks or national forests which he created for them, and for their children, and for their children's children.

Footnotes

CHAPTER 1. The Student Naturalist

1. Theodore Roosevelt, *Theodore Roosevelt an Autobiography*, p. 23.
2. The Roosevelt Library, originally at Roosevelt's birthplace at 28 East 20th Street, was moved in 1943 to Harvard College. It contains the largest collection of Rooseveltiana to be found anywhere.
3. New York *World*, Nov. 16, 1902.
4. *Theodore Roosevelt's Diaries of Boyhood and Youth*, pp. 242–43.
5. *Ibid.*, p. 252.
6. Chapman to author.
7. See bibliography for complete list of Roosevelt's unpublished boyhood manuscripts.
8. Memorial Edition of Roosevelt's Works, Vol. VI, p. 443.
9. R. W. G. Vail, "Letters of Theodore Roosevelt to H. D. Minot," *Colliers*, Dec. 20, 1924.
10. New York *Herald*, Aug. 4, 1901.
11. Unless otherwise indicated, letters by Theodore Roosevelt quoted in this book are to be found in The Theodore Roosevelt Collection at the Harvard University Library.

CHAPTER 2. Some Tests of Strength

1. W. W. Sewall, *Bill Sewall's Story of T. R.*, p. 3.
2. Clara Barrus, *The Life and Letters of John Burroughs*, Vol. II, p. 69.
3. Sewall, *op. cit.*, p. 5.
4. *Ibid.*, p. 3.
5. Theodore Roosevelt, *Outdoor Pastimes of an American Hunter*, p. 339.
6. This bird list of theirs is now a collector's item. Since Roosevelt's death (in 1919) occasional copies have been offered for sale through auction channels, one or two at least bringing as much as $150.00 each.
7. Catherine Drinker Bowen, *Yankee from Olympus*, p. 116.
8. Roosevelt Library Paper.
9. Donald Wilhelm, *Theodore Roosevelt the Undergraduate*, p. 35.
10. Roosevelt Library Paper.
11. Charles G. Washburn, *Theodore Roosevelt, the Logic of His Career*, p. 5.

273

CHAPTER 3. A Change of Course

1. Charles F. Batchelder, *An Account of the Nuttall Ornithological Club.*
2. Batchelder, *op. cit.*, p. 36.
3. Washburn, *op. cit.*, p. 4.
4. *Autobiography*, p. 21.
5. *Bull. Nuttall Orn. Club*, July 1879.
6. Roosevelt Library Paper.
7. Washburn, *op. cit.*, p. 3.
8. J. Laurence Laughlin, *Rev. of Reviews*, Vol. 70, p. 391.
9. Italics mine.
10. *Autobiography*, pp. 24–25.
11. Dr. Mark to author.
12. William Roscoe Thayer, *Theodore Roosevelt*, p. 21.
13. Hermann Hagedorn, *Roosevelt in the Bad Lands*, p. 89.

CHAPTER 4. Ducks and Short-tailed Shrews

1. Letter from Roosevelt to Corinne, June 13, 1881.
2. At last count there are 183 of Roosevelt's birds in the Smithsonian, 46 at Indiana University, 24 in the American Museum, 2 in the Cleveland Museum and 2, appropriately, at the Roosevelt House, 28 East 20th Street, New York City, where Roosevelt was born and where he began his collection.

CHAPTER 5. First Taste of the West

1. *Autobiography*, p. 93.
2. W. W. Sewall, *Bill Sewall's Story of T.R.*, p. 16.
3. Theodore Roosevelt, *Ranch Life and the Hunting Trail*, p. 36.
4. Sewall, *op. cit.*, pp. 15–16.
5. Hermann Hagedorn, *Roosevelt in the Bad Lands*, p. x.
6. Theodore Roosevelt, *Hunting Trips of a Ranchman*, pp. 258–62.
7. *Ibid.*, p. 286.
8. *Roosevelt in the Bad Lands*, p. 28.
9. *Ibid.*, p. 46.

CHAPTER 6. Western Animals and Conservation

1. Theodore Roosevelt, *Ranch Life and the Hunting Trail*, p. 81.
2. *Ibid.*, p. 40.
3. *Ibid.*, p. 39.
4. Theodore Roosevelt, *Hunting Trips of a Ranchman*, p. 225.
5. Theodore Roosevelt, *The Wilderness Hunter*, p. 65.
6. *Works*, Mem. Ed., Vol. III, p. xvi.
7. New York *Nation*, Aug. 14, 1893.
8. Jack Willis, *Roughing It with Roosevelt*, p. 17.
9. *Ibid.*, pp. 15–16.
10. *Ibid.*, pp. 19–23.
11. Theodore Roosevelt, *The Wilderness Hunter*, pp. 305–6.

12. Willis, *op. cit.*, pp. 207–11.
13. *Forest and Stream*, Nov. 2, 1895.
14. *Ibid.*, Nov. 23, 1895.
15. Willis, *op. cit.*, pp. 207–11.

CHAPTER 7. A Natural History Trilogy

1. H. F. Pringle, *Theodore Roosevelt*, p. 115.
2. *Works*, Mem. Ed., Vol. XIV, p. xii.
3. Owen Wister, *The Story of a Friendship*, p. 41.
4. F. E. Leupp, *Atlantic Monthly*, Vol. 109, p. 843.
5. *Hunting Trips of a Ranchman*, p. 12.
6. *Works*, Mem. Ed., Vol. II, p. xxi.
7. Henry Fairfield Osborn, *Impressions of Great Naturalists*, p. 185.
8. *The Spectator*, Jan. 16, 1886.
9. Chicago *Unity*, Sept. 24, 1895.
10. *Works*, Mem. Ed., Vol. I, pp. xiv–xv.
11. From undated clipping in Roosevelt scrapbook.
12. London *Field*, Nov. 25, 1893.
13. Philadelphia *Telegram*, July 26, 1893.
14. *Works*, Mem. Ed., Vol. VI, pp. 449–50.
15. *The Wilderness Hunter*, p. 151.
16. Jack Willis, *op. cit.*, p. 55.
17. *Ibid.*, p. 19.
18. Frederick S. Wood, *Roosevelt as We Knew Him*, p. 12.

CHAPTER 8. "Field Work Also Is Necessary"

1. June 21, 1893.
2. *Report to the Overseers*, Academical Series II, Vol. 7, 1893–1896, Report of the Committee on Zoology.
3. *Ibid.*
4. *Ibid.*
5. *Ibid.*
6. G. H. Parker, Harvard Biological Laboratories, to author, Nov. 20, 1944.
7. G. H. Parker, *The World Expands*, p. 87.
8. *Ibid.*, pp. 87–88.
9. *Science*, Feb. 12, 1932.
10. *Ibid.*

CHAPTER 9. "I Must Have A B & C Dinner"

1. *Works*, Mem. Ed., Vol. 1, p. xviii.
2. G. B. Grinnell (ed.), *Hunting at High Altitudes* (Book of the Boone and Crockett Club), p. 435.
3. Grinnell, *Ibid.*, p. 500.
4. Minute Book of Boone and Crockett Club for 1889.
5. Grinnell, *op. cit.*, pp. 442–453.
6. David Sèville Muzzey, *A History of Your Country*, p. 579.

7. Owen Wister, *The Story of a Friendship*, p. 35.
8. *Ibid.*, p. 36.
9. *Ibid.*, p. 34.
10. *Works*, Mem. Ed., Vol. I, p. xix.
11. *Ibid.*, Vol. I, p. xix.

CHAPTER 10.   Coyotes and *Cervus Roosevelti*

1. *Correspondence of Roosevelt and Lodge*, Vol. I, p. 237.
2. C. Hart Merriam, "Revision of the Coyotes or Prairie Wolves," *Procs. of Biol. Soc. of Washington*, March 15, 1897.
3. *Science*, April 30, 1897.
4. *Ibid.*, May 14, 1897.
5. *Ibid.*, June 4, 1897.
6. L. O. Howard, *Fighting the Insects*, pp. 236–37.
7. *Works*, Mem. Ed., Vol. III, p. xix.
8. *Science*, June 4, 1897.
9. *Nature*, July 15, 1897, pp. 265–68.
10. E. A. Goldman, to author.
11. John Eric Hill, Amer. Mus. of Nat. Hist., to author.
12. *Correspondence of Roosevelt and Lodge*, Vol. I, p. 5.
13. *Procs. Biol. Soc. of Washington*, Dec. 17, 1897.
14. Frank M. Chapman, *Autobiography of a Bird-Lover*, p. 184.

CHAPTER 11.   In the Clutches of the Press

1. *Diaries*, pp. 248–49.
2. N. Y. *Herald*, Jan. 14, 1901.
3. N. Y. *Herald*, Jan. 16, 1901.
4. N. Y. *Herald*, Jan. 19, 1901.
5. N. Y. *Journal*, Jan. 25, 1901.
6. N. Y. *Evening Sun*, Jan. 22, 1901.
7. *Roosevelt-Lodge Correspondence*, Vol. I, p. 484.
8. *Works*, Mem. Ed., Vol. III, p. xv.
9. Theodore Roosevelt, *Outdoor Pastimes of an American Hunter*, p. 32.
10. *Science*, Feb. 12, 1932.
11. *Works*, Mem. Ed., Vol. XVII, p. 118.
12. *The Washington Times*, June 22, 1902.
13. *Theodore Roosevelt's Letters to His Children*, p. 54.
14. *Ibid.*, p. 35.
15. *Ibid.*, p. 19.
16. *Ibid.*, p. 49.
17. *Ibid.*, pp. 199–200.
18. *Ibid.*, p. 147.
19. *Critic*, Nov. 23, 1895.
20. *Letters to His Children*, p. 53.
21. *Ibid.*, p. 135.
22. *Ibid.*, p. 162.
23. *Ibid.*, pp. 47–48.
24. *Ibid.*, pp. 213–16.

25. *Ibid.*, p. 172.
26. *Ibid.*, p. 167.
27. Mark Sullivan, *Our Times*, Vol. II, p. 445.

CHAPTER 12. With Burroughs in Yellowstone

1. April 4, 1903.
2. John Burroughs, *Camping and Tramping with Roosevelt*, p. 6.
3. *Ibid.*, p. 6.
4. Mar. 12, 1903.
5. Burroughs, *op. cit.*, p. viii.
6. *Ibid.*, pp. 34–35.
7. Probably the Uinta ground squirrel (*Citellus armatus*, Kennicott). Its "song" is its alarm note.
8. Burroughs, *op. cit.*, pp. 39–40.
9. *Ibid.*, pp. 46–49.
10. *Ibid.*, p. 66.
11. *Ibid.*, p. 67.
12. *Ibid.*, p. 51.
13. *Ibid.*
14. *Ibid.*, pp. 79–81.
15. *Ibid.*, p. 7.
16. *Ibid.*, pp. 102–3.
17. *Ibid.*, p. 104.
18. Donald Culross Peattie, *A Gathering of Birds*, p. 4.
19. *Ibid.*, p. 1.
20. William Frederic Badè, *The Life and Letters of John Muir*, Vol. II, p. 412.
21. *Ibid.*, Vol. II, p. 412.
22. *Ibid.*, Vol. II, p. 411.
23. *Outdoor Pastimes*, p. 317.
24. *Works*, Mem. Ed., Vol. XII, p. 566.
25. *Ibid.*, Vol. XII, p. 566.

CHAPTER 13. "I'll Back Up Gorgas"

1. Harvey Cushing, *The Life of Sir William Osler* (One Vol. Ed. 1940), pp. 631–32.
2. Mark Sullivan, *Our Times*, Vol. I, pp. 460–61.
3. *Ibid.*, p. 462.
4. Marie D. Gorgas, and Burton J. Hendrick, *William Crawford Gorgas*, p. 196.
5. *Ibid.*, p. 198.
6. *Ibid.*, pp. 199–200.
7. *Ibid.*, p. 202.
8. *Ibid.*, p. 202.
9. *Ibid.*, p. 187.
10. April 19, 1907.
11. Dec. 14, 1903.
12. March, 1906.

CHAPTER 14.   The Nature Faker Controversy

1. *Atlantic Monthly*, March, 1903.
2. Clara Barrus, *The Life and Letters of John Burroughs*, Vol. II, p. 50.
3. *Christian Register*, Dec. 28, 1899.
4. *North American Review*, May, 1903.
5. *Ibid.*, May, 1903.
6. *Outlook*, Sept. 12, 1903.
7. *Science*, Feb. 26, 1904.
8. *Ibid.*, March 4, 1904.
9. Mark Sullivan, *op. cit.*, Vol. III, p. 149.
10. The term "nature fakirs," although attributed to Roosevelt, was coined by Clark. The spelling was later altered to "nature fakers," with a consequent clarification of the sense of the epithet.
11. Philadelphia *Public Ledger*, June 2, 1907.
12. Sullivan, *op. cit.*, Vol. III, p. 154.
13. N. Y. *World*, May 24, 1907.
14. Sullivan, *op. cit.*, p. 155.
15. Philadelphia *Public Ledger*, June 2, 1907.
16. *Ibid.*, June 2, 1907.
17. St. Louis Republican, May 24, 1907.
18. Pittsburgh Press, May 31, 1907.
19. *The Outlook*, June 8, 1907, p. 263.
20. *Everybody's Magazine*, Sept., 1907.
21. Frank Chapman, *Autobiography of a Bird-Lover*, pp. 183–84.

CHAPTER 15.   "Pleased as Punch"

1. *Univ. of the State of N. Y. Bull.*, March 1, 1917, pp. 39–44.
2. *Ibid.*

CHAPTER 16.   A Bird Lover in the White House

1. *Scribners*, Jan., 1908.
2. *Works*, Mem. Ed. Vol. III, pp. 345–347.
3. *Outing*, Sept., 1919.
4. Barrus, *op. cit.*, Vol. II, p. 91.
5. *My Brother*, pp. 226–28.
6. Robert Cushman Murphy to author.
7. *Scribners*, Oct., 1907.
8. Burroughs, *op. cit.*, pp. 102–3.
9. *Ibid.*
10. *Ibid.*, p. 105.
11. *Works*, Mem. Ed. Vol. III, p. 356.
12. *Ibid.*, p. 356.
13. *Ibid.*, p. 357.
14. *Ibid.*, pp. 359–60.
15. Frank Chapman, *Autobiography of a Bird-Lover*, p. 185.

CHAPTER 17. "For the People Unborn"

1. Lewis Einstein, *Roosevelt, His Mind in Action*, p. 91.
2. *Works*, Mem. Ed., Vol. XVII, pp. 120–21.
3. Francis Fevrier Guittard, *Roosevelt and Conservation*, p. 116.
4. *Outlook*, XCVII, pp. 708–9.
5. *Works*, Mem. Ed., Vol. XVIII, p. 135.
6. *Autobiography*, p. 401.
7. *Works*, Mem. Ed. Vol. XVII, p. 119.
8. *Ibid.*, Vol. XVIII, p. 128.
9. Theodore Roosevelt, *California Addresses*, p. 40.
10. *Works*, Mem. Ed., Vol. IV, p. 229.
11. *Ibid.*, Vol. XVII, p. 611.
12. David Fairchild to author.
13. *Works*, Mem. Ed., Vol. XVIII, pp. 166–67.
14. *Nation*, LXXXIV, p. 425.
15. *Rev. of Reviews, Presidential Addresses*, I, p. 328.
16. *Congressional Record*, XL, p. 7888.
17. *Rev. of Reviews, Pres. Addresses*, I, p. 370.
18. *Works*, Mem. Ed., Vol. XIV, p. 569.
19. Frank Chapman, *Autobiography of a Bird-Lover*, pp. 181–82.
20. *Works*, Mem. Ed., Vol. XIV, p. 567.
21. *Ibid.*, p. 567.
22. *World's Work*, XVI (1909), p. 10419.
23. *Chautauquan*, LV (1909), pp. 44–47.
24. L. O. Howard, *Fighting the Insects*, pp. 230–40.
25. *Nation*, LXXXVI, p. 460.
26. *Independent*, LXIV (1908), pp. 1151–1152.
27. *Autobiography*, p. 400.
28. *Ibid.*, p. 410.
29. *Ibid.*, p. 410.
30. To Sidney Brooks, Dec. 28, 1908.
31. Robert LaFollette, *Autobiography*, p. 393.
32. David Seville Muzzey, *A History of Our Country*, p. 578.
33. S. E. Morrison and Henry S. Commager, *The Growth of the American Republic*, II, p. 400.
34. Gifford Pinchot, *The Fight for Conservation*, pp. 94–95.
35. William T. Hornaday, *Vanishing Wild Life*, p. 248.
36. Charles R. Van Hise, *The Conservation of Natural Resources in the United States*, p. 10.
37. *Works*, Mem. Ed., Vol. XV, p. 558.
38. Charles A. Beard and Mary Beard, *A Basic History of the United States*, p. 405.
39. *Works*, Mem. Ed., Vol. XIX, p. 22.
40. *Ibid.*, Vol. IV, p. 227.

CHAPTER 18. Readying for Africa

1. H. F. Pringle, *Theodore Roosevelt*, pp. 18–19.
2. *Ibid.*, p. 184.

3. Correspondence of T.R. and Lodge, Vol. II, p. 347.
4. Lawrence F. Abbot, The Letters of Archie Butt, p. 104.
5. Abbott, *op. cit.*, p. 156.
6. L. O. Howard, *Fighting the Insects*, pp. 241–42.
7. Scrapbook in Roosevelt Library: "Roosevelt in Jungle and Court."
8. Abbott, *op. cit.*, p. 203.

CHAPTER 19.   A Field Naturalist at Work

1. *Works,* Mem. Ed., Vol. V, p. xvii.
2. Henry Fairfield Osborn, *Impressions of Great Naturalists,* p. 175.
3. *Ibid.,* p. 175.
4. *Ibid.*
5. *Roosevelt Wild Life Bulletin,* Vol. I, No. 1, p. 51, Dec. 1921.
6. *Works,* Mem. Ed., Vol. V, p. xvi.
7. Theodore Roosevelt, *African Game Trails,* p. 33.
8. *Ibid.,* pp. 233–34.
9. Clara Barrus, *The Life and Letters of John Burroughs,* Vol. II, p. 116.
10. *African Game Trails,* p. 341.
11. *Works,* Mem. Ed., Vol. V, p. xvi.
12. Theodore Roosevelt and Edmund Heller, *Life-Histories of African Game Animals,* Vol. I, p. 307.
13. *African Game Trails,* p. 182.
14. *Life-Histories of African Game Animals,* Vol. II, p. 605.
15. *Ibid.,* Vol. I, p. 71.
16. *Ibid.,* p. 306.
17. *Roosevelt Wild Life Bulletin,* Vol. I, No. 1, Dec. 1921, p. 50.
18. Frederick S. Wood, *Roosevelt as We Knew Him,* p. 219.
19. *Works,* Mem. Ed., Vol. V, p. xvi.
20. Frederick S. Wood, *Roosevelt as We Knew Him,* p. 215.
21. J. T. McCutcheon, *In Africa,* p. 162.
22. *Works,* Mem. Ed., Vol. IV, p. 454.
23. Kermit Roosevelt, *The Happy Hunting Grounds,* pp. 22–23.

CHAPTER 20.   In the Valley of the Itchen

1. Henry Fairfield Osborn, *Impressions of Great Naturalists,* pp. 171–72.
2. Grey, Viscount of Fallodon, *Twenty-Five Years,* Vol. II, p. 90.
3. *Autobiography,* p. 322.
4. Grey, Viscount of Fallodon, *Fallodon Papers,* p. 68.
5. *Ibid.,* p. 69.
6. *Ibid.,* p. 71.
7. *Ibid.,* p. 71.
8. *The Wilderness Hunter,* p. 66.
9. *Fallodon Papers,* p. 74.
10. *Saturday Evening Post,* Dec. 26, 1931, p. 65. (Letter to David Gray, Oct. 5, 1911.)

CHAPTER 21. T. R. Writes of Africa

1. Kermit Roosevelt, *The Happy Hunting Grounds*, pp. 43–44.
2. J. B. Bishop, *Theodore Roosevelt and His Time*, Vol. II, pp. 361–62.
3. *The Bookman*, Oct., 1910.
4. *African Game Trails*, p. vii.
5. *Ibid.*, pp. vii–viii.
6. *The Bookman*, Oct., 1910.
7. *Ibid.*
8. *Ibid.*
9. *Ibid.*
10. *Natl. Geog. Mag.*, Nov., 1910, pp. 953–62.
11. *Bull. Amer. Geog. Soc.*, Mar. 1915, pp. 190–92.
12. American Museum Journal, March, 1916.

CHAPTER 22. The Concealing Coloration Controversy

1. Frank M. Chapman, *Autobiography of a Bird-Lover*, p. 79.
2. Gerald Thayer, *Concealing Coloration in the Animal Kingdom*, p. 136.
3. *Ibid.*, p. 107.
4. *Ibid.*, p. 153.
5. *Science*, Oct. 7, 1910.
6. *Bird-Lore*, July–August, 1910.
7. *The Auk*, Oct., 1911, pp. 472–80.
8. *African Game Trails*, p. 408.
9. *Bull. Amer. Mus. of Nat. Hist.*, Aug., 1911, p. 132.
10. *African Game Trails*, p. 498.
11. *Ibid.*, p. 494.
12. *The Auk*, Oct. 1912.
13. *Roosevelt Wild Life Bulletin*, Vol. I, No. 1, Dec. 1921, p. 51.
14. *Works*, Mem. Ed., Vol. IV, p. xii.

CHAPTER 23. "To the Land of the Quangley Wee"

1. *Correspondence of Roosevelt and Lodge*, Vol. II, p. 438.
2. J. A. Zahm, *Through South America's Southland*, p. 5.
3. F. M. Chapman, *Autobiography of a Bird-Lover*, p. 216.
4. *Works*, Mem. Ed., Vol. IV, p. xxi.
5. J. A. Zahm, *op. cit.*, p. 17.
6. *Ibid.*, p. 19.
7. George Cherrie, *Dark Trails*, p. 260.
8. *Correspondence of T.R. and Lodge*, Vol. II, p. 444.
9. *Natural History*, XIX, No. 1, pp. 9–10.
10. *Ibid.*
11. Theodore Roosevelt, *Through the Brazilian Wilderness*, p. 301.

CHAPTER 24. The Expedicao Roosevelt-Rondon

1. Theodore Roosevelt, *Through the Brazilian Wilderness*, p. 245.
2. George Cherrie, *Dark Trails*, p. 285.

3. Col. Candido Rondon, *Lectures on The Roosevelt–Rondon Scientific Expedition* (Publicacao No. 43). Rio de Janeiro, 1916, p. 77.
4. Cherrie, *op. cit.*, p. 293.
5. *Ibid.*, p. 295.
6. *Ibid.*, pp. 251–53.
7. *Ibid.*, pp. 300–1.
8. *Ibid.*, p. 309.
9. *My Brother*, p. 278.
10. *Happy Hunting Grounds*, pp. 47–48.
11. *Correspondence of Roosevelt and Lodge*, Vol. I, p. 36.
12. *Amer. Mus. Journal*, Feb. 1915.
13. Feb. 1915.
14. Dec. 19, 1914.

CHAPTER 25. Organizing a Bird Club

1. *Oyster Bay Pilot*, July 9, 1915.
2. Mrs. Richard Derby to author, May 8, 1946.
3. Raymond Gorges, *Ernest Harold Baynes*, p. 231.
4. *Works*, Mem. Ed., Vol. IV, pp. ix–x.

CHAPTER 26. "Only Those Are Fit to Live Who Do Not Fear to Die"

1. *Forest and Stream*, April 24, 1903.
2. Letter from Roosevelt to A. J. Sage, Melbourne, Australia, Oct. 6, 1902.
3. *African Game Trails*, p. 90.
4. Vilhjalmur Stefansson, *The Northward Course of Empire*, pp. 163–64.
5. *Works*, Mem. Ed., Vol. VI, p. 409.
6. *Ibid.*, pp. 415–16.
7. *Ibid.*, p. 445.
8. *Ibid.*, p. 453.
9. *Ibid.*, Vol. III, pp. xvii–xviii.
10. *Ibid.*, Vol. XIV, p. 30.
11. Clara Barrus, *Life of John Burroughs*, Vol. II, p. 278.
12. Hermann Hagedorn, *The Roosevelt Family of Sagamore Hill*, p. 379.
13. *Ibid.*, p. 408.
14. Roosevelt Library Paper.
15. Theodore Roosevelt, *The Great Adventure*, p. 1.
16. *American Museum Journal*, Dec. 1918.
17. Leo Miller to author, July 9, 1945.
18. Frank M. Chapman, *Autobiography of a Bird-Lover*, p. 289.
19. Clara Barrus, *Life of John Burroughs*, II, p. 364.
20. *African Game Trails*, p. ix.

Bibliography

UNPUBLISHED MANUSCRIPTS OF THEODORE ROOSEVELT

About Insects and Fishes, Natural History [1869]
A Jackal Hunt [1873]
Blarina talpoides (Short Tailed Shrew) [No date, obviously youthful]
Buff-fronted Cow Heron (Ardea russata) [1872]
Game Book [1883–1902]
Coloration of Birds [187–]
Field Book of Zoölogy [1876–1879]
Mrs. Field Mouse's Dinner Party [1873]
Notes on the Fauna of the Adirondac Mts. [1871–1877]
Notes on Natural History [No date, obviously youthful]
Ornithology of Egypt Between Cairo and Assouan [1872]
Record of the Roosevelt Museum [1867–1874]
Remarks on Birds (2 vols.) [1874]
Remarks on the Zoölogy of Oyster Bay, L. I. [1874–1876]
Sporting Calendar [1875]
Sou'-sou'-southerly [1881]
Zoölogical Record [1872–1873]

PUBLICATIONS OF THEODORE ROOSEVELT

ROOSEVELT, THEODORE, *African and European Addresses.* New York: G. P. Putnam's Sons, 1910.
———, *African Game Trails,* New York: Charles Scribner's Sons, 1910.
——— and George Bird Grinnell (ed.), *American Big-Game Hunting* (The Book of the Boone and Crockett Club). New York: Forest and Stream Publishing Co., 1893.
———, *Hunting Trips of a Ranchman.* New York: G. P. Putnam's Sons, 1886.
——— and EDMUND HELLER, *Life Histories of African Game Animals.* New York: Charles Scribner's Sons, 1914.
———, *Notes on Some of the Birds of Oyster Bay, Long Island.* [Printer unknown]. March 1879.
———, *Outdoor Pastimes of an American Hunter.* New York: Charles Scribner's Sons, 1905.

——, *Ranch Life and the Hunting Trail*. New York: The Century Co., 1888.

——, *Theodore Roosevelt an Autobiography*. New York: Charles Scribner's Sons, 1922.

——, *Theodore Roosevelt's Diaries of Boyhood and Youth*. New York: Charles Scribner's Sons, 1928.

——, T. S. VAN DYKE, D. G. ELLIOT, and A. J. STONE, *The Deer Family* (Vol. I of American Sportsman's Library edited by Caspar Whitney, in 16 Vols.). New York: The Macmillan Co., 1902.

—— and H. D. MINOT, *The Summer Birds of the Adirondacks in Franklin County, N.Y.*, Salem: Naturalists' Agency (Samuel E. Cassino), Oct. 1877.

——, *The Wilderness Hunter*. New York: G. P. Putnam's Sons, 1893.

——, *Through the Brazilian Wilderness*. New York: Charles Scribner's Sons, 1914.

—— and GEORGE BIRD GRINNELL, *Trail and Camp Fire*, (The Book of the Boone and Crockett Club). New York: Forest and Stream Publishing Co., 1897.

——, *Works*, Memorial Edition (24 vols.). New York: Charles Scribner's Sons, 1923.

——, *A Book-Lover's Holidays in the Open*. New York: Charles Scribner's Sons, 1916.

——, *Good Hunting; in Pursuit of Big Game in the West*. New York: Harper & Brothers, 1907.

—— and GEORGE BIRD GRINNELL, *Hunting in Many Lands* (The Book of the Boone and Crockett Club). New York: Forest and Stream Publishing Co., 1895.

——, *Some American Game*. New York: G. P. Putnam's Sons, 1897.

GENERAL LITERATURE

ABBOTT, LAWRENCE F. (ed.), *The Letters of Archie Butt*. New York: Doubleday, Page & Co., 1924.

AKELEY, CARL E., *In Brightest Africa*. New York: Doubleday, Page & Co., 1920.

BADÈ, WILLIAM FREDERIC, *The Life and Letters of John Muir*. Boston and New York: Houghton Mifflin Co., 1924, 2 vols.

BARRUS, CLARA, *The Heart of Burroughs's Journals*. Boston and New York: Houghton Mifflin Co., 1928.

——, *The Life and Letters of John Burroughs*. Boston and New York: Houghton Mifflin Co., 1925, 2 vols.

BATCHELDER, CHARLES F., *An Account of the Nuttall Ornithological Club*. Cambridge: Nuttall Ornithological Club, 1937.

BEEBE, WILLIAM, *The Book of Naturalists*. New York: Alfred A. Knopf, 1944.

——, *Jungle Peace*. New York: Henry Holt & Co., 1919.

——, G. INNESS HARTLEY, and PAUL G. HOWES, *Tropical Wild Life*. New York: N. Y. Zoological Society, 1917.

BISHOP, JOSEPH BUCKLIN, *Theodore Roosevelt's Letters to His Children*. New York: Charles Scribner's Sons, 1919.

———, *Theodore Roosevelt and His Time.* New York: Charles Scribner's Sons. 1920, 2 vols.

BURROUGHS, JOHN, *Camping and Tramping with Roosevelt.* Boston and New York: Houghton Mifflin Co., 1906.

———, *Under the Maples* (The Complete Nature Writings of John Burroughs) Vol. VI. New York: Wm. H. Wise & Co., 1904–21.

BUTLER, NICHOLAS MURRAY, *Across the Busy Years,* 2 vols. New York: Charles Scribner's Sons, 1939.

CHAPMAN, FRANK M., *Autobiography of a Bird-Lover.* New York: D. Appleton-Century Co., 1933.

CHERRIE, GEORGE K., *Dark Trails, Adventures of a Naturalist.* New York: G. P. Putnam's, 1930.

COWLES, ANNA ROOSEVELT, *Letters from Theodore Roosevelt to Anna Roosevelt Cowles, 1870–1918.* New York: Charles Scribner's Sons, 1924.

CUSHING, HARVEY, *The Life of Sir William Osler.* Oxford: Clarendon Press, 1926, 2 vols.

EINSTEIN, LEWIS, *Roosevelt, His Mind in Action.* Boston and New York: Houghton Mifflin Co., 1930.

FLEXNER, SIMON and JAMES T. FLEXNER, *William Henry Welch and the Heroic Age of American Medicine.* New York: The Viking Press, 1941.

GILMAN, BRADLEY, *Roosevelt the Happy Warrior.* Boston: Little, Brown, & Co., 1921.

CORGAS, MARIE D. and BURTON J. HENDRICK, *William Crawford Gorgas.* New York: Doubleday, Page & Co., 1924.

GORGES, RAYMOND, *Ernest Harold Baynes.* Boston and New York: Houghton Mifflin Co., 1928.

GREY, EDWARD (Viscount Grey of Fallodon), *Fallodon Papers.* Boston and New York: Houghton Mifflin Co. [c. 1926]

———, *Twenty-Five Years, 1892–1916.* New York: Frederick A. Stokes Co., 1925, 2 vols.

CRINNELL, GEORGE BIRD (ed.), *Hunting at High Altitudes* (The Book of the Boone and Crockett Club). New York: Harper & Brothers, 1913.

GRINNELL, GEORGE BIRD (ed.), *American Big Game in Its Haunts.* (The Book of the Boone and Crockett Club). New York: Forest and Stream Publishing Co., 1904.

HAGEDORN, HERMANN, *Roosevelt in the Bad Lands.* Boston and New York: Houghton Mifflin Co., 1921.

———, *The Boys' Life of Theodore Roosevelt.* New York: Harper & Brothers, 1918.

HENDERSON, DANIEL, *Jungle Roads and Other Trails of Roosevelt.* New York: E. P. Dutton & Co., 1920.

HOOVER, IRWIN HOOD (Ike), *Forty-two Years in the White House.* Boston and New York: Houghton Mifflin Co., 1934.

HOWARD, L. O., *Fighting the Insects.* New York: The Macmillan Co., 1933.

IGLEHART, F. C., *Theodore Roosevelt: The Man as I Knew Him.* New York: The Christian Herald, 1919.

JOHNSON, ROBERT UNDERWOOD, *Remembered Yesterdays.* Boston: Little, Brown, & Co., 1923.

JORDAN, DAVID STARR, *The Days of a Man.* Yonkers-on-Hudson, N. Y.: World Book Co., 1922, 2 vols.

KOHLSAAT, H. H., *From McKinley to Harding.* New York: Charles Scribner's Sons, 1923.

LANG, LINCOLN A., *Ranching with Roosevelt.* Philadelphia: J. B. Lippincott Co., 1926.

LEWIS, WILLIAM DRAPER, *The Life of Theodore Roosevelt.* Philadelphia: The John C. Winston Co., 1919.

LODGE, HENRY CABOT, *Selections from the Correspondence of Theodore Roosevelt and Henry Cabot Lodge, 1884–1918.* New York: Charles Scribner's Sons, 1924.

LONG, WILLIAM J., *Wayeeses the White Wolf.* Boston: Ginn and Co., 1907.

——, *Ways of Wood Folk.* Ginn & Co., Boston, 1902.

LORING, J. ALDEN, *African Adventure Stories.* New York: Charles Scribner's Sons, 1914.

MACINTYRE, NIEL [Henderson, Daniel MacIntyre], *"Great Heart," The Life Story of Theodore Roosevelt.* New York: William Edwin Rudge, 1919.

McCUTCHEON, JOHN T., *In Africa.* Indianapolis: The Bobbs-Merrill Co., 1910.

MILLAIS, J. G., *Life of Frederick Courtenay Selous, D.S.O.* New York: Longmans, Green & Co., 1919.

——, *Wanderings and Memories.* London: Longmans, Green and Co., 1919.

MILLER, LEO E., *In the Wilds of South America.* New York: Charles Scribner's Sons, 1919.

OSBORN, HENRY FAIRFIELD, *Impressions of Great Naturalists.* New York: Charles Scribner's Sons, 1925.

PARKER, GEORGE HOWARD, *The World Expands, Recollections of a Zoologist.* Cambridge, Mass.: Harvard University Press, 1946.

PRINGLE, HENRY F., *Theodore Roosevelt.* New York: Harcourt, Brace and Co., 1931.

RIIS, JACOB A., *Theodore Roosevelt the Citizen.* New York: The Outlook Co., 1904.

RIXEY, PRESLEY MARION, *The Life of Presley Marion Rixey:* biography and autobiography. Strasburg, Virginia: Shenandoah Publishing House, 1930.

ROBINSON, CORINNE ROOSEVELT, *My Brother, Theodore Roosevelt.* New York: Charles Scribner's Sons, 1921.

ROOSEVELT, KERMIT, *The Happy Hunting Grounds.* New York: Charles Scribner's Sons, 1920.

ROOSEVELT, THEODORE, JR., *All in the Family.* New York: G. P. Putnam's Sons, 1929.

SETON, ERNEST THOMPSON, *Trail of an Artist-Naturalist.* New York: Charles Scribner's Sons, 1940.

SEWALL, WILLIAM WINGATE, *Bill Sewall's Story of T. R.* New York: Harper & Brothers, 1919.

SMITH, ALFRED CHARLES, *The Attractions of the Nile and Its Banks—A Journal of Travel in Egypt and Nubia,* 2 vols. London: (Murray?) 1868.

STEFANSSON, VILHJALMUR, *The Northward Course of Empire.* New York: The Macmillan Co., 1924.

SULLIVAN, MARK, *Our Times*, Vols. I, II, III, and IV. New York: Charles Scribner's Sons, 1926, 1929, 1930, 1932.

THAYER, GERALD A., *Concealing Coloration in the Animal Kingdom*. New York: The Macmillan Co., 1909.

THAYER, WILLIAM ROSCOE, *Theodore Roosevelt*, Boston and New York: Houghton Mifflin Co., 1919.

UP DE GRAFF, F. W., *Head Hunters of the Amazon*. New York: Duffield and Co. 1923.

WASHBURN, CHARLES G., *Theodore Roosevelt, The Logic of His Career*. Boston and New York: Houghton Mifflin Co., 1916.

WILHELM, DONALD, *Theodore Roosevelt as an Undergraduate*. Boston: J. W. Luce, 1910.

WILLIS, JOHN, *Roosevelt in the Rough*. New York: Ives Washburn, 1931.

WISTER, OWEN, *Roosevelt, The Story of a Friendship*. New York: The Macmillan Co., 1927.

WOOD, FREDERICK S., *Roosevelt as We Knew Him*. Philadelphia: The John C. Winston Co., 1927.

ZAHM, J. A., (H. J. Mozans), *Through South America's Southland*. New York: D. Appleton and Co., 1916.

Index

Abbott, Lyman, 131, 136
Adams, Charles C., 223
Adirondacks, T. R. and, 4; visited by T. R. and Minot, 15, 89
Aedes aegypti, 119
Africa, T. R. and, 186–210; preparation, 186–197; writes Selous and Buxton, 186–187; Smithsonian, 188; animals most eager to shoot, 190; naturalists, 190; liquor, 191; provisions and equipment, 191; clothing, 192; spectacles, 192; African literature, 193, "Pigskin Library," 194–195; Shakespeare, 195; African hunters to White House, 195; precautions, 195; sleeping sickness, 196; knowledge of African animals, 198 *et seq.*; antelopes, 199; knowledge of African birds, 200; curiosity, 201; stomach content of animals, 204; observational powers, 205; concealing coloration, 206 *et seq.*; commands respect of men, 208; success of African expedition, 209; African collection, 209
African Game Trails, 206, 217 *et seq.*; sale of, 218; foreword of, 218; reviews of, 219; Appendix E, 227
Agassiz, Louis, 19; 241
Akeley, Carl, 195, 197, 198, 203, 209
Allen, Francis H., 229
Allen, J. A., 23, 25, 83, 137, 227, 254

American Association for the Advancement of Science, 164
American Big Game Hunting (Boone and Crockett Club book), 73
American Medical Association, The, 121
American Museum of Natural History, T. R. birds displayed at, 7; T. R.'s father helps found, 9; T. R. gives birds to, 34, 162, 235, 240, 254
American Ornithologist's Union, 178
"Animal Surgery," 180
Anopheles, 118
Antelopes (African), 199, 203
Ants, parasol, 244
Audubon, J. J., 2, 160
Audubon Society, 86, 178
Auk, The, 229

Baboon (blue rump), 232
Bad Lands, 38 *et seq.*
Bailey, H. B., 23
Baird, Spencer F., 2
Barbour, Thomas, 230
Batchelder, Charles F., 23
Bates, Henry Walter, 241; *The Naturalist on the Amazons*, 255
Baynes, Ernest Harold, 256, 258
Bear, brown, 101, 102
Bear, grizzly, 44; almost gets T. R., 50, 90
Beebe, William, 142; on T. R.'s contribution to coloration issues, 233; on *Book-Lover's Holidays*, 259; pheasants, 269
Bell, John G., 7

289

Set in Linotype Caledonia
Format by Edwin H. Kaplin
Manufactured by The Haddon Craftsmen, Inc.
Published by HARPER & BROTHERS, *New York*